# Denial of Justice in International Law

# ONE WEEK LOAN

Since the
law was
evolved i
internatic
governm(
swung wi
isations, (

A vast
foreign ir
has given
prospect
national (
that such
to prospe

The p(
exercise (
when Pal
retributio
subject) b
gunships
have no r
the condu
turned, a:
denials of
Massachu

This book examines the modern understanding of denial of justice.

# Denial of Justice in International Law

Jan Paulsson

CAMBRIDGE
UNIVERSITY PRESS

CAMBRIDGE UNIVERSITY PRESS
Cambridge, New York, Melbourne, Madrid, Cape Town, Singapore,
São Paulo, Delhi, Dubai, Tokyo, Mexico City

Cambridge University Press
The Edinburgh Building, Cambridge CB2 8RU, UK

Published in the United States of America by Cambridge University Press, New York

www.cambridge.org
Information on this title: www.cambridge.org/9780521172912

First published 2005
Fourth printing 2007
First paperback edition 2010

*A catalogue record for this publication is available from the British Library*

ISBN 978-0-521-85118-3 Hardback
ISBN 978-0-521-17291-2 Paperback

# Table of Contents

## Table of contents

Table of contents

# *Acknowledgements*

This study grew out of the three Hersch Lauterpacht Memorial Lectures given in Cambridge in November 2003. I thankfully acknowledge the encouragement and support of Sir Elihu Lauterpacht, the founder of Cambridge University's Lauterpacht Research Centre for International Law, and his successors as directors of the Centre, Professor James Crawford SC and Daniel Bethlehem QC.

I have benefited immensely from the constructive criticism and wise counsel of friends who have commented on the lectures and on their development into this volume. Since some of them prefer anonymity, all my expressions of gratitude will remain private.

# Authorities

## International Treaties and Conventions

### *Bilateral treaties and conventions*

*Multinational treaties and conventions*

## Municipal Legislation

*France*

Table of authorities

*Greece*

*Honduras*

*Indonesia*

*Italy*

*Switzerland*

*United Kingdom*

*United States*

Table of authorities

## Decisions of International Courts and Tribunals

*European Court of Human Rights*

*ICJ and PCIJ*

Table of authorities

## Inter-American Court of Human Rights

## Iran–US claims tribunal

## Other

## Decisions of Municipal Courts

### Canada

Table of authorities

Table of authorities

## Arbitral Awards

*International centre for settlement of investment disputes*

## Other awards

## Draft Conventions, Principles, Restatements, Rules, etc.

*American Society of International Law/Harvard Law School*

*International Law Commission (United Nations)*

Table of authorities

Table of authorities

# Abbreviations

| | |
|---|---|
| AJIL | *American Journal of International Law* |
| *Amco II* | *Amco Asia Corp., Pan American Development, Ltd. and PT Amco Indonesia* v. *Republic of Indonesia,* award in the resubmitted case, 5 June 1990, 1 *ICSID Reports* 569 (Lalonde, Magid, Higgins (presiding)) |
| BYIL | *British Yearbook of International Law* |
| de Visscher | Charles de Visscher, 'Le déni de justice en droit international' (1935) 54 *Recueil des cours* 370 |
| ECHR | European Court of Human Rights |
| EHRR | *European Human Rights Reports* |
| Fitzmaurice | Sir Gerald Fitzmaurice, 'The Meaning of the Term 'Denial of Justice'' (1932) 13 BYIL 93 |
| Freeman | A. V. Freeman, *The International Responsibility of States for Denial of Justice* (Longman, London/New York, 1938) |
| ICC | International Chamber of Commerce |
| ICJ | International Court of Justice |
| ICSID | International Centre for Settlement of Investment Disputes |
| ICSID Review | *ICSID Review – Foreign Investment Law Journal* |
| ILC | International Law Commission |
| ILM | *International Legal Materials* |
| *Loewen* | *The Loewen Group, Inc. and Raymond L. Loewen* v. *United States of America,* decision on jurisdiction, 5 January 2001, 7 *ICSID Reports* 434 (Fortier, Mivka, Mason (presiding)), award, 26 June 2003, 7 *ICSID Reports* 451 (Mustill, Mikva, Mason (presiding)) |

| | |
|---|---|
| *Mondev* | *Mondev International Ltd* v. *United States of America*, award, 11 October 2002, 6 *ICSID Reports* 192 (Crawford, Schwebel, Stephen (presiding)) |
| Moore, *Arbitrations* | J. B. Moore, *History and Digest of International Arbitrations to which the United States Has Been a Party* (6 vols., Washington, DC: US Government Printing Office, 1898) |
| NAFTA | North American Free Trade Agreeement |
| *Oppenheim* | Sir Robert Jennings and Sir Arthur Watt (eds.), *Oppenheim's International Law* (9th edn, 2 vols., Harlow: Longman, 1992) |
| PCIJ | Permanent Court of International Justice |
| *Recueil des cours* | *Recueil des cours de l'académie de droit international* |
| RIAA | *Reports of International Arbitral Awards* (United Nations) |
| UN | United Nations |
| Vattel | Emer (or Emmerich) de Vattel, *The Law of Nations or the Principles of Natural Law* (*Le droit des gens, ou principes de la loi naturelle*), trans. Charles G. Fenwick (1916), Classics of International Law (3 vols., Buffalo, NY: William S. Hein & Co., 1995) |

# 1

# The renaissance of a cause of action

By what artifice might a state owe a duty to the world at large to maintain an adequate system for the administration of justice? It is one thing for states to assume obligations at their own diplomatic initiative. Few would question that legal duties will flow from a treaty by which two states promise each other that their nationals will be afforded a certain standard of treatment if they are accused of crimes in the other country, or a multilateral agreement by which each state promises all other signatories to abide by certain rules for international trade and investment. But by what contrivance is a state to be held responsible for an imperfect judicial system? When did any state make promises to that effect?

The answer is that the duty to provide decent justice to foreigners arises from customary international law. Indeed, it is one of its oldest principles.[1] From the Renaissance to the First World War – an international lawyer might say from sometime before Grotius to sometime after Calvo – claims of denial of justice were the staple of international legal disputes. There is nothing surprising here. Like most institutions, the nation state did not emerge full-blown and powerful, but inchoate and vulnerable. The territorial integrity of a polity aspiring to statehood would not long remain inviolate if it failed to warrant that it was not a zone of chaos and lawlessness.

So a paradox emerged; it was precisely in attempting to secure their exclusive jurisdiction over internal legal processes that states accepted the

---

[1] Having reviewed the conventions which proliferated in the sixteenth and seventeenth centuries, Judge Charles de Visscher (as he was to become) wrote in 1935 that the 'numerous treaties which stipulate free and ready access to tribunals do no more than confirm a principle the authority of which is independent of any convention' (de Visscher at p. 374; all translations of quotations from de Visscher are the present author's).

duty to maintain those processes at a minimum international standard. The content of that standard has been a matter of controversy. For many generations, the dominant Latin American view tended to be minimalist. But whatever the debate as to its scope, the principle that a state violates international law if it denies justice to aliens has been universally accepted for centuries.

It is easier to have opinions about a foreigner's claim of denial of justice than to understand its legal foundation. The word 'justice' is often emotive, and sometimes seems to paralyse reflection.[2] Although it was already then among the most venerable notions of unlawful state conduct, Alwyn Freeman began his seminal monograph on the subject in 1938 with the observation that denial of justice was 'one of the most poorly elucidated concepts of international law'.[3] He proceeded to give the matter his own elucidation in 623 pages, demonstrating that the topic, however poorly understood, was hardly bereft of material – whether arbitral awards, diplomatic practice, or academic writings.[4]

In the course of the succeeding three generations, the scope for invoking the grievance of denial of justice has broadened immensely. There are

---

[2] 'This striving towards justice is to all appearances one of man's strongest emotions, which is why reason has the greatest difficulty in controlling it' (Vladimir Bukovsky, Introduction, Arthur Koestler, *Darkness at Noon* (1940; trans. Daphne Hardy, London: Folio Society, 1980)).

[3] Freeman at p. 2.

[4] No work of similar depth appears to have been published subsequently. In his Third Report on Diplomatic Protection for the International Law Commission in 2002, Professor John Dugard expressed his intention to write an addendum on denial of justice, which he considered 'as central to the study of the local remedies rule as is the Prince of Denmark to Hamlet'. International Law Commission (Dugard), Third Report on Diplomatic Protection, UN Doc. A/CN.4/523 (2002) at p. 4, para. 13. (The point is obvious: if exhaustion of local remedies is required, a delinquent state must not be allowed to shunt the grievance into oblivion. This aspect of the problem was perfectly captured by the International Court of Justice in *Case concerning the Barcelona Traction Light and Power Co. Ltd (Belgium v. Spain)* (Preliminary Objections), 1964 *ICJ Reports* 6, at p. 46: '[t]he objection of the Respondent that local remedies were not exhausted is met all along the line by the Applicant's contention that it was, *inter alia*, precisely in the attempt to exhaust local remedies that the alleged denials of justice were suffered'.) The very prospect of such an addendum, however, caused strong headwinds to build up within the Commission, where voices were heard to the effect that the topic of denial of justice appertains to the forbidden realm of so-called primary rules. It appears unlikely that the announced addendum will see the light of day. The draft articles on diplomatic protection studiously avoid any reference to denial of justice for the explicit reason that they seek 'to avoid any suggestion' that they encompass 'primary rule[s]'. International Law Commission (Dugard), First Report on Diplomatic Protection, UN Doc. A/CN.4/506 (2000) at p. 15, para. 40.

two fundamental explanations. First, it has become universally accepted that national courts do not somehow stand apart from other institutions of a state, but are its instrumentalities. They are as much a part of the state as the executive or legislative branches, and their acts and omissions are equally attributable to it. Secondly, and more recently, the incidence of such complaints actually being raised has increased greatly with the emergence of procedures under which victims may act directly, under international law and before international jurisdictions, to seek redress. These procedures have notably been established in human rights treaties, and in treaties for the protection of investments.

Although direct access to the remedies of international law is a dramatic development generally, it is particularly so with respect to claims of denial of justice. In Freeman's day, it was a postulate that claims had to be prosecuted by the victim's state through the channel of diplomatic protection. But a government's foreign relations involve complex and countervailing objectives. Ministries of foreign affairs are disinclined to expend political capital pursuing the claims of individuals or corporations in the single-minded manner indispensable to success in litigation.

The world has changed. Complainants may now pursue states directly. They need not be inhibited by any deference to the fact that the wrong they believed was done to them took the form of a court judgment. Moreover, the number of states of whose conduct they might complain has tripled since 1938. They administer legal systems presenting vastly different degrees of imperfection. Finally, the pace and scope of international exchanges, with their inevitable share of disputes, have increased beyond recognition.

International lawyers therefore inevitably developed a renewed interest in the delict of denial of justice. Although the words come easily to the lips, their meaning is not necessarily fully formed in the mind. What kind of injustice, precisely, is denial of justice? Who commits it? Who is responsible for it? Who corrects it? When does the authority to effect such correction escape the exclusive domain of national institutions? What indeed is the remedy?

If the contours of the ancient landscape surveyed by Freeman were unclear, one should hardly be surprised that the more crowded and frenetic realities of current practice call out even more insistently for the systematic re-examination of a notion as open-textured as this one.

The most salient study in French, still valuable, is de Visscher. Of the numerous articles written on the subject, Fitzmaurice's gem-like study in 1932 captures the essence of the topic.

3

At its most general, the international delict may be stated thus: *a state incurs responsibility if it administers justice to aliens in a fundamentally unfair manner.* The expression is not as nebulous as it may seem. Moreover the fact that rules have open texture is not inconsistent with the presence of a core of settled meaning which resolves most questions in a predictable manner.[5] The words 'administer justice' convey something meaningful, as this study will show, and so does the proviso that we are concerned with violations of international, not national, law. True, the sentence assumes rather than demonstrates the existence of international norms of 'fundamental unfairness'. They require elaboration.

Denial of justice in international law cannot be equated with the notion developed in most municipal systems, where it has the limited meaning of a refusal to hear a grievance. Under national law, a disappointed litigant who has been given full access to the procedures provided within the system – including appeals and possibly mechanisms for revision for mistake, fraud, suppressed evidence and the like – cannot ask for more justice, or different justice. The matter is *res judicata*; the system has given all it has to offer.

International law provides standards by which national systems can be judged from the outside. National courts are, without doubt, instrumentalities of the state, so the state may be judged for the acts or omissions of its courts with respect to aliens. It could not be otherwise. Internationally, the state is a single entity. The rule of law does not allow the very party whose compliance is in question to determine whether it is a transgressor.[6]

To the extent that the decisions of national courts disregard or misapply *international* law, they are subject to international censure like any other organ of a state. But since courts are charged with the administration of

---

[5] This sentence reproduces terms which some readers may recognise as recurrent in H. L. A. Hart, *The Concept of Law* (2nd edn, Oxford University Press, 1994).

[6] 'In the case of international law, an international court is the proper organ finally to make the decision that a rule of international law has been broken. Municipal courts may pronounce on the issue, but it is clear that for the international legal system this cannot be final' (C. F. Amerasinghe, *State Responsibility for Injuries to Aliens* (Oxford: Clarendon, 1967), at p. 215).

The abundant arbitral jurisprudence of the nineteenth century is filled with statements like this: 'It is well settled that the decisions of a court, condemning the property of citizens of another country, are not conclusive evidence of the justice or legality of such condemnation' (*The Orient* (*US* v. *Mexico*), Moore, *Arbitrations* 3229, at pp. 3229–30). Umpire Lieber put it thus in the *Garrison* case: 'It is true that it is a matter of the greatest political and international delicacy for one country to disacknowledge the judicial decisions of a court of another country, which nevertheless the law of nations universally allows in extreme cases. *It has done so from the times of Hugo Grotius*' (*US* v. *Mexico*, Moore, *Arbitrations* at p. 3129 (emphasis added)).

justice, it is tempting to refer to their failure to respect international law as a *substantive* denial of justice. This concept, however, is alien to most national legal systems because they incorporate corrective mechanisms which yield a final result deemed by definition to be right. In other words, denial of justice under international law has been thought to encompass a dimension – *substantive* denial of justice – mostly unknown in national law. (Switzerland, we shall see, is an exception.) There is no need to perpetuate such a confusing contrast between international and national notions. A thesis of this study is that the category of substantive denial of justice may now be jettisoned. When national courts misapply international law, they commit substantive violations which should not be called denials of justice; the state from which they are emanations incurs direct international responsibility for the violation without regard to the branch of government which was involved. Since the acts or omissions of its courts are attributable to the state, their transgressions of international law are those of the state. Nothing is added by giving violations of international law a special appellation only because they are effected by a judicial body.

To the extent that national courts disregard or misapply *national* law, their errors do not generate international responsibility unless they have misconducted themselves in some egregious manner which scholars have often referred to as *technical* or *procedural* denial of justice. Although many national laws recognise this type of denial of justice, municipal concepts vary. Often they are exceedingly narrow; a judge's *refusal to hear* a petition may be severely sanctioned, but that is all. Once a judicial body takes up a matter, violations of procedural codes may naturally be the subject of appeals. This is daily fare for appellate courts, but such grievances have no reason to refer to the concept of denial of justice; the fact that they are being heard means that justice is not being denied. Under international law, the general notion of denial of justice generates liability whenever an uncorrected national judgment is vitiated by fundamental unfairness. Thus it must be, as long as international law does not impose specific supranational procedural rules in the guise of treaties.

Such fundamental instruments as the UN Universal Declaration on Human Rights,[7] the European Convention on Human Rights and the International Covenant on Civil and Political Rights define basic

---

[7] Article 10 of the Universal Declaration of Human Rights ('The world's first international bill of rights', General Assembly Resolution A/RES/217A (III), adopted 10 December 1948) provides: 'Everyone is entitled in full equality to a fair and public hearing by an independent and impartial tribunal, in the determination of his rights and obligations and of any criminal charge against him.'

minimum standards and include norms which must be respected by any judicial system aspiring to international legitimacy.[8] To the extent that such rules emerge, the expression 'denial of justice' may lose currency as petitioners find it more convenient to invoke a breach of specific provisions of the relevant treaty. If so, the general rubric of denial of justice may be redundant in the light of the *lex specialis*, but its substantive tenor is not invalidated.

Although the expression as such does not appear in these and similar texts, the customary international law of denial of justice will continue to influence the way in which international treaties are applied. In turn, the application of treaty provisions will contribute to a modern understanding of the old doctrine. The reason for this inevitable cross-pollination is that the elements of the delict of denial of justice tend to reappear as treaty provisions, for example when they proscribe 'discrimination' or when they require 'fair and equitable treatment'. Thus, a complainant before an international tribunal may allege that a treaty has been breached by reference to its terms without invoking the doctrine of denial of justice by name. When the alleged breach has been committed by a judicial body, however, an assessment of *discrimination*, or *unfairness*, or *protection* immediately invites reference to the way such general notions have been understood in the context of denial of justice.

An illustration is the *Loewen* case, undoubtedly one of the most important international decisions rendered in the field of denial of justice.[9] The complaint alleged breaches of the North American Free Trade Agreement, a treaty which does not contain the expression 'denial of justice' as such. Yet the entitlement to treatment 'in accordance with international law' by virtue of Article 1105 of NAFTA encompasses protection against denials of justice.

With respect to more concrete and specific provisions of modern treaties, to the extent they represent a broad consensus they will inevitably be seen as providing content to the general concepts of customary international law even in cases where such treaties do not apply.

---

[8] See Aleksandar Jaksic, *Arbitration and Human Rights* (Peter Lang Publishing, Frankfurt am Main, 2002); cf. in counterpoint Marius Emberland, 'The Usefulness of Applying Human Rights Arguments in International Commercial Arbitration', (2003) 20 *Journal of International Arbitration* 355. See generally chap. 4 ('Human Rights Law Requirements in International Arbitration') of Georgios Petrochilos, *Procedural Law in International Arbitration* (Oxford University Press, 2004), at pp. 109–165.

[9] *Loewen*, 26 June 2003.

At any rate, greater clarity may be achieved by observing that denial of justice is *always* procedural. The adjective is no longer needed.

State responsibility for denial of justice is justified, indeed required, in order to satisfy the international requirement that states provide for the effective protection of the rights of foreigners, whether those rights have been acquired by operation of national law or imposed by overriding international principles. A foreigner is always entitled to procedural fairness as measured by an international standard. That is the *raison d'être* of the notion of denial of justice. The doctrine of denial of justice is not required to protect substantive rights under international law, for the simple reason that national courts do not have the last word with regard to such rights; courts or tribunals entitled to apply international law will simply correct the failure to observe the right in question. Substantive rights under national law, on the other hand, are created by the state, and are subject to the sovereign authority to legislate, and to interpret. Therefore, the dismissal of a claim of right under national law by the properly constituted national authority, whether correct or incorrect as a matter of national law (as previously or subsequently understood), does not give rise to an international delict unless there has been a violation of due process as defined by international standards.

This study examines the bases on which international jurisdictions may give effect to that essential exception.[10] It will lead to three particularly important insights.

First, we will discover that international fora have no reason to recognise a category of substantive denials of justice. In international law, denial of justice is about due process, nothing else – and that is plenty.

Secondly, many definitions of denial of justice are misleading. The flaw lies in their concentration on individual instances of miscarriage of justice, using an infinite variety of adjectives to convey the egregiousness which undoubtedly is required to conclude that the international delict has indeed occurred. But international law does not impose a duty on states to treat foreigners fairly at every step of the legal process. The duty is to create and maintain a *system of justice* which ensures that unfairness to foreigners either does not happen, *or is corrected*; '[I]t is the whole system of

---

[10] The author should disclose that he was a member of the arbitral tribunals in *Robert Azinian, et al.* v. *Mexico*, award, 1 November 1998, 5 *ICSID Reports* 269; *Himpurna California Energy Ltd* v. *PT. (Persero) Perusahaan Listruik Negara*, award, 4 May 1999, (2000) XXV *Yearbook Commercial Arbitration* 13; and *Generation Ukraine Inc.* v. *Ukraine*, award, 16 September 2003, (2005) 44 ILM 404 which are discussed in various sections of this book.

legal protection, as provided by municipal law, which must have been put to the test.'[11] It is the breach of that duty which constitutes denial of justice. Exhaustion of local remedies in the context of denial of justice is therefore not a matter of procedure or admissibility, but an inherent material element of the delict.[12] Many investment treaties contain a waiver of the exhaustion requirement to the effect that a foreigner may seize an international tribunal without first seeking to use reasonably available national remedies. Such waivers may ensure the complainant access to the international tribunal, yet a claim of denial of justice would fail substantively in the absence of proof that the national system was given a reasonably full chance to correct the unfairness in question. (There is no paradox in the notion of the *substance of a procedural duty*; it is simply the answer to the question: what is due process?)

Thirdly, claims of denial of justice cannot be decided without balancing a number of complex considerations which tend to be specific to each instance. Anyone who insists that international responsibility in this regard may not arise unless it is the product of a perfectly predictable application of objective criteria simply does not accept international adjudication of denial of justice – and to be consistent would have to maintain the same posture with respect to other fundamental matters such as international determinations of 'equitable' delimitation or 'proportional' armed response.

A final introductory comment: current international jurisprudence concerning denial of justice has found a particular expression in the field of foreign investment, perhaps more notably so than in the law of human rights. This may to some degree be the consequence of the fact that investors tend to be better situated to mobilise the resources required to prosecute high-stakes grievances in a sustained manner before international fora. But far more important is the relative paucity of access to effective remedies in the field of human rights. True enough, the European Convention on Human Rights offers the prospect of concrete remedies to millions of Europeans, but practice under the corresponding American and African instruments lags far behind, while the bulk of the world's population, in Asia, does not benefit from a regional human rights

---

[11] *Ambatielos Claim* (*Greece* v. *UK*), 6 March 1956, XII RIAA 83, at p. 120.

[12] *Accord*, A. A. Cançado Trindade, 'Denial of Justice and its Relationship to Exhaustion of Local Remedies in International Law', (1978) 53 *Philippine Law Journal* 404; International Law Commission (Dugard), Second Report on Diplomatic Protection, UN Doc. A/CN.4/514 (2001) at p. 6, para. 10.

convention at all. Moreover, as Professor Dugard wrote in his First Report on Diplomatic Protection for the International Law Commission:

To suggest that universal human rights conventions, particularly the International Covenant on Civil and Political Rights, provide individuals with effective remedies for the protection of their human rights is to engage in a fantasy which, unlike fiction, has no place in legal reasoning. The sad truth is that only a handful of individuals, in the limited number of States that accept the right of individual petition to the monitoring bodies of these conventions, have obtained or will obtain satisfactory remedies from these conventions.[13]

He went on to note that with respect to aliens, although universal and human rights conventions in principle extend protection to all individuals whether nationals or foreigners:

there is no multilateral convention that seeks to provide the alien with remedies for the protection of her rights outside the field of foreign investment.[14]

Dugard was of course examining the expansion of direct access as it relates to the ILC's inquiry into diplomatic protection. To emphasise his point, he observed that although the UN General Assembly in 1985 adopted the Declaration on the Human Rights of Individuals Who are not Nationals of the Country in Which They Live,[15] instead of proposing any enforcement machinery that instrument simply reiterates the alien's right to seek diplomatic protection.

This starkly illustrates the current position: that aliens may have rights under international law as human beings, but they have no remedies under international law – in the absence of a human rights treaty – except through the intervention of their national State.[16]

Investment arbitrations, on the other hand, have proliferated under the multitude of bilateral investment treaties now extant, and, as we shall see, claimants in such cases have rediscovered the grievance of denial of justice and pursued it with vigour.

---

[13] ILC, First Report on Diplomatic Protection at p. 8, para. 25.
[14] *Ibid.* at para. 26.
[15] General Assembly Resolution A/RES/40/144, adopted 13 December 1985.
[16] ILC, First Report on Diplomatic Protection at p. 9, para. 28.

# 2

# The historical evolution of denial of justice*

## Absence of a universal standard

Denial of justice is an elusive concept. Freeman called it that 'innocent-appearing phrase', only to deplore the 'chaotic heterogeneity' of views as to its proper scope. There are two readily apparent reasons why this should be so.

The first is a matter of definition; all kinds of injustice could be referred to as denial of justice, but then the expression could be invoked to complain about the disposition of any grievance. It would thus lack any particular meaning and lose all usefulness. The malleability of the words

---

* The first draft of this chapter was written in the little port of Gustavia, near the modest museum of the island of St Barthelemy and its even more humble library. This happenstance gave rise to one of those welcome diversions of historical research. The town was named after King Gustav III of Sweden, who acquired St Barthelemy in 1784. For the next century, the tiny Caribbean island became Sweden's only durable overseas dominion. The visiting author may perhaps be forgiven for having distracted himself by wondering when the first Swedish national set foot on the island. The true answer (Viktor von Stedingk, an officer of the merchant marine, debarked in 1783) is uninteresting; more entertaining is a false trail, namely the recent discovery that as early as 1633 four vessels with unmistakably Swedish names (*Stockholms Krona, Förgyllda Lejonet, Norrlandskeppet* and *Gefleskeppet*) anchored overnight off the site of what was to become Gustavia. They were part of a fleet embarked on a successful although ephemeral venture to conquer the island of St Martin – visible ten nautical miles away – but had initially, it seems, mistaken their target. More to the point, there was not a single Swede on board; the four ships were flying the flag of Spain, having been seized in San Lucar as reprisal for damage alleged to have been caused to Spanish vessels in the Baltic port of Wismar in Mecklenburg during its occupation by Swedish troops during the Thirty Years' War. The failure of Sweden to make reparations was thus, in Spain's eyes, the denial of justice; the reprisal was the remedy.

*denial of justice* have led states to adopt narrower or broader definitions, as their interests dictate.

The other reason is that some national laws contain their own long-established doctrines of denial of justice, defined in a manner different from that of international law, and sometimes inconsistent with it. These concepts were grounded in the commoners' historical right to demand that local lords hear petitions. They have endured in the prohibition against *non liquet*.[1] The same requirements exist in international law,[2] but the latter certainly requires more. National laws generally demand nothing more than some kind of disposition of the plaint. Even a legally unfounded judgment of inadmissibility is not deemed to constitute a denial of justice, but would stand or fall depending on the availability of other grounds of appeal. The severe sanctions against judges who commit a denial of justice under national law[3] are intuitively consistent with the narrow definition of the delict and the utter rarity of its occurrence. The important point is not that national laws tend to be more restrictive than international law, but that they are varied – different from international law, and differing among themselves. Already in his day, Freeman noted that Switzerland had a uniquely *expansive* jurisprudence with respect to denial of justice. As the Swiss Federal Tribunal put it in 1880, the concept applied to any judicial or administrative act which 'deprives a citizen of any of the essential guarantees granted to him by law'.[4]

The Swiss example is instructive because it demonstrates the different paths national systems may take. Its broad conception stemmed from the interpretation given to the Swiss Federal Constitution of 1874, Article 4(1) of which accords to all citizens 'equality of treatment before the law'. This notion was equated with an expansively defined prohibition of 'denial of justice', both 'formal' and substantive. *Formal* (or procedural) denial of justice was interpreted to include a violation of the right to obtain a ruling on a claim within a reasonable time; to be judged by properly constituted and independent authorities at all levels,

---

[1] See, e.g., Article 4 of the French Civil Code. A digest of national rules with respect to the duty to judge irrespective of legislative lacunae appears in Bin Cheng, *General Principles of Law as Applied by International Tribunals* (Cambridge: Grotius, 1953, repr. 1987), at Appendix 2. See also Hersch Lauterpacht, *The Function of Law in the International Community* (Oxford: Clarendon, 1933), at pp. 63–69.

[2] The rule against declining to judge because of the silence or obscurity of the law has been viewed as a 'fundamental tenet of all legal systems', *Oppenheim*, vol. I, p. 13, note 26.

[3] Article 434-7-1 of the French Penal Code provides, in addition to a fine, for a prohibition against holding public office from five to twenty years.

[4] Quoted in Freeman at p. 93, note 3 (the present author's translation).

irrespective of whether the irregularity had an effect on the decision; not to have a claim rejected due to an inconsequential procedural error[5] (*dépourvue de gravité*); to consult one's court file and present evidence; to obtain a reasoned decision; and even to obtain financial legal assistance. *Substantive* denial of justice included not only a violation of the citizen's right to a correct and uniform interpretation of the law, but also the emblematic right to a decision free of 'arbitrariness' – an expression familiar even to occasional students of Swiss jurisprudence. To ensure uniform application of the law, and hence the equal treatment of its subjects, the Federal Tribunal verifies conformity with established precedents. Arbitrariness is not, moreover, limited to a failure to respect settled law; rare though such findings may be, they may in principle include judgments which are in 'clear contradiction with the factual circumstances'.[6] And when the current Swiss Constitution was promulgated in 1999, it not only retained the original right to equal treatment (in Article 8) but explicitly incorporated (in Article 9) its jurisprudential offshoot, the prohibition of arbitrariness.

In sum, most national laws expressly refer to denial of justice as something less than international law requires, whereas Swiss law has for more than a century gone well beyond anything the international community is yet in a position to prescribe. It is no wonder that non-specialists would have different ideas of what the 'innocent-appearing' phrase means.

Of course other national laws also contain mechanisms to reverse procedural or indeed substantive mistakes.[7] In the common law, they

---

[5] Andres Auer, Giagio Malinverni and Michel Hottelier, *Droit Constitutionnel Suisse* (2 vols., Bern: Staempfli Editions, 2000), vol. II, p. 605, at no. 1272. Swiss jurists employ the phrase '*interdiction de formalisme excessif*'. See *Feuille Fédérale (Journal Officiel) de la Confédération Suisse* (1997) at p. 183; *Recueil officiel des Arrêts du Tribunal Fédéral* 119 Ia 4, at p. 6.

[6] Auer, Malinverni and Hottelier, *Droit Constitutionnel Suisse*, vol. II, p. 534, at no. 1098.

[7] French jurisprudence has developed an exceptional rule of jurisdiction to the effect that the municipal courts will hear a complaint even in the absence of any territorial connection with France if they find that no other legal system considers itself competent to dispose of the matter. The purpose of the rule is expressed as that of avoiding denial of justice; see Pierre Mayer, *Droit international privé* (6th edn, Paris: Montchrestien, 1998), at p. 189. This is another singular use of the expression; it does not denote breach of a duty on the part of any court or indeed legal order, but rather commands the French judge to step in if no one else will. This notion developed in response to the historical refusal of French courts to hear disputes between two foreigners; that *raison d'être* is no longer extant, and denial of justice is today seldom used as a jurisdictional basis; Loïc Cadiet, *Droit judiciaire privé* (3rd edn, Paris: Litec, 2000), p. 243; *but see National Iranian Oil Co. (NIOC) v. Israel*, 2002 *Revue de l'arbitrage* 427.

give effect to notions of natural justice, due process, or appeal for reversible error; in civil law systems, they are sanctioned by codes of procedure. They are thus corrected by the legal system itself and are therefore by definition not viewed as denials of justice. The fact that the Swiss consider a wide range of erroneous lower-court decisions to constitute denials of justice is merely a matter of nomenclature.[8] But when international law considers claims of denials of justice, it evaluates the relevant national system from the outside and from above, in a way which that system by definition cannot do itself.

## Right and might in the law of nations

The origin of the international law of denial of justice may be traced to the medieval rule of private reprisals which emerged when the centre did not hold: when spent empires and kingdoms or principalities could no longer impose their authority.[9] On occasions when ordinary remedies therefore failed, reprisals by private individuals, typically authorised by a letter of marque or warrant from their own sovereign, could be justified as an extraordinary remedy for especially high degrees of injustice: *denegatio justitiae*.[10] Such a wrong would appear whenever judgments were the result of prejudice in favour of one disputant, or desire to please a local ruler – but not if the judgment were simply mistaken. The right would not materialise until appeals had been exhausted. Thereafter, as a number of treaties explicitly provided, extreme measures would not be considered acts of war if justice could not be secured by ordinary means. Justice delayed was recognised as justice denied; the Anglo-Spanish Treaty of 1667, for example, authorised reprisal after six months' notice.[11]

---

[8] In his oral argument on 5 June 1936 in *Losinger Co. Case (Switzerland v. Yugoslavia)*, Professor Georges Sauser-Hall, as Agent for Switzerland, developed the distinctions between municipal and international notions of denial of justice. His point was that the international concept was broader than national ones; he could hardly have argued that the position in his own national law was representative; (1935) PCIJ, Series C, No. 78, 7, at p. 313. The relevance of Sauser-Hall's arguments – and indeed that of the case as a whole – are discussed in Stephen M. Schwebel, *International Arbitration: Three Salient Problems* (Cambridge: Grotius, 1987), at pp. 74–75.

[9] Freeman, at p. 55, note 1, cites da Legano, *Tractatus de Bello, de Repræsaliis et de Duello* (Oxford: Cargenie, 1360), which he found 'apparently remained the most direct attack on this problem for well over two hundred and fifty years'. *Ibid.* at p. 57, note 1.

[10] The expression is echoed in its contemporary Spanish equivalent: *denegación de justicia*.

[11] Treaty of Peace and Friendship between Great Britain and Spain, 13 May 1667 [1667–1668] Consolidated Treaty Series 63.

The objective of the reprisals was typically to compel the original delinquent – who might be a private person – to make reparations since the legal system had proved itself unwilling to do so. The definition of reprisals preferred by de Visscher was this: 'A right granted to a private person by the sovereign authority of which he is a subject to repossess, in times of peace, even by force, his goods or the equivalent thereof, from a foreigner or fellow citizens of the latter, whenever he has not been able to obtain justice by the judicial avenues of the country of his adversary.'[12] Although de Visscher traced one such document back to 1489 (France/Spain), most of the 'long series of treaties' limiting reprisals to instances of denial of justice seem to have emerged in the 1600s.[13]

As states appeared in their modern form, they claimed full control of legal processes ('exclusive jurisdiction') in their territory. With this control came responsibility, including external responsibility for wrongs suffered by foreigners in their territory. The system of reprisals fell into disuse; the injured alien did not need to seek private justice because the foreign state was bound by the law of nations, and would be held to its international responsibility at the initiative of the complainant's own state, which, rather than issuing letters of marque, could exercise the right of diplomatic protection.

Acceptance of international authority to control national dispensation of justice was neither instant nor universal. To the contrary, many states maintained that foreigners should not have any greater entitlement than citizens to challenge the national system. Freeman put it this way:

The principle that foreigners must be content with the treatment which is dispensed by the territorial authorities to nationals is based upon a general presumption *that the laws and their administration are satisfactory in the light of international requirements.*[14]

This passage confuses the problem, and in so doing understates it. For if a general presumption of the type invoked by the author did not exist, it surely would *not* have to be invented. Any party contending that a state's administration of justice is not 'satisfactory in the light of international requirements' must prove it: *actori incumbit probatio*. To posit that this is the result of a presumption is unnecessary and probably wrong. (If a state acting as a claimant wished to demonstrate that it was entitled to the recognition of some right, or absence of liability, as the result of a national judicial decision, it would benefit from no presumption, but would have to

---

[12] De Visscher at p. 371.   [13] *Ibid.* at p. 372.
[14] Freeman at p. 74 (emphasis in the original).

demonstrate that the decision satisfied the international requirement pertaining to the claimed right or to the disavowed responsibility.)

The problem was in fact more serious; some states simply refused to recognise the very existence of 'international requirements' that could trump national standards, and even more emphatically rejected the idea that aliens might be entitled to different treatment from local citizens (because they could claim diplomatic protection and thus trigger proceedings leading to international adjudication).

To understand the context of this reluctance to insist on national treatment, which found its historical spokesman in the Argentinian Carlos Calvo, one must be aware of another difficulty in the transition from the regime of reprisals to that of diplomatic protection, namely the draping of violent interventions in the raiments of international law. Diplomatic protection typically involved a claim that a citizen of the protecting state had been the victim of a denial of justice. If such claims had simply been presented to international tribunals, the matter would not have engendered such controversy and bitterness. The problem was that the old methods of reprisals were revived in the form of gunboat diplomacy and the continued tendency of the powerful to view the right of protection not as an entitlement to stand before an international tribunal, but as a warrant for the use of unilateral force. The *diplomatic* component of the expression 'diplomatic protection' was, in such circumstances, an ironic but hardly subtle fiction.

The apogee of gunboat diplomacy was not reached off the shores of a Latin American port, but rather in Piraeus in 1850, when Lord Palmerston – then Foreign Secretary, five years before becoming Prime Minister – sent the British fleet to seize all ships in the harbour in retribution for the failure of the Greek Government to acknowledge the legal claim of a British subject whose house had been burned down by an anti-Semitic mob angered by the prohibition of the burning in effigy of Judas Iscariot at Easter. This matter became known as the *Don Pacifico* affair, not from the name of a ship but because the victim David Ricardo, born in Gibraltar, was commonly known under this appellation.

For reasons of diplomatic history of no interest here, Palmerston's actions involved a risk of war with France, and the House of Lords censured his foreign policy. A Palmerston ally in the House of Commons moved a contrary resolution in his support. This gave Palmerston the occasion to give his '*Civis Romanus Sum*' oration, which in turn engendered a doctrine of the same name. Here is the nub of it:

As the Roman, in days of old, held himself free from indignity when he could say 'Civis Romanus Sum' [I am a Roman citizen], so also a British subject in whatever land he may be, shall feel confident that the watchful eye and the strong arm of England will protect him against injustice and wrong.

Palmerston went on to spell out the ramifications:

If our subjects abroad have complaints against individuals, or against the government of a foreign country, if the courts of law of that country can afford them redress, then, no doubt, to those courts of justice the British subject ought in the first instance to apply; and it is only on a denial of justice, or upon decisions manifestly unjust, that the British Government should be called upon to interfere.

I say, then, that our doctrine is, that, in the first instance, redress should be sought from the law courts of the country; but that in cases where redress can not be so had – and those cases are many – to confine a British subject to that remedy only, would be to deprive him of the protection which he is entitled to receive.

We shall be told, perhaps, as we have already been told, that if the people of the country are liable to have heavy stones placed upon their breasts, and police officers to dance upon them; if they are liable to have their heads tied to their knees, and to be left for hours in that state; or to be swung like a pendulum, and to be bastinadoed as they swing, foreigners have no right to be better treated than the natives, and have no business to complain if the same things are practiced upon them. We may be told this, but that is not my opinion, nor do I believe it is the opinion of any reasonable man.[15]

Palmerston's rhetoric was effective. The House voted its confidence in his policy; and he went on to become a symbol of British nationalism. Robert Lord Cecil was later to be quoted as reflecting: 'I am aware that, whatever folly or madness an English government may commit, the appeal to the Civis Romanus doctrine is rarely without its effect upon an English audience.'[16]

Palmerston argued that Britain had assisted in securing Greece's independence from Turkey in 1832 on the condition that it become a constitutional monarchy; that when Prince Otho of Bavaria came of age and ascended to the Greek throne his advisers preferred to maintain a 'despotic' rule under which judges 'were at the mercy of the advisers of the Crown' and 'brigandage' was tolerated and indeed rewarded; that Greek soldiers stationed 'within a few minutes' walk' of Don Pacifico's house

---

[15] Parl. Deb., vol. 62, ser. 3, cols. 380–444, 25 June 1850, quoted in E. Root 'The Basis of Protection to Citizens Residing Abroad' (1910) 4 AJIL 517, at p. 522.

[16] Quoted in Joseph H. Park, *British Prime Ministers of the Nineteenth Century: Policies and Speeches* (New York University Press, 1916), at p. 153.

refused to afford protection; that the Greek police refused to search the residences of important people where his stolen jewels might be found; and that the Greek Government dismissed the claim out of hand. Of those who criticised him for employing 'so large a force against so small a Power', he asked rhetorically: 'Is it to be held that if your subjects suffer violence, outrage, plunder in a country which is weak and small, you are to tell them when they apply for redress, that the country is so weak and small that one cannot ask it for compensation?' Should the British government say, 'we cannot give you redress because we have such ample and easy ways of procuring it?'

The *Don Pacifico* affair was only the most notorious of instances where powerful states took it up on themselves to be judge and party when espousing the claims of the real or ostensible victim. As Edwin Borchard was to write in his influential treatise in 1916, *The Diplomatic Protection of Citizens Abroad*, the judgment by one government of the legality of the conduct of another was:

the primary condition for the all too frequent abuse, by strong states, of the rights of weaker countries.[17]

In due course, the twentieth century brought about a consecration of the principle that international conflicts may not be resolved by force, or 'intervention' as the term was used in international law.[18] (The immensity of the suffering of multitudes of civilians during that bloody century doubtless explains the urgent recognition of the norm, so tragically honoured in the breach.) At an intermediate stage, the Drago Doctrine – conceived in the aftermath of the German, British and Italian intervention in Venezuela in 1902–3 – sought to establish the principle that the public debt of a state could never justify armed intervention – provided that the borrowing state accepted international arbitration.[19] Today, the issue is one of adjudication, not force. But achieving a proper balance

---

[17] Edwin Borchard, *The Diplomatic Protection of Citizens Abroad* (New York: The Banks Law Publishing Co., 1916), at p. 331.

[18] The authorities are innumerable. *See* notably Article 8 of the Montevideo Convention on the Rights and Duties of States, Montevideo, 26 December 1933, in force 26 December 1934; Article 3 of the International Law Commission's Draft Declaration on Rights and Duties of States, UN Doc. A/1251 [1949] Yearbook of International Law Commission 287 ('Every State has the duty to refrain from intervening in the internal or external affairs of any other State').

[19] Louis Drago, then the Argentinian Minister of Foreign Affairs, wrote his celebrated note on 29 December 1902 on the occasion of the joint intervention of Great Britain, Italy and Germany against Venezuela. He published a monograph entitled *Cobro*

between external norms and internal freedom to act is still far from complete. It has not been an easy process.

## Objections of weak states

The *Don Pacifico* affair offers instructive parallels in the dominant industrialised countries' attitude toward Latin America. New states there were assisted by Washington and London as they emerged from colonial domination, but their new protectors – having acted on complex motivations ranging from pure geopolitics to commercial opportunity to idealist solidarity with the oppressed – seemed to consider themselves entitled to impose their own ideas of discipline when the fledgling national structures failed to ensure respect for the persons and property of aliens.

So, for example, the Colombian port of Cartagena came to be targeted for subjugation in 1857, just a few years after Palmerston had dispatched the British fleet to Piraeus. The antecedents of the affair involved a vast sale of arms by an influential merchant named James Mackintosh. An early and ardent advocate of recognition of the new states of Latin America, he had addressed the House of Commons in June 1824 in the following terms:

When Great Britain, I hope soon, recognises the states of Spanish America, it will not be a concession to them, because they do not need such recognition; it will be for the own interest of England, to protect commerce and shipping of its subjects, to achieve the best methods of cultivating friendly relations with important countries, and settle, through negotiations, differences that otherwise might end in war.[20]

Mackintosh's enthusiasm for such recognition was fully understandable. In February 1821, he had signed a contract in London with Luis López, a representative of the newly independent Gran Colombia, for the provision of ships, arms and uniforms for 10,000 men. The price was £186,000, paid for by Gran Colombia in government bonds issued with a

---

*coercitivo de deudas publicas* in 1906; his argument is most accessible in English in 'State Loans and their Relation to International Policy', (1907) 1 AJIL 692. The Drago Doctrine was reflected in the Porter Convention of 1907; *see* A. S. Hersley, 'The Calvo and Drago Doctrines', (1907) 1 AJIL 26. *See* also G. W. Scott, 'Hague Convention Restricting the Use of Force to Recover Contract Claims', (1908) 2 AJIL 78; Borchard, *The Diplomatic Protection of Citizens Abroad*, at p. 308 ss.

[20] Quoted in Klaus Gallo, *De la invasión al reconocimiento – Gran Bretaña y el Río de la Plata 1806–1826* (Buenos Aires: A–Z Editores, 1994), at p. 222.

face value of £310,000. The material arrived on time in Cartagena de Indias in April 1822. However, Vice President Santander initially refused delivery in light of the excessive cost. After a debate concerning a renegotiation of the price, none other than Simón Bolívar acknowledged the contract.[21]

The bonds were not repaid. A Colombian minister, Manuel José Hurtado, was sent to London to renegotiate the debt. Attempts to settle amicably failed. Hence the thought that a debt owed by a state recognised by the British Government would be a better credit risk might have crossed Mackintosh's mind when he made his eager speech to the British Parliament.

In 1830, Gran Colombia disintegrated into the states of Nueva Granada (Colombia), Venezuela and Ecuador. Repayment became even more problematic. After many years of renegotiation and failed settlements, British patience ran out. In sharp contrast to the peaceful settlement of disputes prophesied by Mackintosh in 1824, the British Government dispatched a squadron of five warships to Cartagena to pursue his claims. On their arrival at daybreak on 23 April 1857, British Vice Admiral Houston Stewart sent an ultimatum to the Governor, Narciso Jiménez, to pay the outstanding debt or risk bombardment. By an irony of fate, before the deadline expired, tropical disease broke out on the ships and Stewart had to seek the permission of the city authorities to bury the dead in the city cemetery. The magnanimity of the local population in caring for the sick caused him to seek a revocation of the order to bombard which, doubtless in the English spirit of 'fair play', was granted.[22]

It has often been observed in international relations, and elsewhere, that the weak seek the protection of the law, while the strong do not need to be punctilious about its observance. As Solon was remembered to have said, in a dark moment:

---

[21] The case has many parallels with *Jacob Idler* v. *Venezuela*, Moore, *Arbitrations* at p. 3491, discussed at considerable length in the section entitled 'Governmental interference', in Chapter 6.

[22] I am indebted to Nigel Blackaby for providing me with details of this episode, which is described in Eduardo Lemaître, *A Brief History of Cartagena* (Bogotá: Editorial Colina, 1994). This is, broadly speaking, a Colombian version of the events. The story may be told in other ways. But in historical terms, to understand the impulses of Latin American lawyers, perception trumps the facts. Perception is the most important of all realities (even on the premise, much debated in philosophy, that there is any other reality).

Laws are spiders' webs:
If some poor creature comes up against them, it is caught;
but a bigger one can break through and get away.[23]

Experience with the delict of denial of justice in the nineteenth century was so closely associated with unilateral force that it was viewed by the weak as a menace to be resisted. How could it be pretended that a sanction was legitimised by international law in the absence of mutually acceptable, neutral international adjudication?

## The Calvo Doctrine and Clause

Carlos Calvo would have been well aware of the Mackintosh incident. In 1857, he was vice-consul of Argentina in Montevideo at the beginning of an illustrious diplomatic and legal career. Eleven years later, his *Derecho internacional teórico y práctico*, an intellectual assault on gunboat diplomacy, set out a theory of international law which would enter the collective psyche of Latin American and leave its mark well into the late twentieth century. The theory was founded on a basic premise: foreigners who invested in a state (or contracted a debt with a state) should have the same rights to protection as nationals of that state and cannot claim broader protection. If they have suffered a loss, they may only complain to the courts of the host state. As long as the national courts are accessible to them, foreigners have no international recourse. Thus disputes arising from the presence of foreigners are removed from the realm of diplomatic

---

[23] A sustained modern expression is found in the book-length essay of a former US State Department official, Robert Kagan, *Of Paradise and Power: America and Europe in the New World Order* (New York: Alfred A. Knopf, 2003). The author writes at pp. 10–11 that the founders of the US 'knew from their reading of Vattel that in international law, "strength or weakness . . . counts for nothing. A dwarf is as much a man as a giant is; a small Republic is no less a sovereign State than the most powerful Kingdom" [quoting from Gerald Stourzh, *Alexander Hamilton and the Idea of Republican Government*]' (Stanford University Press, 1970, at p. 134). Later generations of Americans, possessed of a great deal more power and influence on the world stage, would not always be as enamoured of this constraining egalitarian quality of international law. In the eighteenth and early nineteenth centuries, it was the great European powers that did not always want to be constrained . . . When the United States was weak, it practiced the strategies of indirection, the strategies of weakness; now that the United Sates is powerful, it behaves as powerful nations do. When the European great powers were strong, they believed in strength and martial glory. Now they see the world through the eyes of weaker powers. These very different points of view have naturally produced . . . differing perspectives on the value and meaning of international law and international institutions.'

protection which on spectacular occasions, as seen, had been exercised in an abusive manner.

Calvo's theory was soon tested. In 1873, a note from the Mexican Minister of Foreign Affairs to the US ambassador affirmed by reference to Calvo's writings that Mexico was not responsible for the harm caused to foreigners during the civil war. The ambassador responded that Dr Calvo was a young lawyer whose theories had not been accepted internationally. This was the first of many rejections of the theory by the United States.

As capital importers, the Latin American states saw the Calvo Doctrine as a means of safeguarding national sovereignty. It removed the unilateral right of the investor's state to interfere militarily or politically on behalf of the investor. If the doctrine had been applied in the Mackintosh contract through the inclusion of the so-called Calvo Clause, the creditor would have had a right of redress only before the Colombian courts for repayment of his debt.

More formal recognition of the Calvo Doctrine came on the occasion of the First International Conference of American States held in Washington in 1889–90, when the *ad hoc* commission for international law recommended adoption of the following propositions 'as principles of American international law:

(1)   Foreigners are entitled to enjoy all the civil rights enjoyed by natives; and they shall be accorded all the benefits of said rights in all that is essential as well as in the form or procedure, and the legal remedies incident thereto, absolutely in like manner as said natives.

(2)   A nation has not, nor recognizes in favor to foreigners, any other obligations or responsibilities than those which in favor of the natives are established in like cases by the constitution and the laws.'[24]

This recommendation was unanimously adopted by the participating Latin American states, with the exception of Haiti.

Taken in its historical and political context, the Calvo Doctrine was an understandable attempt to rid the newly independent states of the trauma of foreign intervention. Latin American states were sometimes able to convince their European partners of its utility. For example, Article 21 of the Treaty of Friendship, Commerce and Navigation between Italy and Colombia of 1892 states:

[24] Adopted on 18 April 1890, quoted in Freeman at p. 714.

Both Contracting Parties wish to avoid disputes which could affect their friendly relationship and agree that in connection with disputes involving private parties arising out of criminal, civil or administrative matters, their diplomatic agents will abstain from intervention, save in case of denial of justice or extraordinary or unlawful delay in the administration of justice.[25]

Latin American governments faced with military or diplomatic action invoked the doctrine frequently. In its most rigid form, the Calvo Doctrine polarised the positions of the United States and Europe, on the one hand, and Latin America on the other. The 'old continent' and the North Americans did not believe that local courts would dispense justice to foreigners, and so rejected the Calvo Doctrine as a whole. Indeed, the Calvo Doctrine replaced one form of unilateralism with another. Insofar as it remained *doctrina hispanoamericana* rather than *doctrina universal* it never became part of customary international law. In order to reach a workable compromise, movement was needed on both sides.

Neutral ground was discovered at the Second International Peace Conference, held in The Hague in 1907, when the Convention for the Peaceful Resolution of International Disputes[26] was prepared. The Latin American states *en masse* signed the Convention, which promoted the institution of compulsory bilateral arbitration treaties. Under these treaties, in the event of a dispute between two states arising out of a private investor's interests, the matter would be resolved neither by gunboats nor local courts, but by an independent arbitral tribunal.

Strict adherence to the Calvo Doctrine was understandable when international law offered no options other than local courts or foreign warships. But the 1907 Convention created a new tool to ensure equality between states at the moment of dispute resolution, notwithstanding vast differences in economic or military power. Examples of early bilateral treaties include the Honduras–Italy Treaty of 1913, which provided for state-to-state arbitration of disputes arising from 'unlawful acts or omissions' of either state or its public authorities that caused financial loss to the nationals of the other state.[27] Pursuant to the Treaty, in the event of such a dispute, Honduras and Italy would sign a special agreement setting out the procedure for the resulting arbitration. If such an agreement were not signed, the arbitration would be conducted by a tribunal appointed by the Permanent Court of Arbitration in The Hague, in accordance with the rules set out in

---

[25] The exception of denial of justice is characteristic; see Note 30 of this chapter below.
[26] [1898–1899] Consolidated Treaty Series 410.
[27] Trattati Convenzioni vol. XXII at p. 391.

the Convention for the Peaceful Settlement of International Disputes of 1899 and the resolutions of The Hague Conference of 1899.

Inter-state arbitration as envisaged by the Italy–Honduras Treaty was clearly an encroachment upon the Calvo Doctrine, since it enabled an aggrieved foreign investor to seek the espousal by its home state of a claim which could then be resolved before an international tribunal. Yet it was also an affirmation of one of the underlying principles of the doctrine: equality between foreign and local citizens. The theme was taken up again in the well-known mixed claims commissions constituted to deal with alleged expropriations, notably in Venezuela and Mexico.[28]

The emergence of such tribunals should not be taken as evidence of harmony and understanding. Latin Americans still resented the fact that agreements to such adjudication were negotiated out of what was for them a position of weakness, and were offended by the eagerness and presumptuousness with which some claimants were obtaining redress for what the local governments simply were not, with the best will in the world, able to ensure for their own citizens. Not all representatives of the industrialised nations displayed the even-handedness of the US Secretary of State Elihu Root, who in a remarkable address to the American Society of International Law in 1910 – two years before winning the Nobel Peace Prize – said the following:

Citizens abroad are too apt to complain that justice has been denied them whenever they are beaten in a litigation, forgetting that, as a rule, they would complain just the same if they were beaten in a litigation in the courts of their own country. When a man goes into a foreign country to reside or to trade he submits himself, his rights, and interests to the jurisdiction of the courts of that country. He will naturally be at a disadvantage in litigation against citizens of the country. He is less familiar than they with the laws, the ways of doing business, the habits of thought and action, the method of procedure, the local customs and prejudices, and often with the language in which the business is done and the proceedings carried on. It is not the duty of a foreign country in which such a litigant finds himself to make up to him for these disadvantages under which he labors. They are disadvantages inseparable from his prosecuting his business in a strange land. A large part of the dissatisfaction which aliens feel and express regarding their treatment by foreign tribunals results from these causes, which furnish no just ground for international complaint. It is very desirable that people who go into other countries shall realize that they are not entitled to have the laws and police regulations and methods of judicial procedure and customs of

---

[28] The literature is abundant, and the awards numerous. A valuable bibliography appears in Freeman at pp. 727–745.

business made over to suit them, or to have any other or different treatment than that which is accorded to the citizens of the country into which they have gone; so long as the government of that country maintains, according to its own ideas and for the benefit of its own citizens, a system of law and administration which does not violate the common standard of justice that is a part of international law.[29]

## The impulse to limit the scope of denial of justice

Since they perceived the rule as too readily traduced into a hypocritical cover for gunboat diplomacy, Latin American jurists came to take the narrowest possible view of the scope of denial of justice (without denying that it was a delict[30]). At the same time, they took the broadest possible view of exhaustion of local remedies as a precondition of the exercise of diplomatic protection. The great debates in the 1960s and 1970s about so-called permanent sovereignty over natural resources suggest that this deeply sceptical attitude was transmitted to the large number of new and insecure states that achieved their independence in the two decades following the Second World War.[31]

These political apprehensions, often emotional, led to the perpetuation of a dialogue of the deaf which endured for at least a hundred years. On the one hand jurists from weaker countries legitimately recoiled from the perceived threat of force under the fig-leaf of the law of nations. Unable to affect the realities of power, they attacked the fig-leaf. On the other hand,

---

[29] Elihu Root, 'The Basis of Protection of Citizens Abroad', (1910) 4 AJIL 517, at pp. 526–527.

[30] In particular, Carlos Calvo himself, as we shall see, accepted this principle. So did his successors; see e.g., J. Irizarry y Puente, 'The Concept of "Denial of Justice" in Latin America', (1944) 43 *Michigan Law Review* 383, at p. 390 (aliens should not be allowed to, *'except in the event of denial of justice*, [invoke diplomatic protection] against a definitive judgment of the courts' emphasis added) and, to identical effect, Clovis Bevilaqua, *Direito publico internacional – A synthese dos principios e a contribuiçao do Brazil* (Rio de Janeiro: Livraria Francisco Alves, 1910), vol. I, at p. 198. Indeed, when the Second International Conference of American States adopted the Convention relative to the Rights of Aliens in Mexico City in 1902, its general rule of national treatment explicitly reserved an exception for international claims in the case of 'manifest denial of justice, or unusual delay, or evident violation of the principles of international law.' Quoted in International Law Commission (Dugard), The Addendum to the Third Report on Diplomatic Protection, UN Doc. A/CN.4/523/Add.1 (2002) at p. 4, para. 8.

[31] Commenting on provisions relating to expropriation in the so-called UN Charter of Economic Rights and Duties of States, General Assembly Resolution, adopted 12 December 1974 (UN Doc. A/RES/3281 (XXIX)), William D. Rogers described them as 'a classic restatement of Calvo', in 'Of Missionaries, Fanatics and Lawyers: Some Thoughts on Investment Disputes in the Americas', (1978) 72 AJIL 1, at p. 5.

jurists fervently seeking the propagation of the rule of law found it inconceivable that any serious scholar would insist that a state, as a subject of international law, could be the judge of the legality of its own conduct.

The frustrations of this dialogue were such that writers who ordinarily expressed themselves in measured tones were unable to resist the temptation of venting their frustration on paper. One lightning-rod was the much-debated Guerrero Report[32] and its suggestions that a decision not to hear a foreigner's petition could not be a denial of justice because of 'the very fact that the local tribunal has been able to give a decision regarding this request' and that it was 'inadmissible' – contrary to the overwhelming weight of doctrine – to consider that delays may constitute a denial of justice. Reflecting on the implications, Freeman yielded to a polemical impulse (uncharacteristically, it must be said) in the following lines:

The possibility of a re-hearing before an international tribunal filled Guerrero with a terrible foreboding and he shrank from this threatened violation of internal sovereignty as from an incurable disease.[33]

Thus ships passed in the night, some piloted by those who could not understand how the rule of international law could be compatible with pure self-assessment, others by those who felt impelled to protect their fragile sovereignty. For the latter, one surmises, the debate was *not one of principle but of control over its application.* They did not in reality have a quarrel with the principle of state responsibility, but a profound distrust for the way it was given effect, whether by overmuscular 'diplomatic' protection or by international adjudicators whom they felt were imposed upon them. Such concerns justified particular insistence on the neutrality of the mechanism for international adjudication. They did not justify the deconstruction of international law. Unfortunately the Latin American voice acquired a reputation for seeking the latter, culminating in the Guerrero Report. That document was characterised by the following conclusion, wholly indefensible from the standpoint of positive law and dominant doctrine:

---

[32] Annexed to questionnaire No. 4 as adopted in 1926 by the Committee of Experts for the Progressive Codification of International Law established by the Assembly of the League of Nations in 1924, League of Nations Document C.196.M.70.1927.V; reproduced in Freeman, Appendix II, at pp. 629–633. The rapporteur, Gustavo Guerrero, was a national of El Salvador.

[33] Freeman at p. 121.

a judicial decision, whatever it may be, and even if vitiated by error or injustice, does not involve the international responsibility of the State.[34]

This proposal was naturally condemned by Freeman, in these terms:

Under this statement of the law, the rendering of *any* decision, regardless of its character, and although it be convincingly demonstrated that the decision was actuated by gross bias or was the result of fraud or bribery, suffices to refute the possibility of a denial of justice.[35]

And again:

Guerrero's view – which typifies the Latin-American attitude – emasculates the rule by which States are responsible for conduct of their judicial organs running counter to international obligations governing the protection of aliens, since it limits denial of justice (and therefore the right of foreign States to intervene diplomatically), to cases which are almost unheard of in the practice of modern States during time of peace. The principle that aliens must be admitted to appropriate judicial recourse for the protection of their rights is one of general international law, quite apart from the common stipulation of numerous treaties that 'nationals of the High Contracting Parties shall have free and unhindered access to the courts and may sue or be sued on the same conditions as nationals of the country.' Consequently, since foreigners almost everywhere have access to courts which render decisions of some kind or another, the effect of the procedural formula is to render the whole notion of denial of justice meaningless.[36]

## Modern political realities

Ministries of Justice are often the poor cousins of government. Many regimes place higher value on their own physical security – internal or external – than on the legal security of their citizens. Ministries of the Interior and Defence stand first in line when budgets are settled. Nor do ordinary citizens necessarily insist that their governments give high priority to providing the material conditions of the best possible administration of justice; for them, health, employment and education are constant concerns, but many go through life without a single day in court. Hence the immediacy of the demands on the Ministries of Public Health, of Labour, or of Education.

Yet investment in justice is not a luxury. Without the rule of law, how can access to health, education, or indeed any form of meaningful

---

[34] Paragraph 6(b) of the Report, quoted in Freeman at p. 122.
[35] Freeman at p. 122 (emphasis in the original).   [36] *Ibid.* at p. 123.

opportunity be properly regulated? How is it possible to achieve economic development, which does not occur without some confidence in
stable expectations?

It takes political maturity to act on such insights. The facts, however,
are plain to see. Poor countries may have powerful presidents and gen-
erals, but they seldom have powerful judges. In poor countries, judges
tend to have far less social status than the leading lawyers who appear
before them. The best and the brightest of graduates are not attracted to a
career on the bench. The quality of justice suffers; so does the general
perception of it; and a vicious cycle works its insidious way into collective
cynicism and despair.

Here and there, idealistic attempts have been made to ensure that
justice is not starved into submission. There have even been constitutional
proclamations that the Justice budget cannot be decreased beneath a
certain proportion of governmental expenditures. But such noble sentiments are all too often simply ignored, or turn out to be vulnerable to
manipulative accounting and other familiar subversions. A decent legal
culture, like any other aspect of culture, cannot be decreed into existence.

It may thus be a source of considerable frustration for a society which
finds it impossible to achieve honest and transparent justice from its own
courts to be told that the treatment to which foreigners claim to be
entitled under international law is superior to that given to local citizens.

The great difficulty is to understand that international adjudication is
not *foreign* adjudication. The citizens of a given country have no stake in
foreign justice; they did not create it, and whatever they may think of its
qualities in the abstract it has no legitimate basis on which to judge them
(unless they venture abroad). Therefore, as long as international justice is
thought of as foreign justice, it will be resisted. The key is the perception of
inclusiveness; when 'we' are part of the processes of international law,
consulted in its formation and benefiting from its protections and remedies, it becomes 'our' law too. The process by which *their law* (meaning the
province of an indifferent and perhaps hostile outside world) becomes *our
law* is extraordinarily complex. The movement is gradual, and not necessarily constant. Different groups of citizens, at different times, have
sharply varied perceptions. Is there a tipping point? If so, how might it
best be attained? These are daunting questions.

Nevertheless, an important movement has been building momentum
in Latin America, the region best known for its suspicion of international
adjudication. In the course of the past two decades, Latin American states
have ratified many bilateral treaties for the promotion and protection of

investment (BITs), and have reversed their initial scepticism with respect to the ICSID Convention of 1965. They were quicker to adhere to the Multilateral Investment Guarantee Agency (MIGA), which also refers to international arbitration.[37] All of these instruments are avatars of the bilateral arbitration treaties that grew out of the 1907 Peace Conference. The most significant feature of BITs is that they give foreign investors the right to initiate international arbitration against the host state to seek a remedy for breaches of the treaty, without requiring any intervention of their own government. Some 300 such treaties involving the region were extant in 2003, more than twice the number four years earlier. Many investors have tested the mechanisms; Latin American states accounted for over 50 per cent of the cases pending the same year before the International Centre for the Settlement of Investment Disputes, the World Bank institution which administers many of these claims.

In addition to BITs, aggrieved parties may be in a position to avail themselves of the options available under the multilateral treaties of the trading regions, such as NAFTA and Mercosur (Brazil, Argentina, Paraguay and Uruguay), which contain similar provisions for intra-regional investment disputes (see NAFTA Chapter 11 and the 1994 Colonia and Buenos Aires protocols for Mercosur). These recall the principles once envisaged at the 1907 Peace Conference, providing a readily accessible neutral forum for the resolution of investment disputes that respects the equality of the parties. By placing arbitration firmly in the hands of the investor, and not the state, they have also effectively depoliticised the remedy. This, as Ibrahim Shihata once wrote, is a principal advantage of providing direct private access to an international forum.[38]

Notwithstanding the practical erosion of the Calvo Doctrine throughout the course of the twentieth century, it has retained a mythical status among public lawyers in Latin America who enshrined it in the constitutions of their states. From Guatemala to Peru and from El Salvador to Bolivia, the Calvo Clause has held a place in the *magna carta*. The developments described above have led to the need to confront the principle of the superior status of international law over domestic law. From its inception, the debate has contained a seed of ambiguity in that, as

---

[37] See C. K. Dalrymple, 'Politics and Foreign Direct Investment: The Multilateral Investment Guarantee Agency and the Calvo Clause', (1996) 29 *Cornell International Law Journal* 161.

[38] Ibrahim Shihata, 'Towards a Greater Depolitization of Investment Disputes: The Roles of ICSID and MIGA', (1986) 1 ICSID Review 1.

Calvo himself readily conceded, foreign complaints were admissible if a state does not at least grant access to its courts. That concession immediately opens the door to question the *quality* of that access; it is difficult to accept that any obligation would be satisfied by a pretence of form. Hence, for example, when the Honduran Constitution of 1982 declares that aliens are entitled to diplomatic protection only in cases of denial of justice,[39] we find ourselves again contemplating the Guerrero–Freeman divide and the utter unlikelihood that any international adjudicator would accept that the former's extreme minimalism reflects international law.

All in all, nearly a century after his death, Calvo's residual legacy in Latin America appears limited. Throughout the region, states have recognised the need to evolve and provide protections for foreign investors as one of the enticements to invest. Once democracy had re-established itself as the norm by the beginning of the 1990s, many countries adopted economic models which included liberal access for foreign investment. In order to attract that investment, the region needed to provide a secure legal framework. A strict approach to the Calvo Doctrine would have been sharply dissuasive.

One should consider that the mischief Calvo sought to combat was the *de facto* perpetuation of the medieval regime of reprisals, with its unilateralist feature of a state being a judge in its own cause, seeking remedies at the mouth of a cannon. The underlying principle of the Calvo Doctrine was to prevent such inequity by insisting on equality between the domestic party and the foreigner, the home state of the investor and the host state of the investment. So if he were with us today, Calvo might justifiably point out that his doctrine supported rather than poisoned the fundamental tenet of international arbitration: his purpose was equal arms, not the pursuit of xenophobia.

Much credit for defusing the tensions surrounding the Calvo Doctrine should be given to the remarkable decision of the Mexico–United States General Claims Commission, under its President Cornelis Van Vollenhoven, in the 1926 case of *North American Dredging Company of Texas* (*US* v. *Mexico*).[40] The claim was for the recovery of nearly a quarter of a

[39] What is true for this reflection of the Calvo Doctrine also holds with respect to the Calvo Clause. As Donald R. Shea concluded in his comprehensive study, most Latin American states would concede the exception of 'a real denial of justice from the contractual ban on intervention'. *The Calvo Clause: A Problem of Inter-American and International Law and Diplomacy* (Minneapolis: University of Minnesota Press, 1955), at p. 36.
[40] 31 March 1926, IV RIAA 26.

million dollars, then a substantial sum of money,[41] on behalf of a company which in 1912 had entered into a contract for dredging the port of Salina Cruz. It contained, in Article 18, a Calvo Clause reading as follows:

The contractor and all persons who, as employees or in any other capacity, may be engaged in the execution of the work under this contract either directly or indirectly, shall be considered as Mexicans in all matters, within the Republic of Mexico, concerning the execution of such work and the fulfilment of this contract. They shall not claim, nor shall they have, with regard to the interests and the business connected with this contract, any other rights or means to enforce the same than those granted by the laws of the Republic to Mexicans, nor shall they enjoy any other rights than those established in favor of Mexicans. They are consequently deprived of any rights as aliens, and under no conditions shall the intervention of foreign diplomatic agents be permitted, in any matter related to this contract.

The Commission had held that, in a parallel case, it had jurisdiction to hear contractual claims. The issue was whether Article 18 defeated jurisdiction in this case. Upholding Mexico's demurrer, the Commission stated that it was not 'impressed' by arguments at the 'extremes', i.e. either wholly endorsing or wholly rejecting Calvo Clauses:

The Calvo clause in a specific contract is neither a clause which must be sustained to its full length because of its contractual nature nor can it be discretionarily separated from the rest of the contract as if it were just an accidental postscript. The problem is not solved by saying yes or no; the affirmative answer exposing the rights of foreigners to undeniable dangers, the negative answer leaving to the nations involved no alternative except that of exclusion of foreigners from business ... By merely ignoring world-wide abuses either of the right of national protection or of the right of national jurisdiction no solution compatible with the requirements of modern international law can be reached.[42]

Having thus identified the difficulty of its task, the Commission proceeded to ask whether there existed any rule of international law that denied an individual:

the right to relinquish to any extent, large or small, and under any circumstances or conditions, the protection of the government to which he owes allegiance.[43]

---

[41] The US Consumer Price Index yields a multiplier of 10.37 from 1926 to 2003.
[42] *North American Dredging Company of Texas*, IV RIAA 26 at p. 27.    [43] *Ibid.* at p. 28.

The Commissioners noted that any such imagined prohibition would run counter to 'the existing laws of progressive, enlightened civilisation' that a person may voluntarily expatriate himself. Why should he not, short of expatriation, be able to undertake by contract to limit his entitlements as a foreigner?

This question the Commission answered in the affirmative, in the process delivering a stinging rebuke both to Palmerstonian imperialism[44] and to the claimant.[45] Nevertheless, the Commission noted that the clause could not take from a foreign national:

his undoubted right to apply to his own Government for protection if his resort to the Mexican tribunals or other authorities available to him resulted in a denial or delay of justice as that term is used in international law.[46]

In the case before it, the claimant's grievance arose under a contract which it had agreed should be subject to the authority of the Mexican courts. The Commission refused to take cognisance of the claim because it was not 'based on an alleged violation of any rule or principle of international law' and therefore fell under the authority of the local courts which the claimant had wrongfully ignored.

The nuanced manner in which the award in *North American Dredging* upheld the relevant Calvo Clause was so successful in terms of articulating a viable distinction that it may be described as a watershed. From 1926 onward, it became exceedingly difficult for foreigners to deny the validity of a Calvo Clause, and equally difficult for the local government to insist that its scope extended to alleged violations of international law.[47] One may note the dissenting voice of Francisco V. García-Amador, who wrote that Calvo Clauses bar *even claims of denial of justice* insofar as such grievances arise from contractual disputes.[48] Yet it is

---

[44] 'Inalienable rights have been the cornerstones of policies like those of the Holy Alliance of Lord Palmerston; instead of bringing to the world the benefit of mutual understanding, they are to weak or less fortunate nations an unrestrained menace.' *Ibid.* at p. 30.

[45] 'The record before this Commission strongly suggests that the claimant used article 18 to procure the contract with no intention of ever observing its provisions.' *Ibid.* at p. 32.

[46] *Ibid.* at p. 30.

[47] A Brazilian scholar has concluded that the *North American Dredging* approach is supported 'by the majority of international arbitral jurisprudence after 1926', Leandro Vieira Silva, 'Latin America and the Concept of "Denial of Justice"' (thesis for an LL M in public international law, Leiden University, 2000, unpublished, at p. 2). Vieira Silva appears to have relied significantly on the primary research of Shea, *The Calvo Clause*.

[48] Francisco V. García-Amador, 'State Responsibility: Some New Problems', (1958) 94 *Recueil des Cours*, vol. II, 369, at p. 458.

difficult to be persuaded by his affirmation that contractual interests and rights are not 'in the same class as the other rights enjoyed by the alien in international law'. There is no corroborative authority for this singular proposition. García-Amador's argument was that contractual rights were less protected because they are matters of volition, and that there is no reason to limit the scope of voluntary relinquishment of rights. The obvious refutation is that no party having access to an international jurisdiction would opt for national courts if that means acceptance to be mistreated and to leave such mistreatment to be appreciated by the very courts which inflicted it.

As a matter of strict logic, one might wonder why an alien – on the path of piecemeal 'expatriation' to use the Commission's analogy – could not waive diplomatic protection with respect to claims under international law as well. The Commission's response was that an alien cannot:

deprive the government of his nation of its undoubted right of applying international remedies to violations of international law committed to his damage. Such government frequently has a larger interest in maintaining the principles of international law than in recovering damage for one of its citizens in a particular case, and manifestly such citizen can not by contract tie in this respect the hands of his Government.[49]

If that is so, a respondent state in a context where there is no issue of diplomatic protection, such as that of claims brought under an investment-protection treaty where the investor exercises an option to bring his grievance before national courts, should be able to argue that that choice extinguishes the possibility of subsequent attempts to seek international remedies, whether or not the breach is one of international law. (The relevant breach of international law in such cases would generally be alleged violation of the treaty itself.)

The unavoidable exceptions would be cases of denial of justice. And that is precisely one of the reasons why this old cause of action is resurgent.

A theoretically interesting question would arise if a foreigner is entitled to access to an international tribunal, say by virtue of a bilateral investment treaty, but has entered into a contract with the state which expressly provides that all disputes relating to that contract, whether relating to grievances allegedly arising under national *or international* law, are to

---

[49] *North American Dredging Company of Texas*, IV RIAA 26, at p. 29.

be exclusively and finally determined by a national court or arbitral tribunal.[50] That an international tribunal entitled to apply international law is not constrained by national law is abundantly clear.[51] But why should international law not respect a contractual stipulation by which the foreigner agrees that all controversies arising out of a given legal relationship are to be determined by a given national jurisdiction? Should the foreigner, like a consumer under national law, be assisted by a presumption that the stipulation is oppressive, and therefore to be disregarded as contrary to international public order? Or should international public order be deemed to reject attempts to exclude the entitlement of international tribunals to apply international law irrespective of the subjective situation of the foreigner? Should the fact that the treaty

---

[50] This issue was reserved in two important cases, *Compañía de Aguas del Aconquija S. A. and Vivendi Universal (formerly Compagnie Générale des Eaux) v. Argentina*, award, 21 November 2000, 5 *ICSID Reports* 296; (2001) 40 ILM 426 (Buergenthal, Trooboff, Rezek (presiding)); and *SGS Société Générale de Surveillance S. A.* v. *Republic of the Philippines*, decision on objections to jurisdiction, 29 January 2004, 8 *ICSID Reports* 518 (Crawford, Crivellaro, El-Kosheri (presiding)).

[51] As the ICJ put it in *Anglo-Norwegian Fisheries case* (*UK* v. *Norway*), 1951 *ICJ Reports* 116, at p. 132, maritime delimitation is not 'dependent merely upon the will of the coastal State as expressed in its municipal law . . . the validity of the delimitation with regard to other States depends upon international law'. Similarly, the ICJ in *Nottebohm* made clear that the internal criteria of nationality were not binding at the level of international law; *The Nottebohm* case (*Liechtenstein* v. *Guatemala*), 1955 *ICJ Reports* 4, at pp. 20–21. Thirty years earlier, the Permanent Court of International Justice had observed that: 'From the standpoint of International Law and of the Court which is its organ, municipal laws are merely facts which express the will and constitute the activities of States, in the same manner as do legal decisions or administrative measures. The Court is certainly not called upon to interpret the Polish law as such; but there is nothing to prevent the Court's giving judgment on the question whether or not, in applying that law, Poland is acting in conformity with its obligations towards Germany under the Geneva Convention' (*Case concerning Certain German Interests in Polish Upper Silesia (Germany v. Poland)* (The Merits), (1935) PCIJ, Series A, No. 7, 5, at p. 19). In sum: 'An act of a State must be characterized as internationally wrongful if it constitutes a breach of an international obligation, even if the act does not contravene the State's internal law – even if under that law, the State was actually bound to act in that way' (James Crawford, *The International Law Commission's Articles on State Responsibility: Introduction, Text and Commentaries* (Cambridge University Press, 2002), at p. 86).

With respect to our subject, Edwin M. Borchard wrote, *in The Diplomatic Protection of Citizens Abroad*, at p. 335: 'It is hardly to be supposed that any foreign state, even among those which have concluded treaties with Latin American republics providing for a renunciation of diplomatic interposition in all cases except denial of justice, would consider itself bound by a municipal legislative interpretation of the term 'denial of justice'.' (States are not to be assumed to legislate in intentional breach of international law. Therefore national laws should be interpreted, if possible, to achieve conformity with international law, *Oppenheim*, vol. I, at p. 82.)

which creates the international jurisdiction establishes an exceptional condition in favour of the state by excluding diplomatic protection, for example by referring to arbitration under the ICSID Convention, Article 27 of which has precisely that effect, imply the transposition into such disputes of the rule of the *North American Dredging* case?

These questions would be likely to generate intense controversy. They are, however, unlikely to arise in practice. It is difficult to imagine a freely negotiated clause by which a party accepts that all of its disputes shall be finally adjudicated by the organs of its co-contractant, even if they turn out to be manifestly biased. Whether or not an economic suicide pact should be countenanced under international law may therefore be left as an open question.

The *North American Dredging* award also stands for the proposition that a Calvo Clause may nullify a waiver of exhaustion of local remedies. The reason is that the treaty under which the Commission operated contained precisely such a waiver, which the Commission deemed to be limited to claims 'rightfully presented', with the effect of barring a claimant who had failed to comply with a fundamental contractual term – namely the Calvo Clause. This aspect of the case was criticised by Freeman[52] and others,[53] and was pointedly disregarded by a domestic commission, composed of three US nationals, established by the US Congress in order to apportion a Mexican settlement *en bloc*.[54] Nevertheless, it retains powerful support[55] and gives rise to this intriguing question: may the harmony between Calvo Clauses, as understood in *North American Dredging*, and the delict of denial of justice be said to be perfected by a similar rule in connection with the latter, to the effect that denial of justice requires exhaustion irrespective of a general waiver? This will be the focus of Chapter 5.

At any rate, the century-old dialogue of the deaf now appears to be largely over. As nations have developed, and their officials have become more accountable to broader strata of their population, their focus is less on why aliens should be entitled to treatment in accordance with international standards and more on why their own citizens should not be accorded the same level of protection even as a matter of national law.

---

[52] Freeman at pp. 481–482.

[53] See, e.g., Edwin M. Borchard, 'Decisions of Claims Commissions, United States and Mexico', (1926) 10 AJIL 536, at p. 540; and K. Lipstein, 'The Place of the Calvo Clause in International Law', (1945) 22 BYIL 130, at pp. 144–145.

[54] The US Commission awarded US$128,627 to the company; see ILC, Third Report on Diplomatic Protection Addendum 1, p. 12, note 44.

[55] Shea, *The Calvo Clause*, at pp. 229–230, note 89.

Governments which continue to represent dictatorships now find it difficult to complain about the international minimum standards enshrined in multilateral treaties such as the UN International Covenant on Civil and Political Rights (1966); regional instruments such as the American Convention on Human Rights (1969) or the African Charter on Human and Peoples' Rights (1981); or in the numerous bilateral treaties for the protection of foreign investments.

If Calvo was the emblematic spokesman of Latin American countries, and of small countries generally, in the nineteenth century, so Eduardo Jiménez de Aréchaga may be viewed as his counterpart in the twentieth century. He was a statesman-scholar who had been both professor of international law and Minister of the Interior in Uruguay[56] before his election to the International Court of Justice and his appointment to the World Bank Administrative Tribunal, both of which he was to serve as President. When Jiménez de Aréchaga gave the General Course in Public International Law at the Hague Academy in 1978, he affirmed that the notion that the conduct of courts is not attributable to governments could no longer be said to reflect international law, and confirmed the international responsibility of states for denial of justice in a broad sense.[57] Perhaps most importantly, he presided over the ICSID arbitral tribunal which in 1988 handed down its jurisdictional decision in the *SPP* v. *Egypt (Pyramids Oasis)* case,[58] a landmark among modern investment arbitrations involving states; it was the first case of a direct international claim brought by a private investor against a state in the absence of an original arbitration agreement between the claimant and the respondent.[59]

Like Calvo but a century later, African scholars who expressed doubts as to the legitimacy of an international legal order in which their newly independent states had not participated have since accepted, as they

---

[56] As well as Rapporteur of the Committee of the Whole in the United Nations Conference on the Law of Treaties (Vienna, 1968–69).

[57] E. Jiménez de Aréchaga, 'International Law in the Past Third of a Century', (1978) 159 *Recueil des Cours*, vol. I, at p. 278.

[58] *Southern Pacific Properties (Middle East) Limited* v. *Egypt*, decision on jurisdiction (No. 2), 14 April 1988, 3 *ICSID Reports* 131 (El Mehdi, Pietrowski, Jiménez de Aréchaga (presiding)). The decision was reached by a two-to-one majority over a comprehensive dissent by the Egyptian member of the tribunal; *ibid.* at p. 163. If Jiménez de Aréchaga had gone the other way, the modern face of investment arbitration would be unrecognisable.

[59] J. Paulsson, 'Arbitration Without Privity', (1995) 10 ICSID Review 232.

must, that 'municipal courts should not be the final judges of the compatibility of national treatment with the standards of international law'.[60]

The surpassingly important point is the ascension of the primacy of international law, grounded in a multitude of international commitments too numerous to mention, and too universal in their origins to admit of complaints that they have been imposed by disproportionate power or other undue influence.

Sometimes these sources of international norms require higher than national standards of treatment, sometimes not. That is a matter of substance, to be enforced by the competent jurisdiction. That, today, means international adjudication.

The history of denial of justice is happily one of declining violence. In its initial medieval tradition, it was the justification of private reprisals under letters of warrant. That type of force was proscribed by the establishment of the monopoly of the state; international delicts came to be prosecuted by the mechanism of diplomatic protection. Such protection could culminate in violent coercion and abuse, but at least it was centralised and subject to some form of systematisation and formal dialogue. If today the international delict has become a principle applied by international tribunals, acting on the initiative of private litigants whose principal hope of remedy is that provided by legal processes, surely the evolution is salutary.

## Summary

National laws offer fundamentally different definitions of denial of justice. It is therefore dangerous to import such definitions into international law. A state's international responsibility arises as a result of the failure of a national legal system to provide due process. International law judges the national system from the outside. This a national supreme court cannot do, because it is a part of the system, and it too must accept that its actions be evaluated by an international authority. The international understanding of denial of justice as a *systemic* failure is inconceivable at the national level.

The origins of the delict of denial of justice were intimately connected with the medieval regime of reprisals. Once states imposed their oligopoly

---

[60] Felix Chuks Okoye, *International Law and the New African States* (London: Sweet & Maxwell, 1972), at p. 179. See also the quotation from Amerasinghe, at Note 6 to Chapter 1, above.

over the system of international protection, private unilateral reprisals were replaced by state-sponsored unilateral reprisals couched in terms of 'diplomatic' protection and espousal of claims of nationals. Vulnerable new states tended to view the delict with misgivings, as a rule too easily abused by the powerful. The legitimacy of unilateral force as an ultimate sanction for denials of justice endured until well into the twentieth century, when international law generally forbade recourse to force as a means of settling disputes.

The Latin American Calvo Doctrine maintained that aliens could have no greater rights than nationals, and that they therefore should be limited to local legal remedies. In its purest expression, the Calvo Doctrine embodies a rejection of international law. It did not win the day. Calvo Clauses, on the other hand, have had a significant impact. Although they have taken many forms, they basically constitute a contractual waiver by aliens, as a condition of entry into a country (notably as traders, builders or investors), not to have recourse to international fora. Even Latin American jurists have, however, accepted the doctrine of the *North American Dredging* award of 1926 to the effect that even though such a clause excludes the international adjudication of contractual or other claims under national law it cannot close the door to international adjudication of violations of international law. The latter category includes denial of justice, and in some cases perhaps *only* denial of justice.

The *North American Dredging* award should also be read to accept that a Calvo Clause may invalidate a general waiver of exhaustion of local remedies. The validity of such waivers in the context of claims of denial of justice merits particular attention. If they are invalid there, the rule of denial of justice is revealed as consistent with Calvo Clauses. This matter will be examined in Chapter 5.

# 3

# Three fundamental developments

## State responsibility for the conduct of the judiciary

Long ago, some authors – and indeed tribunals – argued that it would be wrong to hold a government liable for the conduct of courts having a constitutional mandate to operate independently. Since the government could not, in principle, dictate the conduct of national judges, their acts should not be attributed to the government; unlike the executive and the legislature, they should not be taken to 'represent the expression of its will'.[1] Thus, the Senate of Hamburg, when adjudicating the case of *Yuille, Shortridge & Co.*, a British claim for private losses suffered as a consequence of a Portuguese judgment, declared in its award in 1861 that it would be 'altogether unjust' to require the Portuguese government 'to answer for the misconduct of its courts' since the Portuguese constitution decreed the courts to be 'completely independent of the Government and the latter was consequently unable to exert any influence over their decisions'.[2]

Whatever significance may be attributed to the independence of the judiciary as a matter of internal law, the notion that courts could somehow be separate from their states is unacceptable internationally. As Professor Charles Dupuis wrote in 1924: the state is 'no more entitled to disavow the law of nations by using judicial authority than by a fancy of Parliament or by outrageous conduct of the government'.[3]

---

[1]  T. Baty, *The Canons of International Law* (London: John Murray, 1930), at pp. 127–128.
[2]  21 October 1861, A. de Lapradelle and N. Politis, *Recueil des arbitrages internationaux*, vol. I, 78, at p. 103, para. 30.
[3]  The present author's translation. In the original: 'Il ne lui est pas plus loisible de rompre avec le droit des gens par autorité de justice que par fantaisie de Parlement ou par

Freeman had no hesitation in proclaiming that the notion of national courts as immune from international criticism had come to be held 'generally in abject disrepute'.[4] The argument, he wrote, carries the principle of the separation of powers 'into a domain in which it is irrelevant'; although the courts may be independent of the government, they are not separate from the state. He concluded that:

Whether the infraction of a given obligation under the law of nations proceeds from legislative, administrative, or judicial activity is immaterial ... Only through its component organs does the State exist and function.[5]

As a participant in the processes of international law, the state is always to be perceived as acting as a unit; its various constituent elements are not discrete actors.[6] Parliaments have been known to reject the promptings of the executive; this independence does not mean that acts of legislature are not imputable to the state.

Indeed, in a profound sense the courts cannot from the international perspective be independent of the state, for the reason that they are bound by local legislation. If that legislation itself is violative of international law, the delict cannot be neutralised by being applied through the mechanism of a court judgment.

In an oft-cited passage from his 1978 General Course in Public International Law at the Hague Academy, Judge Eduardo Jiménez de Aréchaga unequivocally confirmed the development Freeman had observed and endorsed forty years before:

in the present century State responsibility for judicial acts came to be recognized. Although independent of Government, the judiciary is not independent of the State: the judgment given by a judicial authority emanates from an organ of the State in just the same way as a law promulgated by the legislature or a decision taken by the executive.[7]

The controversial Guerrero Report of 1930[8] postulated that a national judgment was absolutely sovereign and once rendered could not be questioned internationally on any grounds whatsoever. Apart from any

---

outrecuidance de gouvernement', C. Dupuis, 'Liberté des voies de communication et les Relations internationales' (1924) *Recueil des Cours*, vol. I, 129, at p. 354.

[4] Freeman at p. 31.    [5] *Ibid.* at p. 28.    [6] *Accord*, de Visscher at p. 376.

[7] Jiménez de Aréchaga, 'International Law in the Past Third of a Century', (1978) 159 *Recueil des Cours*, vol. I, at p. 278.

[8] Gustavo Guerrero, Annex to Questionnaire No. 4, Committee of Experts for the Progressive Codification of International Law, Report of the Sub-committee, League of Nations Document C.196.M.70.1927.V.

recourse available under domestic law, it was an inviolable *res judicata*. This notion had been advanced in a judgment of the Supreme Court of Peru in 1927 in order to defeat a Cuban claim against the government.[9] It was curiously resuscitated by the Peruvian President Fujimori seventy years later, as he castigated the Inter-American Court of Human Rights for having dared to question extraordinary decisions of his subservient judiciary in the twilight of his rule (see the section on 'Responses to the anti-international critiques' in Chapter 9). De Visscher, referring back to Guerrero and the Peruvian judgment, wrote simply as follows:

The treatment of foreigners is guaranteed by international law, and it is not within the capacity of national law to limit the state's international obligations by the expedient invocation of the principle of equality [between foreigners and nationals]. As for the principle of *res judicata*, we know that it is applicable only in the internal legal order and may not be invoked in relations between states.[10]

It is no longer seriously possibly to contend that the nature of national judicial bodies is so different from other governmental instrumentalities that the state is insulated from international liability on account of judicial conduct. The ILC Articles on the Responsibility of States for Internationally Wrongful Acts, adopted in 2001, contain the following Article 4(1):

The conduct of any State organ shall be considered an act of that State under international law, *whether the organ exercises legislative, executive, judicial or any other functions*, whatever position it holds in the organization of the State, and whatever its character as an organ of the central government or of a territorial unit of the State.[11]

The ILC Articles are not innovative in this respect; they simply reflect the emergence of a clear consensus. The principle of state responsibility for judicial conduct was not, however, established without a struggle. It is worthwhile examining why the debate was resolved in this way.

If the judiciary were somehow internationally immunised because of its internal independence from the executive, no international wrong could be imputed to the state as a result of judicial acts or omissions. This would be intolerable, because the primary instrumentality of a state giving effect to diplomatic privileges or immunities is the judiciary. A failure to respect such

---

[9] *Cantero-Herrera* v. *Canevaro and Co.*, 25 May 1927, 1927–28 *Annual Digest of Public International Law Cases* 219.

[10] De Visscher at p. 387, citing Gidel's translation of D. Anzilotti's *Course in International Law*, at p. 480.

[11] International Law Commission, Draft articles on Responsibility of States for internationally wrongful acts, UN Doc. A/56/10 (2001) Article 4(1) (emphasis added).

rights is a violation of international law for which the state is responsible. The same would be true if a court purported to assert jurisdiction under a treaty but exceeded the powers defined therein, or if it refused to give effect to rights – like intellectual property rights, or the right to bring suit without providing security for costs – which may be treaty-created. Such delicts establish international responsibility, much like contemporary treaties dealing with the treatment of foreign defendants under criminal law which go to the heart of the matter of denial of justice, for example those requiring timely and specific indictments, or notice to consular agents. International duties would be reduced to pointlessness if the most important agents of their performance, the courts, were immune from criticism of the way they interpret obligations under the relevant treaty.

The theoretical grounds against distinguishing judicial acts from other acts of state instrumentalities have the fortunate consequence of making it unnecessary and irrelevant to question the constitutional choices made by states. It would be difficult and fruitlessly controversial to seek to establish and apply an international definition of judicial bodies (as would be necessary if they were to be given special status). Is a tribunal *judicial* because it is obligatory rather than consensual? If so, the Soviet-era courts of arbitration would probably qualify. Is the test independence? If so, not only would one invite divisive and sensitive debates about ordinary courts, but open the door to claims to immunity by many types of agencies created by the government to deal with the complaints of citizens or to monitor the performance of governmental services; yet such agencies may have the authority to affect the rights of individuals without the semblance of judicial process. Indeed, that is true for a myriad public administrations created under vastly different constitutional regimes. The proper view, as this study seeks to demonstrate, is that *uncorrected* deprivations by such agencies would constitute denials of justice under international law. For this to be so, the ostensible correcting instrumentality, that is to say whatever authority set up to sanction maladministration, cannot be given any greater deference than the initially wrongdoing agency.

A compelling precedent was established in 2001 by the jurisdictional decision of the ICSID tribunal in the *Loewen* case.[12] The claimants alleged that the USA was liable under the North American Free Trade Agreement

---

[12] *Loewen*, 5 January 2001. The Tribunal was composed of Sir Anthony Mason, President, Hon. Abner J. Mikva, and Yves Fortier QC. By the time the Tribunal rendered its final award, *Loewen*, 26 June 2003, which is of capital importance to the subject of this book, Fortier had resigned and been replaced by Lord Mustill.

(NAFTA) for alleged misconduct by the courts of Mississippi. The USA raised five jurisdictional objections. Four were joined to the merits, so the 2001 decision dealt with only the first objection, which was to the following effect:

the claim is not arbitrable because the judgments of domestic courts in purely private disputes are not 'measures adopted or maintained by a Party' within the scope of NAFTA Chapter II.

The claimants alleged that the conduct of the courts of Mississippi had violated the NAFTA obligation (under Article 1105) to provide 'full protection and security' to foreign investors. The USA objected that such obligations can (under Article 1101(1)) arise only from 'measures adopted or maintained' by one of the state signatories to NAFTA. The Tribunal held as follows:

Article 201 defines 'measure' as including 'any law, regulation, procedure, require-ment or practice'. The breadth of this inclusive definition, notably the references to 'law, procedure, requirement or practice', is inconsistent with the notion that judicial action is an exclusion from the generality of the expression 'measures'. 'Law' comprehends judge-made as well as statute-based rules. 'Procedure' is apt to include judicial as well as legislative procedure. 'Requirement' is capable of covering a court order which requires a party to do an act or to pay a sum of money, while 'practice' is capable of denoting the practice of courts as well as the practice of other bodies.[13]

Citing with approval the passage quoted above from Jiménez de Aréchaga, the tribunal noted that the claimants characterised their grievances as arising from violations of international law and a denial of justice. The arbitrators proceeded without hesitation to attribute the acts of the courts of a federated state to the central government, even against the argument that Article 1101(1) of NAFTA constitutes what one might refer to as a narrower jurisdictional *lex specialis*. Their reasoning is worth con-sidering with care, considering the multiplicity of international investment treaties that might be argued to contain specific jurisdictional hurdles:

The question . . . arises whether the words 'measures adopted or maintained by a Party' should be understood, as the Respondent argues, to exclude judicial acts being the judgments of domestic courts in purely private matters. The purpose of Chapter Eleven, 'Section B – Settlement of Disputes between a Party and an Investor of Another Party' is to establish 'a mechanism for the

---

[13] *Loewen*, 5 January 2001, at para. 40.

settlement of investment disputes that assures both equal treatment among investors of the Parties in accordance with the principle of international reciprocity and due process before an arbitral tribunal'. The text, context and purpose of Chapter Eleven combine to support a liberal rather than a restricted interpretation of the words 'measures adopted or maintained by a Party', that is, an interpretation which provides protection and security for the foreign investor and its investment: see *Ethyl Corporation* v. *Canada*, Award on Jurisdiction, June 24, 1998, 38 ILM 708, (where the NAFTA Tribunal concluded that the object and purpose of Chapter Eleven is to 'create effective procedures ... for the resolution of disputes' and to 'increase substantially investment opportunities' (at 83)).

Neither in the text or context of NAFTA nor in international law is there to be found support for the Respondent's submission that 'measures adopted or maintained by a Party', in its application to judicial acts, excludes the judgments of domestic courts in purely private disputes. Neither the definition of 'measure' in Article 201 nor the provisions of Chapters 10 and 17 relating to 'measures' and 'procedures' contain any indication that, in its application to judicial acts, the existence of a measure depends upon the identity of the litigants or the characterisation of the dispute as public or private. An adequate mechanism for the settlement of disputes as contemplated by 11 must extend to disputes, whether public or private, so long as the state Party is responsible for the judicial act which constitutes the 'measure' complained of, and that act constitutes a breach of a NAFTA obligation, as for example a discriminatory precedential judicial decision. The principle that a state is responsible for the decisions of its municipal courts (or at least its highest court) supports the wider interpretation of the expression 'measure adopted or maintained by a Party' rather than the restricted interpretation advanced by the Respondent.

Generally speaking, litigation between private parties is less likely to generate a 'measure adopted or maintained by a Party' but, in some circumstances, private litigation may do so ...

As the Claimants submit, the Mississippi trial court's judgment ordering Loewen to pay O'Keefe $500 million and the Mississippi Supreme Court requirement that Loewen post a $625 million bond were 'requirements' within the meaning of the definition of 'measure' in Article 201, subject to consideration of Article 1121, the principle of finality of judicial acts and the rule of exhaustion of local remedies.

The Respondent argues that the words 'adopted or maintained' in Article 1101 are indicative of an intent to limit Chapter 11 to those actions that involve ratification by government. This limitation, so the Respondent submits, accords with the 'act of state' doctrine. That doctrine is a doctrine of municipal rather than international law ...

Whatever the effect of the act of State doctrine may be, Article 1105, in requiring a Party to provide 'full protection and security' to investments of investors, must extend to the protection of foreign investors from private parties when they act through the judicial organs of the State.[14]

The 'circumstances' referred to in the third paragraph of this passage were left undefined, but obviously included the circumstances that amounted to the miscarriage of justice alleged in this case (and which the subsequent final award found to have existed; see Chapter 6).

One of the last vain attempts by a state to avoid having to account for the actions of its judiciary occurred in *The Last Temptation of Christ* case,[15] involving censorship, where the Government of Chile tried to argue that an act of the judiciary in violation of international law could be attributed to the state only if the executive branch acquiesced in it. The Inter-American Court of Human Rights had no hesitation in holding that 'the international responsibility of the State may be engaged by acts or omissions of any power or organ of the State, whatever its rank, that violate the American Convention'.

## Denial of justice by non-judicial authority

In the past, some authors sought to define denial of justice in such a fashion as to limit it to the conduct of judicial officials. This approach is indefensible. If justice has been denied by officials whose conduct is imputable to the state, it makes no sense to exclude liability because those officials do not have a particular title as a matter of national regulation. The purpose of the delict is to oblige states 'not to administer justice in a notoriously unjust manner' – to repeat Irizarry y Puente's formulation.[16] If it is established that justice has been so maladministered, it is impossible to see why the state should escape sanction because the wrong was perpetrated by one category of its agents rather than another.[17] Surely it would be a denial of justice for the executive to refuse

---

[14] *Ibid.* at paras. 53–58.

[15] *Olmedo Bustos et al.* v. *Chile* (Merits), 5 February 2001, Inter-American Court of Human Rights, Series C, No. 73 at para. 72 (prior censorship of a motion picture held to be a violation of freedom of expression).

[16] Irizarry y Puente, 'Denial of Justice', at p. 406.

[17] To dispose of a trivial issue, obviously formal titles are not decisive; the adequacy of a state's judicial machinery is to be assessed by reference to the conduct of those of its officials who serve in a judicial capacity. Thus, for example, the Portuguese administrative officials who were charged with the registration of deeds which were the focus of the *Croft* case, *UK* v. *Portugal*, 7 February 1856, A. de Lapradelle and N. Politis, *Recueil des arbitrages internationaux*, vol. II, at p. 22 (see the section on 'No responsibility for misapplication of national law' in Chapter 4) were found by the arbitral tribunal to have acted judicially.

to appoint judges to the only jurisdiction competent to hear a particular type of case, or to adopt a decree that has the effect of invalidating the contractual terms of a single contract to the benefit of the government and the detriment of its alien co-contractant; just as it would be a denial of justice for the legislature to edict astronomical filing fees for foreigners. Yet in no such case would the act or omission be that of a judicial officer.

It is impossible to discern any logic behind this approach except an *a priori* objective of reducing the scope of state liability by any means. If that is so, it should be admitted as such and seen for what it is.

As de Visscher wrote:

The important thing as an international matter is not the determination of the state organ to which one may attribute, under constitutional law, the origin of the state's failure in its duty: the sole decisive element is the act in which this failure manifested itself in international relations. If it partakes of the jurisdictional order, one is in the presence of a denial of justice in the meaning we attribute to this expression.[18]

If it is unclear whether a given function 'partakes of the jurisdictional order', de Visscher's view was simply that jurisdictional action is one which leads to a legal conclusion, which, as a matter of national law, is considered to have *res judicata* effect.[19]

Commissioner Van Vollenhoven's opinion in the *Chattin* case of 1927[20] insisted at some length on the need to limit the ambit of denial of justice to claims of wrongdoing by judicial officers and no others. Freeman criticised this approach in 1938.[21] Half a century later, *Amco II* squarely confronted commissioner Van Vollenhoven's statement in *Chattin* to the effect that acts of the judiciary alone can constitute denial of justice, and repudiated it in these terms:

Most arbitral awards do not make this distinction in the context of denial of justice ... the Tribunal sees no provision of international law that makes impossible a denial of justice by an administrative body.[22]

Of course the delict must be circumscribed in such a way as to allow us to identify it and to achieve a useful understanding of the way the

---

[18] De Visscher at p. 391.    [19] *Ibid.* at p. 396.

[20] *USA v. Mexico*, 23 July 1927, IV RIAA 282.    [21] Freeman at p. 21.

[22] *Amco II* at para. 137. *See also* Secretary of State Fish's instructions to his minister in Mexico City on 2 January 1873: 'Where a claimant on a foreign country has, by the law of such country, "the choice of either the judicial or the administrative branch of the Government through which to seek relief," and selects the latter, this does not make the arbitrary decision of the latter against him final and conclusive' (J. B. Moore, *A Digest of International Law* (8 vols., Washington, DC: US Government Printing Office, 1906), vol. VI, at p. 696).

abstraction is intended to affect reality. It is not helpful to postulate, as some writers once were said to have done, that denial of justice corresponds to all violations owed to foreigners under international law.[23] The proposition is so broad that it would become a synonym for *breach*, and therefore meaningless.

But once one accepts as the fundamental postulate of the delict that states have an obligation to maintain a decent and available system of justice, it simply cannot be accepted that the state should be freed from its obligation by the simple expedient of preventing or perverting the judicial process by executive or legislative fiat.[24]

Reading the old awards from the late nineteenth or early twentieth century, one needs to be very careful about arguments or holdings to the effect that the executive and legislative branches of government should be

---

[23] The popular culprits, cited over and over again in the literature, are Professor C. C. Hyde and Dr Fred K. Nielsen. In his two-volume treatise published in 1922, *International Law Chiefly as Interpreted and Applied by the United States*, Hyde wrote as follows: 'A denial of justice, in a broad sense, occurs whenever a state, through any department or agency, fails to observe with respect to an alien, any duty imposed by international law or by treaty with his country.' (2 vols., Little, Brown and Co., Boston, 1922), vol. I, at p. 491.

Nielsen, a US appointee on the US–Mexican Claims Commission, stated in the *Neer* case that: 'a denial of justice may, broadly speaking, be properly regarded as the general ground of diplomatic intervention' (*L. F. H. Neer and Pauline Neer* (*US* v. *Mexico*), 15 October 1926, IV RIAA 60, at p. 64; further similar expressions are quoted in Freeman at p. 98).

Commentators seem to have enjoyed demolishing the 'broad view' of Hyde and Nielsen. Thus, 'If denial of justice is used to refer to all governmental acts … the expression would be robbed of all value as a technical distinction' (Freeman at p. 105). Under this definition, wrote Eagleton, 'the term "denial of justice" would appear to be superfluous and confusing and proper to be eliminated' (*The Responsibility of States in International Law* (New York University Press, 1928), at p. 112). De Visscher wrote, at 386: 'used this way, the expression loses all intrinsic value and is but a source of confusion'. Even President Van Vollenhoven of the Mexican Claims Commission was moved in the *Chattin* case to write that under this conception 'there would exist no international wrong which would not be covered by the phrase "denial of justice"' (*US* v. *Mexico*, 23 July 1927, IV RIAA 282, at p. 286).

Fitzmaurice was no less critical. 'The main objection to this definition', he wrote, 'is that it converts the term into a species of synonym for international delinquency'; he observed that it would appear to cover the imposition of a tax in contravention of a treaty provision, or the failure to provide police protection; Fitzmaurice at p. 95. Yet he was perhaps fairer in acknowledging that Hyde and Nielsen's incidental comments, which Fitzmaurice referred to as 'dicta', but which appear to have sprouted wings and relegated their authors to the role of straw men for several generations, were 'limited by the context' of examining the conditions of diplomatic intervention in the event of failure to give redress for prior wrongful conduct.

[24] Unambiguous support for this conclusion is to be found in Eagleton, *Responsibility of States*, at p. 545; Fitzmaurice, at p. 105; Irizarry y Puente, 'Denial of Justice', at p. 403. The latter refers, *ibid.*, to 'deficiency in the local legislation or arbitrary executive action'.

equally susceptible to engaging the international responsibility of the state as the judicial branch. Often such statements were made against a historical background which gave rise to the view that denial of justice by courts was the only form of injury to foreigners that legitimised international protection. Thus, in ordinary cases of executive action which we would today instantly recognise as expropriatory, the sponsors of the claim, strenuously arguing that the acts of administrative organs of the state could give rise to international responsibility for denial of justice, were seeking to bring the claim within the scope of denial of justice because they did not know what other terms to use to justify the espousal of a claim by the mechanism of diplomatic protection. And so, for example, the US Government in the *Chase* case found itself complaining of the Panamanian Government's failure 'to provide the protection to which the claimant's property rights were entitled under the established principles of international law',[25] and this grievance was naturally thought of as sounding in denial of justice. Many of these cases have nothing to do with denial of justice.[26] Today the alleged wrong would be articulated as a wrongful taking,[27] or a failure of protection.[28] The words 'denial of justice' would never be uttered.[29]

---

[25] *William Gerald Chase (US v. Panama)*, 29 June 1933, VI RIAA 352; the passage quoted from the US memorial appears in B. L. Hunt, *American and Panamanian General Claims Arbitration under the Conventions between the United States and Panama of July 28, 1926, and December 17, 1932*, (US Department of State Arbitration Series, No. 6 (Washington, DC: 1934), 341, at p. 356. The claim was unsuccessful; while governmental authorities adopted inconsistent positions *vis-à-vis* Chase's land rights, there was little discussion of any miscarriage of justice given the fact, acknowledged by the commissioners, that Chase's alleged title had never been clear.

[26] De Visscher at p. 385, perceived precisely this source of misunderstanding in the legal literature, and anticipated its clarification. 'Little by little, however, the authors have come to acknowledge that international responsibility is not reduced to cases of denial of justice, but indeed that denial of justice, even in the domain of protection of foreigners, is but one category among others of conduct giving rise to international responsibility.'

[27] See, e.g., *Wena Hotels Ltd* v. *Egypt*, award, 8 December 2000, 6 *ICSID Reports* 89 (Fadlallah, Wallace, Leigh (presiding)).

[28] See, e.g., *Asian Agricultural Products Ltd* v. *Sri Lanka*, award, 27 June 1990, 4 *ICSID Reports* 245 (Goldman, Asante, El-Kosheri (presiding)); *American Manufacturing and Trading, Inc.* v. *Zaire*, award, 21 February 1997, 5 *ICSID Reports* 11 (Golsong, Mbaye, Sucharitkul (presiding)).

[29] As it happens, the *Chase* case did involve an element within the purview of denial of justice, namely the failure of executive authorities to respect a Supreme Court judgment alleged to be dispositive of Mr Chase's title to disputed lands. The judgment was, however, ambiguous, and this was but an incidental aspect of the case.

This is the context in which it is useful to consider the two famous awards rendered in the *El Triunfo* and *Robert E. Brown* cases.

*El Triunfo*[30] involved an exclusive navigation concession granted by the Government of El Salvador to a corporation whose principal shareholders were US nationals. The concession, which was part of a scheme of macroeconomic importance to develop the port of El Triunfo, took the form of a contract which, after competitive bidding, was signed by the Government in October 1894 and ratified in accordance with the Constitution by the legislature in May 1895. The obligations of the concession holder were fully carried out and the relevant ministers and inspector-general so acknowledged. The port was quickly opened, and from the beginning of 1896 to late 1898 the volume of business of the port was larger than even the most optimistic forecasts, increasing by between 400 per cent and 500 per cent. By the beginning of 1898, the concession holder, called the El Triunfo Company, showed steady net profits (this too acknowledged by the Government's official accountant).

Yet on 14 February 1899 the President of the Republic issued a decree closing the port of El Triunfo, effectively making the concession agreement a dead letter. Three months later, the same concession was granted to citizens of El Salvador.

The ensuing claim is notable in that it involved the breach of a direct contractual relationship with the Government. (*El Triunfo* is one of the classic precedents, cited time and again throughout the twentieth century, in connection with claims relating to international state contracts.) It could also have been articulated as a claim sounding in expropriation or discrimination. The award itself explains the basis of liability as the finding that the concession had been 'arbitrarily and unjustly revoked, destroyed, and cancelled by the Republic of Salvador'.[31] The expression 'denial of justice' does not appear in the award, but figures prominently in the opinion of the two arbitrators forming the majority. They conceived the role of denial of justice in two ways.

First, they noted that before the US could validly exercise its rights of diplomatic protection, it must be shown that the US claimants 'having appealed to the courts of the Republic, have been denied justice by those courts'. This notion gives us the key to a fundamental conceptual

---

[30] *US* v. *El Salvador*, 8 May 1902, XV RIAA 455. Arbitral Tribunal composed of Sir Henry Strong, Chief Justice of the Dominion of Canada; Donald M. Dickinson (US) and Don José Rosa Pacas (El Salvador). Award rendered by a majority (Strong and Dickinson).

[31] *Ibid.* at p. 469.

problem. For in this sense, denial of justice is merely a requirement for diplomatic protection, i.e. a way of restating the need to exhaust local remedies. The arbitrators thus considered that a denial of justice occurred because the wrongful cancellation of the concession was not corrected by national judicial authorities. This approach misapprehends both the exhaustion requirement and the delict of denial of justice.

To exhaust local remedies, it is necessary to attempt to do so, or at least to prove that any attempt would have been futile (see Chapter 5). That may have been the case with respect to the El Triunfo Company, but neither the award nor the majority opinion gives any indication that this issue was explored and evaluated. As for denial of justice, it cannot be a matter of *res ipsa loquitur*; wrongs unconnected with the administration of justice do not automatically become denial of justice because the courts do not correct them. Some act or omission constituting a miscarriage of justice is required.

This brings us to the second way in which the award uses the expression 'denial of justice'. We need to revert momentarily to the facts of this case, which intriguingly anticipated the *Barcelona Traction* saga: foreign owners of an important and prospering enterprise dispossessed by a conspiracy of local rivals abusing corporate procedures to instigate meretricious bankruptcy proceedings. Thus a cabal including a certain Simon Sol, who had led a consortium which had presented an unsuccessful bid at the inception of the project, had taken advantage of the absence of the Company's president; Sol 'assumed the office of president by clear usurpation' and proceeded to adopt an extraordinary resolution to petition for the bankruptcy of the company; within five days, a local court appointed a receiver who immediately took possession of all corporate documents (these were never restored, not even in the course of the arbitration). The American members of the board 'were driven from Salvador in fear of their lives'.

Reacting to these events, on 12 February 1899 the US shareholders called for a meeting for the purpose of restoring the Company's rights by 'turning out the conspirators and installing a representative directorate'. On 13 February, notice of the meeting was published in the Official Journal of the Republic. On 14 February, the President of the Republic, as seen, closed down the port, putting an effective end to the concession. Thus, the majority arbitrators held, 'the Government of Salvador came to the aid of the conspirators and by executive act destroyed the only thing of value worth retrieving through the courts'.

This action may readily have been attacked as a breach of contract or as an unlawful dispossession, and there is every reason to think that it was so perceived by the arbitrators. What is ambiguous is the opinion's approving reference to a US contention to the effect that: 'Justice may as much be denied when it would be absurd to seek it by judicial process as if denied after being so sought'. This comment is apposite with respect to a debate about the need to exhaust local remedies as a precondition to the diplomatic espousal of the claim, or with respect to the sufficiency of an initial miscarriage of justice if there is no reasonable prospect of an effective appellate remedy (see Chapter 5). But to make a lawsuit pointless is not *per se* a miscarriage of justice; conduct having that effect may have no relation to the administration of justice. When the arbitrators went on to say that 'the obligation of parties to a contract to appeal for judicial relief is reciprocal', they showed that they were proceeding on a contractual footing, reproving the Government's unilateral executive abrogation of the concession. In sum, *El Triunfo* is not a precedent which properly belongs in the field of denial of justice. If such a case were to arise today in circumstances of direct access, without the need to show exhaustion of local remedies, the words 'denial of justice' would be out of place in the debate absent any suggestion that the claimants were actually stymied in their efforts to petition the local courts.

*Robert E. Brown*[32] provides an illuminating contrast. Brown was a US national and engineer who had applied in 1895 for 1,200 gold-prospecting licences in South Africa pursuant to a system established under a proclamation by President Kruger of the South African Republic. Kruger withdrew his proclamation on the day following Brown's application. Six days thereafter, the legislature (*Volksraad*) issued a resolution approving the withdrawal of the first proclamation and decreeing that no person who had suffered damage should recover compensation. The High Court of the Republic in due course rendered a judgment in favour of Brown, declaring the *Volksraad* resolution to be unconstitutional, ordering the issuance of the licences, and inviting Brown to sue for damages in the event he were physically prevented from pegging off the 1,200 plots.

An epic battle ensued between President Kruger and Chief Justice Kotzé. Kotzé denounced Kruger as an 'oily old Chadband' and defended his attempts to establish judicial review of the constitutionality of legislation along the lines of what US Supreme Court Chief Justice Marshall had done in the venerable precedent *Marbury* v. *Madison*.[33] Kruger

---

[32] *United States* v. *Great Britain*, 23 November 1923, VI RIAA 120.
[33] US Supreme Court, 5 US (1 *Cranch*) 137 (1803), holding that to determine the constitutional conformity of legislation is 'the very essence of judicial duty'.

countered by describing Kotzé as a lunatic fit for capture and incarceration in an asylum, asserting in his fourth inaugural address in 1889 that 'the testing right [i.e. judicial review] is a principle of the devil', and advised other judges not to follow Kotzé in the devil's way. In the end, might prevailed and Kotzé was removed from office. A reconstituted and more compliant High Court dismissed Brown's motion to determine damages on a technicality in 1898.[34]

Brown successfully appealed to his own government to espouse his claim against Great Britain, as suzerain over the Republic. (The South African Republic was conquered and annexed by Great Britain in 1902.) After protracted negotiations had failed, the claim was disposed of by an international arbitral tribunal in 1923.[35] Like the claimants in the *Loewen* case exactly eighty years later, Brown found to his mortification that his claim for denial of justice was 'undoubtedly' well founded, but that it was inadmissible because Great Britain was not liable for the wrongful acts of the Republic with respect to a pending claim, as opposed to a liquidated debt; the Attorney General of the Colony (as it had become) declared that its courts were still open to Brown.

The tribunal's finding of denial of justice is therefore dictum, but it is still a leading case. (This comment, as we shall see in the section on 'Fundamental breaches of due process' in Chapter 7, is also likely to apply in all respects to *Loewen*.) The arbitrators noted that Brown's claim had consistently been referred to as the 'turning point' in the move to destroy the independence of the High Court. They further found a 'disposition to defeat Brown's claim at any cost', and that his pursuit of damages was rejected, with an assessment of costs against him, although the judgment in his favour had invited him so to proceed. (Another frustrated applicant alleging 'almost identical facts' had been allowed to proceed; the arbitrators had difficulty perceiving the possible technical distinctions between the two cases.) Although Brown was given leave to start a new action, he was advised by his counsel that the effect of the new decision 'was to throw him out of court and deprive him of the benefit of his previous judgment'. A new suit would fly in the face of the *Volksraad*'s edict that no compensation would be due, and the oath of

---

[34] A fuller account of this episode was published by Professor John Dugard in 'Chief Justice versus President: Does the Ghost of Brown v. Leyds NO Still Haunt Our Judges?' *De Rebus* (September 1981), 421, where the author observes that arguably 'this decision and its consequences have contributed more to current South African judicial attitudes than any other episode in our legal history'.
[35] 23 November 1923, VI RIAA 120.

office now required of judges was to the effect that they would defer to the legislature.

The arbitrators concluded that 'if this proceeding were directed against the South African Republic, we should have no difficulty awarding damages on behalf of the claimant'. They noted that there were a number of technical issues as to whether Brown ever held title to specific rights, and that it was correct that 'his legal remedies were not completely exhausted', but:

Notwithstanding these positions, all of which may, in our view, be conceded, we are persuaded that on the whole case, giving proper weight to the cumulative strength of the numerous steps taken by the Government of the South African Republic with the obvious intent to defeat Brown's claims, a definite denial of justice took place. We can not overlook the broad facts in the history of this controversy. All three branches of the Government conspired to ruin his enterprise. The Executive Department issued proclamations for which no warrant could be found in the Constitution and laws of the country. The Volksraad enacted legislation which, on its face, does violence to fundamental principles of justice recognized in every enlightened community. The judiciary, at first recalcitrant, was at length reduced to submission and brought into line with a determined policy of the Executive to reach the desired result regardless of Constitutional guarantees and inhibitions ... In the actual circumstances ... we feel that the futility of further proceedings has been fully demonstrated, and that the advice of his counsel was amply justified. In the frequently quoted language of an American Secretary of State: 'A claimant in a foreign State is not required to exhaust justice in such State when there is no justice to exhaust'.[36]

Freeman concluded that the *Robert E. Brown* award 'assimilated to a denial of justice all the unlawful acts committed to the foreigner's prejudice'. He went on to write:

It was the 'improper deprivation of rights of a substantial character' which, for the arbitrators, constituted the denial of justice. Exactly how or by what State organs that end was accomplished was apparently immaterial.

An identical position was taken in the *El Triunfo Co* case.[37]

Freeman's failure to see the distinctions between the two cases is a matter of considerable importance. In *Robert E. Brown*, there was massive interference in a pending case, with the executive removal of the chief

---

[36] *Ibid.* at p. 129; the US Secretary of State in question was Hamilton Fish; his often-cited dictum appears *in* Moore, *Digest*, vol. VI, at p. 677.

[37] Freeman at pp. 100–101.

judge who had been instrumental in acknowledging Brown's rights and with the legislative reversal of a substantive rule which had already become *res judicata* in Brown's specific case. The implication of the two other branches of government in the administration of justice was direct; the difference with *El Triunfo* was manifest and fundamental.[38]

In sum, Fitzmaurice and Freeman's conclusions to the effect that denial of justice involves 'some misconduct either on the part of the judiciary or of organs acting in connection with the administration of justice to aliens'[39] appear irresistible. Indeed, Freeman quotes a Mexican scholar and diplomat, writing at a time when that country's experiences were not such as to make it enthusiastic about any expansion of the delict, that denial of justice may, in extreme cases, involve 'administrative authorities'.[40] Authors or precedents cited to the effect that denial of justice relates only to actions or omissions of courts on closer analysis appear to have been focused primarily on establishing the proposition that Hyde and Nielsen were wrong,[41] and that denial of justice must relate to some dysfunction of the administration of justice as opposed to any and all breaches of international law that might justify diplomatic intervention. In so doing, such authorities may, *obiter dictum*, have used loose expressions. Once it is established that the relevant act or omission is imputable to the state, it simply cannot matter whether the doors to justice were blocked by executive fiat, legislative overreaching, or judicial obstreperousness.

## Extension of *locus standi*

The actors on the modern international stage are vastly more numerous than in Freeman's day. At the turn of the century, according to the 2001/2002

[38] See also the five awards (*Ruden, R. T. Johnson, Neptune, Ballistini,* and *Romberg*) cited by Eagleton, *Responsibility of States*, at p. 547, note 2828, involving such executive acts as orders forbidding the trial of suits against the treasury and irresistible interventions by a provincial governor to prevent the hearing of a suit.

[39] Freeman at p. 106, agreeing with Fitzmaurice, who referred, at p. 94, to 'actions *in or concerning the administration of justice,* whether on the part of the courts or of some other organ of the state' (emphasis in the original).

[40] '[A]ctos de autoridades administrativas, cuando éstas ejerzan funciones jurisdiccionales con carácter definitivo y sin ulteriores recursos ante los Tribunales de Justicia', Oscar Rabasa, *Responsabilidad Internacional del Estado con Referencia Especial a la Responsabilidad por Denegación de Justicia* ((Mexico: Imprenta de la Secretaria de Relaciones Exteriores, 1933), at p. 35, quoted in Freeman at p. 106, note 2).

[41] See Note 22 of this chapter above.

*Yearbook of International Organizations*, there were nearly 1,000 international intergovernmental organisations and ten times as many international non-governmental organisations. These numbers do not include special bodies created to implement treaties, or the myriad organisations, secular and religious, of what one may call international civil society. Many such organisations may claim both higher representational legitimacy and law-abiding credentials than an unfortunately high number of dysfunctional national governments; indeed, the same may be said of some internationally active private for-profit corporations who believe they can point to an unblemished record of respect for the interests of vast numbers of shareholders and employees, and generally for the rule of law.

Concomitantly, the international system has provided a number of fora where parties other than states, including individuals, are able to raise grievances based on violations of international law. This development is premised on the need to give judicial standing to litigants denied international legal protection with respect to human rights, investments, or the environment. The relevant international instruments are far too numerous to mention exhaustively; suffice it to refer to the European Convention for the Protection of Human Rights and Fundamental Freedoms – a true watershed – Article 34 of which provides that the European Court of Human Rights:

may receive applications from any person, non-governmental organisation or group of individuals claiming to be the victim of a violation by one of the High Contracting Parties of the rights set forth in this Convention on the protocols hereto. The High Contracting Parties undertake not to hinder in any way the effective exercise of this right.

It would be even harder to provide an inventory of the scholarly commentary which has accompanied this development, although it seems necessary and appropriate to single out *International Law and Human Rights*, the highly influential monograph published by Sir Hersch Lauterpacht in 1950, the same year as the European Convention was opened for signature.[42]

[42] In the 9th edition of *Oppenheim* one finds the following succinct footnote: 'The question whether there could be any subjects of international law other than states was at one time a matter of strenuous debate. In the first three editions of this work the view was expressed that states only and exclusively are the subjects of international law. It is now generally accepted that there are subjects other than states, and practice amply proves this. One of the most important pioneers in getting this "modern" view accepted was Sir Hersch Lauterpacht, the editor of the 8th ed of this vol' (*Oppenheim*, vol. I, at p. 16, note 1).

In other words, this development is not recent. As the then Solicitor General of Uganda wrote in 1968, after noting some 'extreme expressions' on the subject:

The position of the individual as a subject of international law has been greatly obscured by a failure to distinguish between the recognition of rights enuring to the benefit of the individual and the enforceability of those rights at his instance ...

At the present stage in the development of international law, generally speaking, individuals lack the procedural capacity to espouse their claims before international tribunals and such claims can be entertained only at the instance of the state of which the individual is a national or in certain circumstances by the international institution of which he is a servant. But it is now only 'generally speaking' true to say that individuals lack procedural capacity to bring claims before international tribunals, and that only states of which they are nationals can espouse such claims. A characteristic trend of modern developments of international law is the granting of procedural capacity to individuals for the protection of certain well-defined rights.[43]

Nor is the notion that foreign investors may have direct access to international tribunals a novelty. Substantive norms and procedural mechanisms for the international protection of foreign investment were actively considered in the 1950s, and gave rise to the so-called Abs–Shawcross Draft.[44] These initiatives were taken up at an intergovernmental level within the framework of the OECD, giving rise in 1967 to a Draft Convention on the Protection of Foreign Property.[45]

Against this background, once-axiomatic declarations to the effect that only states may be subjects of international law fall on modern ears like an echo of an incomprehensible ancient dogma. Private parties are today participants, to a greater or lesser degree, in the international legal process.[46]

[43] Nkmabo Murgerwa, 'Subjects of International Law', in Max Sørensen (ed.), *Manual of Public International Law* (London: Macmillan, 1968), at pp. 265–266.

[44] Draft Convention on Investments Abroad, (1960) 9 *Journal of Public Law* 115; see G. Schwarzenberger, 'The Abs–Shawcross Draft Convention on Investments Abroad', (1961) 14 *Current Legal Problems* 213.

[45] (1968) 7 ILM 117.

[46] International Law Commission (Dugard), First Report on Diplomatic Protection, UN Doc. A/CN.4/506 (2000) at p. 4, para. 4(d), affirmed: 'The work on diplomatic protection should take into account the development of international law in increasing recognition and protection of the rights of individuals and in providing them with more direct and indirect access to international forums to enforce their rights.' See Francisco Orrego Vicuña, 'Individuals and Non-State Entities before International Courts and Tribunals', in J. A. Frowein and R. Wolfrum (eds.), *Max Planck Yearbook of United Nations Law* (The Hague: Kluwer, 2001), vol. V, at p. 53.

True, when in 2001 the ILC finally ended nearly half a century of gestation and gave birth to the Articles on Responsibility of States for Internationally Wrongful Acts, it did not describe how its prescriptions might be invoked by claimants other than states. But this feature of the ILC Articles is readily explained by the fact that the ILC consciously avoided suggesting prescriptions of so-called primary rules. (Broadly, the ILC did not seek to define the primary principles establishing *wrongfulness*, but the secondary rules of *responsibility* once the wrong has been established.) Since the extent to which parties other than states may invoke international responsibility is a function of the primary rule involved, the ILC understandably did not enunciate a general rule of *locus standi*, but left the matter to *lex specialis* such as human rights conventions or, in the case of investor protection, the more than 2,000 bilateral treaties which establish international mechanisms for the invocation by private parties of the responsibility of states.

Accordingly, Article 33(2) states that Part 2 of the ILC Articles (concerning the content of the international responsibility of states) 'is without prejudice to any right, arising from the international responsibility of a State, which may accrue directly to any person or entity other than a State'. Consistently with this statement, the provisions of Part 2 do not identify the party to whom the obligation is owed. Also relevant, in terms of respect for discrete treaty mechanisms, is Article 55 of Part 4 (general provisions) which is entitled '*Lex specialis*' and makes clear that the ILC Articles do not apply 'where and to the extent that ... the implementation of the international responsibility of the State [is] governed by special rules of international law'.

The developments described in this chapter alter immensely the legal landscape in which Freeman and his contemporaries were writing. Yet even in that period, which one might fix roughly as between the two World Wars, there was already a rich body of decisions dealing with claims of denial of justice. (Freeman's table of cases included 457 entries.) It is important to understand the contours of the delict as they had emerged in the 1930s, and to see how they have been developed and clarified in the course of the epochal expansion of the international community since then.

This objective explains the extensive reference to authors such as Freeman, de Visscher and Fitzmaurice. For the rest, this study seeks less to account for what others have written than to consider the thing itself.

# 4

# The modern definition of denial of justice

## Overview

We have seen that the concept of denial of justice was once often used as the rhetorical excuse for interventions by foreign governments acting on behalf of their nationals to obtain reparation for alleged violations of their rights. The triggering event might be *any action deemed to breach international law,* whether or not related to the administration of justice. Forcible intervention was thus justified by the complaint that the initial wrong had not been repaired by national judicial processes.

One consequence of this usage of the expression was that some scholars concluded that it applied only to instances of refusal of redress, so that it would cover failure or extreme delay in the hearing of a complaint, but not cases of miscarriage of justice affecting *defendants*. If the latter were international wrongs, it was said, they would have to be known by some other appellation such as 'manifest injustice', because they were not properly to be understood as justice *denied*, but as justice wrongly *rendered*.

To compound the confusion, some writers and indeed adjudicators concluded that denial of justice could never be a primary wrong, but could only be present when the initial wrong, whatever it may have been, was followed by a failure to correct it. The ensuing habitual coupling of denial of justice with every type of international wrong was doubtless an even more serious consequence of the use of the expression *denial of justice* to legitimise the use of force. The original wrong done to the defendant was blended with the failure of national redress, and the two grievances became the indistinct condition for 'diplomatic' intervention.

These mental constructs have long since been exposed as misleading and unsound. One can of course agree that words should be taken to

57

mean anything at all. Even if one deems a tail to be a leg, however, dogs will still have four legs. We could also agree that any leg should be termed 'a weight-bearing extremity', but that would add nothing to our ability to identify a dog. The unnecessary multiplication of formal causes of action, depending on who has initiated the action, sows confusion. It makes life difficult for lawyers, adjudicators and negotiators of the instruments of international law. So would insistence on the proposition that exactly the same facts that constitute miscarriage of justice, such as the flat refusal to hear a litigant, give rise to one delict if they take place in connection with attempts to redress an 'original wrong' (whether or not connected with the administration of justice), but quite another if they are invoked as the 'primary' wrong. Above all, these quibblings were connected with a preoccupation, namely the justification for diplomatic intervention, which has to do with remedies and not with the elements of responsibility.

These conceptual ambiguities were initially the handiwork of those who were seeking to extend the protection of international law. They undoubtedly included both idealists and opportunists. Whatever their motivation, they were seen by weaker states as providing cover for dubious unilateralism. And so the defenders of those states, which habitually found themselves debtors and respondents to claims of denial of justice, continued to introduce qualifications of their own, equally productive of confusion.

Although all writers on the subject accept that a claim of denial of justice is an international complaint which cannot be disposed of by the very state whose conduct is in question, there was once a wave of commentators seeking with all their might to restrict its definition. The most extreme positions were taken by those who insisted that only a refusal to consider a case could give rise to international responsibility. Once a formal judgment was rendered, no matter how many years after the petition, no matter how unfair the conduct of the trial, indeed no matter how clear the proof of bias or even corruption, it would be an affront to national sovereignty for international adjudicators to examine the actions of the local judiciary. This extreme view would have turned denial of justice into a shimmering mirage. It has no serious proponents in modern international law. (As for the insult to national pride, such emotive comments will always be voiced by the ignorant or the manipulative whenever they find international law to be ill suited to their motives; international law is by definition and in its essence a restriction on national prerogatives.)

A less extreme but in effect equally perverse limitation was the proposition that the expression denial of justice could be used only with respect to the conduct of judicial officers of the state. The support for this proposition is less extensive than some authors have supposed.[1] Some proponents of this theory were interested only in the *a priori* objective of dismantling the international delict of denial of justice. They should be disregarded. As for the others, an examination of their writings suggests that they were primarily concerned with correcting the unacceptable channelling of all international grievances into the delict of denial of justice. In other words, their concern was to achieve agreement to the effect that denial of justice is a meaningful concept only if it is understood as relating to the administration of justice. Once that is established, the issue is simply whether the wrongful acts or omissions are attributable to the state or not. Unless one wishes to open the door to the evisceration of international law by political fiat, it matters not, as argued in greater detail in the section on 'Denial of justice by non-judicial authority' in Chapter 3, whether the internationally wrongful administration of justice is perpetuated by the executive, legislative or judicial branches.

## The difficult emergence of a general international standard

International law would not crumble with the disappearance of the expression 'denial of justice'. Yet if it did not exist it would have to be invented in some other guise, and whatever concept were enlisted in its place would share two of its features: (i) it would have to be expressed as an abstraction[2] and (ii) it could not be applied mechanically.

---

[1] In particular, Cançado Trindade's impressive list of authorities ostensibly favouring the limitation of denial of justice 'to wrong conduct of courts or judges' – including Borchard, Durand, Bevilaqua, Anzilotti, Strisower, Accioly, C. Rousseau, Rolin, 'Oppenheim – Lauterpacht', Brownlie, Kelsen, Castberg, Ago, Brierly – Cançado Trindade, 'Denial of Justice and its Relationship to Exhaustion of Local Remedies in International Law', (1978) 53 *Philippine Law Journal* 404, at p. 411, quickly dissolves into a flood of qualifications and exceptions upon examination of the quoted works.

[2] During the 1954 session of the Institut de Droit International, only a small minority of the participants found merit in the prospect of defining denial of justice by enumeration of instances; the majority favoured overarching formulae, (1954) 45 *Annuaire de l'Institut de droit international* 97. Oliver J. Lissitzyn, 'The Meaning of the Term Denial of Justice in International Law', (1936) 30 AJIL 632, at p. 644, on the other hand, favoured avoidance of the term altogether because of its inconclusiveness, given that 'particular acts or omissions meant to be covered by it can be enumerated and defined expressly'.

If these two related propositions were not accepted, formalism would rule; any state could avoid responsibility for the way its system of justice treats foreigners simply by going through expedient motions.

True, by the study of treaties, precedents and doctrine international adjudicators could seek to decide whether there has been an international delict without using the particular abstraction *denial of justice*, but they would still find themselves struggling with the task of finding meaningful applications of other abstractions that seek to encapsulate an evolving consensus as to the minimum international standard required of national legal systems when they deal with the rights of foreigners. This is unavoidable due to the inexorable inclination of perpetrators of unfairness to cloak their actions in the appearance of fairness.

Freeman gives an account of various tentative codifications which in his day had sought to avoid what was viewed, not without reason, as a fuzzy and controversial notion, unlikely in itself to yield predictability. After noting that 'vagueness is characteristic of growing, living branches of legal science, and allows necessary leeway for the law to pass through its formative periods', he concluded:

the expression should not be tossed aside as incapable of useful service. It is true that considerable controversy rages over its meaning. Yet an imposing body of authority is gradually coming to recognize that its rightful province is synonymous with every failure on the part of the State to provide an adequate judicial protection for the rights of aliens. And as such, 'denial of justice' merits preservation.[3]

International law has already built on this conclusion. It can no longer be seriously maintained that denial of justice means nothing but access to formal adjudication, no matter how iniquitous; nor that state responsibility cannot attach to wrongful acts of the judiciary. And if a foreigner is entitled to the protections of international law, the organs of a state cannot have the last word when such entitlements are invoked. Ignorance, bad faith and the outraged unreasoned rejection of criticism will always be with us, but the controversy of Freeman's day has abated.

The modern consensus is clear to the effect that the factual circumstances must be egregious if state responsibility is to arise on the grounds of denial of justice. If a foreigner has been convicted of a crime by a jury of five and complains that other courts empanel juries of nine for such cases, there is little prospect of concluding that an international standard has

---

[3] Freeman at pp. 182–183.

been violated. On the other hand, if jury members had been allowed to hear the prosecution but not the defence, there can be little doubt that a denial of justice has occurred. International adjudicators do not require an explicit rule or an exactly matching precedent to reach a conclusion in either case. The organs of the state do not necessarily defy the fundaments of a fair legal process by the use of a smaller jury (indeed there is no international standard to the effect that facts must be tried by a jury, even in criminal law). But they do so if they silence an accused.

The indispensable line between fundamental violations and others is easy to draw in the instances just imagined, but other cases are less clearcut. What if the defence is given only thirty minutes to answer the prosecution's hour-long summation? How about five minutes? What if the jury includes only members of a particular religion which is alleged to be hostile to the complaining foreigner, or gives greater weight to the testimony of coreligionists, or to men as opposed to women? What if the judgment looks impressively well-reasoned and balanced, but the trial record shows that important elements of the foreigner's evidence were excluded? Most difficult questions are matters of degree. Sometimes they are given weight only when there is an accumulation of disturbing evidence. These concrete questions are at the heart of the matter, and merit reflection.

A less worthwhile inquiry concerns the taxonomy of state organs to be acknowledged as dispensing justice, or the types of interactions with authorities to be acknowledged as part of the processes of justice. For example, it might be argued that a denial of justice can occur only if an alien is thwarted in his attempt to initiate a suit to protect his rights, but that the expression is inapposite if he is the victim of a miscarriage of justice *as a defendant*; since in the latter case he is by definition before the court, there is no *denial* of justice but rather something that must find another name, such as 'manifest or notorious injustice'. Or it may be posited that internationally unacceptable conditions of arrest or detention are international wrongs of a genus different from denial of justice *stricto sensu* because they occur, as it were, in connection with judicial proceedings rather than as a part of them, and involve the conduct of non-judicial officers. Indeed scholars in times past found it necessary to debate such matters.

The phrase 'denial of justice', no matter how elaborately defined, will never yield instant clarity as to how actual cases are to be decided in a complex and untidy world. It seems futile to develop refined theories about what conduct is encompassed by a given expression of such elasticity. To some extent the debate is one of nomenclature; it does not concern the *existence* of an international delict, but what to call it.

The preferred solution is doubtless to adopt a broad definition that encompasses all aspects of the judicial process. Certainly a detainee held for years without a trial would find it difficult to understand why he is not the victim of a denial of justice simply because no judge ordered his incarceration and the opening gavel for his trial has not yet been brought down. This study proceeds on the premise of a definition such as the one proposed in Chapter 1: the delict of denial of justice occurs when the instrumentalities of a state purport to administer justice to aliens in a fundamentally unfair manner. The interesting debate is not whether international delicts are placed in the right category, but whether they are delicts in the first place.

Grotius conceived two types of denial of justice: (i) where 'a judgment cannot be obtained against a criminal or a debtor within a reasonable time' and (ii) where 'in a very clear case judgment has been rendered in a way manifestly contrary to law'.[4] There are two difficulties with this exposition which have created much confusion over the centuries.

The first problem is that Grotius focused on cases where the complainant was frustrated *as a plaintiff*. This conception of the issue has caused some among the successive generations of scholars to view denial of justice exclusively as a matter of *thwarted redress*. Well into the twentieth century, voices were heard to the effect that denial of justice was 'restricted to those cases in which the alien appears as plaintiff'.[5] Some tribunals reasoned that there must have been some 'original' injustice with respect to which a court thereafter denied redress.[6] But of course a foreigner may suffer from a miscarriage of justice as a defendant; the *Loewen* case is an obvious example. To maintain that denial of justice comes into play with respect to only the wrongful treatment of grievances therefore made it necessary to speak of 'manifest injustice' as a category additional to that of denial of justice. Moreover, this approach suggested that the claimant to whom justice was denied must have been right with respect to his grievance, which logically leads to the unacceptable

---

[4] Hugo Grotius, *De Jure Belli ac Pacis libri tres* (Oxford: Clarendon, 1925), book III, chap. 2.
[5] Clyde Eagleton, 'Denial of Justice in International Law', (1928) 22 AJIL 538, at p. 553. Contra Freeman at p. 151 *et seq.*; de Visscher at p. 393; Fitzmaurice at p. 105.
[6] In the course of colloquy with counsel in the *Cayuga Indians* case, Arbitrator Pound said: 'First there is an injustice antecedent to the denial, and then the denial after it' (*US* v. *Great Britain*; Fred K. Nielsen, *American and British Claims Arbitration under the Special Agreement of August 18, 1910*, at p. 258). This phrase, pithy but misleading (see Freeman's comment at p. 155, n. 1), was cited in the important *Chattin* case in support of the unfortunate conception that the expression 'denial of justice' is inappropriate when 'the courts themselves did injustice', IV RIAA 282, at p. 286.

conclusion that one is entitled to a proper hearing only if one's case is good. Since the substance of the delict of denial of justice is undistinguishable from that of 'manifest injustice' as that phrase was used to cover the special pseudo-category of judicial wrongdoing independent of antecedent injustice, the irresistibly better view is to consider, simply and naturally, that denial of justice covers all situations where a foreigner has been deprived of a proper judicial process, whether he is seeking to establish *or to preserve* legal interests.

Fitzmaurice archly dismissed this as 'a particularly barren distinction of no practical utility', and moreover one of doubtful theoretical validity.[7] The question, he observed, is whether 'a wrong similar in every respect' must be given 'some other name' because it was committed against an alien defendant who is not seeking redress for a prior wrong but is seeking to resist an effort to obtain redress against himself. His analysis in response to this question merits full quotation:

The point is usually obscured by the fact that in nearly all cases an appeal lies, and owing to the familiar rule that all appeals must be exhausted before formal diplomatic intervention can take place, such intervention can, in fact, when the time comes, usually be based on a failure to redress a previous wrong, i.e. in the case of a defendant, on the improper failure, due e.g. to a lack of impartiality, on the part of a higher court to redress the injury caused by a wrong judgment in a lower one. But it is possible to conceive a case where this would not be so. Imagine that A sues B, a foreigner, for money lent. The court quite properly decides in favour of B, it being clear that he never borrowed the money. A appeals. The court of appeal confirms the judgment. A appeals to the final court of appeal. This court, being clearly prejudiced against B on the ground that he is a foreigner, reverses the previous judgments, and condemns him to pay. Most people would say that this would constitute a denial of justice. Yet it would not consist in a failure to redress a previous injury done to B. On the contrary it would constitute an original wrong done to him.

This instance brings into glaring relief the unreality of the distinction between a denial of justice committed by the courts, and an original wrong or *in*justice committed by them. The distinction may be sound in theory, but it is unreal in practice. In either case there is a failure on the part of the courts to do justice, and in either case there is a failure to render to the injured party the justice which he had the right to expect in a court of law; in other words a denial to him of justice – be he plaintiff or defendant. But the distinction, even if it be valid in pure theory, becomes still more unreal when considered in connexion with the by no means unusual class of case, to which attention has already been drawn, where the

---

[7] Fitzmaurice at p. 105.

parties before the court are neither plaintiff nor defendant, but as it were both – where each seeks to establish a right and to contest the other's right but without alleging any actual injury. If in such a case a court, e.g. the highest court of appeal, delivers a judgment against one of the parties, a foreigner, which obviously constitutes a flagrant piece of dishonesty, clearly involving the international responsibility of the state, can it be said with any real justification that the party in question has not suffered a denial of justice because there has been no failure by the court to redress a prior wrong (when none was asserted) and that the wrong committed by the court must be called by some other name?

The conclusion to be drawn seems to be that, at any rate for all practical purposes, every injury involving the responsibility of the state committed by a court or judge acting officially, or alternatively every such injury committed by any organ of the government in its official capacity in connexion with the administration of justice, constitutes and can properly be styled a denial of justice, whether it consists in a failure to redress a prior wrong, or in an original wrong committed by the court or other organ itself.[8]

Fiztmaurice found support for this view in the following passage from Borchard:

Whether it is technically possible or desirable to make the distinction where courts are involved between primary and secondary injuries, for example, whether it is practical to say where a mob or the executive controls the courts in a case where the alien is a defendant, that a denial of justice has not occurred, but only an 'unjust judgment', seems rather doubtful. Foreign Offices would probably not make the distinction, nor have international tribunals or writers generally.[9]

The expression 'manifest injustice' of itself is an unhappy one, because it is irremediably ambiguous; it could refer to either an unjust judgment or an unfair trial. This ambiguity is precisely the second difficulty with the Grotian formulation. A judgment 'rendered in a way manifestly contrary to law' could be vitiated either because the court disregarded the procedural code or because it misapplied principles of liability. If anything is clear about the international law of denial of justice, it is that it does not concern itself with bare errors of substance. Fitzmaurice wrote that it 'hardly seems necessary to give authority for the proposition that mere error of fact or mere error in the interpretation of the national law does

---

[8] *Ibid.* at pp. 107–109.
[9] (1929) I *Zeitschrift für ausländisches öffentliches Recht und Völkerrecht* 223, quoted in Fitzmaurice, at p. 109.

not *per se* involve responsibility', but went on to quote eloquent and categorical passages to that effect from four awards.[10]

Grotius' discussion of this subject was incidental; he was not proposing a new doctrine to reflect the limits of the territorial prerogatives of emerging nation states, but simply considering all grievances that might be said to legitimise war. The true intellectual father of denial of justice was Vattel, who in 1758 proposed a systematic approach to the illegitimate *refusal* of justice under three heads:

- not admitting foreigners to establish their rights before the ordinary courts,
- delays which are ruinous or otherwise equivalent to refusal,
- judgments 'manifestly unjust and one-sided'.[11]

Two centuries of debate focused on the third category. (No serious international lawyer contests either of the first two.) That phrase – 'manifestly unjust and one-sided' – is the heart of this study. Much may lie in the two adjectives. *Unjust* is not enough, the conjunctive *and* signifies that something more is required. *One-sided* then opens the door to the manner in which the process was conducted; all fundamental rules of procedure are, after all, intended to ensure the absence of partiality. The proper reaction to discrimination, fraud, bias, malice or harassment, abuse of form, or arbitrariness should not engender controversy in principle; they are proscribed. But to anticipate the greatest difficulty of our subject, it should follow that gross or notorious injustice – whatever the words used – is not a denial of justice merely because the conclusion appears to be demonstrably wrong in substance; it must impel the adjudicator to conclude that it could not have been reached by an impartial judicial body worthy of that name. (Thus the unexplained disregard of a century of unbroken jurisprudence might be viewed with suspicion if it happens to benefit powerful local interests arrayed against a politically controversial foreigner.[12])

---

[10] *Ibid.* at p. 111, note 1.    [11] Vattel, Book II, at para. 350.

[12] As Spain's Counter-Memorial in *Barcelona Traction* put it, a state is liable for erroneous judicial decisions, or *mal jugé*, only if it is found that the relevant courts exhibited some degree of 'bad faith or discriminatory intention'. Quoted in Eduardo Jiménez de Aréchaga, 'International Responsibility of States for Acts of the Judiciary', in W. G. Friedmann, L. Henkin and O. J. Lissitzyn (eds.), *Transnational Law in a Changing Society – Essays in Honor of Philip C. Jessup* (New York: Columbia University Press, 1972), 171, at p. 179. An example of a legal basis for a national judgment so outlandish that it is rejected by the international tribunal is the peculiar notion of *res judicata* in the *Idler* case, discussed in the section on 'Gross incompetence' in Chapter 7.

Freeman quoted De Visscher's formulation of denial of justice, namely:

toute défaillance dans l'organisation ou dans l'exercice de la fonction juridic-
tionnelle qui implique manquement de l'Etat à son devoir international de
protection judiciaire des étrangers,[13]

and offered the observation that 'it may well be wondered whether any
future jurist will be able to improve upon'[14] that definition. One might
object that the word 'definition' does not easily apply to a sentence which
includes the unexplained words 'failure', 'duty', and 'judicial protection'.

Certainly Freeman's own attempt, offered almost apologetically in
light of the author's admiration for de Visscher's phrase, can be criticised
on the same basis. He wrote:

If there is anything even remotely approaching a tendency toward a uniform
definition in recent doctrinal utterances, it is to apply the phrase 'denial of justice'
to all unlawful acts or omissions engaging the State's responsibility in connection
with the entire process of administering justice to aliens.[15]

This is circular. No insight is required to understand that 'unlawful acts or
omissions' give rise to responsibility. What we want to know is precisely
*what makes them unlawful*. All we can say, as we try to apprehend the sense of
such oft-recurring intensifiers as *shocking*, or *surprising*, is that the issue is
one of *fundamental unfairness*. Since the days of de Visscher and Freeman,
we have learned to live with inherently elastic concepts relating to the
international legitimacy of national judicial processes. The fundamental
conventions of human rights which have come into being since then have
struggled to do better than to refer to abstractions such as *fair trials*.[16] Yet

---

[13] In de Visscher at p. 390, quoted in Freeman at p. 162 ('any shortcoming in the
organisation or exercise of the jurisdictional function which involves a failure of the
state to live up to its international duty of extending judicial protection to foreigners').
[14] Freeman at p. 163.   [15] *Ibid.* at p. 161.
[16] Although one must recognise the contribution of the United Nations on the specific
issue of the independence of the judiciary and of lawyers: see, e.g., Commission on
Human Rights resolution 2003/43 'Independence and impartiality of the judiciary,
jurors and assessors and the independence of lawyers', UN Doc. E/CN.4/2003/L.11/
Add.4, at p. 57; Basic Principles on the Independence of the Judiciary, adopted by the
Seventh United Nations Congress on the Prevention of Crime and the Treatment of
Offenders, UN Doc. A/CONF.121/22/Rev.1, at p. 59; Basic Principles on the Role of
Lawyers, adopted by the Eighth United Nations Congress on the Prevention of Crime
and the Treatment of Offenders, UN Doc. A/CONF.144/28/Rev.1, at p. 118; and
General Assembly resolutions A/RES/43/153, adopted 8 December 1988, A/RES/
48/137, adopted 20 December 1993, and A/RES/58/183, adopted 18 March 2004,
all on 'Human rights in the administration of justice'.

political consensus has been reached as to the articulation of those general principles, and international adjudicators have been able to give them life. An international legal *culture* emerges that enables us to perceive *in concreto* the boundaries of national discretion – with more or less certainty, as always in the life of the law, the closer we find ourselves to the boundary beyond which the international delict arises. The situation is the same with respect to denial of justice. And so perhaps a phrase will do, such as Irizarry y Puente's succinct formulation: 'the international obligation of the state not to administer justice in a notoriously unjust manner'.[17] As seen above, *unfair* might be preferable to *unjust*, because it denotes not just error, but fault. At any rate, and whatever assistance may be provided by precedents and by crystallising general principles relating to due process, the perception of what is fundamentally unfair will, in the difficult cases, ultimately be a matter of subjective discernment.

Before concluding these reflections on the contemporary standard, it seems appropriate to suggest that it is time to put aside the confrontational vocabulary which was perhaps unavoidable in the convulsive period of decolonialisation which gathered momentum in the wake of the Second World War and culminated in the watershed year of 1960. One can understand how Judge Guha Roy could have written in 1961 that the protection of rights obtained in a colonial regime 'cannot for obvious reasons carry with them in the mind of the victims of that abuse anything like the sanctity the holders of those rights and interests may and do attach to them', and that universal adherence cannot be expected to accrue to a law of state responsibility which 'protects an unjustified status quo or, to put it more bluntly, makes itself a handmaid of power in the preservation of its spoils'.[18] But we are no longer talking about the perpetuation of rights originating in King Leopold's shameful private domain, or handed down from colonial concessions. Half a century has gone by, and we are now concerned with the reliability of legal rights and interests defined by autonomous governments who have encouraged foreigners to rely on them. To deny the capacity of sovereign states to generate international acquired rights is to condemn them to suffer a handicap tantamount to perpetual credit-unworthiness. It is to deprive them of the most powerful of tools in the vast process of economic development.

---

[17] J. Irizarry y Puente, 'The Concept of 'Denial of Justice' in Latin America', (1944) 43 *Michigan Law Review* 383, at p. 406 (emphasis omitted).
[18] S. N. Guha Roy, 'Is the Law of Responsibility of States for Injuries to Aliens a Part of Universal International Law?' (1961) 55 AJIL 866.

## An evolving standard

One of the insights of the modern conception of denial of justice is that its evolution is bound to continue. A good and uncontroversial illustration of this perception is provided by *Mondev*.

As the arbitral tribunal found,[19] the principal admissible issue in the case concerned 'the content of the notion of denial of justice' under the international law minimum standard of treatment of aliens (as that is applicable under NAFTA). Referring with approval to the award in *Pope & Talbot*,[20] the tribunal found that this was an evolutionary standard to be informed by practice, including treaties. In its intervention as a third-party signatory of NAFTA, Mexico noted that the customary international law standard 'is relative and that conduct which may not have violated international law [in] the 1920s may very well be seen to offend internationally accepted principles today'; the core idea is that 'of arbitrary action being substituted for the rule of law'.[21] For its part, Canada in its intervention noted that its 'position has always been that customary international law can evolve over time, but that the threshold for finding violation of the minimum standard of treatment is still high'.[22] Canada referred to the conception of customary international law articulated by the Claimants Commissions of the interwar years, notably that of the Mexican Claims Commission in the *Neer* case which found a requirement that, for there to be a breach of international law, 'the treatment of an alien ... should amount to an outrage, to bad faith, to wilful neglect of duty, or to an insufficiency of governmental action so far short of international standards that every reasonable and impartial man would readily recognize its insufficiency'.[23]

In oral argument, the respondent United States itself acknowledged that 'like all customary international law, the international minimum standard has evolved and can evolve'.[24]

The *Mondev* tribunal immediately noted that cases like *Neer* did not involve the treatment of foreign investment, but rather the physical safety of aliens. Neer himself had been killed by armed men who were not alleged to have been carrying out government instructions. The complaint was rather that the authorities were lax in their investigation and

---

[19] *Mondev* at para. 99.
[20] *Ibid.* at para. 105, *Pope & Talbot Inc.* v. *Canada*, award on damages, 31 May 2002, 7 *ICSID Reports* 148, at para. 59 (Greenberg, Belman, Dervaird (presiding)).
[21] *Mondev* at para. 108.   [22] *Ibid.* at para. 109.
[23] *L. F. H. Neer and Pauline Neer* (*US* v. *Mexico*), 15 October 1926, IV RIAA 60, at pp. 61–62.
[24] *Mondev* at para. 124.

pursuit. The *Mondev* tribunal was unwilling to assume that the protection of foreign investment in treaties like NAFTA was 'confined to the *Neer* standard of outrageous treatment'.[25] It also noted that:

To the modern eye, what is unfair or inequitable need not equate with the outrageous or the egregious. In particular, a State may treat a foreign investment unfairly and inequitably without necessarily acting in bad faith . . . the content of the minimum standard today cannot be limited to the content of customary international law as recognised in arbitral decisions in the 1920s.[26]

In an oft-quoted sentence, it added:

A judgment of what is fair and equitable cannot be reached in the abstract; it must depend on the facts of the particular case.[27]

This sentence was qualified by the consideration that an arbitral tribunal 'may not simply adopt its own idiosyncratic standard of what is 'fair' or 'equitable', without reference to established sources of law'.[28]

## Relationship with specific rights created by international law

If a bilateral treaty requires the authorities of one state to notify the consular authorities of the other state within seven days of its indictment of any national of the latter for a capital crime, a treaty violation will be extant on the eighth day of an unnotified indictment. Such a violation of international law clearly arises in connection with the administration of justice, but it is not necessarily a denial of justice. The national authorities have breached a specific international engagement which creates a constraint on the administration of justice, but that does not mean that it constitutes a breach of general principles of law. True, general principles of international law are not static, and may come to embrace material provisions of treaties provided that the latter reflect sufficiently broad and constant state practice. A single treaty, however, is most unlikely to create a general principle of law and thus does not establish criteria of denial of justice.

So too international awards create obligations which may establish constraints on national legal systems. That does not mean that refusal to abide by such awards constitutes a denial of justice. The well-known *Martini* case of 1930[29] illustrates a type of recurring confusion in this regard. Rendered by a tribunal presided by Östen Undén, a former Swedish Minister of Foreign

---

[25] *Ibid.* at para. 115.  [26] *Ibid.* at paras. 116 and 123.  [27] *Ibid.* at para. 118.
[28] *Ibid.* at para. 119.  [29] *Italy* v. *Venezuela*, 3 May 1930, II RIAA 975.

Affairs, this award observed that a prior, related award, issued in 1904[30] and finding the state liable for certain illegal acts causing damage to a railroad and mining enterprise, constituted an international obligation for Venezuela. It held accordingly that a subsequent Venezuelan judgment contradicting the findings of that award constituted a 'manifest injustice' under the terms of a new arbitration agreement entered into by Italy and Venezuela. The 'manifest injustice' standard had been imposed on the tribunal by the arbitration agreement as an issue it was mandated to decide; 'manifest injustice' is of course one way of characterising a so-called substantive denial of justice. But this was not denial of justice; it was the violation of an international obligation to respect the prior arbitral award as a *res judicata*.

In *Feldman* v. *Mexico*,[31] the Government of Mexico conceded that the arbitral tribunal could find that a Mexican law violated the relevant treaty (the North American Free Trade Agreement) even if the Mexican courts upheld the national law in question; the arbitrators put the matter squarely as follows: 'this Tribunal is not bound by a decision of a local court if that decision violates international law'.[32] In *Himpurna* v. *Indonesia*, the arbitral tribunal rejected the proposition advanced by the respondent state to the effect that the arbitrators would not have the authority 'to consider whether there has been a violation of international law – which is part of the law of Indonesia – if such consideration might lead to disregard of an Indonesian court decision'.[33]

This concept may be usefully examined by reference to Article 2(3)(a) of the US/Bahrain Treaty concerning the Encouragement and Reciprocal Protection of Investment,[34] which provides that:

Each Party shall at all times accord to covered investments fair and equitable treatment and full protection and security, and shall in no case accord treatment less favorable than that required by international law.

In her letter to the President recommending the Treaty, the US Secretary of State noted that in addition to the explicit reference to 'fair and equitable treatment' and 'full protection and security':

---

[30] *Italy* v. *Venezuela*, 8 July 1904, X RIAA 644.
[31] Award, 16 December 2002, 7 *ICSID Reports* 341 (Covarrubias Bravo, Gantz, Kerameus (presiding)).
[32] *Ibid.* at para. 140.
[33] *Himpurna California Energy Ltd* v. *Indonesia*, interim award, 26 September 1999, (2000) XXV *ICCA Yearbook Commercial Arbitration* 109 (de Fina, Abdurrasyid, Paulsson (presiding)), at p. 181.
[34] Signed on 29 September 1999, (2000) 39 ILM 252.

The general reference to international law also implicitly incorporates the fundamental rules of customary international law regarding the treatment of foreign investment.[35]

Such a provision naturally opens the door to liability, as found by an international tribunal, for denial of justice as a 'fundamental rule of customary international law'. But denial of justice is not the only rule of international law. If other rules are disregarded by national courts to the detriment of an alien entitled to rely on this provision, the judgment is not compliant with international law and should properly be disregarded by an international tribunal competent to apply the treaty. But that does not mean that there has been a denial of justice.

This is an area where it is difficult to agree with Freeman, who was either wrong or unhelpfully ambiguous when he wrote that denial of justice 'in the international sphere' is 'designed ... to guarantee and safeguard the rights of aliens. It should therefore be found necessary to modify the traditional procedural definition.'[36] In his view, the 'obligations implicit in the concept of denial of justice' extend beyond 'the procedural operation of the judicial mechanism' to:

embrace the substantive treatment which must be accorded to aliens by the courts or whatever other organs the State may have charged with the function of dispensing justice.[37]

Was Freeman postulating that the breach of international law should be deemed to be a denial of justice whenever it is done by judicial authorities? That seems to be the case, for it is difficult to see why he would otherwise be propounding an extension of the rule. Yet it is impossible, without ignoring the natural meaning of words, to see what this had to do with denial of justice. As Fitzmaurice had written only a few years before:

the judgments of municipal courts applying international law will, if they mis-apply international law, *ipso facto* involve the responsibility of the state (at any rate if acted upon) even though rendered in perfect good faith by an honest and competent court.[38]

And Jiménez de Aréchaga put his finger on the problems when he wrote, thirty years on, that:

---

[35] Lucy Reed, Jan Paulsson and Nigel Blackaby, *Guide to ICSID Arbitration* (The Hague: Kluwer, 2004), at p. 179.
[36] Freeman at p. 178.   [37] *Ibid.* at p. 51.   [38] Fitzmaurice at p. 110.

the obvious objection is that denial of justice and State responsibility are not co-extensive expressions, and that State responsibility for acts of the Judiciary does not exhaust itself in the concept of denial of justice.[39]

This objection is clearly well founded. A court which refuses to comply with a treaty obligation to dispense with bonds as *cautio adjudicatum solvi* will by definition violate an international obligation, but it is not a denial of justice – unless the bond is unreasonable in amount, or discriminatory.

A significant theoretical weakness of de Visscher's important Course at the Hague Academy is to be found in his unsuccessful attempt to clarify the debate as to the circumstances under which the substance of a national judgment may be challenged internationally. He thought that the contours of the problem could be better understood if one distinguished instances in which the state had guaranteed predetermined judicial outcome from situations where there was no such guarantee. The first hypothesis, according to de Visscher, involved such undertakings as the non-requirement of a bond as security for costs or the duty to respect an arbitral award duly rendered in accordance with an international agreement.[40]

This construction is of no assistance, for the simple reason that a violation of an independent international obligation, whether by a court or any other organ of the state, is irrelevant to the discussion of denial of justice. A national court judgment violative of international law does not pose any conceptual difficulty. There is no need to find any exacerbated error, contaminated by bad faith or by gross incompetence. There is no presumption of compliance with international law. A simple error suffices. A simple difference of opinion on the part of the international tribunal is enough; it has plenary powers to rule on the alleged international wrong as it sees fit.

In other words, the difficult hypothesis is the *only* hypothesis we must wrestle with in connection with denial of justice. What is the dividing line between what the Senate of Hamburg, in *Yuille, Shortridge and Co.*, referred to as 'failure of justness' and 'total absence of justice'? De Visscher suggested the following:

[39] Jiménez de Aréchaga, 'International Responsibility' in M. Sørensen (ed.), *Manual of Public International Law* (London: Macmillan, 1968), at p. 555.

[40] De Visscher referred, at p. 402, to the *Martini* case, which, as seen, involved the rejection of an award by the Venezuelan courts, leading to a further international arbitration against that state.

In international relations, a decision manifestly rendered against all justice may no longer be considered as a work of justice. The protection of the foreigner by the internal procedures has proved itself to be ineffective. Under the appearances of legality, the international duty of protections is violated; recourse to the international forum is open.[41]

In considering the egregiousness of the wrongfulness of a national judgment applying national law, de Visscher observed that international arbitrators had on occasion deduced 'manifest injustice' from extrinsic circumstances such as pressure or corruption affecting the judges, or, by reference to the *Robert E. Brown* award, evidence of collusion between the legislature, the government and the judiciary. He concluded, however, that in the great majority of cases the judgment itself furnishes the *éléments d'appréciation* which might lead to the conclusion that it was motivated by bias against the foreigner reflected in the 'extreme defectiveness of its reasoning'.[42]

## No responsibility for misapplication of national law

The general rule is that the final word as to the meaning of national law should be left with the national judiciary. Vattel's admonition remains pertinent:

In all cases open to doubt a sovereign should not entertain the complaints of his subjects against a foreign tribunal nor undertake to exempt them from the effect of a decision rendered in due form, for by doing so he would give rise to continual disturbances.[43]

As seen above, Fitzmaurice wrote in 1932 that it hardly seemed necessary to cite authority to the effect that 'mere error in the interpretation of the national law does not *per se* involve responsibility'.[44] We may indeed refer to this proposition as the general rule. De Visscher put it as follows:

The mere violation of internal law may never justify an international claim based on denial of justice. It may be that the defectiveness of internal law, the refusal to apply it, or its wrongful application by judges, constitute elements of proof of a denial of justice, in the international understanding of the expression; but in and of themselves they never constitute this denial.[45]

---

[41] *Ibid.* at p. 404.    [42] *Ibid.* at p. 407.    [43] Vattel, vol. II, at para. 350.
[44] Fitzmaurice at p. 111, note 1.    [45] De Visscher at p. 376.

In sum:

*Errare humanum est*: error in good faith excludes responsibility.[46]

The general rule may be illustrated by *Denham*,[47] which involved an inheritance dispute between a widow and another woman, Andrea Gonzalez, by whom the widow's late husband had had five children. These children would not, under Panamanian law, have had a share in the estate without a will. Their mother presented for probate a will which purported to give her children a greater interest in the estate than that which Panamanian law would have granted to the widow in the absence of a will. The document was drawn up in dubious circumstances as Mr Denham lay dying, and his widow expressed her intention to challenge it. To avoid litigation, the two women decided to reach an accommodation by which the estate was divided equitably between the deceased's legitimate and illegitimate descendants. The controversial will was abandoned, and the settlement was judicially approved as the basis for a decree determining the succession.

Two years later, Sra Gonzalez brought suit to have the settlement agreement set aside and the estate redistributed in accordance with the will she had originally presented. She argued that the will would have given her children more than they obtained under the settlement, and that she had not had the right, under Panamanian law, to compromise the rights of minors without the approval of the court.

The Panamanian court held in favour of Sra Gonzalez's children, stating that she had:

disposed gratuitously of part of the property which belonged to them by law, according to the testator's order, without having the legal authorization to do so.

The Panamanian Supreme Court upheld this judgment, stating in part that the minors 'had been deprived of a great part of their patrimony . . . without complying with tutelary formality'.

The American Agency brought proceedings on behalf of Mrs Denham, alleging a denial of justice in that the courts had made unjustified assumptions of non-existing facts, namely (a) that there was a valid will, and, (b) at any rate, it was untrue that there had been a failure to

---

[46] *Ibid.* at p. 382.
[47] *Lettie Charlotte Denham & Frank Parlin Denham (US v. Panama)*, 27 June 1933, VI RIAA 334.

comply with formalities; a court decree had given effect to the settlement agreement insofar as it affected the minors, and Article 1501 of the Civil Code did not invalidate this disposition, since it provided only that no effect shall be given to a mother's compromise with respect to the rights of children under her tutelage 'without judicial authorisation'.

The Commission rejected the American complaint, finding 'no evidence of any manifest violation of law or of manifest bad faith application of law or in weighing the evidence filed by the parties'.

What needs to be stressed is that the Commission refused to substitute its judgment for that of the Panamanian courts. The case thus illustrates the powerful general rule that the final interpretation of a municipal law should be left to the municipal judiciary.

The *Croft* arbitration between the United Kingdom and Portugal[48] also illustrates the firmness of the general rule. The British claimants in that case had certain interests in a gift estate. In order to establish those interests, a certain type of registration, known as *insinuation*, was required. The claimants had sought to obtain that registration, but their application was dismissed by a judgment which held it to be premature, and advised its presentation upon the death of the donor. When the Crofts ultimately returned to do so, the relevant Portuguese officials refused to recognise the prior judgment. The claimants objected that this action violated the law governing registration and the rights recognised by the earlier judgment. Acting as arbitrator, the Senate of Hamburg held that even if the refusal had been wrongful, there was no violation of the law of nations as the case did not fall under any of the three types of denial of justice enumerated by Vattel (no access to a forum, excessive delay, or a 'manifestly unjust and partial decision').

*Yuille, Shortridge & Co.* was another claim brought to arbitration before the Hamburg Senate by the UK against Portugal.[49] The problem was that a Portuguese court of appeal had rather astonishingly held that the claimant, a corporate entity, was liable for the personal debts of one of its shareholders. The UK argued that the judgment was an egregious injustice. Once again relying on Vattel, the arbitral tribunal disagreed, holding that there was:

---

[48] 7 February 1856, de Lapradelle and Politis, *Recueil*, vol. II, at p. 22.
[49] 21 October 1861, *ibid.* at p. 101.

neither denial of justice nor a simulacrum of form, because it was the Court of Appeal which had judged on the basis of legal principles, however poorly applied to the facts.[50]

Freeman criticised this arbitral decision on the grounds that it seemed to leave no international remedy against the substance of a judgment applying national law – 'no matter how erroneous, manifestly unjust or both'. He criticised the arbitral tribunal for interpreting Vattel's 'manifest injustice' in an overly restrictive way, and wrote that 'one may well conjecture whether the point at issue in the *Yuille, Shortridge & Co.* case would not have been decided differently if presented today'.[51]

Since the claim was successful on another ground, the arbitral tribunal's comments were *obiter dictum*. There may have been more to the matter than can be gleaned from the available summary. Indeed the Hamburg Senate may have been careless in making this observation. That does not mean, however, that Freeman is necessarily right in suggesting that the conclusion should have been an exception to the general rule. A better approach would be to test the Portuguese judgment against a standard of gross incompetence, and to have the claim fail or succeed depending on whether the record justified the conclusion that on that basis it could be considered procedural denial of justice.

The general principle that misapplication of national law is not a denial of justice has been confirmed in more recent jurisprudence.

*Mondev* involved claims against the United States arising out of a decision rendered by the Massachusetts Supreme Judicial Court (the SJC), as well as the US Supreme Court's decision to refuse to hear an appeal from that decision. Through a US subsidiary, Mondev had entered into a commercial real estate development contract with the City of Boston and the Boston Redevelopment Authority (BRA). The relevant entity ultimately owned by Mondev, called Lafayette Place Associates (LPA), brought a suit against the City and BRA. The contract involved a multi-faceted project, but a dispute arose specifically with respect to LPA's alleged right to an option to build on a certain site in the event the City decided to remove structures and to install an underground parking garage. A jury entered substantial verdicts against both defendants. The trial judge rejected the jury's verdict against BRA by reason of a Massachusetts statute giving BRA immunity from suit. He did not disturb the verdict against the City. The SJC upheld the judge's

[50] *Ibid.* at p. 103; the author's translation.  [51] Freeman at p. 335.

judgment as concerned BRA, but reversed it with respect to the City. Thus both jury verdicts in favour of LPA were ultimately overturned.

Mondev's claim of denial of justice focused on three aspects of the contractual claim against the City. It also challenged the dismissal of its tort claim against the BRA on the grounds that the United States should not be able to avoid international responsibility by local enactments purporting to confer immunity on governmental bodies. This aspect of the case will be considered in the section on 'Absolute denial of access through state immunity' in Chapter 6.

As for the three complaints arising from the dismissal of the contractual claim against the City, the SJC essentially reasoned that the plaintiff under the law of Massachusetts was required to put the non-performing party in breach. Concretely, this meant that LPA was required to follow steps defined in the contract to put the City on notice that it demanded performance. There was no 'outright refusal' by the City to perform, and the evidence did not reveal a notice sufficiently specific to satisfy the law as established in a precedent from 1954. The Supreme Judicial Court noted that its analysis applied particularly in the case of 'a complex and heavily regulated transaction such as this one, where public entities and public and elected officials with changing policies and constituencies are involved, and the transaction spans many years', and it went on to note a dictum of Justice Holmes that '[m]en must turn square corners when they deal with the Government'.[52] By inference, neither LPA nor Campeau had turned such corners, and thus 'LPA was not excused from its obligation to put the city in default'. Mondev argued that the judgment involved a 'significant and serious departure' from case law, and that it was exacerbated by its failure to consider whether its allegedly new approach should apply retrospectively.

The arbitral tribunal expressed doubts that the Massachusetts court had applied the law in a novel fashion. It noted that 'all legal systems' must define the conditions under which an agreement in principle to transfer real property may be made legally effective. Even if the court in this case had made new law, 'its decision would have fallen within the limits of common law adjudication'.[53] As for the reference to the Holmesian

---

[52] *Mondev* at para. 130, citing *Rock Island, Ark. & La. R. R.* v. *United States*, 254 US 141, 143 (1920).

[53] *Mondev* at para. 133. The quality of the reasoning in the *Mondev* award is of such a calibre as to pre-empt dissent. A less sophisticated tribunal might have been less successful in defusing concerns that the national courts had moved the goalposts to the detriment of the foreign party. It seems fair to say that the case may leave a

pronouncement, the arbitrators accepted that it 'stands in some tension' with the proposition that 'governments are subject to the same rules of contractual liability as are private parties'. They continued:

> To the extent that it might suggest the contrary, the 'square corners' rule might raise a delicate judicial eyebrow. Indeed a governmental prerogative to violate investment contracts would appear to be inconsistent with the principles embodied in Article 1105 and with contemporary standards of national and international law concerning governmental liability for contractual performance. But in the Tribunal's view, the SJC's remark was at most a subsidiary reason for a decision founded on normal principles of the Massachusetts law of contracts, and the SJC expressly disclaimed any intention to absolve governments from performing their contractual obligations. In its context the remark was merely supplementary and was not itself the basis for the decision.[54]

The *Waste Management II*[55] case involved a concession agreement between a US-controlled corporation called Acaverde and the City of Acapulco. The agreement contemplated that the City would establish an irrevocable line of credit with a development bank known as Banobras (Banco Nacional de Obras y Servicios Publicos) to guarantee 'all payments' to the concessionaire. (Banobras was 'partly owned and substantially controlled by Mexican government agencies'.) A credit agreement was duly signed between the local government and Banobras, but it was limited to an amount equal to six monthly payments. On the other hand, Banobras was given the right to divert federal payments to the local government as a means of effecting reimbursement under the line of credit.

In the course of twenty-seven months of operations, Acaverde issued invoices amounting to 49 million pesos. Only 7 million were paid: somewhat more than 2 million by the City and somewhat less than 5 million by Banobras. There was controversy as to whether Acaverde had fully performed its obligations.

Acaverde brought local arbitral proceedings against the City under the concession agreement. It also initiated cases in the Mexican federal courts against Banobras under the credit agreement, as an alleged third-party beneficiary. The arbitration was discontinued without any decision. The court cases were dismissed both at first instance and on appeal. The US

---

disquieting sense of possible discrimination in the minds of reasonable readers; the case was, one surmises, more finely balanced than the arbitrators cared to say.

[54] *Ibid.* at para. 134 (notes omitted).
[55] *Waste Management, Inc.* v. *Mexico*, award, 30 April 2004, (2004) 43 ILM 967 (Civiletti, Magallón Gómez, Crawford (presiding)).

parent corporation subsequently brought international arbitral proceedings pursuant to Chapter 11 of the North American Free Trade Agreement. The international arbitral tribunal was led to examine whether either the arbitration or the court proceedings had constituted a denial of justice.

The issue arising out of the discontinued arbitral proceedings (whether the refusal of the City of Acapulco to pay its share of the advance payment on account of the fees of the arbitrators could be deemed a denial of justice) is discussed in the section on 'Repudiation by a state of an agreement to arbitrate' in Chapter 6.

The federal court proceedings against Banobras involved claims in respect of unpaid invoices. There were two separate actions, relating to invoices from 1996 and 1997 respectively. The first action gave rise to a judgment at first instance on 7 January 1999, upholding Acaverde's standing to sue but dismissing the claim on the merits on the ground that the invoices had not been submitted to the City in the required manner so as to demonstrate the City's acceptance. An appeal was dismissed on 11 March 1999 on the grounds that the Banobras line of credit was to come into play only in the event of the debtor's lack of liquidity; absent proof of accepted invoices, and given the formal notice to Banobras of a dispute between the City and Acaverde as to the performance of the latter, it was not proved that the non-payment was due to illiquidity. A constitutional action was dismissed on 6 October 1999. Although this final court agreed with Acaverde that the court of first instance had erred in its interpretation of the credit agreement, Acaverde had not proved that the City had received and accepted its invoices; unstamped photocopies were not sufficient for this purpose.

The second action resulted in an initial judgment of 12 January 1999 dismissing the claim without prejudice on the grounds that Acaverde could not claim against Banobras before arbitrating its claim against the City under the concession agreement. An appeal was rejected on 18 February 1999; a request for reconsideration was rejected on 25 February 1999. Finally, a constitutional action was rejected on 20 May 1999 on the grounds that although Acaverde was entitled to resist the non-retroactive applicability of new rules of judicial procedure it had waived any such objection given the way it had initiated and pursued the action.

Reviewing the record of these unsuccessful parallel actions, the international arbitral tribunal noted that the credit agreement did not guarantee the entirety of the City's indebtedness under the concession agreement. Therefore 'the federal proceedings were in any event incapable of resolving Acaverde's most important grievance'. That being said, the tribunal reached its conclusion as follows:

Certain of the decisions appear to have been founded on rather technical grounds, but the notion that the third party beneficiary of a line of credit or guarantee should strictly prove its entitlement is not a parochial or unusual one. Nor was it unreasonable, given the limitations of the Line of Credit Agreement, for the court in the second proceedings to insist that Acaverde comply with the dispute settlement procedure contained in the Concession Agreement, notice of the dispute with the City having been given to Banobras.[56]

The tribunal also noted that there was no evidence of collusion between the City and either the national arbitral institution referred to in the concession agreement (CANACO) or the federal courts. As for Acaverde's claim that the City adopted a 'difficult and obstructive' litigation strategy which itself amounted to a denial of justice, the tribunal observed that 'a *litigant* cannot commit a denial of justice unless its improper strategies are endorsed and acted on by the court, or unless the law gives it some extraordinary privilege which leads to a lack of due process'.[57] Ultimately, 'it was not a denial of justice for the federal courts to insist on prior action against the City'[58] – an initiative which Acaverde chose not to pursue to its resolution.

In *Azinian et al.* v. *Mexico*,[59] the grievance arose from the termination of a waste-disposal concession by the *ayuntamiento* (city council) of a Mexico City suburb. The termination had been unsuccessfully challenged before three levels of Mexican courts. The tribunal stated that it was:

evident that for the Claimants to prevail it is not enough that the Arbitral Tribunal disagree with the determination of the *Ayuntamiento*. A governmental authority surely cannot be faulted for acting in a manner validated by its courts unless the courts themselves are disavowed at the international level.[60]

The arbitrators found the fact that the Claimants had raised no complaints against the Mexican courts and did not allege a denial of justice to be fatal to their claims:

For if there is no complaint against a determination by a competent court that a contract governed by Mexican law was invalid under Mexican law, there is by definition no contract to be expropriated.[61]

---

[56] *Ibid.* at para. 129.   [57] *Ibid.* at para. 131.   [58] *Ibid.* at para. 132.
[59] 1 November 1998, 5 *ICSID Reports* 269 (Civiletti, von Wobeser, Paulsson (presiding)).
[60] *Ibid.* at para. 97 (emphasis omitted).   [61] *Ibid.* at para. 100.

Noting that a 'clear and malicious misapplication of the law' is a type of denial of justice – which 'doubtless overlaps with the notion of "pretence of form" to mask a violation of international law' – the arbitral tribunal went on to observe that no such wrongdoing had been alleged, and that the evidence showed that the findings of the Mexican judgments 'cannot possibly be said to have been arbitrary, let alone malicious'. To the contrary the arbitrators found that there was ample evidence of misrepresentations by the Claimants' representatives in the conclusion of the concession.

But how precisely is one to understand the possibility that international responsibility may be extant in the event the judgment on the merits evidences impermissible bias? Although de Visscher, as seen above, clearly spelled out the general rule – *errare humanum est*, with no international responsibility for violations of national law – he then went on to write that complaints against the substance of a national judgment may 'exceptionally' be heard 'if it is shown that under the colour of justice rendered, justice was denied'.[62] Is this to be understood as an exception to the general rule, or something else?

The erroneous application of national law cannot, in itself, be an international denial of justice. Unless somehow qualified by international law, rights created under national law are limited by national law, including the principle that by operation of the fundamental rule of *res judicata* a determination by a court of final appeal is definitive. So even if an instance of municipal *mal jugé* is given weight by international adjudicators when determining that there has been a denial of justice, on the footing that rights created under national law have been so blatantly disregarded as to compel conviction with respect to violation of international standards proscribing discrimination, bias, undue influence, or the like, it remains the case that the international wrong is not the misapplication of national law.

## Demise of substantive denial of justice

Three generations ago, conventional doctrine was expressed confidently by Freeman as follows:

practice, as well as the overwhelming preponderance of legal authority, recognises that not only flagrant procedural irregularities and deficiencies may justify diplomatic complaint, but also gross defects in the substance of the judgment itself.[63]

---

[62] De Visscher at p. 395.    [63] Freeman at p. 309.

The distinction has, it seems, been perpetuated by repetition; writers continue to describe denial of justice as either *procedural* or *substantive*.

Yet in modern international law there is no place for substantive denial of justice. Numerous international awards demonstrate that the most perplexing and unconvincing national judgments are upheld on the grounds that international law does not overturn determinations of national judiciaries with respect to their own law. To insist that there is a *substantive* denial of justice reserved for 'grossly' unconvincing determinations is to create an unworkable distinction. If a judgment is *grossly* unjust, it is because the victim has not been afforded fair treatment. That is the basis for responsibility, not the misapplication of national law in itself.

Extreme cases should thus be dealt with on the footing that they are so unjustifiable that they could have been only the product of bias or some other violation of the right of *due process*. Once again, Fitzmaurice merits extensive quotation:

if all that a judge does is to make a mistake, i.e. to arrive at a wrong conclusion of law or fact, even though it results in serious injustice, the state is not responsible.

There can be no question of the soundness of the above position. Yet, as every one who has had any practical experience of the matter knows, the rule that a state is not responsible for the *bona fide* errors of its courts can be, and all too frequently is, made use of in order to enable responsibility to be evaded in cases where there is a virtual certainty that bad faith has been present, but no conclusive proof of it . . .

One of the chief difficulties in applying the rule that the *bona fide* errors of courts do not involve responsibility lies in the fact that the question of whether there has been a 'denial of justice' cannot, strictly speaking, be answered merely by having regard to the degree of injustice involved. The only thing which can establish a denial of justice so far as a judgment is concerned is an affirmative answer, duly supported by evidence, to some such question as 'Was the court guilty of bias, fraud, dishonesty, lack of impartiality, or gross incompetence?' If the answer to this question is in the negative, then, strictly speaking, it is immaterial how unjust the judgment may have been. The relevance of the degree of injustice really lies only in its evidential value. *An unjust judgment may and often does afford strong evidence that the court was dishonest, or rather it raises a strong presumption of dishonesty. It may even afford conclusive evidence, if the injustice be sufficiently flagrant, so that the judgment is of a kind which no honest and competent court could possibly have given.*[64]

---

[64] Fitzmaurice at pp. 112–113 (emphasis added).

The most difficult cases in this respect are evidently those where there is strong suspicion, but no proof, of bad faith. Fitzmaurice's solution was as follows:

> In almost all such cases it is probable that the court will have committed some more or less serious error, in the sense of a wrong conclusion of law or of fact. This suggests that the right method is to concentrate on the question whether the court was competent rather than on whether it was honest. The question will then be, was the error of such a character that no competent judge could have made it? If the answer is in the affirmative, it follows that the judge was either dishonest, in which case the state is clearly responsible, or that he was incompetent, in which case the responsibility of the state is also engaged for failing in its duty of providing competent judges.[65]

And we can go further. Pleading for Spain in *Barcelona Traction*, Paul Guggenheim conceded that a presumption of judicial bad faith or *culpa late* could arise, in the case of 'exceptionally outrageous or monstrously grave' *breaches of municipal law*. In such cases, he added, it must be shown that 'one can no longer explain the sentence rendered by any factual consideration or by any valid legal reason'.[66] Three decades earlier, the government of Venezuela, in its memorial in the *Martini* case, had similarly acknowledged that 'not an erroneous judgment, but a gross error, an inexcusable error' could give rise to international responsibility.[67]

This approach may give rise to more controversy and discord than one would wish to see in the international realm where national sensitivities are acute. Pragmatically, it may be wiser to consider that if in such difficult cases the perpetrators of the unfairness are incapable of dissimulating their conduct under the cover of formally irreproachable reasoning, they are equally likely to be guilty of serious procedural missteps and on that account provide better justification for finding denial of justice; to declare that judgments under national law are rationally unsustainable

---

[65] *Ibid.* at pp. 113–114. De Visscher conceived, at 381, that part of a state's international obligation concerns the 'proper recruitment of judges' (*recrutement convenable des magistrats*); and, at 394, that its duty is to 'place at the disposal of foreigners a judicial organisation capable, by the laws that regulate it *as well as by the men who comprise it*, of achieving the effective protection of their rights' (emphasis added).

[66] CR 69/25, 23 May 1969, quoted in Jiménez de Aréchaga, 'International Responsibility of States', at p. 185.

[67] Quoted in de Visscher at p. 406, note 1. The Venezuelan government's comment was, however, irrelevant. The issue was not whether a Venezuelan judgment repudiating an international award was an error, inexcusable or not, of national law, but whether it violated an international undertaking to respect that award.

may expose the international jurisdiction to the criticism that it does not have an adequate intellectual foundation in the relevant national law.

It may seem that this discussion seriously undercuts the conclusions of the previous section (the general rule of non-revision) as well as the title of the present one. What needs to be understood is that even if in extreme cases the substantive quality of a judgment may lead to a finding of denial of justice, the objective of the international adjudicator is *never* to conduct a substantive view. As Fitzmaurice put it in the lengthier of the two quotations above: 'it is immaterial how unjust the judgment may have been'.[68]

The demonstration of this proposition requires that one consider two questions: does a judicial organ of a state which violates international law thereby automatically commit a denial of justice? Absent a violation of international law, may such an organ commit a denial of justice by erroneously applying its national law? The answer to each question is negative.

## Judgments in breach of international law

When a national judiciary renders a decision violative of international law, a tribunal having jurisdiction to apply international law is free, *indeed required*, to substitute its judgment for that of the national court if it disagrees with the way the latter has interpreted or applied international law. Such is the necessary consequence of treating national courts, as one must, as neither more nor less than an instrumentality of the state; and of excluding, as one must, that the state be judge and party in its own case.

It does not follow that the national court's misapplication of international law is a denial of justice. We have already considered this matter in the section of this chapter entitled 'Relationship with specific rights created by international law'. If a court has violated a treaty, the state to which its actions are imputed is internationally responsible in the same way as any other agency of the state. The fact that the culpable agency is charged with the administration of justice does not justify or require a special nomenclature.

So if two countries sign a treaty under which they agree that the citizens of each, when before the other's courts, are entitled to trials in the course of which able-bodied witnesses will not be heard unless they stand on one leg when testifying, a court which neglects that requirement may violate international law by reason of its breach of the treaty, but does not

---

[68] Fitzmaurice at p. 112.

commit a denial of justice under international law. (If a vast and durable majority of states came to require one-legged testimony, the requirement might be absorbed into customary international law, and thus relevant to the assessment of claim of denial of justice, but that is a different matter.)

For a more realistic illustration, imagine that a national of a state which is not a party to the New York Convention on the Recognition and Enforcement of Foreign Arbitral Awards presents an ordinary commercial arbitral award rendered in Edinburgh for enforcement in Indonesia. Under local rules, all foreign awards intended to be enforced in Indonesia must be presented to the Central Jakarta District Court. The matter is heard after due notice, in observance of unobjectionable procedures and without any suggestion of bias. There is, in other words, no procedural denial of justice. Nevertheless, the petition is dismissed because the applicant is not a national of a state signatory to the New York Convention and because he has not presented a certificate from Indonesian consular services in Edinburgh.

Such is in fact the tenor of the Indonesian Supreme Court Regulation no. 1990/1, which provides in Article 5(4) that a petition for the enforcement of a foreign arbitral award must be accompanied by, among other things:

(c) a statement from the Indonesian diplomatic representative in the country where the said foreign arbitral award was issued, declaring that the country of the petitioner is bilaterally bound with Indonesia in an international convention concerning the recognition and enforcement of a foreign arbitral award.[69]

To deny enforcement because of the applicant's nationality is a clear violation of the New York Convention. The only permitted condition of reciprocity permitted under the New York Convention is that the *place of arbitration* (e.g. Edinburgh) be in a country (e.g. the United Kingdom) which is also a party to the Convention. The requirement of a consular certificate is certainly also a violation of the Convention, given that Article V of that instrument provides that such a petition may be refused only if one of a limited set of exceptions apply; those exceptions do not include the absence of such a certificate. (Moreover, Article III forbids 'substantially more onerous conditions ... than are imposed on the recognition and enforcement of domestic arbitral awards'.) One need only consider that there exist a multitude of plausible places of arbitration where there are no Indonesian consular services, not to mention the

---

[69] 'Indonesia', *in* (1991) XVI *International Handbook on Commercial Arbitration* 398, at p. 400.

unlikelihood that a member of any consular staff would readily take it upon himself – in the absence of any directives or standardised procedures – to study the file of the arbitration and then execute an *ad hoc* certificate at the behest of a foreigner who wishes to use it to collect money in Indonesia, and thus very likely against an Indonesian party.

Since the Regulation itself contradicts an international treaty, the responsibility of Indonesia could be invoked immediately by any state which is a party to the Convention, even in the absence of any refusal of enforcement in a particular case, on the basis that every signatory state has an interest in seeing that awards rendered in its territory are reliable pursuant to the terms of the Convention. Indonesia's liability would be founded on the breach of international *lex specialis* (the Convention), not on a denial of justice.

And once the Indonesian courts make a decision to refuse enforcement on grounds which are violative of international law, there is a clear international wrong which has no relation to any inherent defect in the Indonesian court proceedings. Responsibility for such a delict could be invoked either by the disappointed applicant's state or by the applicant directly before any competent international tribunal.

If an international tribunal has been given the authority to apply international law, it has the authority and the duty to apply it in its entirety, including the fundamental concept that the pronouncements of a national judiciary, properly viewed as no different from other instrumentalities of its state, are not binding in international adjudication whenever they purport to assess the international legality of action by the very state of which it is an organ.

Finally, one may consider the hypothesis of a national law which by its terms creates a denial of justice, or which is held by a court to create a denial of justice. (Instances might be decrees to the effect that persons of a particular nationality may no longer have standing in court, or to the effect that previously agreed arbitral tribunals are divested of jurisdiction; or decrees *interpreted by judges* to have such effect.) Might it not be said that these are substantive denials of justice, because they require determinations that the national laws or judgments are wrong? Freeman seemed to think so when he wrote that:

a judgment which is perfectly valid under municipal law may work a denial of justice because the law itself is contrary to international law.[70]

_____
[70] Freeman at p. 310.

A better view is that the validity under national law of such a decree or judgment is irrelevant when reviewed at the international level. The question is whether the national decree or judgment operates a denial of justice *under the criteria of international law*. The denial of justice, once more, is not substantive error, but fundamental unfairness as understood by reference to international norms.

## Judgments in breach of national law

Whenever an international tribunal rejects a decision founded on a national judicial authority's interpretation of its own law, it does so for reasons which are properly understood as based on a determination that the process was defective.

As Commissioner Nielsen put it in an often-quoted passage from his opinion in the *Neer* case: 'strict conformity by authorities of a government with its domestic law is not necessarily conclusive evidence of the observance of legal duties imposed by international law, although it may be important evidence on that point'.[71]

It is not easy for a complainant to overcome the presumption of adequacy and thus to establish international responsibility for denial of procedural justice. The fact that the international tribunal seized of the matter may believe it would have applied national law differently – 'mere error' – is in and of itself of no moment.

Yet some authorities continue to suggest that substantive denial of justice may exceptionally occur with respect to national law. In the first award rendered in the much-discussed *Vivendi* v. *Argentina* case,[72] the arbitral tribunal stated, *obiter*, that the effect of a contractual jurisdiction clause referring to municipal courts was that no claim could arise against the state unless:

the Claimants were treated unfairly in those courts (denial of procedural justice) or if the judgments of those courts were substantively unfair (denial of substantive justice) or otherwise denied rights [under a relevant bilateral treaty].[73]

---

[71] *L. F. H. Neer and Pauline Neer (US v. Mexico)*, 15 October 1926, IV RIAA 60, at p. 64.

[72] *Compañía de Aguas del Aqonquija and Vivendi Universal (formerly Compagnie Générale des Eaux)* v. *Argentina*, award, 21 November 2000, 5 *ICSID Reports* 296; (2001) 40 ILM 426. (Award partially annulled on grounds irrelevant here, 3 July 2002; 6 *ICSID Reports* 340; (2002) 41 ILM 1135.)

[73] *Ibid.* at para. 80.

It is useful to examine a precedent said to support this proposition. In the *De Sabla* case,[74] decided by the US–Panama General Claims Commission in 1932, the claimant's grievance was that her land had been treated as though it were public property, and as such had been granted to other individuals. The Government answered that under Panamanian law applications for land grant were approved unless opposition were made, and that the claimant's failure to make opposition meant that the grants of parcels of her land were lawful. The Commission held to the contrary that the adjudication of the grants by the public administrator was wrongful:

Since the land laws by their terms contemplated the adjudication only of public lands, and since the result of granting adjudications on private property was to deprive the owner of his property without compensation, the burden of persuasion on this issue is clearly on Panama. She has failed to sustain it . . .

The legislative intent clearly was, not that private owners should have to protect their rights by constant oppositions, but that adjudications should be made only on lands shown to be public on the [national land] map, and that the Administrators should reject of their own accord applications for lands appearing as private property on the map.[75]

Freeman categorises this case as an exception to the general rule that misapplication of national law is not a denial of justice.[76] His analysis is unpersuasive. The case does not stand as an exception to the general principle just mentioned; it falls more convincingly either under the category of violation of the substantive international rule against dispossession without compensation, or yet again as a *procedural* denial of justice; as the Commission itself wrote, the Panamanian 'machinery of opposition, as actually administered, did not constitute an adequate remedy to the claimant for the protection of her property'.[77]

From time to time, the literature in the field has referred to three types of exceptions to the general rule described in this chapter under the heading 'No responsibility for misapplication of national law'. In fact the discussion would be clearer if it were recognised that there are, properly speaking, no exceptions to the rule.

The first false exception is that of judgments vitiated by bad faith however perceived: fraud, bias, dishonesty or malice. The reason why this is not a true exception to the rule is that such cases have nothing to

[74] *Marguerite de Joly de Sabla (US v. Panama)*, 29 June 1933, VI RIAA 358.
[75] *Ibid.* at p. 360.　[76] Freeman at pp. 346–347.　[77] *De Sabla*, VI RIAA 358, at p. 363.

do with the degree of deference international law gives to the *substantive* content of judgments applying national law. They involve situations where the defect of the judgment lies in its circumstances and not its content, and are therefore properly to be understood as *procedural* denials of justice.

The second false exception is that of judgments in contravention of international law. Here again, such cases have nothing to do with the degree of deference international law gives to the meaning attributed to national law by the national judiciary. Although they are instances of *substantive* denials of justice, they do not purport to overrule the national judge's determination of his own law; to the contrary, they accept it as such – and then rule on the consequences of any violation of *international* law inherent in that determination.

The third false exception is that of gross incompetence; a judgment so poor that it cannot be accepted as the verdict of a legal system worthy of the name. The point is not that the international tribunal considers that it would have applied the national law differently; that would plainly be insufficient to establish a denial of justice.

The Senate of Hamburg did not provide much illumination when it wrote, in a dictum in *Cotesworth & Powell*, that states are responsible for judgments pronounced or executed in 'flagrant violation of the law' or when they are 'manifestly unjust'. Such expressions invite rather than resolve controversy. Writers like Fitzmaurice and de Visscher provide better elucidation when they suggest that there must be an element of bad faith or culpable negligence. As de Visscher put it, one needs to distinguish:

the simple *mal jugé*, to be equated with judicial error, from grave and manifest injustice stemming from aggravated fault or from malice toward foreigners as a group or toward the nationals of a particular country.[78]

If no judge could reasonably have reached the challenged decision, the inference is that it was not rendered by an independent judicial mind deciding according to its conscience. What is required is that the international tribunal be persuaded that the error was of a kind which no 'competent judge could reasonably have made'.[79] Needless to say, the burden of proof is difficult to sustain.

True, unlike the first two false exceptions, such a remarkable instance would indeed be one where international law declines to defer to the national judgment. But this is not because of an ordinary disagreement. Rather it reflects a grave defect in the legal system, and therefore a failure

---

[78] De Visscher at p. 399.    [79] Fitzmaurice at p. 114.

to abide by the obligation to provide an acceptable mechanism to hear the grievances of foreigners.

## Confirmation of the distinction

The distinction proposed above between injury to foreigners under internal and international law was given similar importance in James Fawcett's study in 1954 in the analogous context of 'The Exhaustion of Local Remedies: Substance v. Procedure?'[80] With respect to violations of internal law, as Fawcett perceived, international responsibility arises only from acts or omissions of the defendant state's authorities *in the course* of the alien's attempts to secure redress, and not as a function of the outcome. The exhaustion of local remedies rule is hence a material necessity before any international responsibility may be established, in the same way as it is a material element of the international delict of denial of justice (see Chapter 5). To the contrary, a violation of international law by national authorities has quite unrelated consequences for exhaustion of remedies, on the one hand, and denial of justice, on the other. In this hypothesis, exhaustion is a *procedural* precondition for diplomatic protection (with a number of consequences, e.g. with respect to issues of prescription, waiver and the date of satisfying nationality requirements); but the violation, whatever it is, will not be a denial of justice at all but a breach of another obligation of international law.

With a remarkable economy of expression, Dugard captured all strands of reflection in the following formulation:

> where the injury is caused by an act constituting a violation of municipal law but not of international law, international responsibility commences only after the exhaustion of local remedies resulting in a denial of justice.[81]

## State responsibility for subdivisions

As a matter of national law, a host of familiar problems surround the constitutional basis upon which the central government may enter into international obligations on behalf of a federated state.

---

[80] (1954) 31 BYIL 452.

[81] International Law Commission (Dugard), Second Report on Diplomatic Protection, UN Doc. A/CN.4/514 (2001) at p. 30, para. 61; see also p. 32, para. 63. *Accord*, G. Fitzmaurice, 'Hersch Lauterpacht – The Scholar as Judge', (1961) 37 BYIL 53; Ian Brownlie, *Principles of Public International Law* (6th edn, Oxford University Press, 2003), at p. 473.

As a matter of contract law, there are also a number of issues peculiar to the relationship that may be created by a foreign investor and the government of a province entitled to act in its name and to answer for its debts.

These weighty subjects are beyond the scope of this book. A federated state which has entered into international obligations cannot escape them by attributing allegedly unlawful acts or omissions to its subdivisions. (The obligations of customary international law do not, of course, require positive acknowledgement, but are a consequence of statehood.) Freeman wrote that international responsibility:

attaches itself to all States no matter what their political structure may be and even though their internal organization be such that, as in federal systems of government, the nation may be unable to fulfill it by actions through agencies under its direct control . . .

Neither the practical nor legal domestic difficulties inherent in the particular political system chosen by the territorial State may be pleaded in bar of the claims advanced by other States.[82]

With respect to the proposition that a federal state is responsible for its component units, the International Law Commission's commentary to Article 4 ('Conduct of organs of a State') of its Articles on Responsibility of States for Internationally Wrongful Acts cites eleven cases in a 'consistent series of decisions to this effect'.[83] It observes that it is 'equally irrelevant whether the internal law of the State in question gives the federal parliament power to compel the component unit to abide by the State's international obligations',[84] quoting the *Pellat* case to the effect that responsibility 'cannot be denied, not even in cases where the federal Constitution denies the central Government the right of control over the separate states or the right to require them to comply, in their conduct, with the rules of international law'.[85]

As the International Court of Justice put it succinctly in 1999: 'the Governor of Arizona is under the obligation to act in conformity with the international undertakings of the United States'.[86] (If it were argued that the Governor did not have a constitutional duty to respect international

[82] Freeman at pp. 369–370.
[83] James Crawford, *The International Law Commission's Articles on State Responsibility: Introduction, Text and Commentaries* (Cambridge University Press, 2002), at p. 97.
[84] *Ibid.*
[85] *Estate of Hyacinthe Pellat (France v. Mexico)*, 7 June 1929, V RIAA 534, at p. 536.
[86] *LaGrand (Germany v. US) Provisional Measures*, 1999 *ICJ Reports* 9, at p. 16, para. 28.

law as a matter of national law, this simply means that international adjudicators will hold the federal state responsible for the breach – a variation of the constant theme that international law must trump national law in the same way that national law trumps the individual volition of citizens.[87])

This proposition is illustrated by the *Loewen* case, in which the US Government's liability for the miscarriage of justice perpetrated by the courts of Mississippi was acknowledged in principle. (As we shall see in Chapter 5, the claim failed for other reasons.) The pleadings of the parties in that case provided a wealth of references to authority; they are readily available[88] and will not be repeated here.

What is perhaps more surprising is that the subject had considerable antecedents in the United States. The issue was raised by a US President (Harrison) in his annual State of the Union address in 1891, and his precise words were repeated with approval by one of his successors (McKinley) in the latter's State of the Union address in 1900. This extraordinary attention of the part of successive heads of state of one of the best-known federated nations to such a technical issue was the product of a crisis in US relations with Italy as a consequence of five instances of multiple lynchings of Italian immigrants by American mobs. In all instances – in Louisiana, Colorado and Mississippi – the victims were in the custody of local police or penitentiary officers. On the first occasion (involving the lynching of eleven Italians in New Orleans, apparently as a result of allegations that they had been involved in murderous 'machinations of a secret society called the Mafia'), President Harrison said this:

Some suggestions growing out of this unhappy incident are worthy the attention of Congress. It would, I believe be entirely competent for Congress to make offenses against the treaty rights of foreigners domiciled in the United States cognisable in the Federal courts. This has not, however, been done, and the Federal officers and courts have no power in such cases to intervene either for the protection of a foreign citizen or for the punishment of his slayers. It seems to me to follow, in this state of the law, that the officers of the State charged with police and judicial powers in such cases must, in the consideration of international questions growing out of such incidents, be regarded in such sense as Federal agents as to make this Government answerable for their acts.[89]

---

[87] See Note 51 of Chapter 2 above.
[88] On a number of Internet websites rapidly identifiable by any leading search engine.
[89] Moore, *Digest*, vol. VI, at p. 840, para. 1026.

Further incidents of lynchings of Italian nationals took place under the presidency of Grover Cleveland, prompting the latter to ask Congress – 'without discussing the question of liability of the United States' – to appropriate monies for 'reasonable pecuniary provision' for the victims or their families.

In 1900, after five prisoners of Italian origin were taken from jail and hanged by a mob in Tallulah, Louisiana, McKinley noted that there still was no legislation of the type proposed by Harrison and commended its reconsideration by Congress. He reiterated *in extenso* the passage quoted above from Harrison's State of the Union address of 1891.[90]

In sum, the internal laws of a state cannot insulate its international liability. Nor does it appear ever to have been argued that an alien who knows about the internal regime waives any objection when he enters the country. Whatever rights a state may have to bar the alien's entry, once he is admitted the minimum standards of international law apply.

## Attempts at codification

The word 'codification' appears in the title of a collection of texts published in 1974 by three eminent scholars who had been particularly involved in the work of the International Law Commission on State Responsibility (Professor García-Amador) and in the elaboration, under the aegis of the Harvard Law School, of the 1961 Draft Convention on the International Responsibility of States for Injuries to Aliens (Professors Sohn and Baxter).[91] Of course their use of the word should not disguise the fact that these efforts were merely aspirational; they were *attempts* at codification.[92]

---

[90] *Ibid.* at pp. 845–848.

[91] F. V. García-Amador, Louis B. Sohn and R. R. Baxter, *Recent Codification of the Law of State Responsibility for Injuries to Aliens* (Dobbs Ferry, NY: Oceana, 1974).

[92] The governments which generated the Charter of the United Nations were firmly opposed to conferring on the United Nations legislative power to enact binding rules of international law. They also rejected proposals to give the General Assembly the power to impose conventions on states by vote. There was, however, strong support for conferring on the General Assembly the more limited powers of study and recommendation for the purpose of 'encouraging the progressive development of international law and its codification' (UN Charter, Article 13(1)(a)). When the International Law Commission was established in 1947, its Statute provided that the 'Commission shall have for its object the promotion of the progressive development of international law and its codification'. Article 15 makes a distinction 'for convenience' between *progressive development* as 'the preparation of draft conventions on subjects which

Graver reservations must be made with respect to earlier efforts. In his Report to the ILC, García-Amador decried that international case law on denial of justice, 'considered as a whole, do[es] not yield any general and objective criteria applicable to situations which occur in reality'. He immediately went on to refer to previous proposed codifications, which he contended offered 'surer guidance'; although not always agreeing 'on the definition of the acts and omissions which give rise to responsibility, they do in general agree remarkably on fundamental points'.[93]

He was demonstrably wrong. There may have been some justice in his critique of the body of precedents, but that will always be so with respect to the application of fundamental open-textured principles such as 'equitable delimitation', 'proportional response', or, with regard to our subject, 'fair trial'. This study seeks to prove that the international jurisprudence is not chaotic. But García-Amador was flatly in error about what he said he perceived as remarkable agreement on fundamental points in early texts proposing formulation of an international rule of denial of justice. This is manifest in his own citations.

He first referred to the 1927 Guerrero Report, which had been so thoroughly discredited by Freeman[94] (whose own seminal work was curiously not cited by García-Amador). That report, which stands as a high-water mark of Latin American attempts to minimise the ambit of the international delict, was irreducibly focused on affirming what type of conduct should *not* be deemed a denial of justice, rather than on the contrary. It proposed, for example:

That a State has fulfilled its international duty as soon as the judicial authorities have given their decision, even if those authorities merely state that the petition, suit or appeal lodged by the foreigner is not admissible.

That proposition naturally left only the narrowest scope for responsibility:

Denial of justice consists in refusing to allow foreigners easy access to the courts to defend those rights which the national law accords them. A refusal of the competent judge to exercise jurisdiction also constitutes a denial of justice.[95]

---

have not yet been regulated by international law or in regard to which the law has not yet been sufficiently developed in the practice of States' and *codification* as 'the more precise formulation and systematization of rules of international law in fields where there already has been extensive State practice, precedent and doctrine'.

[93] García-Amador, Sohn and Baxter, *Recent Codification*, at p. 24, reprinting paras. 133 ss of the author's Second Report to the ILC, UN Doc. A/CN.4/106 (1957).

[94] See the quotations in the section on 'The impulse to limit the scope of denial of justice' in Chapter 2.

[95] League of Nations Document C.196.M70.1927.V, at p. 104.

There is a blindingly obvious omission from this proposal: any qualitative requirement of the processes of national courts.

In this respect the Guerrero Report was wholly at odds with other texts quoted by García-Amador. For example, the Institute of International Law had proposed, in Article V(3) of its draft on the International Responsibility of States for Injuries on their Territory to the Person or Property of Foreigners adopted in Lausanne the same year, findings of liability whenever 'the tribunals do not offer the guarantees which are indispensable to the proper administration of justice'.[96]

Proposition 5(4) of the so-called 'Bases of Discussion' drafted by the Preparatory Committee of the Hague Conference in 1930 suggested that an unappealable judgment would constitute a denial of justice if it 'is irreconcilable with the treaty obligations or the international duties of the State'.[97] As discussed at length in this chapter, such a proposition is unhelpful; there is no purpose in duplicating an existing duty by incorporating its breach in the concept of denial of justice.

The Montevideo Conference of American States in 1933, following closely on Guerrero's conception, specified that the scope of denial of justice 'shall always be interpreted restrictively, that is, in favor of the sovereignty of the State in which the difference may have risen'.[98] This promotion of a special rule of evidence for denial of justice happily seems to have found no echo in the jurisprudence, which contents itself with the general principles that a claimant must prove his case and that it is not lightly to be concluded that the organs of a state consciously violate international law.

Other inter-American texts made it clear that wrongfulness could be determined only in accordance with municipal law,[99] thereby amputating the fundamental basis of an international obligation.

The 1929 Harvard-sponsored draft Convention on the Law of Responsibility of States for Damages Done in Their Territory to the Person or Property of Foreigners represented a significant advance. Its

---

[96] (1928) 22 AJIL 330 (Special supplement).    [97] Freeman at p. 634.

[98] The International Conferences of American States, First Supplement, 1933–1940 (Washington, DC: Carnegie Endowment for International Peace, 1940), at p. 92; Freeman at p. 722.

[99] García-Amador, Sohn and Baxter, *Recent Codification*, at p. 25; see, e.g., the Santiago Conference of American States in 1923; Freeman at p. 717; defining, as denial of justice, cases where 'the fundamental rules of the procedure *in force in the country* have been violated' (emphasis added).

Article 9 made a commendable effort at specificity (which moved it all the further away from Guerrero's minimalism):

A state is responsible if an injury to an alien results from a denial of justice. Denial of justice exists when there is a denial, unwarranted delay or obstruction of access to courts, gross deficiency in the administration of judicial or remedial process, failure to provide those guarantees which are generally considered indispensable in the proper administration of justice, or a manifestly unjust judgment. An error of a national court which does not produce manifest injustice is not a denial of justice.[100]

But the most extreme antipode to the Guerrero Report is to be found in the 1961 Draft Convention on the International Responsibility of States for Injuries to Aliens,[101] which defines denial of justice under three articles. The first two – captioned 'Denial of Access to a Tribunal or an Administrative Authority' and 'Denial of a Fair Hearing' – were innovative only in their attempt at exhaustiveness. The title to Article 8 would clearly lift some eyebrows: 'Adverse Decisions and Judgments'. Its content would do more than that; subparagraph (b) makes clear that the authors of the draft were proposing that a judgment should be held internationally wrongful 'if it unreasonably departs from the principles of justice recognized by the principal legal systems of the world'.[102] In view of what the present chapter of this book has sought to establish by way of positive international law, it should not be surprising that the award in *Amco II*, by an ICSID tribunal presided by Rosalyn Higgins, flatly referred to this Draft Convention generally as being 'of doubtful weight as persuasive authority of international law'.[103]

García-Amador's own reports for the ILC are extensive and interesting. For present purposes, it is sufficient to note that by 1961 – the year before he left the ILC – the draft which appeared as an addendum to his sixth report treated our subject in two ways: implicitly, among the definitions in Article 1 of 'rights of aliens', and explicitly, under Article 3 entitled 'Acts and omissions involving denial of justice'.[104] Article 1 provided:

---

[100] Harvard Law School, *Research in International Law, II, Responsibility of States* (Cambridge, MA, 1929) at p. 134; (1929) 23 AJIL 133, at p. 173 (Special supplement).

[101] (1961) 55 AJIL 548. This text was to a considerable degree based on the 1929 Harvard draft, above.

[102] *Ibid.* at p. 551.   [103] *Amco II* at para. 123.

[104] International Law Commission (García-Amador), Sixth Report on State Responsibility, Addendum, UN Doc. A/CN.4/134/Add. 1 (1961).

## The modern definition of denial of justice

1. For the purpose of the application of the provisions of this draft, aliens enjoy the same rights and the same legal guarantees as nationals, but these rights and guarantees shall in no case be less than the 'human rights and fundamental freedoms' recognized and defined in contemporary international instruments.

2. The 'human rights and fundamental freedoms' referred to in the foregoing paragraph are those enumerated below:

    . . .

    (d) The right to a public hearing, with proper safeguards, by the competent organs of the State, in the substantiation of any criminal charge or in the determination of rights and obligations under civil law;

    (e) In criminal matters, the right of the accused to be presumed innocent until proved guilty; the right to be informed of the charge made against him in a language which he understands; the right to present his defence personally or to be defended by a counsel of his choice; the right not to be convicted of any punishable offence on account of any act or omission which did not constitute an offence, under national or international law, at the time when it was committed; the right to be tried without delay or to be released.

Article 3 read thus:

1. The State is responsible for the injuries caused to an alien by acts or omissions which involve a denial of justice.

2. For the purposes of the foregoing paragraph, a 'denial of justice' shall be deemed to occur if the courts deprive the alien of any one of the rights or safeguards specified in article 1, paragraph 2(c), (d) and (e), of this draft.

3. For the same purposes, a 'denial of justice' shall also be deemed to occur if a manifestly unjust decision is rendered with the evident intention of causing injury to the alien. However, judicial error, whatever the result of the decision, does not give rise to international responsibility on the part of the State.

4. Likewise, the alien shall be deemed to have suffered a denial of justice if a decision by a municipal or international court in his favour is not carried out, provided that the failure to carry out such decision is due to a clear intention to cause him injury.

This bifurcation of the subject illustrates a development which had taken a concrete and important form in 1950 when the European Convention of Human Rights was promulgated. Like Article 1 of the just-quoted draft, that Convention does not use the expression 'denial of justice', but gives its principal substantive elements the force of positive international treaty-based law. (As noted in Chapter 1, the general heading *denial of justice* may lose currency in *lex specialis*, but its substance and its influence will remain.)

Still, viewed on the whole, the old attempts at codification are of limited value. Worse, when taken in isolation they can lead to great error. Fortunately, drafts remain drafts, and we can today benefit from the cross-fertilisation of the customary international law of denial of justice and the important jurisprudence that has arisen pursuant to the positive international legislation to be found in modern treaties, notably in the realm of human rights. They will enrich Chapters 6 and 7 of this study.

## Summary

No enumerative approach to defining denial of justice has succeeded in the past, and there are no prospects that one will emerge in the future. Rather, as with the norms of due process that have developed with respect to the protection of human rights, international adjudicators will perforce have to confront the task of giving concrete content to the notion of 'fundamental fairness in the administration of justice'.

Denial of justice is always procedural. There may be extreme cases where the proof of the failed process is that the substance of a decision is so egregiously wrong that no honest or competent court could possibly have given it. Such cases would sanction the state's failure to provide a decent system of justice. They do not constitute an international appellate review of national law.

A national court's breach of other rules of international law, or of treaties, is not a denial of justice, but a direct violation of the relevant obligation imputable to the state like any acts or omissions by its agents.

These are the conclusions that emerge from this chapter. At the heart of the matter lies an irreducible difficulty: the notion of fundamental procedural fairness. Defenders of the conduct of national authorities will in all difficult cases be able to insist with vehemence that there has been no *proof* that they have failed to meet minimum standards. These are issues of degree and judgment, and ultimately come down, as we shall see in Chapter 9, to acceptance or rejection of international adjudication.

To observe this difficulty is not, however, to concede that there is something extraordinary about denial of justice that requires apology for the elasticity of the concept. Law (international and national alike) knows many such notions. It is not possible to 'prove' in an absolute sense that a party has acted in *reasonable* reliance on the representations of another, or that it has taken *reasonable* or *proportional* steps to mitigate damages or to protect itself. Any law student could multiply the examples. It is possible only to prove such propositions *to the satisfaction of a trier of fact*. So once again the issue is whether one accepts to yield sufficient national sovereignty to respect the judgment of international jurisdictions.

To say that a concept is inherently difficult is not to say that it is *confusing*. So why did Freeman and the other leading writers of his day – de Visscher, Fitzmaurice, Eagleton – decry their subject as one of such confusion? If they were right, should one not admit that the subject remains confused?

They were right, but their conclusion no longer holds. The confusion of their time was artificial. It was born of the impulse to expand the notion of denial of justice to encompass every form of international wrong, due to the fact that demands for international reparation were once invariably articulated as responses to denials of justice. *Any wrong would thus be spoken of as a denial of justice because it was not remedied by national justice.* Moreover, unnecessary fictions were created to the effect that denial of justice related only to the mishandling of claims rather than defences, and that a denial of justice was necessarily a second wrong in the failure to correct an initial wrong. The notion of 'manifest injustice' emerged to cover the cases of mistreated defendants, or of maladministration of justice independent of a separate initial wrong. These were indeed confusing concepts, and they were compounded by the fact that the delict was invariably prosecuted by the means of diplomatic protection, which meant that the victim of a wrong had to demonstrate the failure of local remedies; denial of justice thus slipped into a usage in which it was confused with the precondition for raising any number of delicts.

These confusions have dissipated. We know that there are many inter-national wrongs apart from denial of justice. *El Triunfo* today would be a case of contract breach, or of expropriation, and the claim would stand or fall without a word of denial of justice. Direct access to international jurisdictions without the diplomatic espousal of claims has made it unnecessary to resort to fictions to demonstrate exhaustion of local remedies. The alleged wrong is not a denial of justice. There is no need to allege that national courts prevented a remedy by the means of a denial of justice; it is sufficient to invoke their simple refusal to grant the remedy. (No matter how perfectly a national court system administers a claim of expropriation, its decision is subject to plenary international review to the extent that the matter includes the breach of an international duty.) If the alleged wrong is a denial of justice, as we shall now see in Chapter 5, exhaustion is required as a matter of substance, and this is true even if it has been waived or dispensed with as a matter of procedure.

# 5

# Exhaustion of local remedies and denial of justice

## The case for exhaustion

In *Loewen*, where the documentation put before the arbitral tribunal was particularly exhaustive, the final award noted that:

No instance has been drawn to our attention in which an international tribunal has held a State responsible for a breach of international law constituted by a lower court decision when there was available an effective and adequate appeal within the State's legal system.[1]

The absence of such instances is unsurprising. International law attaches state responsibility for judicial action only if it is shown that there was no reasonably available national mechanism to correct the challenged action. In the case of denial of justice, finality is thus a substantive element of the international delict. States are held to an obligation to provide a fair and efficient *system* of justice, not to an undertaking that there will never be an instance of judicial misconduct. Writing as rapporteur to the International Law Commission, James Crawford put it this way:

an aberrant decision by an official lower in the hierarchy, which is capable of being reconsidered, does not of itself amount to an unlawful act.[2]

---

[1] *Loewen*, 26 June 2003, at para. 154. The proposition articulated in the quoted paragraph should be understood as limited by the context of the claim of denial of justice. As a general statement of international responsibility, it is likely too wide.

[2] International Law Commission (Crawford), Second Report on State Responsibility, UN Doc. A/CN.4/498 (1999) at para. 75. Commenting on the ILC Draft Articles in 1998, the UK expressed itself as follows: 'Corruption in an inferior court would not

The correctness of this proposition is not open to doubt. Freeman traced it back to the medieval regime of reprisals, which were considered lawful when there was, as da Legnano wrote in 1360,[3] 'a failure of remedy (*propter defectum remedii*) arising from the neglect of those who govern'. It followed that the injured alien could look to external force (including his own, with the permission of his prince) only if he was unable to obtain reparation from the local sovereign. By the twentieth century, Freeman wrote, this had been transformed into 'the rule that local remedies must first be exhausted'.[4] He cited numerous precedents[5] and made the following sensible observation:

Ample protection against arbitrary violations of the local law will normally be afforded within the State itself by the conventional means of appeal to a superior court. Ruling improperly on evidence, erroneously charging a jury, exceeding the decorous limits of judicial restraint with prejudicial effects for one of the parties (such as openly insulting the claimant's attorney before the jury), emotionally addressing the jurymen with the aim of kindling their hostility, and the like will usually find rectification in the wisdom of the reviewing bench.[6]

Against this background, Freeman gave the following reasons for the perpetuation of the rule[7]:

- the outcome of national appeals may make international action unnecessary;
- facts that emerge in the course of such appeals may deter international action on behalf of the aliens;
- 'the presumption of uniformity between national institutions and the requirements of international law' is overcome only 'by a denial of justice against which there is no effective appeal';
- inter-state friction is lessened;

violate [the duty to provide a fair and efficient system of justice] if redress were speedily available in a higher court', International Law Commission, Draft Articles on State Responsibility, Comments and Observations Received from Governments, UN Doc. A/CN.4/488 (1998) at p. 69. See also the *Green, Bum, The Ada, Smith* and *Blumhardt* cases rendered by Umpire Thornton in *US* v. *Mexico* cases, Moore *Arbitrations* at p. 3139 and following, as well as *The Mechanic* (*Corwin* v. *Venezuela*), *ibid.* at p. 3210. The *Jennings, Laughland & Co.* award (*US* v. *Mexico*), *ibid.* 3135, at p. 3136 declared: 'The Umpire does not conceive that any government can thus be made responsible for the misconduct of an inferior judicial officer when no attempt has been made to obtain justice from a higher court.'

[3] *Tractatus de Bello, de Repraesalus et de Duello*, ch. CXXIII, quoted in Freeman at p. 55.
[4] Freeman at p. 56.  [5] *Ibid.* at p. 403 *et seq.*  [6] *Ibid.* at pp. 291–292 (notes omitted).
[7] *Ibid.* at pp. 416–417.

- 'the gravity and exceptional character of international responsibility' is respected by limiting claims to those 'really worthy of consideration'.

Moreover, as Nsongurua Udombana, a Nigerian scholar, has more recently pointed out:

local remedies are normally quicker, cheaper, and more effective than international ones. They can be more effective in the sense that *an appellate court can reverse the decision of a lower court, whereas the decision of an international organ does not have that effect,* although it will engage the international responsibility of the state concerned.[8]

All of these reasons, however, militate in favour of the exhaustion rule with respect to *all* claims of state responsibility, not only in connection with claims of denial of justice. Indeed, the exhaustion requirement has long been established as a general principle of international law.[9] As such, it is applicable to claims presented by diplomatic protection under a treaty even if it is not expressly mentioned therein.[10]

### *Loewen* and the problem of waiver

A problem then arises by reason of the fact that waivers of the exhaustion requirement have been made in many treaties. International arbitrations

---

[8] Nsongurua Udombana, 'So Far, So Fair: The Local Remedies Rule in the Jurisprudence of the African Commission on Human and Peoples' Rights', (2003) 97 AJIL 1, at p. 9 (emphasis added). W. Michael Reisman was able to encompass all of these considerations in a single sentence: 'The domestic remedy rule is founded on principles of economy, localization of delict and remedy, and good faith', *in Nullity and Revision: The Review and Enforcement of International Judgments and Awards* (New Haven, CT: Yale University Press, 1971), at p. 364.

[9] *Panevezys–Saldutiskis Railway (Estonia* v. *Lithuania),* (1939) PCIJ, Series A/B, No. 76, 3; see generally the Separate Opinion of Judge Sir Hersch Lauterpacht in *Certain Norwegian Loans (France* v. *Norway),* 1957 ICJ Reports 9, at pp. 34–66, A. A. Cançado Trindade, *The Application of the Rule of Exhaustion of Local Remedies in International Law: Its Rationale in the International Protection of Individual Rights* (Cambridge University Press, 1983). (The *application* of the principle to deny admissibility in *Panevezys–Saldutiskis Railway* is, however, open to considerable doubt; Judge Erich's analysis in his dissent, at pp. 52–53, seems a far more realistic assessment, consistent with the approach of international tribunals before and since, from *Robert E. Brown to ELSI; accord.,* Reisman, *Nullity,* at p. 369.)

[10] 'If there is a positive utility to the exhaustion rule – and it is submitted that there is – an argument for automatic waiver other than through an express compromise is not persuasive', Reisman, *Nullity,* at p. 365, n. 18. This doctrinal view was given jurisprudential confirmation in *Elettronica Sicula SpA (ELSI) (US* v. *Italy),* 1989 *ICJ Reports* 15, at para. 50: 'the Chamber finds itself unable to accept that an important principle of customary international law should be held to have been tacitly dispensed with, in the absence of any words making clear an intention to do so'.

governed by the ICSID Convention are a salient example. In ICSID arbitrations, the exhaustion rule does not apply unless the respondent state made an express 'condition of its consent' to that effect when adhering to the Convention. Hundreds of bilateral investment treaties have also opened the door to arbitration without the exhaustion requirement.

Is the consequence of such waivers that the requirement does not apply to claims of denial of justice? If not, why should such claims be different from any other claims of breaches of international law?

The *Loewen* tribunal found itself struggling with this issue. As we shall see in the section on 'Fundamental breaches of due process' in Chapter 7, the arbitrators concluded that 'by any standard of measurement' the trial of which the claimant complained 'was a disgrace'.[11] That conclusion was not enough to give rise to international responsibility; it was necessary to determine whether the grievance nevertheless failed for want of adequate pursuit of appeal. The arbitrators found that Loewen could not succeed for want of a demonstration that 'no reasonably available and adequate remedy under United States municipal law' was open to it. Thus the claim was bound to fail for failure to pursue local remedies; indeed the award reads as though the burden was on the complainant to *disprove* the existence of reasonably available remedies.[12]

*Loewen* arose under NAFTA, Article 1121(1)(b) of which requires any claimant who wishes to bring international arbitration to waive its 'right to initiate or continue before any administrative tribunal or court ... any proceedings' relating to the grievance. Loewen argued that this provision implicitly eliminated the exhaustion requirement. The US government, according to the tribunal, 'appears to acknowledge ... that the Article relaxes the local remedies rule to a partial but limited extent, without defining or otherwise indicating what that extent is or may be'.[13]

So the arbitrators needed to distinguish claims of denial of justice from other claims brought before international tribunals. They therefore insisted that the former requires respect for a 'finality' rule which is *substantive* in character, whereas other claims are subject to a merely *procedural* rule of exhaustion which governs their admissibility. Indeed, the award studiously avoids using the word 'exhaustion' with respect to

---

[11] *Loewen*, 26 June 2003, at para. 119.

[12] *Ibid.* at para. 2. This finding – like most of the award – was *obiter*; the case was dismissed by reference to a threshold issue of standing: failure to satisfy a 'diversity of nationality' requirement under the North American Free Trade Agreement.

[13] *Ibid.* at paras. 145–146.

claims of denial of justice, as though paraphrases, such as 'challenged through the judicial process'[14] or that 'the judicial process be continued to the highest level',[15] might suffice to create a special category. Thus it seems – for the award is not explicit on this score – that the waiver of the general exhaustion rule should not be considered to achieve waiver of the special finality requirement that applies with respect to claims of denial of justice.

This may have been a convenient way to reach the desired outcome. The reasons summarised by Freeman remain valid today, as does the point that local appellate bodies are in a position to reverse illegitimate decisions. They all militate in favour of the exhaustion of national remedies before a claim of denial of justice may be internationalised. But does not each one of them equally militate in favour of exhaustion with respect to international responsibility for *all* wrongs imputable to a state? And who is to say that sovereign states do not have the right to waive the exhaustion requirement in whatever context they choose? There must be some defensible foundation for distinguishing claims of denial of justice; it is no answer to invent labels like *substantive* or *finality* and to declare arbitrarily that they define a higher threshold of admissibility.

Judge Jiménez de Aréchaga may have been searching for just such a distinction when he wrote that it is:

an essential condition of a State being held responsible for a judicial decision *in breach of municipal law* that the decision must be a decision of a court of last resort, all remedies having been exhausted.[16]

This makes sense. If municipal legislation violates *international* law, there is no need to raise a claim of denial of justice; the legislature's wrongful act is imputable to the state as a specific breach of the relevant duty under international law. If it is not in itself violative of international law, it may nevertheless be *interpreted* or *applied* by a court in a manner that contravenes international law. But such a misinterpretation or misapplication of the national law can hardly be considered to be an expression of the minimally adequate legal system which international law requires states to maintain until it is confirmed in the manner which is part and parcel of the system – i.e. including ordinary and reasonably available forms of

---

[14] *Ibid.* at para. 159.  [15] *Ibid.* at para. 161.
[16] E. Jiménez de Aréchaga, 'International Law in the Past Third of a Century' (1978) 159 *Recueil des cours*, vol. I, p. 278, at p. 282 (emphasis added).

appeal.[17] Therefore there is no transgression unless there has been at least an attempt to take the matter to the highest level.

So far so good, but it is well short of a complete answer. Many if not most claims of denial of justice – including the one raised in *Loewen* – allege that the initial trial immediately violated *international law* because it was conducted, as Loewen's was found to have been, in a manner falling short of international standards. The complainant would therefore contend that it is unnecessary to show, in Jiménez de Aréchaga's phrase, 'a breach of municipal law'. Why should waiver of the exhaustion of remedies not open the door to an immediate international claim?

When drafting its final award, the *Loewen* tribunal had to confront the fact that its earlier jurisdictional decision had contained the following passage:

the rule of judicial finality is *no different from* the local remedies rule. Its purpose is to ensure that the State where the violation occurred should have an opportunity to redress it by its own means, within the framework of its own domestic legal system.[18]

Now faced with the problem that the waiver of one thing should logically imply the waiver of whatever is 'no different from' it, the arbitrators had to backtrack. 'This statement requires qualification', they wrote, explaining that the finality rule 'means that this requirement and the local remedies rule, though they may be similar in content, serve two different purposes'.[19]

This is rather perplexing. How can the assertion that a rule exists in itself 'mean' that it serves a different purpose from another rule? Absent any elucidation in the award, one would need mystical powers to divine the 'different purposes' invoked by the arbitrators. After all, in cases where the exhaustion requirement has been waived, ICSID arbitrators

---

[17] '[W]here the action complained of is a breach of the local law but not initially of international law, the international responsibility of the State is not engaged by the action complained of: it can only arise out of a *subsequent* act of the State constituting a denial of justice to the injured party seeking a remedy for the original action of which he complains', J. E. S. Fawcett, 'The Exhaustion of Local Remedies: Substance or Procedure?' (1954) 31 BYIL 452, at p. 456.' Here the local remedies rule operates as a substantive bar to an international claim as no claim arises until a denial of justice can be shown.' International Law Commission (Dugard), Second Report on Diplomatic Protection, UN Doc. A/CN.4/514 (2001) at p. 31, para. 62.

[18] *Loewen*, 5 January 2001, at para. 71 (emphasis added).

[19] *Loewen*, 26 June 2003, at para. 159.

have accepted as admissible a claim of expropriation by way of the armed take-over of a hotel by 'up to perhaps two dozen' uniformed men acting at the behest of an Indonesian army pension fund even though there had been no attempt to achieve redress through the Indonesian courts – indeed in the absence of any formal decree of expropriation.[20] Similarly, a claim for failure to ensure 'full protection and security' on the occasion of an anti-guerrilla raid by counter-insurgency forces who destroyed a shrimp farm was held admissible without giving the state the opportunity to offer redress by local remedies.[21] Yet again, another investor successfully pursued an expropriation claim before ICSID in the absence of any decree to that effect, on the basis of a finding of fact that the state acted as though there had been an expropriation, notably through an administrative memorandum which spoke of the relevant enterprise as being under state control, even though there had been no judicial challenge.[22] There is no mystery: these claimants did not have to give local courts an opportunity to consider their grievances before seizing international tribunals because there had been a waiver of exhaustion of such remedies. So why should the result not be the same when a trial court has disgraced itself?

Nor is it any answer to observe, as the *Loewen* tribunal did with a bow to the International Court of Justice's judgment in *ELSI*,[23] that an important principle of international law should not readily be deemed to have been 'tacitly dispensed with'.[24] The exhaustion rule is indubitably an 'important principle', yet it is unambiguously and routinely waived in investment treaties, as well as in the investment chapter of the North American Free Trade Agreement. The difficulty remains: is there something which causes the exhaustion requirement to be more inalienable with respect to denial of justice than with respect to other claims?

It is difficult to resist the impression that the arbitrators regretted that their previous jurisdictional decision (decided, it should be noted, when one of the members of the tribunal was a different arbitrator) had asserted that the rule of finality 'is no different from the local remedies rule', since that assertion does not sit comfortably with the fact that they ultimately determined to deal with the matter not as an issue of admissibility, but as

---

[20] *Amco Asia Corp. et al.* v. *Indonesia*, award, 20 November 1984, 1 *ICSID Reports* 413 (Foighel, Rubin, Goldman (presiding)); *Amco II.*

[21] *Asian Agricultural Products Ltd* v. *Sri Lanka*, award, 27 June 1990, 4 *ICSID Reports* 245 (Goldman, Asante, El-Kosheri (presiding)).

[22] *Benvenuti and Bonfant srl* v. *Congo*, 8 August 1980, 1 *ICSID Reports* 330 (Bystricky, Razafindralambo, Troller (presiding)).

[23] *US* v. *Italy* 1989 *ICJ Reports* 15.   [24] *Loewen*, 26 June 2003, at para. 160.

one of the merits. The local remedies rule is, of course, traditionally considered as a matter of admissibility.[25]

The *Loewen* tribunal's final attempt to explain its conclusion was thus to wax teleological. If the exhaustion requirement were held waived:

it would encourage resort to NAFTA tribunals rather than resort to the appellate courts and review processes of the host State, an outcome which would seem surprising, having regard to the sophisticated legal systems of the NAFTA Parties. Such an outcome would have the effect of making a State potentially liable for NAFTA violations when domestic appeal or review, if pursued, might have avoided any liability on the part of the State. Further, it is unlikely that the Parties to NAFTA would have wished to encourage recourse to NAFTA arbitration at the expense of domestic appeal or review when, in the general run of cases, domestic appeal or review would offer more wide-ranging review as they are not confined to breaches of international law.[26]

But this will be recognised as nothing more than a restatement of the reasons summarised by Freeman, and an incomplete one at that. Once again, the explanation does not point to a distinguishing feature to justify that other claims not be subject to the same threshold.

Ultimately, we are left with this somewhat anticlimactic pronouncement (as though the arbitrators felt that the fact of their having tried so valiantly to come up with a justification entitled them to credit for having achieved it):

One thing is, however, reasonably clear about Article 1121 and that is that it says nothing expressly about the requirement that, in the context of a judicial violation of international law, the judicial process be continued to the highest level.[27]

One can only wonder why at this point the arbitrators found the matter only 'reasonably' clear; it is as clear as day that Article 1121 breathes not a word of the specific case of responsibility for judicial acts. They could have said that it was *perfectly* clear; the response would still be: 'so what?'

## Exhaustion as a substantive requirement of denial of justice

Yet the *Loewen* tribunal was surely right. Freeman's list of reasons *are* intuitively more compelling with respect to claims of denial of justice than

---

[25] Indeed Article 44 of the ILC's Articles on State Responsibility, which articulates the local remedies rule, is entitled 'Admissibility of claims': ILC Draft Articles on Responsibility of States for internationally wrongful acts, UN Doc. A/56/10 (2001).
[26] *Loewen*, 26 June 2003, at para. 162.    [27] *Ibid.* at para. 161.

in connection with other allegations of international wrongs. We must, it seems, try again to find a rationale for the arbitrators' conclusion. To return to first principles, the question is this: even when exhaustion is otherwise not required, is the international delict of denial of justice, unlike other violations of international law, consummated only after the ordinary and reasonably accessible appeals process has run its course?

To repeat: states may, and do, enter into treaties that provide for direct access by foreigners to international tribunals without first having to exhaust local remedies. Such waivers give foreigners the assurance that internationally wrongful conduct will not be swept under the rug indefinitely.

In the particular case of denial of justice, however, claims will not succeed unless the victim has indeed exhausted municipal remedies, or unless there is an explicit waiver of a type yet to be invented. (An *ad hoc compromis* might do.) This is neither a paradox nor an aberration, for it is in the very nature of the delict that a state is judged by the final product – or at least a *sufficiently* final product – of its administration of justice. A denial of justice is not consummated by the decision of a court of first instance. Having sought to rely on national justice, the foreigner cannot complain that its operations have been delictual until he has given it scope to operate, including by the agency of its ordinary corrective functions.

Perhaps the strongest argument for this special treatment of claims of denial of justice is that it avoids interference with the fundamental principle that states should to the greatest extent possible be free to organise their national legal systems as they see fit. Conscious of the public demand for greater speed, they may wish to provide for a great number of local courts even if they do not have the resources to staff them with the highest-quality jurists. They may institute accelerated procedures on the understanding that most litigants prefer rough justice now to perfect justice in their dotage. They may allow lay volunteers to sit on commercial tribunals of first instance. The state can make such compromises because of its confidence in its appellate mechanisms. If aliens are allowed to bypass those mechanisms and bring international claims for denial of justice on the basis of alleged wrongdoing by the justice of the peace of any neighbourhood, international law would find itself intruding intolerably into internal affairs. For a foreigner's international grievance to proceed as a claim of denial of justice, the national system must have been tested. Its perceived failings cannot constitute an international wrong unless it has been given a chance to correct itself.

When on the other hand the alleged delict has been committed by officials who are not carrying out a function susceptible to judicial review, the issue is simply whether their acts are imputable to the state or not. If so, responsibility for the delict is in principle extant even in the absence of any attempt to seise a higher authority. Claimants are of course unlikely to pursue international claims against a state for the misdeeds of lower-level officials; overwhelming common sense will command that an attempt be made to go over their heads to administrative superiors before engaging the expense of launching an international claim. (A well-advised potential claimant will also be aware that the quantum of recovery may be compromised in the absence of any attempt to mitigate.)

But a trial judge who misconducts himself simply does not commit a fully constituted international delict imputable to the state. States do not have an international obligation to ensure that no individual judge is ever guilty of a miscarriage of justice. The obligation is to establish and maintain a *system* which does not deny justice; the system is the whole pyramid.[28]

---

[28] The failure to pursue local remedies may be given weight in assessing the substantive justification for claims other than denial of justice. In contrast to the three cases involving respectively Indonesia (*Amco Asia et al.* v. *Indonesia*, 1 *ICSID Reports* 376), Sri Lanka (*Asian Agricultural Products Ltd* v. *Sri Lanka*, 4 *ICSID Reports* 245), and *Congo* (Brazzaville) (*Benvenuti and Bonfant srl* v. *Congo*, 1 *ICSID Reports* 330), see *Generation Ukraine Inc.* v. *Ukraine*, award, 16 September 2003, (2005) 44 ILM 404 (Salpius, Voss, Paulsson (presiding)), where the lack of attempts to seek local redress persuaded the arbitrators that there had in fact been no expropriation: '20.30 . . . it is not enough for an investor to seize upon an act of maladministration, no matter how low the level of the relevant governmental authority; to abandon his investment without any effort at overturning the administrative fault; and thus to claim an international delict on the theory that there had been an uncompensated virtual expropriation. In such instances, an international tribunal may deem that the failure to seek redress from national authorities disqualifies the international claim, not because there is a requirement of *exhaustion* of local remedies but because the very reality of conduct tantamount to expropriation is doubtful in the absence of a *reasonable* – not necessarily exhaustive – effort by the investor to obtain correction . . . 20.33 No act or omission of the Kyiv City State Administration during this period, whether cumulatively or in isolation, transcends the threshold for an indirect expropriation. This Tribunal does not exercise the function of an administrative review body to ensure that municipal agencies perform their tasks diligently, conscientiously or efficiently. That function is within the proper domain of domestic courts and tribunals that are cognisant of the minutiae of the applicable regulatory regime. In the circumstances of this case, the conduct cited by the Claimant was never challenged before the domestic courts of Ukraine. More precisely, the Claimant did not attempt to compel the Kyiv City State Administration to rectify the alleged omissions in its administrative management of the Parkview Project by instituting proceedings in the Ukrainian courts. There is, of course, no formal obligation upon the Claimant to exhaust local remedies before resorting to ICSID arbitration

A tacit recognition of this fundamental element of denial of justice was provided by *Feldman* v. *Mexico*,[29] a case which arose under NAFTA and was decided by an ICSID Additional Facility Tribunal. The arbitrators quoted with approval the reasoning expressed in *Azinian* v. *Mexico* to the effect that 'a governmental authority surely cannot be faulted for acting in a manner validated by its own courts unless the courts themselves are disavowed at the international level'. Faced with a claimant who argued that unfavourable regulatory actions of the Ministry of Finance and Public Credit (in alleged disregard of both a Supreme Court precedent and a specific agreement made with the claimant) constituted denial of justice, the arbitral tribunal had to go further than *Azinian*, where there was no challenge to the relevant Mexican court decisions. In rejecting the claim, the *Feldman* award noted that Mexican judicial and administrative procedures were at all relevant times open to the claimant, that he had indeed won one such court application to the Supreme Court, and that court review of the adverse regulatory decisions was available.[30]

The proposed Article 12 of the Second Report on Diplomatic Protection prepared for the International Law Commission by John Dugard affirms that the local remedies rule is a procedural precondition to the prosecution of an international claim, and not a substantive norm. This proposition seems consistent with the views expressed by Judge Lauterpacht in *Norwegian Loans*,[31] but contrary to those of the first Lauterpacht lecturer, Judge Schwebel, in the *ELSI* case.[32]

For present purposes, it is possible, and indeed right, to sidestep this controversy (which is not a Lauterpacht–Schwebel debate, but a notorious matter of discussion among international legal scholars[33]).

pursuant to the BIT [Ukraine–United States Bilateral Investment Treaty]. Nevertheless, in the absence of any *per se* violation of the BIT discernible from the relevant conduct of the Kyiv City State Administration, the only possibility in this case for the series of complaints relating to highly technical matters of Ukrainian planning law to be transformed into a BIT violation would have been for the Claimant to be denied justice before the Ukrainian courts in a *bona fide* attempt to resolve these technical matters.' (Emphasis in the original. Compare *Oil Field of Texas, Inc.* v. *Iran*, award, 8 October 1986, 12 Iran–US Claims Tribunal Report 308, where the finding of expropriation depended in significant part on 'the Claimant's impossibility to challenge the Court order in Iran', *ibid.* at para. 43.)

29 Award, 16 December 2002, 7 *ICSID Reports* 339.    30 *Ibid.* at para. 140.

31 *France* v. *Norway* 1957 *ICJ Reports* 9, at p. 41.

32 *US* v. *Italy* 1989 *ICJ Reports* 15, at pp. 115–116.

33 Judge Roberto Ago once compiled a bibliography of the different schools of thought: *ILC Yearbook* 1977, vol. II, A/CN.4/SER.A/1977/Add.1(78.v.2) at 135–137. De Visscher had no hesitation in declaring the exhaustion requirement to be a *règle de procédure*. He then wrote, at 421: 'It affects less the existence of responsibility than the

The proposition advanced is that the very definition of the delict of denial of justice encompasses the notion of exhaustion of local remedies. There can be no denial before exhaustion.[34] (To put it more precisely, the offending state must be given a reasonable opportunity to correct actions which otherwise would ripen into delicts.) The aptness or otherwise of Dugard's proposed Article 12, as it applies to other international delicts, is simply *hors propos*. To take one step further: denial of justice is by definition to be distinguished from situations where international wrongs materialise before exhaustion of local remedies; there is no impediment to perceiving, in accordance with Dugard's report, that exhaustion of local remedies with respect to such wrongs is a waivable procedural precondition.[35]

This analysis impels us to revert to the subject of Calvo Clauses. The fundamental effect of such Clauses, generally accepted as such since the

conditions for initiating the claim.' The word *less* is uncomfortable; if the matter truly was so clear to de Visscher, he might have expressed himself in a more absolute manner, and written *not*. At any rate, the quoted sentence would get a claimant nowhere with respect to a denial of justice; there is no way to 'initiate a claim' which has not matured, i.e. the elements proving 'the existence of responsibility' are not extant before the national system has been given an opportunity for correction. The exhaustion rule adopted by the ILC Articles on the Responsibility of States for Internationally Wrongful Acts in 2001 appears in Article 44(b), which is entitled 'Admissibility of claims'. (It refers to the non-exhaustion of any *available* and *effective* local remedy.) The commentary does not, however, suggest that exhaustion is purely procedural; James Crawford, *The International Law Commission's Articles on State Responsibility: Introduction, Text and Commentaries* (Cambridge University Press, 2002), at pp. 264–265.

[34] The *Mondev* award was therefore in error when it asserted that 'under NAFTA it is not true that the denial of justice rule and the exhaustion of local remedies rule "are interlocking and inseparable"'. *Mondev* at para. 96 (quoting C. Eagleton, *The Responsibility of States in International Law* (New York University Press, 1928), at p. 113).

[35] It is possible that the actions of a lower court may breach international obligations under a treaty. Jiménez de Aréchaga noted in 1968 that 'State responsibility for acts of the Judiciary does not exhaust itself in the concept of denial of justice', in 'International Responsibility', in Max Sørensen (ed.), *Manual of Public International Law* (London: Macmillan, 1968), at p. 555. For example, a treaty may contain promises of 'fair and equitable treatment' which are held not to be confined to matters covered by the customary law of denial of justice; breaches of such promises may not require the exhaustion of local remedies. Or a treaty may be held to contain promises of 'transparency' the breach of which is consummated by a lower court. (The example is suggested by the controversy engendered by the *Metalclad case*; see *Metalclad Corp.* v. *Mexico*, award, 30 August 2000, 5 *ICSID Reports* 209 (Civiletti, Siqueiros, Lauterpacht (presiding)), and its partial annulment in British Columbia, *Mexico* v. *Metalclad Corporation*, 2 May 2001, *ibid.* at 236. Such grievances must find their basis in the *lex specialis* of the treaty; for want of the exhaustion of local remedies, they have not matured as claims of denial of justice.

*North American Dredging* case,[36] is to deny to international tribunals the power to try (or review) dispositions of national law.[37] Conduct which is alleged to generate immediate international responsibility may of course be brought to such international forums as may have jurisdiction *ratione personae*. But claims that arise because of the manner in which the national system has administered justice do not fall within the scope of authority of international adjudicators until that system has finally disposed of the claim submitted to it, and such an international wrong is not consummated until its remedies have been exhausted. Our conclusion is in harmony with the operation of the Calvo Clause. Put another way, *Loewen* is consistent in principle with *North American Dredging*.

## The qualification of reasonableness

In the *Montano* case discussed at greater length in Chapter 6, the Umpire of the US–Peruvian Claims Commission (General Herran) rejected the US Government's objection of non-exhaustion of local remedies and went on to uphold a significant Peruvian claim. He wrote notably:

> The obligation of a stranger to exhaust the remedies which nations have for obtaining justice, before soliciting the protection of his government, ought to be understood in a rational manner, that such obligation does not make delusive the rights of the foreigner.[38]

The Peruvian claimant, Esteban Montano, had obtained a federal judgment in his favour, but it remained unenforced due to the negligence of the marshal charged with its execution in California. The US Government apparently considered that the claimant should now lodge a complaint against the marshal, and thus seemed to be saying, in General Herran's ironic phrase, that 'what Montano gained by the sentence was the right to bring forward another complaint'. The Umpire was satisfied that 'the claimant had exhausted the ordinary means of obtaining justice'.

---

[36] See the section on 'Modern political realities' in Chapter 2.

[37] The well-informed reader will not miss the broad parallel with the effect of contractual forum clauses analysed in the cases of *SGS Société Générale de Surveillance S.A.* v. *Pakistan*, decision on jurisdiction, 6 August 2003, 8 *ICSID Reports* 406 (Faurès, Thomas, Feliciano (presiding)) and SGS *Société Générale de Surveillance S.A.* v. *Philippines*, decision on jurisdiction, 29 January 2004, 8 *ICSID Reports* 518 (Crawford, Crivellaro, El-Kosheri (presiding)).

[38] *Peru* v. *US*, Moore, *Arbitrations* 1630 at p. 1637.

Similarly, in the exotic saga of the high-stakes feud between a French lawyer and entrepreneur named Antoine Fabiani and his Venezuelan in-laws, the Roncayolos, the international tribunal embodied in the President of the Swiss Federation noted that in the light of a series of '*dénégations de justice notoires*' it would be unacceptable to ask of Fabiani that he must then ask for a ruling about his claim of denial of justice – from the very courts 'of which for years he had fruitlessly demanded the execution of an irreproachable award ... notwithstanding that the higher supervising administrative and judicial authorities had been put on notice of the illegalities committed'.[39]

The victim of a denial of justice is not required to pursue improbable remedies. Nor is he required to contrive indirect or extravagant applications beyond the ordinary path of a frontal attempt to have the judgment by which he was unjustly treated set aside, or to be granted a trial he was denied. This issue is sometimes referred to as one of an *exception* to the rule of exhaustion; a more apt expression would be that it is a *qualification* necessary to establish the inherent limits of the rule.

Debates concerning the plausibility of a remedy yet to be solicited are naturally likely to generate serious controversy. Jurisprudence and commentary reflect much hard thinking about the criteria that should properly allow a claimant to consider that his claim of denial of justice is mature, and thus that he is not required to pursue further local remedies. The competing suggestions of appropriate criteria are sophisticated and merit careful attention.

Yet before exposing ourselves to the rarefied atmosphere of this debate, we may fortify ourselves with the oxygen of a simple guiding proposition, namely that it must be possible for international adjudicators to examine the plausibility of the alleged remaining remedy without actually requiring that the claimant try it.

Ultimately, one cannot know whether a remedy would have been adequate or effective unless one actually seeks to rely on it. If the rule were so strict as to require an attempt in every case, the supposed qualification would be wiped out by its very definition; the most remotely *conceivable* remedy must be attempted.

No proposed criteria should be adopted if they lead to such an extreme result. It would imply the abandonment of international review, for it would be sufficient for a respondent state to *assert* that some residual

---

[39] *Antoine Fabiani (no. 1) (France* v. *Venezuela)*, Moore, *Arbitrations* 4878 at p. 4904 (the present author's translation).

remedy might still be availing. In Secretary of State Hamilton Fish's famous phrase: 'A claimant in a foreign state is not required to exhaust justice in such state when there is no justice to exhaust'.[40] The ICJ Chamber which decided the *ELSI* case gave useful content to this abstraction. In the interest of succinctness, it suffices to cite the introduction of Judge Schwebel's dissenting opinion, where he sets out his *agreement* with the judgment in this 'paramount' respect:

the Judgment applies a rule of reason in its interpretation of the reach of the requirement of the exhaustion of local remedies. It holds not that every possible local remedy must have been exhausted to satisfy the local remedies rule but that, where in substance local remedies have been exhausted, that suffices to meet the requirements of the rule even if it may be that a variation on the pursuit of local remedies in the particular case was not in fact played out. It has of course long been of the essence of the rule of exhaustion of local remedies that local remedies need not be exhausted where there are no effective remedies to exhaust. It may be said that the Chamber has done no more than to reaffirm this established element of the rule. In fact it has reaffirmed it, but in doing so the Judgment makes a contribution to the elucidation of the local remedies rule by indicating that, where the substance of the issues of a case has been definitively litigated in the courts of a State, the rule does not require that those issues also have been litigated by the presentation of every relevant legal argument which any municipal forum might have been able to pass upon, however unlikely in practice the possibilities of reaching another result were. The United States of America submitted that the claims brought by it were admissible since 'all reasonable' local remedies had been exhausted; in substance, the Chamber agreed, and rightly so. Its holding thus confines certain prior constructions of the reach of the rule of exhaustion of local remedies to a sensible limit.[41]

---

[40] J. B. Moore, *Digest of International Law* (8 vols., Washington, DC: US Government Printing Office, 1906), vol. VI, at p. 677.

[41] *US* v. *Italy* 1989 *ICJ Reports* 15, at p. 94. Italy had argued that Raytheon, the aggrieved US corporation, could have brought an action founded on Article 2043 of the Italian Civil Code, which generally requires the reparation of 'wrongful damages' caused by wilfulness or fault. Italy argued that this provision had been frequently and successfully invoked by individuals against the Italian State. Accordingly, the unsuccessful attempts of ELSI's trustee in bankruptcy (pursued to the level of the Court of Cassation) to obtain an indemnity on account of an allegedly illegal requisition by the Mayor of Palermo of plant and machinery, leading to the insolvency of the company, was argued not to constitute sufficient exhaustion by its US parent corporation. Rejecting this argument, the ICJ Chamber stated that it appeared 'impossible to deduce ... what the attitude of the Italian courts would have been'; Italy had not discharged the burden 'to show, as a matter of fact, the existence of a remedy which was open to the United States stockholders and which they failed to employ' (*ibid.* at p. 47).

There can be no hesitation if the international tribunal is satisfied as a matter of fact that theoretically available local remedies are incapable of altering a decision, e.g. in the face of an executive order forbidding suits against the treasury[42] or in the face of executive subversion of judicial authority.[43] Michael Reisman has also suggested that the pendency of internal judicial proceedings should not inhibit international actions if the former are based on internationally unlawful legislation; he gave the example of the South African apartheid government's Terrorism Act.[44]

The plausibility of the remedy posited by the respondent US Government was critical to the outcome of the 2003 award in *Loewen*, where the claim was rejected on the merits for failure to show 'that Loewen had no reasonably available and adequate remedy under United States municipal law in respect of the matters of which it complains'.[45] (To be accurate, the award states that such would have been the claimants' fate had it been able to overcome the issue of standing which doomed their case at any rate, namely the failure of a 'diversity of nationality' requirement under the North American Free Trade Agreement.[46]) Before we revert to this remarkable case, some issues of principle merit consideration.

The question of futile remedies that arises with respect to denial of justice is analogous to the one arising in connection with the obligation to exhaust local remedies before seeking diplomatic protection. The Second Report on Diplomatic Protection to the ILC proposed a text requiring recourse to 'all available local legal remedies', defined as those 'which are of right open to natural or legal persons before judicial or administrative courts or authorities whether ordinary or special'.[47] In subsequent debates within the ILC, the point was made that the remedies in question must also be *adequate or effective*. In due course, the Third Report proposed alternative negative formulations, namely that local remedies need not be exhausted if they are:

---

[42] *Ruden (US v. Peru)*, Moore, *Arbitrations* 1653, at p. 1655.
[43] As in the *Robert E. Brown case* (*US v. Great Britain*, VI RIAA 120), discussed in John Dugard, 'Chief Justice versus President: Does the Ghost of Brown v. Leyds NO Still Haunt Our Judges?' *De Rebus* (September 1981), where the South African President overruled the courts and ultimately dismissed judges unwilling to swear that they would not review the constitutionality of decrees.
[44] Reisman, *Nullity*, at p. 365.   [45] 26 June 2003, at para. 2.
[46] *Ibid.* at para. 237.   [47] ILC, Second Report on Diplomatic Protection at p. 3.

(1) 'obviously futile', or
(2) 'offer no reasonable prospect of success', or
(3) 'provide no reasonable possibility of an effective remedy'.

The Special Rapporteur's reason for proposing negative formulations – i.e. *exceptions* – relate to his analysis of the burden of proof:

> the burden of proof in respect of the availability and effectiveness of local remedies will in most circumstances be on different parties. The respondent State will be required to prove that local remedies are available, while the burden of proof will be on the claimant State to show that such remedies are ineffective or futile.[48]

The relevance in terms of denial of justice is direct and evident. (And what goes for 'the claimant state' in espousal cases also goes for any other claimant.)

It is a matter for determination by the international forum, on a case-by-case basis, whether a remedy is *reasonably available*, in terms of either adequacy or efficacy. Unilateral affirmations should not be given conclusive effect, whether they are made by the claimant (typically on the basis of advice from jurisconsultants) or by the respondent state. To proceed otherwise would violate the principle of equality of the parties before the international forum. The following pronouncement of the Permanent Court of International Justice should therefore be read with caution:

> The question whether or not the Lithuanian Courts have jurisdiction to entertain a particular suit depends on Lithuanian law and is one on which the Lithuanian Courts alone can pronounce a final decision ... Until it has been clearly shown that [they] have no jurisdiction ... the Court cannot accept the contention ... that the rule as to the exhaustion of local remedies does not apply.[49]

The notion expressed by the phrase 'it has been clearly shown' should be read liberally, with the adjunction *by any convincing means*, rather than as requiring proof of a formal dismissal.[50]

---

[48] International Law Commission (Dugard), Third Report on Diplomatic Protection, UN Doc. A/CN.4/523 (2002), at p. 6, para. 19.

[49] *Panevezys–Saldutiskis Railway* (1939) PCIJ, Series A/B, No. 76, 3, at p. 19.

[50] *Accord*, ILC, Second Report on Diplomatic Protection. Professor Reisman's sharp criticism of the PCIJ's 'momentary inability to grasp [the issue] in a realistic manner ... constitutes an exceptional indiscretion in international jurisprudence', Reisman, *Nullity*, at p. 369, would presumably lead that author to concur emphatically.

Still, what exactly needs to be shown? Which of the three formulations proposed by Dugard carries the weight of authority and the conviction of sound policy?

The second formulation – *offer no reasonable prospect of success* – is overly favourable to the claimant, to such a degree that one may be tempted to view it as a straw man, placed at one extreme of the debate to provide favourable contrast with the middle ground. To begin with, it could have the perverse consequence that a poor case could more easily be brought before an international forum than more meritorious ones, precisely because the claimant did not have reasonable prospects of success before the national courts. For the purposes of the analysis of the maturity of claims of denial of justice, the availability of local remedies must logically proceed on the hypothesis that the appeal is factually accurate and legally well-founded as formulated; for it is only if the international forum can be persuaded that even a deserving complainant has nowhere to turn that the denial of justice can be deemed consummated. Finally, this formulation would be a departure from the weight of jurisprudence and authority, since national legal systems are presumed to function properly. They should not be found wanting simply because a litigant does not like his chances and convinces an international tribunal that he is indeed unlikely to prevail.

The first formulation stands at the other extreme, but does have some jurisprudential support. Credit for the expression 'obviously futile' has gone to the arbitrator in the *Finnish Ships* case,[51] Justice Algot Bagge of the Swedish Supreme Court, and so he too is criticised for the perceived excessive severity of this test. But when one considers what he actually did and decided, it seems unlikely that Bagge would recognise himself as a champion of the rule he is said to have authored. What he confronted was a controversy about the existence of appealable points of law. He examined the points available to the claimant and concluded that they were 'obviously' insufficient to justify a revision of the controversial initial judgment. There is no warrant for concluding that his finding that the claimant had a compelling case for maturity of his international action means that equally compelling demonstrations must be made in all cases before non-exhaustion is excused. His claimant was simply far above the threshold. Referring to his award in a scholarly publication many years later, Bagge himself wrote:

---

[51] *Finland* v. *Great Britain*, 9 May 1934, III RIAA 1479.

it would not be reasonable to require that the private party should spend time and money on a recourse which *in all probability* would be futile.[52]

The present author finds himself fully persuaded to endorse the middle ground represented by the third formulation: a 'reasonable possibility of an effective remedy'. It is directly reproduced from the separate opinion of Sir Hersch Lauterpacht in the *Norwegian Loans* case.[53] The concept of *reasonable possibility* rather than *reasonable prospect*, coupled with that of an 'effective remedy', which focuses on the availability in principle of a workable mechanism rather than the prediction of an outcome in a given case, imposes a considerable burden on the claimant, yet does not require proof of 'obvious futility'.

In his review of the precedents, Professor Dugard categorised the circumstances in which local remedies have been found to be ineffective and futile as follows[54]:

- the local courts have no jurisdiction over the dispute;
- the national legislation justifying the acts of which the alien complains will not be reviewed by the courts;[55]
- the local courts are notoriously lacking in independence (Dugard cites the classic case of *Robert E. Brown*; in more recent times, one could imagine Peru under the Fujimori regime as a context in which proof would be extant; see the *Constitutional Court* case[56]);
- a consistent and well-established line of precedents adverse to the alien;

---

[52] A. Bagge, 'Intervention on the Ground of Damage Caused to Nationals, with Particular Reference to Exhaustion of Local Remedies and the Rights of Shareholders', (1958) 34 BYIL 162, at pp. 166–167 (emphasis added).

[53] *France* v. *Norway* 1957 *ICJ Reports* 9, at p. 39.

[54] ILC (Dugard), Third Report on Diplomatic Protection at pp. 14–17, paras. 38–44.

[55] This category is unlikely to be relevant to claims of denial of justice; the paradigm case is that of a decree of expropriation, which of itself is not a denial of justice, but a separate international wrong. As such, it could be susceptible either to direct action (without the requirement of exhaustion of local remedies) or to diplomatic protection (subject to an exhaustion requirement which could give rise to a new international wrong in the case of a denial of justice). See *Robert Azinian, et al.* v. *Mexico*, award, 1 November 1998, 5 *ICSID Reports* 269 (Civiletti, von Wobeser, Paulsson (presiding)).

[56] *Constitutional Court case (Aguirre Roca, Rey Terry, and Revoredo Marsano v. Peru)* (Merits), 31 January 2001, Inter-American Court of Human Rights, Series C, No. 71. Local applications for the remedy of *amparo* (constitutional protection) were held illusory and defective because of the unjustified delay in ruling upon them. See J. M. Pasqualucci, *The Practice and Procedure of the Inter-American Court of Human Rights* (Cambridge University Press, 2003), at p. 132.

- the local courts do not have the competence to grant an appropriate and adequate remedy;
- the absence of an adequate system of judicial protection.

Another instance of pointlessness of further recourse was described by Östen Undén, sole arbitrator in the *Treaty of Neuilly* arbitration, as follows:

the rule of exhaustion of local remedies does not apply generally when the act charged consists of measures taken by the government or by a member of the government performing his official duties. There rarely exist local remedies against the acts of the authorized organs of the state.[57]

De Visscher cited[58] this passage in support of his argument that it must be possible to act directly on the international level to challenge the application of a measure, legislative or executive, against which the law of the relevant state offers no legal recourse. Otherwise, he reasoned, international law would be subordinated to internal juridical arrangements, an 'unacceptable result, contrary to the autonomy of the international legal order'.[59]

One writer has also suggested that local remedies should be deemed exhausted 'if the cost involved in proceeding considerably outweighs the possibility of any satisfaction resulting'.[60] This proposition may be doubtful with regard to exhaustion in the context of diplomatic protection, but it is not to be assumed that the requirement is to be understood in precisely the same way in specific instances of denial of justice.

---

[57] *Arbitration under Article 181 of the Treaty of Neuilly (Greece v. Bulgaria)*, 4 November 1931, (1934) 28 AJIL 760, at p. 789. Undén was appointed by the Council of the League of Nations. He issued the award in French, and it was published in the original in *Uppsala Universitets Årsskrift* (yearbook), vol. 1932 (Prog. 1) and 1933 (Prog. 2). The passage reproduced above refers to '*les actes des organes les plus autorisés de l'Etat*', which means that the translation should have used the expression '*most* authorised organs'.

[58] De Visscher at p. 424, note 2.   [59] *Ibid.* at p. 424.

[60] David R. Mummery, 'The Content of the Duty to Exhaust Local Remedies', (1965) 59 AJIL 398, at p. 401. In one of his decisions as Umpire of the commission under the US/Mexico Convention of 4 July 1876, *Benjamin Burn (US v. Mexico)*, Moore, *Arbitrations*, at p. 3140, Sir Edward Thornton explicitly acknowledged *in dictum* that the issue of exhaustion might have a factual dimension as well as a purely legal one. While dismissing the claim for failure of 'a man of some education and determination' living in the capital to bring an appeal, he observed:

'In distant parts of the country, where the inferior judge is perhaps the only authority within reach, and where the foreigner may be poor, uneducated, and isolated, such a proceeding [in the supreme court] might be almost impossible.'

## Application of the reasonableness qualification in *Loewen*

In *Loewen*, the Canadian claimant's grievance arose out of a verdict rendered against it by a Mississippi jury in the amount of US$500 million, all but US$25 million of which was on account of 'emotional distress' and 'punitive damages'.[61] Loewen believed that there had been serious judicial misconduct and appealable errors. Yet its attempts to appeal, so Loewen alleged, had been frustrated in circumstances described by the arbitral tribunal as follows:

> Loewen sought to appeal the $500 million verdict and judgment but was confronted with the application of an appellate bond requirement. Mississippi law requires an appeal bond for 125% of the judgment as a condition of staying execution on the judgment, but allows the bond to be reduced or dispensed with for 'good cause'.

> Despite Claimants' claim that there was good cause to reduce the appeal bond, both the trial court and the Mississippi Supreme Court refused to reduce the appeal bond at all and required Loewen to post a $625 million bond within seven days in order to pursue its appeal without facing immediate execution of the judgment. According to Claimants, that decision effectively foreclosed Loewen's appeal rights.

> Claimants allege that Loewen was then forced to settle the case 'under extreme duress'. Other alternatives to settlement were said to be catastrophic and/or unavailable. On January 29, 1996, with execution against their Mississippi assets scheduled to start the next day, Loewen entered into a settlement with O'Keefe under which they agreed to pay $175 million.[62]

As seen, the victim of a denial of justice is not required to pursue ineffective appeals. Loewen could not complain on this account; the appeal procedure existed, and there was no reason to doubt that it would have been practically effective if the appeal had succeeded. As the arbitrators wrote, the issue was rather the *reasonable availability* of the remedy. Quoting with approval commentary to the effect that claimants should be permitted 'to introduce evidence of the practical workings of justice', such as excessive orders of security for costs, the arbitrators put it thus:

> Availability is not a standard to be determined or applied in the abstract. It means reasonably available to the complainant in the light of its situation,

---

[61] Mr Raymond Loewen was also a claimant as an individual shareholder; reference to 'Loewen' in the singular is made for convenience.

[62] *Loewen*, 26 June 2003, at paras. 5–7.

including its financial and economic circumstances as a foreign investor, as they are affected by any conditions relating to the exercise of any local remedy.

If a State attaches conditions to a right of appeal which render exercise of the right impractical, the exercise of the right is neither available nor effective nor adequate. Likewise, if a State burdens the exercise of the right directly or indirectly so as to expose the complainant to severe financial consequences, it may well be that the State has by its own actions disabled the complainant from affording the State the opportunity of redressing the matter of complaint. The scope of the need to exhaust local remedies must be considered in the light of these considerations.[63]

With these factors in mind, the arbitral tribunal analysed Loewen's situation as follows. Loewen did lodge an appeal to the Mississippi Supreme Court. The appeal was expected to last 6–24 months. In the meanwhile, if Loewen did not post the bond of US$625 million its assets would be subject to enforcement, in Mississippi and elsewhere, up to the judgment amount of US$500 million. Loewen was financially unable to provide a bond in that amount. O'Keefe announced that it would pursue aggressive enforcement initiatives. Loewen applied to the trial court for a stay of enforcement against a bond of US$125 million, i.e. 125 per cent of the compensatory damages component of the judgment. O'Keefe argued against the application, referring to Loewen's distressed share price and the pendency of other lawsuits which might erode Loewen's assets and make it unable to pay the full US$500 million judgment amount if its appeal failed. The motion was denied, as was a subsequent petition before the Mississippi Supreme Court. Neither of these denials, in the arbitrators' view, transgressed international minimum standards; each was 'at worst an erroneous or mistaken decision'.[64] Coming on the back of such egregious failures at the trial level, as described in the section on 'Fundamental breaches of due process' in Chapter 7, this tolerance can hardly fail to raise many readers' eyebrows.

Loewen was thus in the position that it could pursue the appeal, but subject to the risk of execution. Its only alternatives were: (a) to make a negotiated settlement with O'Keefe; (b) to file for bankruptcy; or (c) to try to interest the US Supreme Court in its predicament on the grounds that the bond requirement violated constitutional guarantees of due process, given the likelihood of irreparable harm before appellate review.

In these circumstances, Loewen put an end to its travails by paying O'Keefe US$175 million to settle the dispute. The tribunal was left to

---

[63] *Ibid.* at paras. 169–170.   [64] *Ibid.* at paras. 189 and 197.

consider whether, given its alternatives, Loewen had pursued reasonable local remedies.

To proceed with the appeal while exposed to the imminent danger of enforcement would have exposed the company to 'the inevitable consequence that Loewen's share price would collapse'; it was not a 'reasonably available remedy'.

As for the option of reorganisation under the Bankruptcy Code, the arbitrators were hesitant. They noted that although it would have resulted in a stay of execution, and the company could continue to conduct its business under court supervision, such a course of action would have restricted its initiatives and perhaps depressed its share price. All in all, they expressed the view that 'no doubt there are some situations in which it would be reasonable to expect an impecunious claimant to file [for bankruptcy protection] in order to exercise an available right of appeal', and the reasonability of doing so depended to some extent on Loewen's reasons for entering into the settlement agreement (see below).

With respect to the envisaged petition to the US Supreme Court (as well as an attempt to achieve collateral review before a Federal District Court), each side submitted reports from law professors. The arbitral tribunal found itself unable to do more than to say that there was 'a prospect, at most a reasonable prospect or possibility', of success.[65]

Given the refusal to reduce the bond – 'an act for which the Respondent is responsible in international law' – did Loewen have 'a reasonably available and adequate remedy' in the US federal courts? The arbitral tribunal rejected the argument that the settlement agreement in itself should be deemed a voluntary abandonment of local remedies:

It may be that the business judgment was inevitable or the natural outcome of adverse consequences generated by the impugned court decision ... If, in all the circumstances, entry into the settlement agreement was the only course which Loewen could reasonably be expected to take, that would be enough to justify an inference or conclusion that Loewen had no reasonably available and adequate remedy.[66]

One might be puzzled at the idea that the responsibility of the USA could depend on an act – the refusal to reduce the bond – which the arbitral tribunal had said did not violate international minimum standards. Perhaps it should be interpreted as meaning that a non-violative act for which the state is responsible could nevertheless propel a violative act (the original

---

[65] *Ibid.* at para. 211.  [66] *Ibid.* at paras. 214–215.

judgment) over the threshold of the exhaustion requirement because it did not *allow* the aggrieved party a reasonably practical opportunity to overturn the judgment. For many of us, that will be over-rarefied, and we will draw the conclusion that the refusal to reduce the bond was also deemed to be an infringement of international law, no matter what the arbitrators had said about it before they got to this point in the award.

The matter will remain academic, however, since the arbitrators, rather abruptly, identified 'the central difficulty in Loewen's case' as being its failure to present evidence 'disclosing its reasons for entering into the settlement agreement in preference to pursuing other options'. Stating that the 'onus of proof rested with Loewen', they concluded that they could not decide that settlement was Loewen's only reasonable option, since 'we are simply left to speculate on the reasons which led to the decision to adopt that course rather than to pursue other options'. To the contrary, one could but conclude, so they found, that Loewen failed to pursue its remedies, and had therefore not demonstrated a violation of international law; it would have failed even if it had retained Canadian nationality to the end.

The award contains a postscript, all the more curious for appearing under the caption 'conclusions' inserted after the dispositive orders. Noting that they had 'criticised the Mississippi proceedings in the strongest terms' and concluded that 'there was unfairness here towards the foreign investor' which engendered a 'natural instinct' to correct 'a miscarriage of justice', the arbitrators nevertheless concluded that they were constrained by the limits of international law. No one can quarrel with this conclusion. If that was indeed so, the apology was unnecessary, and will therefore appear to many as disconcerting. Indeed, since the thrust of the 'conclusion' is that international tribunals cannot interfere in internal affairs unless it does so 'in the last resort', it relates only to the dismissal of the case on the merits – as though this passage had been written before the arbitral tribunal decided that the complaint would be dismissed for failure of a formal jurisdictional requirement of citizen-ship. In the end, the arbitrators thus seemed to be apologising for not giving effect to a dictum. Given this avowed sympathy for the victim, and given the fact that an international remedy would apparently have been available if the evidence had shown the settlement had been the only reasonable alternative, one is left to wonder why the arbitrators *did not ask for* such evidence as there might be – and then let the chips fall where they may. An international tribunal faced with a claim for denial of justice is not an appellate jurisdiction required to deal with an immutable factual record. As we shall see throughout Chapters 6 and 7, the real difficulty of denial of justice is less legal principle than the evaluation of facts.

The idea that there was no evidence of Loewen's deliberations about its options in the wake of this corporate catastrophe, or that it would have refused to provide it to the tribunal, would strike any reader of the award as absurd. Certainly Loewen offered explanations to the writer who covered the case for *The New Yorker*.[67]

It therefore did not come as a total surprise when Raymond Loewen, in his individual capacity, requested the arbitral tribunal to issue a supplemental decision in September 2003. His request contained some startling revelations – at least to outsiders to the case. It now transpired that significant proof had indeed been presented to the arbitral tribunal in relation to the prospects of an appeal to the US Supreme Court. That evidence had taken the form of a declaration of an independent member of Loewen's Board of Directors, who happened to be a former Minister of Justice and Prime Minister of Canada, to the effect that Loewen had formed a Special Committee to consider the corporate response to the Mississippi proceedings. That Special Committee had procured legal advice, and concluded that further recourse was practically doomed to fail.

The legal advice in question had been given by a highly qualified US consultant who concluded that: (i) the likelihood of obtaining Supreme Court review was 'exceedingly remote'; and (ii) a collateral attack in a US federal court of first instance was so clearly 'foreclosed' by the one of the most famous decisions in US judicial history, *Pennzoil* v. *Texaco*, that *even the attempt* might be sanctionable as abusive. Naturally such opinion evidence is subject to contrary opinion, or to the tribunal's own assessment of its credibility. What is aberrant is to ignore it, indeed to declare that there had been no attempt to adduce evidence of this kind.

Loewen Inc. itself might have had a basis on which to complain about the award, but ran the risk that any request for reconsideration or annulment would fall on deaf ears due to the great reluctance to disturb international *res judicata*. But the same conclusion did not

---

[67] 'Even if, by some miracle, he did manage to post the $625 million bond, and avoid immediate bankruptcy, that in itself would have serious repercussions for the company. The premium payments and interest would amount to tens of millions of dollars, and it would affect the warranties and covenants made to banks that had financed the acquisition of several hundred funeral homes.' Jonathan Harr, 'The Burial', *The New Yorker*, 1 November 1999, at p. 93.

necessarily apply to Raymond Loewen himself, who as a shareholder of Loewen Inc. (approximately 15 per cent) had an independent right to assert compensable damages under Article 1116 of NAFTA. This claim was not pronounced upon by the arbitral tribunal, in what Mr Loewen considered a case of *infra petita*. In his motion for reconsideration of this undecided claim, referring to the three major themes of the putative final award, he pointed out first: that the substantive denial of justice, albeit *in dicta*, was made surabundantly clear in the tribunal's emphatic findings of an 'outrage' imputable to the US Government; secondly that the nationality requirement which was fatal to Loewen Inc. did not affect him because he had always remained Canadian; and thirdly that he was in a position to point with insistence to evidence which the arbitrators said was not there. The arbitral tribunal could hardly have upheld this motion without admitting to considerable embarrassment. Instead, in what is destined to remain a controversial ending to this case, the arbitrators issued a six-page decision[68] asserting that its dismissal of all claims 'in their entirety' should be understood as 'necessarily' resolving Mr Loewen's Article 1116 claim; they referred in particular to their prior disinclination to accept the Loewen thesis that the settlement which put an end to the US court actions was consistent with the duty to exhaust local remedies.

In *Amco II*, Indonesia argued that the acts of its administrative agency in revoking an investment licence 'could not themselves constitute a wrong in international law, if unlawful, but that only a failure of the courts to rectify them could constitute such a wrong'.[69] The award noted this argument, but dealt with it by giving two non-answers: (i) denial of justice may be committed by an administrative body, not just a court; and (ii) the behaviour of the investment board transgressed the criteria of denial of justice as established in international precedents. This stance cannot be squared with *Loewen*, nor is it consonant with the analysis developed in this study. National responsibility for denial of justice occurs only when the system as a whole has been tested and the initial delict has remained uncorrected. It may be that the *Amco II* tribunal took account of the fact that the investment board sought and received Presidential approval for its decision and concluded that any appeal would have been futile. But then the arbitrators should have said

---

[68] Decision on Request for a Supplementary Decision, 13 September 2004, 10 *ICSID Reports* [forthcoming].
[69] *Amco II* at para. 137.

so, and justified their position in the light of the international standard, which, as discussed above, requires that claimants avail themselves of 'a reasonable possibility of an effective remedy'.

## No fresh starts at the international level

Aliens should not be able to pursue a state for denial of justice because it failed to deal fairly with contentions made for the first time after an international forum has been seized. All arguments to be raised at the international level must also have been invoked in the municipal proceedings. The arbitral tribunal put it thus in the *Finnish Ships* case:

> all the contentions of fact and the propositions of law which are brought forward by the claimant Government ... must have been investigated and adjudicated upon by the municipal Courts.[70]

More recently, the Appeals Chamber of the International Criminal Tribunal for the Former Yugoslavia has held that 'a party should not be permitted to refrain from making an objection to a matter which was apparent during the course of the trial and to raise it only in the event of an adverse finding against that party'.[71]

In Professor Daniel O'Connell's apt phrase, international law has thus adopted 'the rule common to municipal systems that a litigant cannot have a second try if, because of ill-preparation, he fails in his action'.[72] O'Connell noted that it follows from this proposition that the exhaustion rule requires not only the pursuit of appeals, but also, while the earlier proceedings were in progress, that the complainant availed himself of existing procedural mechanisms (such as calling witnesses and discovering documents) essential to the prosecution of his case.

---

[70] *Finland* v. *Great Britain*, 9 May 1934, III RIAA 1479, at p. 1502. See also Jiménez de Aréchaga, 'Past Third of a Century' 282: '[A] State cannot base the charges made before an international tribunal or organ on objections or grounds which were not previously raised before the municipal courts.'

[71] *Prosecutor* v. *Delalic and others*, 20 February 2001, Case No. IT–96–21–A at para. 640. The complainant in *Delalic* was able to demonstrate that one of the judges had slept through portions of the trial, but his counsel had not raised the point before the lower court. In *Gregory* v. *United Kingdom*, 25 February 1997, (1998) 25 EHRR 577, the European Court of Human Rights attached importance, at para. 45, to the fact that defence counsel had remained passive when a juror in a criminal case complained to the judge that there was racial bias within the jury.

[72] D. P. O'Connell, *International Law* (2nd edn, London: Stevens & Sons, 1970), at p. 1059.

As the *Ambatielos* case showed, this concept may impose a daunting task on a foreigner's advocate when faced with tactical choices in a trial. The commission in that case, starting with the proposition that it is 'the whole system of legal protection, as provided by municipal law, which must have been put to the test',[73] made clear that the failure to have called a witness – whom Greece itself argued would have provided decisive evidence in favour of a different outcome – may be fatal.

## Effect of forks in the road

Many investment treaties make it clear that a foreign claimant must elect his remedy, and that such an election is irreversible.

This requirement does not prevent the complainant from pursuing separate causes of action before different fora. Indeed, there are circumstances where he obviously *must* do so because his preferred forum does not have subject matter jurisdiction over all causes of action. Broadly speaking, the conceivable causes of action may include:

(a)   violations of law[74] which do not contravene treaty rights;
(b)   breaches of a contract which do not contravene treaty rights, or are subject to an exclusive[75] contractual choice of forum;
(c)   violations of treaty rights.

The fact that a claimant goes to a national court with respect to (a), or that he seizes the contractually designated forum with respect to (b), does not constitute an election not to bring (c) before the relevant international forum.

Before considering how a claim of denial of justice falls to be processed in the context of such *forks in the road*, to use the now common expression, it is useful to consider how they have been held to operate generally. The guiding principle, that of 'the essential basis of claim', was established in the *Vivendi* case. This ICSID arbitration resulted in a first award[76] which was partly annulled by an *ad hoc* committee operating pursuant to

---

[73]   *Greece* v. *UK*, 6 March 1956, XII RIAA 83, at p. 120.

[74]   This will typically mean violation of *national* law; violations of *international* law would generally contravene treaty rights.

[75]   Exclusivity may for all practical purposes be forced upon an initially non-exclusive contractual forum clause by operation of the relevant treaty, if it provides that non-use of that clause is a precondition for one of the arbitral mechanisms made available by the treaty. See Lucy Reed, Jan Paulsson and Nigel Blackaby, *Guide to ICSID Arbitration* (The Hague: Kluwer, 2004), at pp. 58–59.

[76]   *Compañía de Aguas del Aconquija S.A. and Vivendi Universal (formerly Compagnie Générale des Eaux)* v. *Argentina*, award, 21 November 2000; 5 *ICSID Reports* 296; (2001) 40 ILM 426.

Article 52 of the ICSID Convention.[77] The case arose from a dispute under a concession contract entered into by a French company and its Argentine affiliate, on the one hand, and Tucumán, a province of Argentina, on the other, for the operation of a regional water and sewerage system. Although the concession contract provided that the parties would submit disputes to the local administrative courts, the claimants did not bring any disputes before the local courts. They instead filed claims against Argentina under the France–Argentina bilateral investment treaty (BIT), seeking damages for actions that related not just to breach of the BIT but also to breach of the concession contract.

The first arbitral tribunal found that it had jurisdiction, but proceeded to dismiss all of the treaty breach claims on grounds that they were inextricably linked with questions of interpretation of the concession contract, which, so the arbitrators held, were reserved for the local courts under the dispute resolution clause of that contract. The committee empanelled for the annulment proceeding set aside this part of the award, finding that the tribunal had exceeded its authority by refusing to rule on the merits of the treaty claims over which it had jurisdiction, even if there was an overlap between the contract and treaty claims. The committee emphasised the legal distinction between the two categories of claim:

As to the relation between breach of contract and breach of treaty in the present case, it must be stressed that Articles 3 [fair and equitable treatment] and 5 [expropriation] of the BIT do not relate directly to breach of a municipal contract. Rather they set an independent standard. A state may breach a treaty without breaching a contract, and *vice versa*, and this is certainly true of these provisions of the BIT. The point is made clear in Article 3 of the ILC Articles, which is entitled 'Characterization of an act of a State as internationally wrongful':

The characterization of an act of a State as internationally wrongful is governed by international law. Such characterization is not affected by the characterization of the same act as lawful by internal law.

In accordance with this general principle (which is undoubtedly declaratory of general international law), whether there has been a breach of the BIT and whether there has been a breach of contract are different questions. Each of these claims will be determined by reference to its own proper or applicable law – in

---

[77] *Compañía de Aguas del Aconquija S.A. and Vivendi Universal (formerly Compagnie Générale des Eaux)* v. *Argentina*, decision on annulment, 3 July 2002, 6 *ICSID Reports* 340; (2002) 41 ILM 1135 (Crawford, Fernàndez-Rozas, Fortier (presiding)).

the case of the BIT, by international law; in the case of the Concession Contract, by the proper law of the contract, in other words, the law of Tucumán.[78]

The Committee proceeded to develop an 'essential' or 'fundamental basis of the claim' test:

In a case where the essential basis of a claim brought before an international tribunal is a breach of contract, the tribunal will give effect to any valid choice of forum clause in the contract ...

On the other hand, where 'the fundamental basis of the claim' is a treaty laying down an independent standard by which the conduct of the parties is to be judged, the existence of an exclusive jurisdiction clause in a contract between the claimant and the respondent state or one of its subdivisions cannot operate as a bar to the application of the treaty standard. At most, it might be relevant – as municipal law will often be relevant – in assessing whether there has been a breach of the treaty.[79]

In the subsequent *SGS* v. *Pakistan* case, another ICSID tribunal applied *Vivendi*'s 'essential basis' test to dismiss certain claims for lack of jurisdiction. The tribunal found that an arbitration clause in the parties' pre-inspection services contract, which called for arbitration in Pakistan, to be 'a valid forum selection clause *so far as concerns the Claimant's contract claims which do not also amount to BIT claims'*.[80]

Claims properly initiated before a national court or an arbitral tribunal established by contract fall to be decided by that court or tribunal. Whatever international jurisdiction that may be available under a treaty would not, absent unusual circumstances, be in a position to hear such claims. *They include claims of denial of justice provided that their 'essential basis' has been set forth as part of the cause of action.*

But that will not be so in the more likely case that the alleged denial of justice takes place in the course of the action before such a court or contractually stipulated arbitral tribunal. The claimant was by definition ignorant of a wrong which had not occurred at the time the complaint was formulated.

[78] *Ibid.* at paras. 95–96.   [79] *Ibid.* at paras. 98 and 101 (footnotes omitted).
[80] *SGS Société Générale de Surveillance S.A.* v. *Pakistan*, decision on jurisdiction, 6 August 2003, 8 *ICSID Reports* 406 at para. 161 (emphasis in the original). In *SGS Société Générale de Surveillance S.A.* v. *Philippines*, decision on jurisdiction, 29 January 2004, 8 *ICSID Reports* 518, yet another tribunal, while making it clear that it did not believe that contractual claims are in principle excluded as a grievance under investment treaties, and thus explicitly disagreed with the analysis of the arbitrators who decided the *SGS* v. *Pakistan* case, in practical terms reached a similar result.

## Summary

Since denial of justice implies the failure of a national legal system as a whole to satisfy minimum standards, the wrong does not occur until reasonable attempts have been made to secure the remedies available within that system. Waivers of the requirement of exhaustion of local remedies are effective with respect to other claims over which international adjudicators have jurisdiction, but only insofar as they are dispensable preconditions for seizing the international forum. With respect to denial of justice, they are indispensable; the claim simply cannot be said to exist until the self-correcting features of the national system have failed. On the other hand, claimants do not have to seek to avail themselves of remedies which offer no reasonable prospect of success. And it is important to bear in mind the frequently quoted statement of Sir Hersch Lauterpacht to the effect that the rule of exhaustion of local remedies is 'not purely technical' but one which 'international tribunals have applied with a considerable degree of elasticity'.[81]

The issue of exhaustion of local remedies relates to the admissibility of claims and must be distinguished from issues of jurisdiction. An international tribunal either has jurisdiction or not. Any consideration to the effect that it might have been *reasonable* for the parties to establish international jurisdiction is entitled to no weight if they have not done so. A tribunal's ruling on a jurisdictional demurrer is almost invariably open to review. The rule of exhaustion of remedies, on the other hand, gives the international tribunal plenary authority to determine the ripeness of the claim in light of its evaluation of the circumstances facing the claimant. Since the requirement of exhaustion is a substantive element of the delict rather than a prerequisite of the authority of the tribunal, a finding by an arbitral tribunal that there was an adequate exhaustion of remedies should be no more subject to review than any other factual determination.

Treaties which require an election of remedies, with the result that a claimant chooses an irreversible direction at a fork in the road, do not preclude claims of denial of justice before an international tribunal with respect to acts or omissions which were not encompassed in the petition made to an initially elected national forum. The most obvious instance would be an allegation of denial of justice in that very forum.

---

[81] *Certain Norwegian Loans*, 1957 *ICJ Reports*, 9, at p. 39.

# 6

# Denial of justice by outside interference

This chapter – and the next – describes a field which is anything but limited to a handful of precedents. Given the prodigious expansion of international commercial arbitration over the past half-century (the increase of trade being its fundamental cause, and the 1958 New York Convention on the Recognition and Enforcement of Foreign Arbitral Awards its primary instrument) modern practitioners may be excused for believing that we are living in an unprecedented golden age of international arbitration. They would be surprised to learn how vast international arbitral jurisprudence was in the nineteenth century. In the period between 1814 and 1898, for example, one study enumerated no less than 158 different international tribunals, including the celebrated commissions created in 1853 between Britain and the US; in 1868 between Mexico and the US; and in 1880 between France and the US.[1] All of these bodies were created by treaty, some to resolve only one dispute, but others to deal with many cases over a period of years.

Denial of justice was a dominant theme in early international arbitrations. We have already examined the reason in Chapter 4. Denial of justice was the primordial private grievance to give rise to diplomatic protection. Indeed, claims whose true basis were quite different – such as expropriation or breach of contract – were frequently cast as denials of

[1] W. Evans Darby, *International Tribunals: A Collection of Various Schemes Which Have Been Propounded, and of Instances since 1815* (London: Peace Society, 1899), at pp. 285–304 (Darby titled this little annex: 'The Proved Practicability of International Arbitration'). The list did not include the commissions created under the famous Jay Treaty, UK/US, 8 *Stat.* 116, which was concluded in 1794 for the purpose, *inter alia*, of adjudicating claims of British creditors who were unsatisfied by their treatment at the hands of US courts, and vice versa.

justice on the conceptual basis that the initial wrong had not been repaired by the local judicial system. There is therefore a multitude of instances in which nineteenth and early twentieth-century international adjudicators applied the doctrine concretely.

By the time Freeman concluded the research for his monograph in 1938, many more international adjudicators had rendered international awards, including (to name only the most prominent ones) those of the British–US commission created in 1910; the several arbitral tribunals established by Germany and Austria-Hungary, on the one hand, and various allied powers, on the other; the Mixed Claims Commission created by treaty in 1921 between Germany and the US; the several commissions set up under seven treaties concluded by Mexico with the US, France, Germany and Britain between 1923 and 1928; and the US – Panama Commissions created by treaties in 1928 and 1932. Freeman's 'Table of Cases' (almost exclusively decisions of international tribunals or commissions) listed no less than 457 entries. Even so, his work was but a survey which, despite its immense value as such, gives only an imperfect picture of the wealth of underlying materials that comprises this jurisprudence.

Any scholar with access to these materials will quickly find that an in-depth examination of a single individual case – including not only the ultimate decision but often also three or even more lengthy individual opinions, memorials by the litigating states, and the record of the under-lying procedures alleged to have comprised the denial of justice – is often at least a full day's work. For a proper comprehension of these precedents, it is not sufficient to understand critical distinguishing facts. One must also examine how the claim and defences were pleaded, and, perhaps most crucially, be aware of specific limitations often included in the treaties that created the international bodies, both with respect to the types of liability that would in principle be justiciable and with respect to the kind of relief that could be awarded.

Claimants who say they are victims of denial of justice often have long stories to tell. It is in the nature of the thing; frustration born of repeatedly thwarted efforts is what creates the sense of injustice. Thus the patterns of behaviour said to comprise denial of justice are often kaleidoscopic. A legislated denial of justice is likely to be coupled with executive interfer-ence (or even be a manifestation thereof); breaches of due process may be just as logically categorised as instances of arbitrariness or gross incom-petence. The categories of Chapters 6 and 7 overlap to such a degree that they may seem artificial. Still, the approach of this monograph must be thematic. (The alternative would be a massive case digest.) Hence the reader will notice different aspects of the same case appearing in different sections, and on occasion may feel required to cross-refer with the assistance of the index to get a fuller picture.

It might appear logical to distinguish grievances relating to civil jurisdictions from complaints relating to the administration of penal law. It is true that some elements are unique to each category. There is also, however, substantial overlap between the two with respect to important elements of what international adjudicators have found to be at the core of due process. The least repetitive approach is therefore to proceed by themes, with indications where appropriate of those aspects which are peculiar to either civil or penal proceedings.

## Jurisprudence under human rights treaties

Our study is aided by the emergence of a new and formidable body of jurisprudence under human rights treaties. Foremost among these international instruments is the European Convention on Human Rights, Article 6(1) of which provides that:

In the determination of his civil rights and obligations or of any criminal charge against him, everyone is entitled to a fair and public hearing within a reasonable time by an independent and impartial tribunal established by law.

This fundamental provision has been and will in all certitude continue to be relied upon by numerous litigants before both international and national jurisdictions. The elements of Article 6(1) merit individual consideration:

 (i)   it applies to the whole legal process: the determination of civil as well as criminal cases;
 (ii)  a fair hearing means adequate notice and an adequate opportunity to examine and rebut evidence;
 (iii) a public hearing excludes secret special tribunals;
 (iv)  justice delayed may be justice denied;
 (v)   the independence of tribunals is vitiated if they are controlled or intimidated by the executive branch of government;
 (vi)  the impartiality of tribunals is vitiated if they are controlled or intimidated by powerful individuals or groups;
 (vii) the notion of tribunals established by law excludes extraconstitutional *ad hoc* jurisdictions or 'popular tribunals' set up by the executive branch or a mob.

These elements recur in other international texts, such as Article 14(1) of the (United Nations) International Covenant on Civil and Political Rights and Article 8 of the American Convention on Human Rights. They are recurrent features in the various instances of denial of justice considered in this chapter and in Chapter 7.

## Denial of access to justice

The right of access to courts is fundamental and uncontroversial; its refusal the most obvious form of denial of justice. Legal rights would be illusory if there were no entitlement to a procedural mechanism to give them effect. The notion of *free access to courts* was given the following elucidation in the *Ambatielos* arbitration:

the foreigner shall enjoy full freedom to appear before the courts for the protection or defence of his rights, whether as plaintiff or defendant; to bring any action provided or authorised by law; to deliver any pleading by way of defence, set off or counterclaim; to engage Counsel; to adduce evidence, whether documentary or oral or of any other kind; to apply for bail; to lodge appeals and, in short, to use the Courts fully and to avail himself of any procedural remedies or guarantees provided by the law of the land in order that justice may be administered on a footing of equality with nationals of the country.[2]

Although Article 6(1) of the European Convention of Human Rights did not in terms create a right of access in 1975, the European Court of Human Rights held, in *Golder* v. *UK*, that such a right was *inherent*: 'It would be inconceivable ... that [Art. 6(1)] should describe in detail the procedural guarantees afforded to parties in a pending lawsuit and should not first protect that which alone makes it in fact possible to benefit from such guarantees, that is, access to a court.'[3]

This holding was controversial. Counsel for the UK (Sir Francis Vallat) argued in his oral submissions that 'the Government of the United Kingdom had no idea when it was accepting Article 6 ... of the Convention that it was accepting an obligation to accord a right of access to the courts without qualification'.[4] This was an overstatement; the jurisprudence of the European Court since then, as we shall see, has been characterised precisely by the challenge of defining appropriate

[2] *Greece* v. *United Kingdom* award, 6 March 1956, 23 ILR 306, at p. 325.
[3] *Golder* v. *United Kingdom*, 21 February 1975, (1975) 1 EHRR 524, at para. 35.
[4] *Ibid.*, quoted in the separate opinion of Judge Sir Gerald Fitzmaurice, at para. 39, note 24.

qualifications. Still, given the importance of his contribution to our subject forty-three years earlier,[5] it is interesting to read Sir Gerald Fitzmaurice's lengthy dissenting opinion. He disagreed that prison authorities had prevented access to courts when they forbade a prisoner from consulting a solicitor with a possible view to instituting civil action against a guard who had accused him of participating in a disturbance.[6] But, he wrote, even if his view of the facts was wrong, as a matter of principle:

The conclusion I draw from the nature of the successive texts [of the draft Convention] ... is that the contracting States were content to rely de facto on the situation whereby, in practice, in all European countries a very wide measure of access to the courts was afforded; but without any definite intention on their part to convert this into, or commit themselves to the extent of, a binding international obligation on the matter ... This type of obligation cannot, for reasons already stated, be internationally acceptable unless it is defined and particularized, and its incidence and modalities specified. The Convention does not do this; and the Court, with good reason, does not compound the misconceptions of the Judgment by attempting a task that lies primarily within the competence of governments. As the Judgment itself in terms recognizes [in para. 39(2)]: 'It is not the function of the Court to elaborate a general theory of the limitations admissible in the case of convicted prisoners, nor even to rule in abstracto on the compatibility of ... the [United Kingdom] Prison Rules ... with the Convention'. But if it is not the function of the Court to elaborate restrictions on the right, then a fortiori can it not be its function to postulate the right itself which is one that cannot operate in practice without the very restrictions the Court declines to elaborate.[7]

In antiquity the protection of the law could lawfully be openly withheld from foreigners. In modern international life, even the least sympathetic government understands the benefit of being seen as attached to the rule of law, and therefore tends to give the foreigner his day in court. What better illustration than the Stalinist show trials of the value ascribed, in terms of propaganda, to a semblance of respect for the forms of a legal process? (See the section on 'Pretence of form' in Chapter 7.)

---

[5] Fitzmaurice.

[6] The Prison Rules 1964, a statutory instrument, permit a prisoner in an English prison to consult a legal adviser in connection with matters that do not concern an ongoing litigation to which the prisoner is a party only with the leave of the Home Secretary. Golder applied for such leave in order to consult a solicitor about the possibility of bringing a libel claim against a prison guard who had made a statement, following a prison riot, implicating Golder as a participant in the disturbance. The Home Secretary denied Golder's application, and Golder submitted a complaint to the European Commission of Human Rights.

[7] *Golder* v. *United Kingdom*, 21 February 1975, (1975) 1 EHRR 524, separate opinion of Fitzmaurice, at para. 46.

Today, a claim is therefore unlikely to be based on the absolute refusal of access to justice, but rather the refusal of access under reasonable conditions.

Article 6(3)(b) of the European Convention provides specifically with respect to criminal trials that the accused must be afforded 'adequate time and facilities for the preparation of his defence'. The European Court held that Greece breached this principle in a case where an air force captain was convicted of disclosing military secrets.[8] He was first sentenced by the Permanent Air Force Court to two-and-a-half years' imprisonment. He petitioned the Courts-Martial Appeal Court, which appointed two experts to consider the significance of the technical data on guided missiles which the defendant had communicated to a private enterprise. The defendant was also allowed to appoint experts. Four days of hearings were conducted; nineteen witnesses were heard. The appellate judgment maintained the conviction, but reduced the sentence to a suspended term of five months on the grounds that the disclosed secrets had been trivial.

The problem for the European Court related to the handling of the final appeal to the Court of Cassation (*Areios Pagos*). Under the Military Criminal Code, such an appeal had to be lodged within a period of only five days. Although the appellate judgment was read out in the defendant's presence, it did not contain the Appeal Court's answers to six detailed questions deemed to be decisive on the issue of guilt. Accordingly the defendant was in a position to only file a one-page petition to the *Areios Pagos*, perforce expressed in general terms. The six answers of the Appeal Court were communicated to him forty-eight days after the judgment. At that point in time, his ability to expand the petition was severely circumscribed.[9]

In these circumstances, the European Court, while noting the 'considerable freedom' enjoyed by states in 'the choice of appropriate means' to satisfy Article 6 of the Convention, affirmed that national courts must nevertheless:

indicate with sufficient clarity the grounds on which they based their decision. It is this, inter alia, which makes it possible for the accused to exercise usefully the rights of appeal available to him.[10]

---

[8] *Hadjianastassiou* v. *Greece*, 16 December 1992, (1993) 16 EHRR 219.

[9] '[A]dditional submissions may be taken into account only if the initial appeal sets out at least one ground which is found to be admissible and sufficiently substantiated.' *Ibid.* at para. 36.

[10] *Ibid.* at para. 33.

In the premises:

> the rights of the defence were subject to such restrictions that the applicant did not have the benefit of a fair trial.[11]

Government officials have found a number of indirect ways to frustrate access to justice. Their effect is a denial of justice. In his important study in 1935, Judge de Visscher reasoned that that access to court was denied *de facto* whenever a legal system imposed 'abusive formalities or conditions, such as the requirement of a manifestly exaggerated bond'.[12] In the *Ballistini* case, local officials ignored requests to deliver copies of documents which were formally necessary for him to bring an action.[13] Venezuela once promulgated a decree (in 1873) to the effect that any plaintiff 'exaggerating' the amount of his injury may be fined or imprisoned.[14] In modern times, government officials faced with vast foreign debts have taken measures destroying the profitability of investments and then threatened further sanctions if the investors sought international remedies. Granting an amnesty to parties who have committed torts or contractual breaches may obviously have the effect of operating as an obstacle to judicial relief. Freeman describes such examples, and the consensus in the course of the Conference on the Codification of International Law in 1930 that such amnesties may constitute denial of justice.[15]

The case of *Philis* v. *Greece*[16] before the European Court of Human Rights involved a less obvious hindrance. It concerned a national decree under which engineers could not directly institute court actions to claim for fees, but had to request that the Technical Chamber of Greece do so on their behalf. The government stated that the purpose was to protect engineers from pressure to accept excessive reductions of fees from powerful employers, and thus to secure the rights of engineers to a 'compulsory minimum scale of fees'. The system also allowed the Chamber to secure payment of a compulsory insurance contribution. Philis did not approve of the way his claims were presented by the Chamber, which used counsel of its, not his, choice. He sought to initiate

---

[11] *Ibid.* at para. 37.    [12] De Visscher at p. 395.

[13] J. H. Ralston, *Venezuelan Arbitrations of 1903* (Washington, DC: US Government Printing Office, 1904), at p. 503. A similar incident was part of the epic *Fabiani* case, Moore, *Arbitrations* at p. 4878, at 4903.

[14] Freeman at p. 232. An extreme form of obstacle was illustrated by the *Caccavilli* case, where the President of Santo Domingo (General Heureaux) had orchestrated a condemnation of Caccavilli in order to dispossess him. Caccavilli appealed, and was assassinated on the way to the hearing. Freeman at p. 231, note 4.

[15] *Ibid.* at p. 232.    [16] 27 August 1991, (1991) 13 EHRR 741.

an action directly. The Athens Court of Appeal ruled that he lacked requisite capacity. He then came to the European Court, alleging that he had been deprived of his right of access to a court. His complaint was upheld. The Court recognised that the right of access to courts is not absolute, but affirmed – in one of many iterations of this expression – that limitations on such access must not be so great 'that the very essence of the right is impaired'. By that test, there had been a violation since Philis 'was not able to institute proceedings, directly and independently'.[17]

Judge Pettiti, the lone dissenter of the nine judges, reasoned that if the Chamber refused to bring proceedings, or did so incompetently, the plaintiff could sue the Chamber for its inaction or negligence; therefore there was not a definitive impairment of the right of action. This conclusion is unappealing. Philis was interested in suing his debtor, not in initiating a conflict with his own professional association. And the notion of a right to complain about negligent prosecution of his claim seems unrealistic. A litigant is not content with a level of representation which escapes censure as negligent; he seeks total commitment, not adequacy.

In sum, the UK's pleadings in the *Golder* case were wrong in apprehending that the European Court would recognise 'a right of access to the courts without qualification'. Limitations are accepted when they are motivated by a legitimate purpose, when the means are proportional to that objective, and when 'the very essence' of the right is not impaired. The perception of international adjudicators as to what constitutes *essence* and *impairment* cannot be encapsulated in an *a priori* definition. The *Philis* case suggests that the right of access to justice, beyond the right to a fair trial before a lawful tribunal, also includes the liberty to decide whether, when and how one pursues or protects one's legal rights.

## Absolute denial of access through state immunity

There is one area where states, by statute or judicial precedent, make no pretence of debating the need to establish reasonable *limitations* on access to courts. Rather, they make access flatly impossible.

Special governmental immunities from suit by definition exclude access to the courts in the determination of civil rights. This raises the spectre of denial of justice, just as it could defeat the objectives of human rights conventions. The European Court of Human Rights has confronted this problem in a number of cases. In *Fogarty* v. *United Kingdom*, the Court observed that:

[17] *Ibid.* at paras. 59 and 65.

it would not be consistent with the rule of law in a democratic society or with the basic principle underlying Article 6(1) [of the European Convention on Human Rights] – namely that civil claims must be capable of being submitted to a judge for adjudication – if, for example, a State could, without restraint or control by the Convention enforcement bodies, remove from the jurisdiction of the courts a whole range of civil claims or confer immunities from civil liability on large groups or categories of persons.[18]

*Fogarty* involved a claim by a former employee of the United States Embassy in London who considered she had been the victim of victimisation and discrimination under the UK Sex Discrimination Act 1975. The US invoked its immunity from civil proceedings under the UK State Immunity Act 1978. The plaintiff was advised that this assertion of immunity was irresistible; there was no means by which a court or tribunal in the UK could entertain her grievance. She therefore brought action against the UK before the European Court.

The European Convention does not require that the 'civil rights and obligations' which must be determined by a fair trial have a particular substantive content beyond those explicitly set forth in the treaty itself. The contrary would, to say the least, have made its signature a political unlikelihood. The European Court has established a procedural/substantive distinction as a tool to understanding that its role is to protect the procedural entitlement to obtain a fair hearing of such substantive rights and obligations which may be alleged to exist under local law. As the Court said in *Fogarty*: 'Certainly the Convention enforcement bodies may not create by way of interpretation of Article 6(1) a substantive civil right which has no legal basis in the State concerned.'[19] The UK sought to argue that the applicant did not have a substantive right under domestic law due to the operation of State immunity. The Court rejected this argument; the rights claimed were explicitly recognised under the Sex Discrimination Act, and the Court was therefore 'satisfied that the grant of immunity is to be seen not as qualifying a substantive right but as a procedural bar'.[20]

---

[18] *Fogarty* v. *United Kingdom*, 21 November 2001, (2002) 34 EHRR 12, at para. 25, citing *Fayed* v. *United Kingdom*, 21 September 1994, (1994) 18 EHRR 393, at para. 65.

[19] *Fogarty* v. *United Kingdom*, 21 November 2001, (2002) 34 EHRR 12, at para. 25.

[20] *Ibid.* at para. 26. One must therefore question the arbitral tribunal's dictum in the case of *Mondev* (discussed below in this section) to the effect that the Boston Redevelopment Authority's entitlement to statutory immunity under the law of Massachusetts 'arguably' was a matter of 'substance rather than procedure in terms of the distinction under Article 6(1) of the European Convention'. *Mondev* at para. 144. The counter is obviously that the tort of international interference in contractual relations is established in Massachusetts law, and the issue is whether immunity was a procedural bar.

Nevertheless, the Court held by sixteen votes to one that there had been no violation of Article 6(1) of the European Convention. It noted that the right of access to court is not absolute, but may be limited in a manner left to 'a certain margin of appreciation' as long as:

- the 'very essence' of the right is not impaired;
- the limitation pursues 'a legitimate aim';[21]
- there is a 'reasonable relationship of proportionality between the means employed and the aim sought to be achieved'.

The Court had no difficulty in accepting that the grant of sovereign immunity pursues a legitimate aim: 'complying with international law to promote comity and good relations between States'.

As for proportionality, measures which 'reflect generally recognised rules of public international law on State immunity cannot be regarded as imposing a disproportionate restriction on the right of access to court'.

*Fogarty* should be compared with another judgment rendered the same day. In *McElhinney* v. *Ireland*, the applicant seized the Irish courts to seek damages against the UK Secretary of Defence for personal injury caused by the alleged tort of a British soldier. The Irish Supreme Court held that the case could not proceed by reason of the defendant's sovereign immunity; the acts complained of related to an incident at a military checkpoint and therefore must be regarded as *jus imperii*. McElhinney then seized the European Court of Human Rights, claiming that his right to a trial had been impaired. Ireland answered that the European Convention should be interpreted in the light of public international law, which had long been understood as requiring sovereign immunity with respect to governmental acts of foreign states: 'The limitation on the applicant's right of access to court had a legitimate objective, namely compliance with generally recognised principles of international law and the promotion of harmonious relations, mutual respect and understanding between nations.'[22]

The applicant countered that: (i) modern international law has evolved to permit actions for personal injuries caused or occurring in the territory of the forum state; (ii) the limitation could not be said to pursue a 'legitimate aim' in the absence of evidence that relations between the

---

[21] In *Ashingdane* v. *United Kingdom*, 28 May 1985, (1985) 7 EHRR 528, at para. 57, the Court had already held, at para. 58, that the avoidance of the 'mischief . . . of [officials] being unfairly harassed by litigation' was a legitimate aim.

[22] *McElhinney* v. *Ireland*, 21 November 2001, (2001) 34 EHRR 322, at para. 28.

UK and Ireland would have deteriorated significantly if the action had been heard; and (iii) the limitation could not be deemed 'proportionate' as the UK State Immunity Act 1978 did not grant immunity to foreign governments for this type of action.

The European Court took this occasion to restate in a nutshell the principles of its jurisprudence in this regard:

> The right of access to court is not, however, absolute, but may be subject to limitations; these are permitted by implication since the right of access by its very nature calls for regulation by the State. In this respect, the Contracting States enjoy a certain margin of appreciation, although the final decision as to the observance of the Convention's requirements rests with the Court. It must be satisfied that the limitations applied do not restrict or reduce the access left to the individual in such a way or to such an extent that the very essence of the right is impaired. Furthermore, a limitation will not be compatible with Article [6(1)] if it does not pursue a legitimate aim and if there is no reasonable relationship of proportionality between the means employed and the aim sought to be achieved.[23]

In the light of these principles, the Court said with respect to the case before it that measures 'which reflect generally recognised rules of public international law on State immunity cannot be regarded as imposing a disproportionate restriction', and 'it is not possible, given the present state of development of international law, to conclude that Irish law conflicts with general principles'.

This judgment was rendered by a majority of twelve votes to five. Among the dissenters, Judge Rozakis stated that 'the balancing exercise of weighing the various interests involved' should have led to a different outcome given the trend toward limiting sovereign immunity. He referred to 'a rather weak invocation of a State's interest'. Three other dissenters referred to Article 12 of the International Law Commission's Draft Articles on Jurisdictional Immunities of States and Their Property, which would exclude sovereign immunity in the case of actions for compensation for personal injury caused in the forum state, and noted that this provision had not encountered 'significant challenges'. Judge Louraides added:

> In present democratic society an absolute immunity from judicial proceedings appears to be an anachronistic doctrine incompatible with the demands of justice and the rule of law ... It is correct that Article 6 may be subject to inherent limitations, but these limitations should not affect the core of the right.

---

[23] *Ibid.* at para. 34.

Procedural conditions such as time-limits, the need for leave to appeal etc. do not affect the substance of the right. But completely preventing somebody from having his case determined by a court, without any fault on his part and regardless of the nature of the case, contravenes, in my opinion, Article [6(1)] of the Convention.

In *Mondev*, a case which arose under the investment protection chapter of the North American Free Trade Agreement (NAFTA), the claimant argued that a Massachusetts state agency known as the Boston Redevelopment Authority (BRA) had committed the tort of intentional interference with contractual relations. (As described in the section on 'No responsibility for misapplication of national law' in Chapter 4, the claimant had sought to exercise an option, agreed with the City of Boston, to acquire rights to develop a site whose value had greatly appreciated.) Although a jury had upheld this claim, its verdict was set aside by the trial judge under the Massachusetts Tort Claims Act, which gives immunity for intentional torts to public employers which are not independent corporate entities. The judge's decision was affirmed on appeal by the Supreme Judicial Court of Massachusetts.

Mondev was a Canadian corporation and thus entitled to invoke NAFTA. It argued before the international tribunal that conferring such immunity was itself a failure to provide 'full protection and security' to its investment, in violation of Article 1105(1) of NAFTA. The United States answered that customary international law does not require statutory authorities to be generally liable for their torts. Therefore it could not be said that the immunity of the BRA infringed Article 1105(1).

This led to a detailed discussion of a number of novel considerations. The US argued that governmental immunity from tort actions has a long history as a matter of both federal and Massachusetts law. Although the general immunity was abrogated at the federal level in 1946 and in Massachusetts in 1978, various actions remained impossible – including precisely suits alleging interference with contractual rights. The US argued, moreover, that there are no legal systems where the liability of officials are identical to those of private parties; the US approach should not be viewed as exceptional in international terms.

Mondev countered that the conferral on a public entity of a 'blanket immunity' from suit for tortious interference violated the express duty under NAFTA to provide 'full protection and security'.

Responding to these arguments, the tribunal defined its starting position as follows:

circumstances can be envisaged where the conferral of a general immunity from suit for conduct of a public authority affecting a NAFTA investment could amount to a breach of Article 1105(1) of NAFTA. Indeed the United States implicitly accepted as much. It did not argue that public authorities could, for example, be given immunity in contract vis-à-vis NAFTA investors and investments.[24]

Moreover, the arbitrators stated that statutory immunity from tort actions could also violate Article 1105(1), for example if an investor whose on-site staff had been assaulted by the police 'could well claim that its investment was not accorded "treatment in accordance with international law including ... full protection and security"'.[25]

With respect to the specific tort of interference with contractual relations, however, the arbitrators reasoned that there may be sound reasons why a regulatory body should be protected against claims brought by private parties disgruntled by the grant or refusal of permissions which have an impact on commercial relations. Having to defend such actions might be deemed unacceptably distractive. This 'is a matter for the competent organs of the State to decide', and Mondev's claim therefore failed.

In its original Notice of Arbitration,[26] Mondev had cited a startling sentence from the judgment of the Massachusetts Supreme Judicial Court, which made no attempt to de-emphasise the effect of immunity: 'It is perfectly possible for a governmental entity to engage in dishonest or unscrupulous behaviour as it pursues its legislatively mandated ends.'[27] The proscription of 'unfair or deceptive practices in the conduct of any trade or commerce' was established by a Massachusetts statute. Prior case law under that statute held that it did not apply in terms to parties motivated by 'legislative mandate, not business or personal reasons'.[28] This led immediately to the provocative statement quoted above. Mondev pointed out that this was not a situation where the local law did not contain the substantive rule on which it had sought to rely (successfully so – with the jury). To the contrary, the wrong was clearly defined, but a mischievous separate law purported to insulate the wrongdoer. Referring to the offending sentence in the SJC's judgment, Mondev argued: 'Such a rule clearly violates contemporary

---

[24] *Mondev* at para. 151.   [25] *Ibid.* at para. 152.
[26] 1 September 1999, available at <http://www.international-economic-law.org/ Mondev/mondev.pdf> at para. 113.
[27] *Lafayette Place Associates* v. *Boston Redevelopment Authority & another*, 427 Mass. 509, at p. 535; 694 NE 2d 820, at p. 836 (1998).
[28] *Poznik* v. *Massachusetts Medical Professional Insurance Association*, 417 Mass. 48, at p. 52; 628 NE 2d 1 (1994).

international standards for foreign investor–host government commercial relations.'[29]

The US countered by quoting Freeman: 'The organization of ... courts, the procedure to be followed, *the kind of remedies instituted, the laws themselves,* are left to the State's own discretion.'[30] That surely did not take the matter very far. The quotation is not actually from Freeman, but, as he acknowledged, from the Memorial of the UK Government in the *Finnish Ships* case. Freeman immediately continued, in his own words, to make clear that 'this delegation is not complete' – and that is of course the whole debate. But that feature was in the first instance ignored by the US; its pleadings argued that: 'Mondev has made no attempt to prove that customary international law mandates that sovereigns adopt laws subjecting themselves to liability for intentional tort.'[31] This was an ambitious way to put the issue; one might well have asked, instead, whether customary international law allows sovereigns to adopt laws to insulate themselves from liability.

In the better-refined arguments of its Rejoinder,[32] the US noted that the international system generally operates on the basis that 'State municipal courts routinely dismiss proceedings in favour of a more convenient foreign forum, finding such a forum to be adequate even where the cause of action pleaded in the forum State does not exist in the foreign court or is materially different there.'[33] This observation misses the mark in that the law of Massachusetts had explicitly recognised the cause of action raised against the BRA. So the US defence ultimately depended on the proposition that deference must be given to different national solutions with respect to the amenability to suit of public bodies. As the European Court of Human Rights has said, it is 'no part of the Court's function to substitute for the assessment of the national authorities'[34] and access to

---

[29] Notice of Arbitration, 1 September 1999, available at <http://www.international-economic-law.org/Mondev/mondev.pdf> at para. 113.

[30] Freeman at p. 79 (emphasis added by the US).

[31] Counter-Memorial on Competence and Liability, 1 June 2001, available at <http://www.state.gov/documents/organization/14710.pdf> at p. 52.

[32] Rejoinder on Competence and Liability, 1 October 2001, available at <http://www.state.gov/documents/organization/14711.pdf>.

[33] *Ibid.* at p. 27, citing *DiRienzo* v. *Chodos*, 232 F.3d 49, 57 (2d Cir. 2000) ('The mere fact that the foreign and home fora have different laws does not ordinarily make the foreign forum inadequate'); as well as *La Société du Gaz de Paris* v. *Les Armateurs Français*, House of Lords, (1925) 23 Ll L Rep 209, at p. 210 (affirming decision of Scottish lower court granting motion for dismissal on *forum non conveniens* grounds despite possible unfavourable law in France).

[34] *Ashingdane* v. *United Kingdom*, 28 May 1985, (1985) 7 EHRR 528, at para. 57.

courts may 'vary in time and in place according to the needs and resources of the community and of individuals'.[35]

There are nevertheless difficulties in trying to square the result in *Mondev* with the conclusions of the important study authored by Judge de Visscher in 1935. Mondev involved a conflict between local policies concerning the efficiency of public administration (as enhanced by protection from distracting lawsuits) and the requirements of international law. The latter, in de Visscher's view, include the availability of at least one court to examine the merits of a claim. The general rule must be, he wrote, that a judgment declining jurisdiction is a denial of justice if there is no other avenue for complaint.[36] He cited an article by Professor Charles Durand to the effect that: 'One cannot be said to have had access to the courts if only to be told that one is not entitled to formulate a demand.'[37]

In a passage of obvious relevance to the particular circumstance of *Mondev* – as indeed to any other case of claimed immunity under local law – de Visscher wrote that the absence of any jurisdiction competent to hear a complaint for damages caused by prejudicial administrative acts would be internationally wrongful if this absence is due to 'a measure of discrimination against foreigners'.[38] Moreover, whenever the state has entered into a contractual relationship with an alien, it must 'place at his disposal internal legal means for ensuring its fulfilment'.[39] This particular point was at the heart of Judge Schwebel's analysis, half a century later, of 'denial of justice by governmental negation of arbitration'.[40] The fulfilment of an arbitration agreement, one hardly needs to say, is to participate loyally in the arbitration.

The principle of immunity collided with that of the right of access to justice in the case of *UNESCO* v. *Boulois*,[41] where the international organisation had concluded a contract containing an arbitration clause but later rejected the claimant's attempt to initiate proceedings under the

---

[35] *Golder* v. *United Kingdom*, 21 February 1975, (1975) 1 EHRR 524, at para. 38. To say that access may be *variable* should not, however, be taken as meaning that it is infinitely so. There must be limits to national discretion, lest the principle of international accountability wither away.

[36] De Visscher at p. 396.

[37] 'La responsabilité internationale des Etats pour déni de justice', 1931 *Revue générale de droit international public* 696, at p. 713, quoted at de Visscher at p. 396, note 4.

[38] *Ibid.* at p. 395.     [39] *Ibid.* at p. 396, note 1.

[40] Stephen M. Schwebel, *International Arbitration: Three Salient Problems* (Cambridge: Grotius, 1987), at pp. 108 and following.

[41] 19 June 1998, 1999 *Revue de l'arbitrage* 343.

clause on the grounds that there was no dispute as to performance. The claimant then requested the President of the *Tribunal de grande instance* to order that an arbitral tribunal be constituted. He so ordered, and UNESCO appealed to the Court of Appeal of Paris. UNESCO's petition was dismissed. To accept the claim of immunity, said the Court, would be to prevent the claimant from having his case heard. The arbitral tribunal, not UNESCO, had the authority to decide whether there was a bona fide dispute. To deprive the claimant of access to the agreed arbitral jurisdiction would be 'contrary to *ordre public* because it would be a denial of justice and a violation of the terms of Article 6(1) of the European Convention on Human Rights'.

The difficulty of this matter is to discern the line of demarcation between cases of 'acceptable' immunity, on the one hand, and, on the other, the *Ruden*[42] and *R. T. Johnson*[43] awards, where the Peruvian Government had forbidden that judgments be pronounced in actions against the treasury, resulting in refusal by the courts to assume jurisdiction. It is far more likely that a legislative attempt to avoid legal responsibility by creating immunity for public bodies will be characterised as denial of justice if the legislation is special rather than general, if it emerges after a conflict has arisen and seems calculated to have an effect on it, or if it is discriminatory in its effect. De Visscher saw the point quite clearly – as an exception to the 'general rule' he posited[44] – when he wrote that:

one cannot consider a denial of justice to inhere in the absence of judicial or administrative recourse against measures taken by superior authorities of the State, the legislature or the government to the extent that this absence results from the general legislation of the State and not from a measure of discrimination against aliens.[45]

Today, international legal developments have transformed the ability of states to circumscribe legal recourse by such 'general legislation'. Treaties, such as the European Convention and its Article 6(1), in effect mandate general rights of redress, although the debate as to the residual national right to restrict access in a proportionate manner and for a legitimate interest remains open, as *McElhinney* v. *Ireland*[46] illustrates.

---

[42] *US* v. *Peru*, Moore, *Arbitrations* at p. 1653.     [43] *US* v. *Peru*, *Ibid.* at p. 1656.
[44] A judgment declining jurisdiction is a denial of justice if there is no other avenue of complaint: de Visscher at p. 396.
[45] *Ibid.* at p. 395.     [46] 21 November 2001, (2001) 34 EHRR 322.

## Targeted legislation

It is not unknown for states to trash the law to defeat the claims of unpopular foreigners. Hot-headed politicians may seek public favour by advancing narrow conceptions of the national interest by law or decree. If local courts defer to such laws or decrees, they may incur the international responsibility of their state on account of gross incompetence in failing to recognise either fundamental strictures on the retroactive application of laws, or evident acquired rights. But a more straightforward analysis may lead to the conclusion that the legislature itself has interfered in the judicial process to such an extent as to create a denial of justice. Two famous examples will suffice. They both involved attempts to defeat contractual rights.[47]

A Presidential Order of Bangladesh purporting to extinguish the contractual obligations of a state company gave rise to an ICC arbitration and an award which found it 'painfully, clear ... that the Disputed Debts Order was made for the sole purpose of being injected as a spoliatory measure into the present arbitration'.[48]

A decree of the Portuguese Council of Ministers purporting to suspend contractual rights of cancellation in favour of a state-owned shipyard by extending a delivery date by two years was disregarded by an arbitral tribunal of the Netherlands Arbitration Institute as contrary to 'concepts

---

[47] Professor Robert Jennings (as he then was) noted in 1961 that while some authors among previous generations of scholars – Borchard (in 1919), Hyde (in 1945) and Jessup (in 1949) – had gone 'so far as to maintain that international law did not permit intervention founded only upon an alleged breach of a State contract', they nevertheless considered that 'an arbitrary or confiscatory amendment of a State contract is in itself a tort', 'State Contracts in International Law', (1961) 37 BYIL 156, at p. 159. In diplomatic correspondence in 1860, the US Government observed that when its nationals do business with citizens of a foreign country, or enter into private contracts abroad: 'it is not to be expected that either their own or the foreign Government is to be made a party to this business or these contracts, or will undertake to determine any disputes to which they may give rise. The case, however, is very much changed when no impartial tribunals can be said to exist in a foreign country, or when they have been arbitrarily controlled by the Government to the injury of our citizens. So, also, *the case is widely different when the foreign Government becomes itself a party to important contracts, and then not only fails to fulfill them, but capriciously annuls them*, to the great loss of those who have invested their time and labor and capital from a reliance upon its own good faith and justice.' (Letter of 3 May 1860 from Secretary of State Cass to Mr Dimitry, in F. Wharton (ed.), *A Digest of the International Law of the United States* (3 vols., 2nd edn, Washington, DC: US Government Printing Office, 1887), vol. II, at p. 615), emphasis added.)

[48] *Société des Grands Travaux de Marseille* v. *East Pakistan Development Corporation*, award, (1980) V *Yearbook Commercial Arbitration* 177 (Andrew Martin QC, sole arbitrator), at p. 181.

of public policy and morality common to all trading nations' notwith-standing that the contract was subject to Portuguese law.[49] The decree was couched in general terms; its benefit was conferred on any Portuguese company which had been 'declared to be in a critical economic condi-tion'; but it thus gave the government unfettered discretion to apply the decree to a single state enterprise facing a difficult litigation.

The victims of such manipulations are, of course, not only unpopular foreigners. In the exceptionally important case of *Stran Greek Refineries and Stratis Andreadis* v. *Greece*, an *ad hoc* tribunal had rendered a significant award against the state.[50] The headnote in the case report instantly encapsulates the point: 'Legislative annulment of arbitration award'.[51] This annulment took the form of a law enacted by Parliament affirming that contracts entered into in the period 1967–74 (when a military dictatorship ruled the country) were repealed – and that that effect extended to any arbitration clauses contained in them.[52] Accordingly any arbitral tribunals constituted under such contracts would 'no longer have jurisdiction', and their awards 'shall no longer be valid and enforce-able'.[53] It should be observed that the Greek Government had: (a) initially insisted on arbitration (obtaining rulings by the Athens Court of First Instance and the Athens Court of Appeal deferring to the arbitration clause in the relevant contract); (b) participated in the proceedings; and (c) subsequently lost its challenges to the award before the same two courts. The law was promulgated while the government's challenge to the award before the Court of Cassation was pending. The Court of

---

[49] *Settenave Estaleiros Navais de Setubal SARL* v. *Settebello Ltd* (McCrindle, Vischer, Brunner (presiding)), unpublished, described in W. Laurence Craig, William W. Park and Jan Paulsson, *International Chamber of Commerce Arbitration* (3rd edn, Dobbs Ferry, NY: Oceana, 2000), at p. 104, note 28; and in *Settebello Ltd* v. *Banco Totta and Acores*, Court of Appeal of England [1985] 1 WLR 1050.

[50] In the amounts of some US$16 million, some 116 million drachmas, and half a million French francs, all expressed as of 1978.

[51] *Stran Greek Refineries and Stratis Andreadis* v. *Greece*, 9 December 1994, (1995) 19 EHRR 293.

[52] The government later argued, before the European Court of Human Rights, that: 'The democratic legislature had been under a duty to eradicate from public life the residual traces of measures taken by the military regime. Mr Andreadis had been a giant of the economy and the scheme that he had envisaged had at the time been on a huge scale for a country the size of Greece. Moreover, the announcement of the scheme had led, before the fall of the military regime, to one of the largest anti-dictatorship demonstrations.' *Ibid.* at para. 45. This political argument was rejected by the Court in these terms: 'by rejoining the Council of Europe on 28 November 1974 and by ratifying the Convention, Greece undertook to respect the principle of the rule of law.' *Ibid.* at para. 46.

[53] Law No. 1701/1987, Official Gazette 25 May 1987.

Cassation then dismissed a challenge to the constitutionality of the law and declared the award to be void.

The European Court of Human Rights held that Greece 'infringed the applicants' rights under [Article 6(1)] by intervening in a manner which was decisive to ensure that the – imminent – outcome of proceedings in which it was a party was favourable to it'.[54]

## Repudiation by a state of an agreement to arbitrate

There is no longer a vast gulf between national and international standards with respect to the right to the fair administration of justice. Both national legislation and international law tend to seek to impose upon states the duty – *in principle*, the realist will add – to treat nationals as well as international law requires them to treat foreigners. Today, procedural rights under 'European law', that is to say the international law of treaties, are frequently invoked by Europeans when they appear before their home courts.

Thus, in principle, or as one might say with a pejorative connotation *in theory*, there is nothing to fear from national norms; they tend to conform to international standards. Yet experience has shown, time and time again, that it is crucial for the foreign victim of miscarriages of justice to achieve a neutral (i.e. international) adjudication of his grievance. Whatever the rosy rhetoric about the equality of treatment of nationals and foreigners, the very fact of being foreign creates an inequality. The foreigner's obvious handicap – his lack of citizenship – is usually compounded by vulnerabilities with respect to many types of influence: political, social, cultural.

How international law deals with the purported restriction of a foreigner's access to a previously accepted international forum is therefore a matter of paramount importance. We have already seen, in the immediately preceding section on 'Targeted legislation', how the European Court of Justice concluded that a Greek law designed to void the authority of an arbitral tribunal once it had rendered an award unfavourable to the government was a violation of the right to a fair trial, which it held to 'preclude any interference by the legislature with the administration of justice designed to influence the judicial determination of the dispute'.[55]

---

[54] *Stran Greek Refineries and Stratis Andreadis* v. *Greece* (1995) 19 EHRR 293, at para. 50.
[55] *Ibid.* at para. 49. Another notable feature of the case emerged by reason of the claim that Greece had violated not only Article 6(1) of the European Convention on Human

(The 'judicial' determination in question was whether the Greek Court of Cassation should annul the award.) That section also recalled the infamous *East Pakistan Development Corporation* and *Settebello* cases.

In the first Lauterpacht Lectures in 1983, Judge Stephen Schwebel devoted one of his three presentations to what he called 'Denial of Justice by Governmental Negation of Arbitration'.[56] This important contribution builds on valuable research, analysing a series of particularly significant cases from the first half of the twentieth century. Many of these cases may have faded from the consciousness of scholars, practitioners and adjudicators. *Schwebel's work brings them into current focus and is indispensable to any in-depth consideration of this subject.* Rather than to summarise a text that deserves a full reading, we will consider some subsequent precedents.

*Himpurna* v. *Indonesia*,[57] an arbitration under the UNCITRAL Rules, arose out of an alleged governmental guarantee of the performance of the national electricity company, PLN, under a power supply agreement. The government had confirmed its undertaking to arbitrate in formal Terms of Appointment executed at a time when PLN's liability had not been established – and pursuant to which the claimant agreed to postpone the arbitration against the government until and unless PLN was held

Rights (the right to a fair trial) but also Article 1 of Protocol No. 1, which declares every person's entitlement to 'the peaceful enjoyment of his possessions'. The Court agreed – unanimously – with the Applicants' thesis that as of the moment the offending law was voted by the Parliament, they had a 'right' in the sums awarded which should be equated to a 'possession' within the meaning of the just-quoted phrase. The implications of this holding will not escape students of investment treaties, which invariably protect property rights. Interference with arbitral awards is thus subject to censure on a foundation additional to the obvious duty to afford 'fair and equitable treatment'. (Given the fact that choses in action may be assigned for value, a case could be made for the proposition that the logic of *Stran Greek Refineries* would extend to pre-award interference with the arbitral process.)

56 This is the title of Part II of *International Arbitration: Three Salient Problems*. The origins of Judge Schwebel's contemplation of this topic may be traced to an article he co-authored with J. Gillis Wetter in 1966, 'Arbitration and the Exhaustion of Local Remedies', (1966) 60 AJIL 484; reprinted in Stephen M. Schwebel, *Justice in International Law: Selected Readings* 171 (Cambridge: Grotius, 1994), with a new postscript at 191. The thrust of the original article was put in a nutshell (with approval) by O'Connell: 'Where a State and an alien agree to arbitrate disputes relating to a contract in terms that indicate that it is to be the exclusive remedy ... no other local remedy may be exacted', D. P. O'Connell, *International Law* (2nd edn, London: Stevens & Sons, 1970), at p. 1059.

57 *Himpurna California Energy Ltd* v. *Indonesia*, interim award, 26 September 1999; final award, 16 October 1999, extracts in (2000) XXV *Yearbook Commercial Arbitration* 109 (de Fina, Abdurrasyid, Paulsson (presiding)). Two other awards, for all substantive purposes identical, were handed down the same days in the parallel case brought by Himpurna's sister company, Patuha Power Ltd.

liable for damages. After PLN had been held guilty of breach of contract[58] and had failed to pay the damages awarded, the government argued that the arbitral process should be suspended because of two procedural developments.

One of those developments came to attract considerable notice, but is not of direct relevance to the notion of denial of justice. It concerned the *de facto* withdrawal of the Indonesian arbitrator in the final stages of the arbitration. It transpired that representatives of the government physically prevented him from attending the final hearings and instructed him to cease communication with the other members of the arbitral tribunal. (The findings of fact of the remaining members of the tribunal in relation to this incident[59] were confirmed by the missing arbitrator, who at the time of the incident was Chairman of the Indonesian National Arbitration Association, and a former Deputy Attorney General of Indonesia, when his memoirs were published in 2003.[60]) Under the circumstances, the truncated tribunal, relying on international precedents to the effect that an unauthorised withdrawal of an arbitrator is unlawful and is not entitled to paralyse the original intent of parties having agreed to arbitration, proceeded to render a final award.[61]

Of greater present interest was an event which occurred prior to the interference with the arbitrator, namely the government's attempt to halt the arbitral proceedings by successfully applying for an injunction from the Indonesian courts. This injunction was obtained at the behest of Pertamina, the Indonesian national oil and gas company.

The question for the arbitral tribunal was whether it was bound to cease its work as a result of the injunction. It found that the initiative of the municipal court was attributable to the state. It also found, after a detailed review of the laws under which Pertamina existed and functioned, that the company was wholly subservient to the government. It noted that

---

[58] *Himpurna California Energy Ltd* v. *PT (Persero) Perusahaan Listruik Negara*, award, 4 May 1999, (2000) XXV *Yearbook Commercial Arbitration* 13 (de Fina, Setiawan SH, Paulsson (presiding)). Another award, for all substantive purposes identical, was handed down the same day in the parallel case brought by Patuha Power Ltd.

[59] (2000) XXV *Yearbook Commercial Arbitration* 154–166.

[60] The relevant chapter is published *in extenso* in 18(6) *Mealey's International Arbitration Report* 29 (H. Priyatna Abdurrasyid, 'They Said I was Going to be Kidnapped').

[61] See V. V. Veeder, 'The Natural Limits to the Truncated Tribunal: The German Case of the Soviet Eggs and the Dutch Abduction of the Indonesian Arbitrator', in R. Briner, L. Y. Fortier, K. P. Berger and J. Bredow (eds.), *Law of International Business and Dispute Settlement in the 21st Century – Liber Amicorum Karl-Heinz Böckstiegel* (Cologne: Bredow, 2001).

although the government alleged that it was obligated to yield to the injunction and not to participate in the arbitration, it had presented no evidence of any attempts on its part to convince the court not to issue the injunction. To the contrary, the government had explicitly reserved 'its right' to seek orders of contempt of court and the sequestration of the claimant's assets if the latter were to pursue the case.

The tribunal concluded that the government did not have a valid excuse for declining to participate further in the arbitral proceedings. It held that 'to prevent an arbitral tribunal from fulfilling its mandate in accordance with procedures formally agreed to by the Republic of Indonesia is a denial of justice', and that the government was in default under the Terms of Appointment. The tribunal accordingly proceeded to fulfil its mission even though the government declined to participate further. (Written memorials having been provided by both sides, the only remaining phase involved the hearing of witnesses. Without changing the legal place of arbitration, Jakarta, the tribunal summoned the parties to such a hearing at the Peace Palace in The Hague, using its authority under Article 16(2) of the applicable UNCITRAL Arbitration Rules, which provides that the arbitral tribunal 'may hear witnesses and hold meetings for consultation among its members at any place it deems appropriate, having regard to the circumstances of the arbitration'. The government sought to obtain an injunction from the District Court of The Hague. Its application was denied.[62] That set the stage for the incident at Schiphol Airport, where Indonesian officials intercepted the Indonesian arbitrator and prevailed upon him to return to Jakarta without communicating with the other arbitrators. In the event, the hearing was exceedingly brief, as the government did not appear to avail itself of the opportunity to question witnesses, and the claimant was content to let the written witness statements speak for themselves.)

For present purposes, the nub of *Himpurna v. Indonesia* may be found in the following holding: 'it is a denial of justice for the courts of a State to prevent a foreign party from pursuing its remedies before a forum *to the authority of which the State consented*, and on the availability of which the foreigner relied in making investments explicitly envisaged by that State'.[63]

---

[62] *Indonesia v. Himpurna California Energy Ltd, et al.*, Order of the President of the *Arrondissementsrechtbank* (Court of First Instance), The Hague, 21 September 1999, (2000) XXV *Yearbook Commercial Arbitration* 469.

[63] (2000) XXV *Yearbook Commercial Arbitration* 109, at pp. 182–183 (emphasis added).

Judge Schwebel commented as follows:

The holdings of these Tribunals that a State commits a denial of justice under international law when its courts lend themselves to interdiction and frustration of international arbitral processes are particularly significant. In classical international law, a State denies justice when its courts are closed to foreign nationals or render judgments against foreign nationals that are arbitrary. In modern international law, a State denies justice no less when it refuses or fails to arbitrate with a foreign national when it is legally bound to do so, or when it, whether by executive, legislative or judicial action, frustrates or endeavours to frustrate international arbitral processes in which it is bound to participate. These cases are of exceptional importance in recognizing and applying this cardinal principle.[64]

In the *Waste Management II* case described in the section on 'No responsibility for misapplication of national law' in Chapter 4, the claimant sought to extend this notion to the effect that a denial of justice arises where the government simply makes it burdensome (not impossible) to use the arbitral mechanism. The foreign investor's subsidiary had entered into a concession agreement with the City of Acapulco. The agreement called for arbitration under the Rules of Mexico's National Chamber of Commerce (CANACO). A claim was brought for non-payment by the City of fees owed on account of services rendered by the concessionaire. The City objected to the jurisdiction of the arbitral tribunal on the grounds that the concession agreement was necessarily subject to the jurisdiction of Mexican administrative courts. It also asked a Mexican court to halt the arbitration for the same reason. When CANACO asked for an advance payment from each party on account of the arbitrators' fees, the City refused to pay. The claimant thus faced the prospect of having to fund the arbitration alone. Given the position taken by the City, the claimant withdrew its case.

The City was clearly entitled to raise jurisdictional objections without being deemed to commit an international delict. Even if the objection had

---

[64] 'Injunction of Arbitral Proceeding and Truncation of the Tribunal', (2003) 18(4) *Mealey's International Arbitration Report* 33, at p. 38 (notes omitted). In *Bechtel Enterprises International (Bermuda) Ltd et al* v. *Overseas Private Investment Corporation*, award, 3 September 2003, (2004) 16 World Trade and Arbitration Materials 417 (Renfrew, Kay, Layton (presiding)), a tribunal operating under the Rules of the American Arbitration Association held that the Indian courts and various entities controlled by or representing the Indian Government had 'enjoined and otherwise taken away Claimants' international arbitration remedies . . . in violation of established principles of international law, in disregard of India's commitments under the UN Convention as well as the Indian Arbitration Act'. The Claimants were held entitled to recover under an insurance policy covering expropriation.

been absurd, the delict would have arisen only if the Mexican legal system had upheld it. To the contrary, CANACO rejected a preliminary jurisdictional argument by the City on the grounds that it was a matter for the arbitral tribunal. As for the court proceedings relating to arbitrability, they were never concluded. The international arbitral tribunal observed that Mexican jurisprudence suggested that the City's objection would fail. At any rate, it was sufficient that the investor had not demonstrated the contrary. It is thus only in connection with the issue of fees that *Waste Management II* is of particular interest in connection with claims of denial of justice by way of impeding recourse to arbitration.

The tribunal noted that the deposit sought was 'very large by local standards' (the equivalent of some US $500,000). On the other hand, 'the claim was large and threatened to be complex'. Although the international arbitrators would have deemed 'evidence of collusion between CANOCO and the City' to be 'very material', the evidence before the tribunal showed that CANOCO 'apparently behaved in a proper and impartial way'. The tribunal concluded that 'the discontinuance of the arbitration, a decision made by the Claimant on financial grounds, did not implicate the Respondent in any internationally wrongful act'.

This outcome was without doubt correct. Frustrating as it may seem to claimants, there is no absolute international duty to finance arbitral proceedings. True, under some rules of arbitration such participation is to be deemed a contractual undertaking, and there is support for the proposition that a non-payment in connection with arbitration under such rules entitles the moving party to relief by way of summary judgment.[65] Yet the amount requested by the tribunal or the arbitral institution may be the consequence of the articulation of what the respondent deems to be an abusive or tactically inflated claim. Nor is the rule universal; some rules of arbitration avoid this type of dispute-within-a-dispute by providing that the claimant must pay the entire advance. It cannot be posited that the refusal of a public respondent to contribute to the costs of arbitration immediately generates an international wrong imputable to the state.

Might it be said that the frustration of an agreed arbitral mechanism exposes the author of the mischief to the possibility that other legal systems will organise alternative arbitral proceedings in order to overcome the potential denial of justice? The question may seem far-fetched, and so it may be. Nevertheless that was the thrust of an unusual and

[65] See Georgios Petrochilos, *Procedural Law in International Arbitration* (Oxford University Press, 2004), at p. 126 and the sources cited there.

much-commented-upon judgment in 2001, *National Iranian Oil Company (NIOC)* v. *Israel*,[66] in which the Paris Court of Appeal appointed an arbitrator at the request of NIOC in order precisely to remedy a prospective denial of justice. The dispute had arisen from a contract entered into in 1968 for the construction of an oil pipeline. It contained an *ad hoc* arbitration clause calling for the nomination of one arbitrator by each party. In the event the two arbitrators so named failed to select the third member of the arbitral tribunal, the President of the International Chamber of Commerce was to make the appointment. There was no provision for an appointing authority in the event one of the parties failed to make its nomination. Nor was a seat of arbitration specified.

The dispute arose in 1994. Relations between Iran and Israel had profoundly deteriorated in the aftermath of the Iranian revolution of 1979. When NIOC sought to initiate arbitral proceedings, Israel failed to name an arbitrator. NIOC therefore asked the President of the *Tribunal de grande instance* of Paris to do so, as it was entitled to do under Article 1493 of the New Code of Civil Procedure in cases where France is the seat of the arbitration, or French procedural law is otherwise applicable.

The French judge rejected the application on jurisdictional grounds, noting that neither of those two requirements was fulfilled. In reaching his initial decision, he observed that Israeli law provides for judicial appointment of an arbitrator in the event of party default, and that therefore NIOC had not established a denial of justice. NIOC therefore explored the possibility of seizing the Israeli courts, only to be informed by its Israeli lawyers that any attempt on its behalf to initiate proceedings before an Israeli court would be rejected as a result of a prior judicial determination (in an unrelated case, but apparently having an effect equivalent to *stare decisis*) that Iran was an 'enemy state'. NIOC therefore returned before the Parisian judge.

Once again, he rejected NIOC's application. Denial of justice as an independent basis of jurisdiction of the courts of France, he reasoned, is not demonstrated unless the plaintiff proves – in addition to showing some connection between the dispute and France – that it is practically impossible for him to seize a foreign jurisdiction; the judge was not satisfied that it was impossible for NIOC to seek relief from either an Israeli court (since the prior judicial refusal to hear Iranian parties might be overturned) or an Iranian court.

[66] 2002 *Revue de l'arbitrage* 427; *aff'd Cour de cassation*, 1 February 2005, *Gazette du Palais*, 27–28 April 2005 at p. 34.

This decision was reversed on appeal. Two elements of this reversal raised the eyebrows of many scholars and practitioners. The first concerns the rule to the effect that there is no recourse against the decisions of judges who make orders when asked to do so in aid of arbitration; the Court of Appeal circumvented this restriction by declaring an exception if the lower court judge, as it found here, had exceeded his powers or violated a fundamental procedural norm. The other concerns the apparent lack of jurisdiction of the French courts, which the Court of Appeal overcame by creating, in effect, a third basis of jurisdiction under Article 1493, namely 'if a denial of justice abroad is established'. The Court added that 'the right for a party to an arbitration agreement to have its claims submitted to an arbitral tribunal is a rule of public policy'. Nevertheless, French judicial intervention could not occur unless it is 'justified by a link with France'. In the case at hand, it found that a sufficient link was extant because of the reference to the ICC, which notwithstanding its international functions and personnel is a French legal entity and has its headquarters in Paris.

Leaving aside jurisdictional issues, the Court's finding of a denial of justice may be defended as such, but hardly in its reasoning. It is not necessarily the case that a party to an arbitration agreement has 'a right to have its claims submitted to an arbitral tribunal'; the proposition may sound well-intentioned, but the expression of an intent to create an arbitral mechanism is not sufficient to overcome the failure to specify or refer to a reliable arbitral mechanism. One can only wonder what support the Court thought it had for such a wide-sweeping pronouncement.

The arbitration agreement may be defective; there may have been a precondition to arbitration which has not been met; or the claim may be unarbitrable according to some applicable law. A court's judgment that these, or other, grounds make it inappropriate to name an arbitrator is not readily to be equated to a denial of justice, nor should it readily be overturned by the courts of another country. The fact that a party is frustrated in its attempts to initiate arbitral proceedings is not, in and of itself, a denial of justice. Arbitral justice is not the only justice; a party which finds that its attempt to create an arbitral mechanism fails must also prove that it could not avail itself of such jurisdictions as are competent in the absence of a workable arbitration agreement. Such proof is not satisfied by speculation as to the inimical attitudes of the courts that might be seized (e.g. those of Israel), or as to the unlikelihood that they would be respected by the recalcitrant party (e.g. an assumption that Israel would not accept an Iranian judicial decision as legitimate).

The analysis is different when the dispute involves a state as a party, and that state refuses to give effect to its promise to arbitrate. The denial of justice in *NIOC* v. *Israel* did not require inaction of the Israeli courts; it was consummated when the government refused to name an arbitrator. This was a denial of justice not because all parties have a right to the implementation of their arbitration agreement, but because the government had made a promise to a foreign party that the justice it would vouchsafe was that of arbitration. The failure to respect this promise, as demonstrated above, is an international delict. Applying international law as a part of French law, the French courts (assuming once more that they had jurisdiction) would be entitled to find that there had been a denial of justice.

There was therefore a conceivably adequate basis for the Court of Appeal of Paris to reach the conclusion it did, but the same cannot be said for the remedy it ordered. For a court or tribunal to find that there has been a denial of justice is one thing; but quite another to proceed to administer justice in the place of the delinquent state. As will be seen in Chapter 8, the proper remedy lies in damages, and may involve an assessment of the merits of the dispute. In the annals of international law, *NIOC* v. *Israel* appears to be a unique case of judicial substitute performance, perhaps confirming the adage that hard cases make bad law.

## Governmental interference

Although the independence or otherwise of the courts is irrelevant for the purpose of attributing international responsibility for judicial acts or inaction to a state (see Chapter 3), it may be quite fundamental in terms of proving the grievance. Whenever aliens have a dispute with the executive, it is difficult to accept that the municipal courts may properly deal with the matter if they are not independent. Moreover, the requirement of exhausting local remedies would be pointless if the relevant institutions did not possess the autonomy necessary for impartial judgment.[67] In sum, the absence of an independent judiciary may be fatal to

---

[67] This requirement of independence encompasses not only the judiciary, but also other crucial institutions in the justice system, most notably lawyers and other advocates, as recognised by the United Nations. The UN has espoused not only the Basic Principles on the Independence of the Judiciary (adopted by the Seventh United Nations Congress on the Prevention of Crime and the Treatment of Offenders, UN Doc. A/CONF.121/22/Rev.1, at p. 59) calling on governments to guarantee the independence of the judiciary and enshrine it 'in the Constitution or the law of the country', but also the Basic Principles on the Role of Lawyers (adopted by the Eighth

the defence of a state against a claim of denial of justice in cases where executive governmental acts were under review.

There are two dominant precedents. The first is *Robert E. Brown*,[68] which has been sufficiently described in the section on 'Denial of justice by non-judicial authority' in Chapter 3. The second is *Idler*.

The full story of Jacob Idler's dealings with Simon Bolívar's armies would require not pages, but volumes. During four years, from 1817 to 1821, described in the award as 'the most uncertain perhaps in the long struggle of the Spanish – American provinces for liberty',[69] Idler and his associates shipped vast quantities of arms and army stores to Venezuela, where these supplies were used in the great liberation. In the end, a number of invoices and other charges, totalling nearly a quarter of a million dollars,[70] remained unpaid. It so remained for seventy years. The matter attracted the attention of the press and politicians. It was the object of repeated parliamentary debates in Washington as well as in Caracas. Lengthy intergovernmental negotiations continued until 1866, when a treaty was signed calling for international adjudication of the claim. But that experience was not a success. As Jackson Ralston was to write in 1929: 'The integrity of the conduct of the commission was attacked by Venezuela, and its career forms the blackest spot in the history of arbitrations.'[71] Another twenty years went by until a new commission was formed under a treaty signed in 1885, this time 'one of the ablest up to that time'.[72]

United Nations Congress on the Prevention of Crime and the Treatment of Offenders, UN Doc. A/CONF.144/28/Rev.1, at p. 118) that promulgate various guidelines for governments in order to ensure that lawyers are able to perform their functions as an element in the justice system effectively and appropriately.

[68] *US* v. *Great Britain*, 23 November 1923, VI RIAA 120.

[69] *Jacob Idler* v. *Venezuela*, Moore, *Arbitrations* at p. 3491, at 3493.

[70] Venezuela's annual revenue was estimated in 1885 as only five million dollars; Rice Report of the House Foreign Affairs Committee, cited in Moore, *Arbitrations* at pp. 1669–74.

[71] J. Ralston, *International Arbitration from Athens to Locarno* (Stanford University Press, 1929), at p. 221. It was not only Venezuela which complained about this commission, which comprised two nationals of Venezuela and one of the US and sat in Caracas, but also disappointed US claimants. The US Congress determined that there had been fraud in the appointment of the umpire, and that the US commissioner had extorted fees from successful claimants, H. R. Rep. No. 787, 44th Cong., 1st Sess. at VI (1875), referred to in W. Michael Reisman, *Nullity and Revision: The Review and Enforcement of International Judgments and Awards* (New Haven, CT: Yale University Press, 1971), at p. 495. Both the House and the Senate recommended that the US stop all payments to successful claimants and that a new commission be created.

[72] *Ibid.* This commission sat in Washington. The aggregate amount it awarded to the US claimants was lower than that of its predecessor.

But we must return in time. While Idler's programme of supplies was still under way, Venezuela united with New Granada to form the Republic of Colombia. The pre-existing debts of each component of the new state were acknowledged as a national debt by the Colombian Congress in 1821. Bolívar became president of the new Republic, which was divided into ten subentities; one of them was called the Department of Venezuela. Bolívar himself examined the Idler invoices in 1827 and decided that they should be paid from the general treasury in Bogotá. The matter was then complicated by a suit against Idler in Caracas brought by the treasurers of the Venezuelan Department on account of alleged failures to credit past payments. Nevertheless in late 1828 the Colombian secretary of the treasury wrote to Idler that 'His Excellency [Bolívar] has directed me to say that the government acknowledges the justness of your claim, but that the present circumstances of the treasury do not permit its payment. You are therefore to wait some time further in the assurance that soon you will be paid.'

The very next day Idler was ordered by the *intendente* of Caracas not to leave the jurisdiction until the suit against him had been resolved. On 1 January 1830, Venezuela reasserted its independence. The following week the treasury court in Caracas ordered that the Idler account be determined by an umpire, a certain G. B. Sprotto. The latter then issued an award in favour of Idler, albeit with a substantial deduction on account of past overpayments. Notwithstanding this award, the Caracas prefecture issued an order dated 31 August 1830 to the effect that Idler should provide a bond or other security for the 'balance now standing against him' (*sic*) and that thereafter a new calculation of his accounts would be undertaken.

Idler did not comply with this order, nor did the courts – at this stage – accommodate the executive branch. To the contrary, in August 1831 Sprotto's award was confirmed in court. That confirmation was disallowed on appeal; a certain José Cadenas was appointed as 'revising umpire' and rendered a lengthy award in September 1832. This decision was also in Idler's favour, although it further reduced his balance (but by less than $2,000). The court of first instance ordered that Cadenas' award be communicated to both parties. Each of them assented in writing to its entry. The court then declared that the government should pay its debt to Idler; this judgment was affirmed by the superior court. The treasury nevertheless refused to make payment, now raising the objection that only the Supreme Court of Justice had authority to deal with the matter. Idler then petitioned the Supreme Court which, in December 1832, after 'a review of the case from its inception', found against the government and declared that its judgment 'settles forever the matter'.

That turned out to be a hollow declaration. The council of government quickly took up the matter and resolved, notwithstanding the Supreme Court judgment, not to make payment until Idler had presented his case to unidentified 'plenipotentiaries' who 'are to be appointed' and who would *apportion the debt of Colombia*. Six weeks later, the Supreme Court sought to assert its authority and decreed that this resolution was entitled to no effect:

because otherwise the validity and strength given by law to the final decisions of the courts of justice of competent jurisdiction, upon full knowledge of the facts and the law of the case, and in faithful compliance with the precepts of law, would be weakened and destroyed.[73]

This assertion of authority did not secure the release of any funds from the executive branch, which simply disregarded the Supreme Court. By now Idler had been away from home for ten years; he decided to return to the US and to petition his own president.

In his absence, and without notice to him, the council of government prepared a 67-page analysis of the case which it submitted to the Supreme Court along with a motion that it annul its previous judgment. Two of the four judges excused themselves from hearing this application. They were replaced by appointees 'from the Caracas bar'. Idler received notice of this action by letter rogatory only twelve days before the expiration of the time limits for his appearance. He made no appearance; nor did he appoint counsel. The Supreme Court declared in 1837 that it was not competent to annul its previous affirmation of a lower-court judgment; the matter properly belonged to the inferior court. The matter was then taken up before the Superior Court of Caracas, with no notice to Idler. A new judgment was entered, purportedly 'restoring the whole subject to the condition in which it was' on the date of the order of 31 August 1830 – i.e. before the Cadenas award. The council of government quickly 'complied' with this decision and informed a commission sitting in Bogotá (charged with the task of adjusting the accounts between the separated countries) that 'nothing remained to Idler than to pay what he owed'.

This was far from the end of the story. 'Suffice it to say, almost every, if not every, administration from Jackson's to Grant's contributed to [the diplomatic history of the case] under the almost constant stress of urgency by the contractors or their descendants.'[74] But the facts already stated are sufficient for an understanding of the international award ultimately rendered pursuant to the US–Venezuela treaty of 1885.

The award is of a length that excludes full treatment in these pages. Its four key conclusions are:

(i) The composition of the Supreme Court when it dealt with the resubmitted case in Idler's absence was illicit.[75]

(ii) The purported defeasance of Idler's contractual rights was based on an extraordinary notion of ancient Spanish law to the effect that the sovereign could invoke an exceptional so-called mechanism of *restitutio in integrum*, by which individuals could avoid contractual undertakings entered into on their behalf when they were minors. The commission clearly considered it preposterous to attempt to extend this privilege to the Venezuelan Government.[76] It held that the alleged doctrine, said to operate so as to undo contracts and indeed judgments, could not be invoked against Idler.

(iii) The Superior Court of Caracas had had no jurisdiction. Jurisdiction would have existed in the case of an 'action upon the record', i.e. not an independent suit but a sequel to a case where Idler could still have been deemed an active party, but such an action was time-barred; nor could it have been deemed to have been commenced by the mistaken application to the Supreme Court.[77]

(iv) Venezuela had committed a denial of justice. The American Minister at Caracas was officially told in 1840 that the judicial proceedings had finally determined that the matter of Idler's claim should be treated as an 'administrative and economic question of the government' rather than a 'judicial proceeding'. Now, the government was 'disposed' to proceed to a new determination of accounts which Idler and his attorneys would be free to attend. The commission concluded: 'The government thus interpreted the judgments as taking the case out of the hands of the courts, to be proceeded with in a nonjudicial – *i.e.* 'administrative and economic' – manner before its own account-ing officers of the treasury, as it might be disposed to direct. That is, in effect, the government proposed to decide the Idler case itself.

---

[75] A key passage of the commission's reasoning is reproduced in the section on 'Manipulation of the composition of courts' in this chapter.

[76] A key passage of the commission's reasoning is reproduced in the section on 'Gross incompetence' in Chapter 7.

[77] A key passage of the commission's reasoning is reproduced in the section on 'Illegitimate assertion of jurisdiction' in Chapter 7.

*The litigation before the courts was put an end to,* and thereby the contracts, in so far as they remained unfulfilled (if there were any), were for all practical purposes annulled; for the government's action and reiterated opinion left no room for question what it would do. We have seen *restitutio* could not reach these contracts. It is believed it never contemplated such results as to judgments.

The supreme court for the case knew – must have known – that the order of August 31 was impossible of execution, and had been from the very day of its entry nearly ten years before. Its affirmance [*sic*] of the alleged superior court judgment annulling proceedings back to that order, leaving it to stand, could have had but one purpose – to switch the case from the lines of judicial determination; in short, to dismiss it. We have no hesitation in saying the *effect* of these judgments was a denial of justice.[78]

By any standards, the *Idler* case appears as a remarkable instance of governmental manipulation of the judicial branch. The commission noted that the government had communicated with the Supreme Court about the case before making its ultimate application for reversal.[79] The commission also stressed that the government had previously assented to the entry of an award rendered by a local court-appointed umpire, and then refused to pay it. In these circumstances:

the reorganization of the court so as to change its *personnel,* and the substitution of a temporary *fiscal* for the regular officer, for this one case, both, too, in violation of the Colombian statute extended still to Venezuela; the fact that this was the first and the last time the republic in its own behalf ever claimed a right to the ancient remedy, asserted in the right of succession from the Spanish King, when Spain had abolished it more than two hundred years before, except in a few cases among which the Idler case could not by possibility be classed; the final decree exactly in accordance with the prayer of the treasurers, in their report of May 2, 1829, and the wishes of the government; and the practical outcome, namely, *the ending of the litigation* and virtual extinction of the contracts so far as they were not yet satisfied; one considering these things can not, as seems to us, well escape the

---

[78] Moore, *Arbitrations,* at pp. 3516–3517 (emphasis in the original).

[79] In *The Orient (US* v. *Mexico),* the US–Mexican Commission, under the Convention of 11 April 1839, considered evidence that a government official had 'agreed' with a judge to confirm the validity of the confiscation of a vessel. The Commission observed: 'A judge who would thus, two weeks in advance of a trial and before the testimony was examined, pledge himself to make a particular decision, would not be likely to be very scrupulous in the examination of the evidence, and certainly could claim no very great degree of respect for his decision', Moore, *Arbitrations,* at p. 3231.

conviction that it was the voice of Idler's opponents which found expression in the judgments of 1838 and 1839, and not that either of justice or of the supreme court of justice.

A foreign citizen in litigation with a sovereign before his own courts is entitled to no special favors; but ... 'ordinary justice' is his right in the eye of the public law. This Idler did not get. The 'justice' attempted to be meted out to him, whatever else could be said of it, was certainly not *'ordinary* justice.'

Our conclusion is, from the foregoing considerations, that the proceedings *in restitutio* were, as against Idler, and are, as against the claimants, a nullity. This is the best we can say of them.[80]

## Manipulation of the composition of courts

One of the findings of the US–Venezuela commission in the *Idler* case, discussed in some detail in the preceding section on 'Governmental interference', was that when it rendered a judgment repudiating its own previous decisions in the matter, thus dramatically reversing the foreign claimant's fortunes, the Supreme Court was constituted illicitly. The commission reasoned as follows:

The difficulty is not that the court at Caracas was filled by members from the bar for this case, or that two judges made the appointments. But *that this was done without the authority of law.* If such a proceeding has a parallel in common-law jurisprudence it has escaped our notice. Venezuela could, of course, constitute her courts as she desired, but having established them, it was Idler's right, if his affairs were drawn in litigation there, to have them adjudicated by the *courts constituted under the forms of law.* There are instances where the action of tribunals presided over by *de facto* judges, acting under color of authority, has been upheld upon satisfactory grounds, but we think the doctrine would not apply in such a case as this. If the Colombian law of 1830 was in force when the court was organized for the Idler case, as seems to have been the fact, the judges were prohibited from exercising any *'other powers than those which are assigned to them,'* and as the power of appointment was not among those assigned *to the minority of the court,* the acts of the two judges in appointing the other two *ad hoc,* were not only not under color of law, but in violation of its express provisions. A body so constituted could not have legal validity. Its acts could not bind absent parties. They would be utterly void.[81]

No further comment seems necessary, except perhaps to observe that exceptional jurisdictions immediately puts international adjudicators on

[80] Moore, *Arbitrations,* at p. 3517 (emphasis in the original).
[81] *Ibid.* at pp. 3508–3509 (emphasis in the original).

their guard. *Ad hoc* reorganisation of the legal process cannot fail to raise the spectre of executive fiat.[82]

## Excessive public pressure

A theme recurrent in international awards relates to litigants' legitimate expectation that they be judged in an atmosphere of dispassionate serenity. In such circumstances, the issue is not so much a specific defect in the process as the failure to secure an environment within which neutral justice can be achieved.

In *Solomon*,[83] for instance, the claim was decided against Panama on the grounds that imprisonment of a US national had been 'sustained, not by the ordinary motive of punishing an offense, but by strong local sentiment'.[84] The dissenting commissioner observed that the influence attributed to 'strong popular feeling ... is a mere assumption and not a proved fact'.[85] *Proof* that general animosity towards a foreigner has in fact influenced the course of justice is indeed unlikely to be established as a fact. Such a conclusion is more likely to be derived from the combination of the existence of grounds for belief that there was prejudice and a demonstrably suspect administration of the case. The latter, absent any other explanation, leads the international adjudicator to the conclusion that the former is likely to have influenced the outcome. The *Solomon* case itself provides an illustration of this approach by inference.

Solomon had come to Panama with a detachment of the US Army which was sent to the Chiriqui province to supervise elections in 1918. Although the detachment stayed on to assist in maintaining public order, Solomon was honourably discharged and went to work for William Chase, who operated the San Juan ranch. It will be recalled that Chase unsuccessfully brought a claim of his own relating to the non-recognition by the Panamanian legal system of his title to that significant property.[86] The commission noted that the US Army detachment had the duty of

---

[82] In *Fabiani, ibid.* 4878, at p. 4882, the constitution of the State of Falcon-Zulia was altered at the instigation of Fabiani's local enemies so that a judge could be replaced by the Governor – who was the brother of Fabiani's arch-enemy's lawyer – from a list of 'advocates and citizens'. This was one of several elements which convinced the President of the Swiss Confederation, sitting as sole arbitrator, that multiple instances of denial of justice had been committed.
[83] *Abraham Solomon (US* v. *Panama)*, 29 June 1933, VI RIAA 370.   [84] *Ibid.* at p. 373.
[85] *Ibid.* at p. 375.
[86] See the section on 'Denial of justice by non-judicial authority' in Chapter 3.

assisting local police in arresting offenders against US nationals residing in Chiriqui, and that 'their presence was extremely distasteful both to the public and to the authorities in Panama'. Moreover, the public perception was that the real purpose of the US soldiers' presence was 'to protect Chase in his alleged wrongful possession of San Juan'. Solomon's association with the soldiers was 'a ground for local enmity'; his employment by Chase 'accentuate[d his] unpopularity'.

The events that gave rise to Solomon's imprisonment were the following. Solomon apprehended a trespassing poacher named Villamonte, and turned him over to a US soldier. They both testified that their intention was to turn him over to the police in a town twelve hours' journey away. While preparing for the trip, the US soldier locked up Villamonte, who escaped before the expedition could head out.

It appears that some Panamanian officials became extraordinarily determined to seize upon this incident to put Solomon away. An initial complaint was made to the local mayor, who conducted an investigation but found that there were no grounds for complaint. (Article 1575 of the Panamanian Administrative Code allowed private persons to apprehend trespassers under certain conditions.) The mayor was quickly replaced; the new appointee instituted proceedings. A municipal judge was commissioned to conduct another investigation into a charge that Solomon had wounded Villamonte; his conclusion was that there was no evidence to that effect. Many months later, another judge nevertheless ordered Solomon arrested for wounding and imprisoning Villamonte. Solomon was ultimately incarcerated for one year on the sole charge of having imprisoned Villamonte. The US Agent observed that although Solomon's condemnation had been secured principally on the testimony of Villamonte, the trial court subsequently ordered the latter's prosecution for perjury on account of his statements in the proceedings.

The Commission stated that in its opinion 'there was no justification for convicting Solomon for the particular offense of which he was found guilty'. It noted that even if Article 1575 of the Administrative Code did not avail Solomon, the penalty under Article 491 of the Penal Code for wrongfully apprehending a person for the purpose of turning him over to the authorities was a fine, not imprisonment. The courts had found Solomon guilty of violating Article 488, dealing with criminal sequestration. The uncontradicted evidence was that Villamonte had been locked up by the US soldier, not Solomon: 'there was no evidence in the record to sustain a finding that Solomon did not intend to turn Villamonte over to the police'.

Under these circumstances, the Commission found Solomon's conviction and imprisonment to have been 'a palpable injustice'. The concluding two paragraphs of the decision focused on the impact of local sentiment rather than on a lack of proper legal foundation for the conviction:

> The fact that four separate investigations were instituted against Solomon, the fact that the charge was changed to illegal imprisonment after an earlier charge of wounding had been dropped for lack of evidence, and that the case was revived after being moribund for months, the unexplained change of trial judges during the final proceedings, the fact that the Fiscal in his address to the lower court denounced the [American] soldiers, [whose presence was distasteful to Panaman citizens] emphasized Solomon's connection with them, and quite improperly went out of his way to excite hostility to Solomon by reciting a story about him which had no relation to any evidence in the record, all taken together lend credence to the theory that the proceeding was sustained, not by the ordinary motive of punishing an offense, but by strong local sentiment. The Commission cannot avoid the conclusion, arising largely out of Panama's own evidence and contentions, that the claimant's conviction was unconsciously influenced by strong popular feeling. So to hold is not to cast any personal aspersions on the judges involved. The unavoidable susceptibility of local judges to local sentiment is a matter of common knowledge. One of the primary purposes of international arbitration is to avoid just such susceptibility, and to remedy its consequences.[87]

The standard commentary on the work of the US–Panama Claims Arbitrations is worth quoting with respect to *Solomon*:

> The circumstances of this case, as shown by the evidence and as defined by the International Tribunal, exemplify clearly the fact that unless international justice is to be frustrated by sentimental considerations, the review of the decisions of courts of last resort is a necessity, although perhaps, on occasion, a disagreeable necessity. National sentiment naturally revolts at the thought of submitting the judgment of a supreme tribunal to the scrutiny of international inquiry under a charge of being a perversion of justice ... The history of international arbitration demonstrates clearly, however, that 'local sentiment, prejudice, and pressure' occasionally, though perhaps unconsciously, outweigh the normal and predominating instinct of worthy men to do justice at all times, even as judges of their fellow men ... To maintain that cases in which there may possibly have been such failure of justice shall not be submitted to the scrutiny of an impartial, international tribunal is, of course, to sacrifice the cause of international justice

---

[87] *Abraham Solomon (US v. Panama)*, 29 June 1933, VI RIAA 370, at p. 373.

on the altar of local pride and sentiment ... When it shall have become universally recognized, as it virtually is at present, that the judgments of supreme municipal courts with respect to the rights of foreigners are properly subject to review by international tribunals, the occasions for such review will naturally decrease.[88]

With respect to the final paragraph of the award, the reporter observed that:

denials of justice, recognizable by international tribunals, must not, of necessity, proceed from judgments contaminated or influenced by improper motives of the local judge, as has so frequently and unwisely been stated or implied by authorities in the past. Such decisions as this, which assists in making clear that denial of justice, as understood in international law, may proceed from the innocent or unconscious weaknesses of human nature, or from unique and uncontrollable circumstances, as well as from such human weaknesses as make for the conscious and purposeful corruption or perversion of justice, are valuable contributions in the sane development of international law.[89]

Freeman cited *Solomon* as an example of an exception to the general rule against the international reversal of national applications of national law, i.e. as an instance of substantive denial of justice. For reasons stated in the section on 'Judgments involving a breach of national law' in Chapter 4, it is rather an illustration of why there is no exception; the Commissioners did not presume to correct the Panamanian judiciary's conception of the crime of false imprisonment, but rather held that Panama had failed to ensure circumstances under which Solomon could be fairly tried. This is *procedural* denial of justice.

Freeman wrote that he was 'frankly troubled' by the difficulty of reconciling the notion that misapplication of municipal law is not sufficient to constitute a denial of justice with the outcome in *Solomon* (with which he was yet broadly in agreement). The impossible task of applying a 'manifest injustice' standard disappears if one simply drops the insistence on finding exceptions to the rule, and rather concentrate on whether the evidence is sufficient to conclude that there was procedural denial of justice.

---

[88] Bert L. Hunt, *American and Panamanian General Claims Arbitration under the Conventions between the United States and Panama of July 28, 1926, and December 17, 1932*, US Department of State Arbitration Series, No. 6 (Washington, DC, 1934), at pp. 488–489.
[89] *Ibid.* at p. 490.

## Failure to execute judgments

Governments are not obliged to satisfy judgments in favour of foreigners against parties who might be insolvent, or who find ways to evade payment. But they are held to the duty of providing officials who with reasonable diligence and without discrimination put the *imperium* of the law at the service of foreign judgment creditors. In the *Fabiani* case, the President of Swiss Confederation, sitting as sole arbitrator, noted that the Government of Venezuela had a constitutional duty to *'assurer l'administration de la justice'*.[90] Not only did the government not do so, but the President of the Republic (Guzman Blanco) subverted the very purpose of the arbitral award which Fabiani was seeking to enforce against a dishonest local ex-partner by approving the fraudulent assignment of a railroad contract. Other valuable maritime transport contracts were accorded to an accomplice of Fabiani's adversary, with the effect of insulating the assets of the award debtor.[91] Finding denial of justice in the non-execution by the Venezuelan court of an arbitral award rendered in France between private French and Venezuelan businesses, the arbitrator included in the delict such executive acts and omissions as bore 'so immediately or approximately upon the execution of said award as to have an appreciable effect thereon'.[92]

Denial of justice thus includes the failure to execute a final judgment.[93] The judgment of the European Court of Human Rights in *Timofeyev v. Russia* contains a remarkable factual description of the practical difficulties faced by the applicant when he sought to enforce his judgment against the state before national courts: the obscurity of the judgment in identifying the payor within the state administration, unlawful inaction by the bailiff, meretricious interventions by authorities claiming powers of supervisory review, and, in the end, the silent refusal to respond at all. The unanimous judgment held that 'the applicant should not pay the price of

---

[90] *Antoine Fabiani (no. 1) (France v. Venezuela)*, Moore, *Arbitrations*, 4878, at p. 4900.

[91] *Ibid.* at pp. 4883 and 4888.

[92] *Ibid.* at p. 4878. This was the award at the centre of yet a further case, when the unrelenting claimant (by his government) sought to claim further damages from the French–Venezuelan Commission, contending unsuccessfully that the Swiss award had not disposed of all claims he was entitled to have heard under a protocol between the two states; *Antoine Fabiani (no. 2) (France v. Venezuela)*, 31 July 1905, X RIAA 83.

[93] L. A. Podesta Costa and José Maria Ruda (eds.), *Derecho internacional público* (2 vols., Buenos Aires: TEA, 1984), vol. II, at p. 214; *accord* A. O. Adede, 'A Fresh Look at the Meaning of the Doctrine of Denial of Justice under International Law', 1976 *Canadian Yearbook of International Law* 86.

these omissions of the State' and that it was 'unacceptable that a judgment debt is not honoured for such a long period of time'. In a key passage, the judges held that the 'right to a court' enshrined in Article 6(1) of the European Convention on Human Rights:

would be illusory if a Contracting State's domestic legal system allowed a final, binding judicial decision to remain inoperative to the detriment of one party. It would be inconceivable that Article [6(1)] should describe in detail procedural guarantees afforded to litigants – proceedings that are fair, public and expeditious – without protecting the implementation of judicial decisions; to construe Article 6 as being concerned exclusively with access to a court and the conduct of proceedings would be likely to lead to situations incompatible with the principle of the rule of law which the Contracting States undertook to respect when they ratified the Convention. Execution of a judgment given by any court must therefore be regarded as an integral part of the 'trial' for the purposes of Article 6.[94]

This proposition has an established tradition in the customary international law of denial of justice, as seen in the *Fabiani* case. It is essential that the duty is understood as extending beyond the formal judicial order of execution; that may be only the beginning of the judgment creditor's travails.

A brilliant illustration is the *Montano* case, a grievance presented to the US–Peruvian Claims Commission constituted under a treaty of 1863 which resulted in a remarkable success for the Peruvian claimant (Esteban Montano).[95] He was the owner of a vessel which in 1851 sank in the Bay of San Francisco due to pilot error. Successfully pursuing the pilots' association, which enjoyed a monopoly granted by the state of California, he was awarded the then considerable amount of US$24,151 by a US federal district court. He entrusted the judgment to a federal marshal, who proved ineffectual in securing enforcement. The marshal declined to make levy on a pilot boat which, as the award put it, 'was known as the property of the licensed pilots' association'. The marshal apparently relied on a statement by a third party claiming to have purchased the boat. He therefore demanded a bond of indemnity, which Montano did not give. Moreover, the marshal did not seek to levy on the surety which the association was legally bound to maintain in return for its monopoly, apparently on the lame excuse that someone had

---

[94] *Timofeyev* v. *Russia*, 23 October 2003, [2003] ECHR 546, at para. 40.
[95] *Peru* v. *US*, Moore, *Arbitrations*, at p. 1630. The case is also sometimes referred to as *The Eliza*.

told him that such an effort would be pointless because the association had not in fact complied with its duty to furnish the sureties.

The US Attorney General contested the claim, arguing that there were two classes of 'officers of the law', namely those who represented the proprietary interests of the government, and those who 'were the agents of society itself, and were appointed only by the government in its capacity of *parens patriae*'. The latter could be prosecuted for malfeasance, but did not attract governmental liability.

The Umpire (General Herran) firmly rejected the US Government's arguments. The marshal, he wrote,

neglected the means at his disposal . . . The sentence of the court was not made effective through the fault of the public officer who was under obligation to execute it.[96]

The Umpire concluded that the US Government had been guilty of a denial of justice and ordered it to pay to Montano the amount of his judgment, plus eight years' interest from the date of the failure of enforcement. (The award was expressed 'in the current money of the U.S.'. The US Government chose to pay him in currency worth only about $15,000 in gold. Montano protested, and thereafter successfully prosecuted a second claim before the subsequent Peruvian Claims Commission, established by a treaty of 1868.)

## Inadequate measures against perpetrators of crimes against foreigners

States have an international obligation, recognised by impressive historical authority,[97] to take adequate steps to apprehend and punish

---

[96] *Ibid.* at p. 1635. See also *De Sabla*, where parcels of the claimant's land had been adjudicated to various individuals with the alleged justification that the public administrator was bound to make such adjudications in favour of unopposed applicants for the land. The Commission determined that 'the machinery of opposition, as actually administered, did not constitute an adequate remedy to the claimant for the protection of her property'. *De Sabla* (*US v. Panama*), 29 June 1933, VI RIAA 358, at p. 363.

[97] See the lengthy footnote in Freeman at p. 369. A typical statement appears as follows in the *Janes* case (*US v. Mexico*), Claims Commission, United States and Mexico, Opinions of Commissioners, Washington 1927, 108, at para. 19: 'non punishment must be deemed to disclose some kind of approval of what has occurred, especially so if the Government has permitted the guilty parties to escape or has remitted the punishment by granting either pardon or amnesty'.

the perpetrators of crimes against foreigners. This type of denial of justice has lapsed into relative desuétude.

In some cases this grievance is only part of the context of a broader complaint which accuses the state of direct wrongdoing as well. Thus, in the *Don Pacifico* episode, the acts for which the state was criticised were in themselves constitutive of denial of justice (i.e. discrimination and prejudice in a wilful cover-up). In modern cases, the failure to prosecute private violence has been invoked in support of claims of expropriation, by way of seeking to show complicity or manipulation.[98] But claims based on a failure to prosecute alone have become quite rare. In part this may be because at one time they provided convenient excuses for powerful states to engage in gunboat diplomacy against new states whose primary failure was institutional underdevelopment. Such attitudes today tend to meet acute resistance internationally. Another explanation may lie in the observation that private claimants, who are more interested in material remedies than in reparation for insult, find that their objectives are better served by invoking the duty of 'protection and security' as articulated in numerous treaties.'[99]

Anyone interested in the prosecution of allegations of denial of justice in times past would find it rewarding to study the instances of relevant state practice which arose in the 1890s when the US Government was faced with a series of claims raised by Italy on behalf of families of a number of its nationals lynched by mobs. The first episode occurred in New Orleans, where vengeful rioters killed eleven Italian immigrants charged with the murder of the chief of police, alleged to have been the product of 'machinations of a secret society called the Mafia'. Of the eleven, five had not been tried, three had been acquitted and three were facing a retrial. The Italian minister at Washington demanded that the persons who attacked the jail be apprehended and punished, and reserved the right of his government to seek other reparations. The secretary of state communicated to the minister a copy of a telegraph to the governor

---

[98] *Amco Asia Corp. et al.* v. *Indonesia*, 20 November 1984 and 5 June 1990, 1 *ICSID Reports* 377 (original proceedings: Foighel, Rubin, Goldman (presiding); resubmitted case: Lalonde, Magid, Higgins (presiding)); *Wena Hotels Ltd* v. *Egypt*, 8 December 2000, 6 *ICSID Reports* 89 (Fadlallah, Wallace, Leigh (presiding)).

[99] *See, e.g., Asian Agricultural Products Ltd* v. *Sri Lanka*, award, 27 June 1990, 4 *ICSID Reports* 245 (Goldman, Asante, El-Kosheri (presiding)); *American Manufacturing & Trading, Inc.* v. *Zaire*, award, 21 February 1997, 5 *ICSID Reports* 11 (Golsong, Mbaye, Sucharitkul (presiding)).

of Louisiana, in which it was said – in the ornate prose of the age – that the President of the United States:

deeply regretted that the citizens of New Orleans should have so disparaged the purity and adequacy of their own tribunals as to transfer to the passionate judgment of a mob a question which should have been judged dispassionately and by settled rules of law.[100]

These sonorous phrases were not followed by action satisfactory to Italy, which withdrew its minister. Relations between the two countries were not improved when a grand jury made a report which excused those who participated in the attack on the jail; none was indicted. More than a year later, in his State of the Union address to Congress in December 1892, President Harrison expressed his government's 'reprobation and abhorrence' of the lynching, and noted that an indemnity of 125,000 francs, or US$24,330, had been paid, allowing the full restoration of diplomatic relations.[101]

Similar lynchings of Italians in police custody took place in Colorado in 1895, in Louisiana in 1896 and again in 1899, and in Mississippi in 1890. On these occasions, indemnities were proffered by the US Government with greater speed. In his State of the Union address of 1899, President McKinley referred to:

the public duty to take cognisance of matters affecting the life and rights of aliens under the settled principles of international law no less than under treaty stipulation.

He observed that in the case of the 1899 incident in Louisiana the perpetrators had not been indicted by local authorities, a failure he characterised as 'a miscarriage'; lauded the Italian Government's 'most temperate and just representations'; called for legislation to 'confer upon the Federal courts jurisdiction in this class of international cases where the ultimate responsibility of the Federal Government may be involved'; advised that 'in accordance with precedent, Congress make gracious provision for indemnity to the Italian sufferers'; and invited 'the attention of my countrymen to this reproach upon our civilization'.[102]

In a world facing the perils of terrorism and failed states, it may be asked whether the delict of denial of justice may be invoked as a foundation for

---

[100] J. B. Moore, *A Digest of International Law* (8 vols., Washington, DC: US Government Printing Office, 1906), vol. VI, at p. 838, para. 1026.
[101] *Ibid.* at pp. 840–841.   [102] *Ibid.* at p. 848.

the international responsibility of states which do not pursue perpetrators of terrorist crimes who find refuge within their borders. Although the traditional paradigm involves individuals as victims, there is no reason why a state could not invoke denial of justice as a violation of international law. Nevertheless two factors militate against claims by a state on this basis. The first is that the objective of the complaining state is not apology or monetary compensation, but rather extraterritorial police actions. The second is the fact that the doctrine of denial of justice has for centuries focused on the respondent state's failure to police activity within its borders. The issues raised in such a context would involve burning contemporary controversies about the scope of justified self-defence, notably under the Charter of the United Nations. This political debate would overwhelm any attempt to view the matter through the doctrinal prism of denial of justice.

## Wrongful measures of physical coercion

International tribunals have been quick to censure national authorities who disregard due process in the administration of criminal justice. A routine case, *Stetson*,[103] presented before the US–Mexican commission under the Treaty of 4 July 1868, involved a brig seized in 1858 by authorities in Tampico, then under siege by General Garza. The master was imprisoned. His release occurred only upon the arrival of a US man-of-war. The commissioners had no difficulty holding that the local authorities should either have warned the brig away, or, if there was a bona fide reason for capturing her, have instituted proper judicial proceedings. A significant award was entered against the Mexican Government.

On the other hand, there is little sympathy for claimants who act in ignorance of local laws. In the *Selkirk* case before the same commission,[104] the Umpire, Francis Lieber, had little patience for the captain and owner of a vessel who travelled upriver in the mistaken belief that he had been authorised to do so. His papers, wrote Lieber, 'were simply incongruous with his presence in that river'. After the vessel had been libelled, the 'proper court of law' gave a decision within two months, stating as its opinion that Selkirk was guilty of nothing more than 'want of judgment', and levying a fine of 200 dollars and costs. Selkirk was told that he could either appeal or pay. He did neither, but instead abandoned his vessel and returned to the US, where he brought his complaint to the Department of

---

[103] *Stetson's case (US v. Mexico)*, Moore, *Arbitrations*, at p. 3131.   [104] *Ibid.* at p. 3130.

State seeking compensation for the loss of the vessel. Lieber was unsparing. Selkirk, he said, did not 'seem to have taken any rational steps in the matter'. His conclusion was this:

The umpire willingly adopts the view which the Mexican court seems to have taken, and ascribes the irregular conduct of claimant to a serious want of judgment, or his unfitness, in an intellectual point of view, for the part he had assumed as captain or master of his own vessel in foreign ports where the Spanish language is spoken; but neither equity nor justice permits us to allow his claim. He might himself have easily avoided the difficulty.[105]

In principle, international law recognises the right of a state to organise the enforcement of laws on its territory in such manner as it may reasonably choose. Aliens are bound to respect local law. They may suffer inconvenience, such as detention for questioning, when the state acts to prevent or punish crime.[106] Their property may be subjected to conservatory measures ordered by a judge in connection with legal disputes. Such often disagreeable exposure to the ordinary process of municipal law must be tolerated without complaint unless mandatory principles of international law have been neglected or specific requirements of treaties have not been met.

Charges against an individual must be articulated by a competent official and specify the legal basis of the accusation. Gross mistreatment in connection with apprehension or detention violates international standards. An alien's property may not be confiscated on mere assertions of contraband or the like.

---

[105] *Ibid.* at p. 3131.

[106] The *Bullis* case, involving a US national convicted in Venezuela of the illegal possession of arms, considered that: 'Bullis was arrested, tried, and convicted in strict accordance with the laws of Venezuela, to which he was at the time subject, and in conformity with the usual procedure of its courts; that his trial was not unnecessarily delayed; that he was provided with counsel; that he was allowed to communicate with the representative of his Government; that there was no undue discrimination against him as a citizen of the United States, nor was there, in his trial, any violation of those rules for the maintenance of justice in judicial inquiries which are sanctioned by international law. It does not appear that he was subjected to any unnecessarily harsh or arbitrary treatment during his imprisonment. The respondent Government has incurred no liability to this claimant. Every nation, whenever its laws are violated by anyone owing obedience to them, whether he be a citizen or a stranger, has a right to inflict the prescribed penalties upon the transgressor, if found within its jurisdiction; provided always that the laws themselves, the methods of administering them, and the penalties prescribed are not in derogation of civilized codes'; *Henry C. Bullis (US v. Venezuela)*, IX RIAA 231, at p. 232.

The standard for treatment of foreign prisoners is neither necessarily that of their countries of origin nor that of the local carceral system. A state cannot escape liability by pleading that it treats all prisoners equally, whether national or foreign, or that it does not have the means to provide humane custodial conditions (edible food, medical attention, rudimentary sanitation and a modicum of respect for human dignity). The relevant test is whether aliens are treated in conformity with universal standards. They also prohibit unjustified delay in bringing a detained alien suspect to trial.

These minimum requirements are uncontroversial, and indeed would doubtless be understood by decent people everywhere without the need for learned consultations.

More controversial issues in the area of criminal law relate to the notion of excessive bail and the opportunity to consult counsel. There have been cases where disproportionate bail was deemed a denial of justice[107]; and cases where reasonable periods of *incommunicado* were upheld.[108]

Acquittal, whether at first instance or appeal, does not in and of itself open the gate to recovery for wrongful imprisonment if the proceedings were based on probable cause and were conducted in accordance with established procedures (which themselves satisfy minimum international standards, and in particular are not corrupted by malice or arbitrariness). The same principle applies, with the same qualifications, if an alien is released prior to trial. In Freeman's memorable phase:

'Protection' does not imply that a foreign citizen must be elevated to a pedestal of privileges above the law and treated as a juridical *enfant gâté*.[109]

---

[107] E.g. *Chattin case (US v. Mexico)*, 23 July 1927, IV RIAA 282; *Jones's case (US v. Spain)*, Moore, *Arbitrations*, at p. 3253.
[108] E.g. *Kaiser case (US v. Mexico)*, Claims Commission, United States and Mexico, Opinions of Commissioners, Washington 1929, at p. 80.
[109] Freeman at p. 212. (*Enfant gâté* means 'spoiled child'.)

# 7

# Denial of justice by the decision-maker

## Refusal to judge

It may appear odd that a national court ill disposed towards a foreigner would refuse to decide. Why would an antagonistic judge not rather render an unfavourable judgment or order?

The answer may be that the adverse judgment is difficult to justify, and – most of all – open to appeals before higher jurisdictions less likely to protect parochial interests. Such a chauvinistic impulse may explain the fate that befell the engineering firm Revpower Limited in 1993 when it sought to enforce an award rendered in Shanghai against a Chinese state-owned enterprise based in that city (the Shanghai Far-East Aero-Technology Import and Export Corporation).[1] Its application for enforcement was filed with all requisite supporting documents in the Intermediate People's Court. Since China was bound by the New York Convention on the Recognition and Enforcement of Foreign Arbitral Awards, a decree of enforcement should in principle have been forthcoming. Instead, the assigned judge simply refused to put the case on the docket. If Revpower had had access to an international forum, it could plainly have held the central government internationally responsible for the denial of justice.

As one might expect, a malingering court is likely to make some show of activity. The international tribunal then faces the challenge of determining whether there was in fact a disguised refusal to deal with the case. The

---

[1] *See* Jan Paulsson and Alastair Crawford, '1994 Revision of CIETAC Rules Promises Increased Neutrality in Arbitration in China', (1994) 9(6) *Mealey's International Arbitration Report* 17, at pp. 18–19.

leading precedent is perhaps the *Fabiani* case,[2] decided in 1896 by the President of the Swiss Confederation, acting by special authority as sole arbitrator under the Franco-Venezuelan treaty of 1864. Fabiani had secured a private arbitral award in his favour in France in 1880. It had been duly granted *exequatur* by the competent court in that country. He presented the award for enforcement in Venezuela, only to be met with a long series of meretricious suspensions and interlocutory appeals, culminating in the refusal of a *tribunal d'exception*, especially selected to deal with his case, even to schedule a meeting. Fabiani, who had been bankrupted in the meanwhile, made a substantial recovery on account of the denial of justice.[3]

## Delay

Freeman devoted an entire chapter to the topic of 'Unreasonable Delay in Administering Justice'.[4] In the *Fabiani* case referred to in the preceding section, the sole arbitrator (President Lachenal) wrote as follows:

Upon examining the general principles of international law with regard to denial of justice, that is to say, the rules common to most bodies of law or laid down by doctrine, one finds that denial of justice includes not only the refusal of a judicial authority to exercise his functions and, in particular, to give a decision on the request submitted to him, but also wrongful delays on his part in giving judgment.[5]

Freeman stated that 'ever since the era of private reprisals it has been axiomatic that unreasonable delays are properly to be assimilated to absolute denials of access … attempts to deny that continuous unwarranted postponements of judicial action violate international law are now of the rarest occurrence'.[6] As he noted, delays may be 'even more ruinous' than absolute refusal of access, because in the latter situation the claimant knows where he stands and take action accordingly, whether by seeking diplomatic intervention or exploring avenues of direct legal action.

What constitutes 'unreasonable delay' depends on a number of factors. Perhaps the most important feature in criminal proceedings is whether the claimant was imprisoned awaiting trial. *Chattin*[7] was kept in detention for some five months while unsuccessfully appealing to the court. The

---

[2] *No. 1 (France v. Venezuela)*, Moore, *Arbitrations*, at p. 4878.    [3] *Ibid.* at pp. 4884 and 4902.
[4] Freeman, chap. X, at pp. 242–263.
[5] *Antoine Fabiani (no. 1) (France v. Venezuela)*, Moore, *Arbitrations*, 4878, at p. 4895; the translation from the French appears in Freeman at p. 242.
[6] Freeman at pp. 242–243 (notes omitted).
[7] *US v. Mexico*, 23 July 1927, IV RIAA 282.

presiding commissioner observed that whereas Chattin's appeal from his decree of imprisonment was formulated on 11 July 1910, it was not remitted to the appellate court until 12 September 1910.

In civil cases, defendant states have sought to excuse delays by reference to overcharged dockets. Such arguments have not met with success; as the Anglo-Mexican Claims Commission put it in the *El Oro Mining and Railway Co.* case, refusing to countenance a failure by the relevant Mexican authority to render a decision within some nine years:

> the amount of work incumbent on the Court, and the multitude of lawsuits with which they are confronted, may explain, but not excuse the delay. If this number is so enormous as to occasion an arrear of nine years, the conclusion cannot be other than that the judicial machinery is defective.[8]

The French Conseil d'Etat, the highest court in administrative matters, has held that the State is liable by virtue of Articles 6(1) and 13 of the European Convention on Human Rights for its failure to ensure, as a part of its obligation to respect the rights of a *procès equitable*, that judgments are rendered within a reasonable period of time. For example, in a decision rendered in 2002,[9] the Conseil d'Etat found such liability where the administrative tribunal of Versailles took seven and a half years to rule on a 'request which did not present any particular difficulty'. To determine whether the duration was reasonable, the Conseil d'Etat emphasised the need to evaluate the matter concretely and in its entirety, taking into account its degree of complexity, the conduct of the parties in the course of the proceedings, as well as any known facts pointing to a legitimate interest in celerity. (In that case, the claimant was a public works contractor aged 72 at the date of his petition.)

Depending on the circumstances, French courts have sanctioned judges for setting over-lengthy intermediate deadlines, such as one and a half years for the defendant's written pleadings in a civil case, ten months for the constitution of a labour tribunal, or forty months for an appeal from such a tribunal.[10]

## Illegitimate assertion of jurisdiction

This is a natural complement to tampering of the judiciary by the executive or legislative branches. (See the section on 'Manipulation of the

---

[8] Quoted in Freeman at p. 259.
[9] Conseil d'Etat, *Garde des sceaux, Ministre de la justice/M. Magiera*, 28 June 2002.
[10] Loïc Cadiet, *Droit judiciaire privé* (3rd edn., Litec, Paris, 2000).

composition of courts' in Chapter 6.) The government stacks the courts in its favour, or selects compliant judges to sit on special tribunals. If the tactic is to work, the manipulated court must go along with it. In such circumstance, its assertion of jurisdiction will be internationally illicit.

In the *Idler* case, the Venezuelan Government had filled vacancies on the Supreme Court in an unlawful manner. Idler was summoned by letters rogatory to appear before that court. He failed to do so. The Supreme Court decided that the matter in fact should be heard by a lower-level court, and sent the case to be decided there. This occurred without notice to Idler. A judgment unfavourable to him was handed down, and approved by the Supreme Court. The commission reasoned that if the facts necessary to give a court jurisdiction do not exist, 'the record will be a nullity in the eyes of a controlling authority', and continued as follows:

The fact that the supreme court of its own motion sent the record down to the superior court does not help the matter, for it is immaterial whether the suit was begun there at its instance or not. The question is when and whether it was *therein* instituted.

The objection to this record is by no means technical. No notice, legal or other, was received or sent to Jacob Idler about the suit in the superior court, the only court having jurisdiction to entertain it in the first instance (unless it be the treasury court, where it never was), as is conceded on all hands. The letters rogatory directed him to appear in the *supreme court* in a suit instituted *there*. If the summons was legal it only gave him notice of what that court *in that* case – not in another instituted in an inferior tribunal and subsequently appealed to it – might lawfully adjudge. The notice directing him, away in a distant land, to appear in one court when the business affecting his interests was to be done in another, was worse than none at all, for it was misleading. Even if no notice had been required, and one had nevertheless been given, whose tendency was thus to mislead, we are inclined to think the act, from the standpoint of justice, would vitiate the whole proceedings. Receiving the notice in 1837, at Philadelphia, that a suit had been begun against him in *restitutio* in the supreme court of Venezuela in June 1836, he – charged at most with a knowledge of the law as it was declared to be – could well have said to himself, 'I shall not undertake the hazards of a journey or incur the expense to appear. The court has no jurisdiction and can not grant the prayer of the government, and it is now too late to bring the suit in the court which had jurisdiction.'[11]

---

[11] *Jacob Idler* v. *Venezuela*, Moore, *Arbitrations* 3491, at pp. 3514–3515.

## Fundamental breaches of due process

This is the heart of the matter. What may seem intolerably warped to one lawyer may strike another, depending on cultural differences, as an innocent error at most. Any international censure of national court proceedings may therefore incur the criticism that the international adjudicators are substituting their judgment about matters as to which reasonable persons can disagree, and which therefore should not be subject to review.

In the *Chattin* case decided by the Mexican–US Commission in 1927, for example, the Presiding Commissioner (Cornelis Van Vollenhoven, an estimable Dutch international lawyer of his time) wrote this:

Irregularity of court proceedings is proven with reference to absence of proper investigations, insufficiency of confrontations, withholding from the accused the opportunity to know all of the charges brought against him, undue delay of the proceedings, making the hearings in open court a mere formality, and a continued absence of seriousness on the part of the Court.[12]

There was much in this with which Fernandez MacGregor, the Mexican Commissioner, could agree:

To prevent an accused from defending himself, either by refusing to inform him as to the facts imputed to him or by denying him a hearing and the use of remedies; to sentence him without evidence, or to impose on him disproportionate or unusual penalties, to treat him with cruelty and discrimination; are all acts which *per se* cause damage due to their rendering a just decision impossible.[13]

Yet this passage comes from a fervent *dissent*, in which the following sentences read as follows:

But to delay the proceedings somewhat, to lay aside some evidence, there existing other clear proofs, to fail to comply with the adjective law in its secondary provisions and other deficiencies of this kind, do not cause damage nor violate international law. Counsel for Mexico justly stated that to submit the decisions of a nation to revision in this respect was tantamount to submitting her to a regime of capitulations. All the criticism which has been made of these proceedings, I regret to say, appears to arise from a lack of knowledge of the judicial system and practice of Mexico, and, what is

---

[12] *US* v. *Mexico*, 23 July 1927, IV RIAA 282, at p. 295.  [13] *Ibid.* at p. 312.

more dangerous, from the application thereto of tests belonging to foreign systems of law.[14]

Chattin was an American employee of a Mexican railroad company who, along with others, had been convicted of embezzlement (a ticket scam) and imprisoned. The majority of the commissioners concluded that there had been 'a most astonishing lack of seriousness on the part of the Court'. They delved far into the details of the record to criticise the lack of diligence in fact-finding. Moreover, they noted with disapproval the absence of 'any such thing as an oral examination or cross-examination' – an observation which was bound to trigger Fernandez MacGregor's disapproval given the differences in national practice as to the importance of oral hearings. What most profoundly disturbed the majority was clearly the weight given by the court to anonymous written accusations submitted by the railroad company, and the doubt that subsisted as to whether they were even seen by Chattin's lawyer before judgment.

Fernandez MacGregor responded that he did not believe that the accused had been ignorant of any charges or evidence, 'for the simple reason that the records found in a criminal process are not secret, according to Mexican law'. Nor did the Mexican Constitution require that an accused be confronted with every witness. His review of the record led him to the conclusion that the convicting judge had not relied on the secret information; in any event, the facts had been established by cumulative means. Finally, he rejected any criticism of the duration of the 'trial proper' as having 'lasted five minutes at the most' on the grounds that such criticism ignores the basic criminal process in a system, like Mexico's, where all evidence tends to be adduced in preliminary phases of investigation, during which all rights should be observed, with the result that the parties frequently have nothing to add on the occasion of the final public hearing.

---

[14] *Ibid.* This debate may be compared to the way the arbitrators dealt with one of the aspects of the *Mondev* case, where the claimant argued that a particular matter should have been remanded to a civil jury as the proper trier of fact. The arbitral tribunal disagreed, in these terms:

'Questions of fact-finding on appeal are quintessentially matters of local procedural practice. Except in extreme cases, the Tribunal does not understand how the application of local procedural rules about such matters as remand, or decisions as to the functions of juries vis-à-vis appellate courts, could violate the standards embodied in Article 1105(1). On the approach adopted by Mondev, NAFTA tribunals would turn into courts of appeal, which is not their role.' *Mondev* at para. 136.

This dissent appears consonant with the views expressed by the US government in diplomatic instructions in 1855, which observed that while the practice in Austria of holding defendants *incommunicado* 'is certainly revolting to our notions of justice and humane treatment', it was not 'peculiar to that government' and would not be the subject of international complaints by the US. The US Government's analysis was as follows:

The system of proceeding in criminal cases in the Austrian government, has, undoubtedly, as is the case in most other absolute countries, many harsh features and is deficient in many safeguards which our laws provide for the security of the accused; but it is not within the competence of one independent power to reform the jurisdiction of others, nor has it the right to regard as an injury the application of the judicial system and established modes of proceedings in foreign countries to its citizens when fairly brought under their operation. All we can ask of Austria, and this we can demand as a right, is that, in her proceedings against American citizens prosecuted for offences committed within her jurisdiction, she should give them the full and fair benefit of her system, such as it is, and deal with them as she does with her own subjects or those of other foreign powers. She can not be asked to modify her mode of proceedings to suit our views, or to extend to our citizens all the advantages which her subjects would have under our better and more humane system of criminal jurisprudence.[15]

Fortunately, substantial international consensus has emerged today with respect to a number of fundamental matters, in a manner which would sharply reduce the tolerance of 'national peculiarities' reflected in this instruction. This consensus owes much to recent jurisprudence, not only in the area of human rights but also in that of international arbitrations of both a public and private law nature where assessments of the finality of arbitral awards by an impressive multitude of international and national jurisdictions have found much common ground. But a great deal of that consensus has existed for a long time.

The three international arbitrators who rendered the *Loewen* award in 2003 were all eminent retired common law judges. The words they used to describe the treatment of the Canadian investor at the hands of American courts included these: 'a disgrace', 'the antithesis of due process', and 'a miscarriage of justice'. How they reached those conclusions is a matter of great interest.

---

[15] Instructions of Secretary of State Marcy to his chargé at Vienna, 6 April 1855, J. B. Moore, *A Digest of International Law* (8 vols., Washington, DC: US Government Printing Office, 1906), vol. VI, at p. 275.

Any consideration of *Loewen* must however begin with the observation that the award upheld a motion to dismiss for lack of jurisdiction. That motion, raised after the oral hearing on the merits, succeeded on the grounds that the claims had been assigned to an entity owned and controlled by a United States corporation. This, the arbitrators held, defeated a NAFTA requirement of diversity of nationality as between claimants and the relevant respondent state. In other words, the arbitral tribunal did not have jurisdiction to decide the case on the merits. Everything the arbitrators had to say on the subject of denial of justice is therefore *obiter dictum*. As for the continuous-nationality issue, they decided it on the basis that it was not explicitly dealt with in NAFTA and thus fell under general principles of 'customary international law'. These, the arbitrators felt, should lead to the conclusion that the claimant must maintain the relevant nationality until the date of the award – 'through the date of the resolution of the claim', as the tribunal put it.[16] There is nothing in the award to indicate that the arbitrators had considered the special addendum on 'continuous nationality and the transferability of claims' prepared by the ILC's rapporteur on diplomatic protection, Professor Dugard, in early 2000.[17] They wrote only that Loewen had *contended* such a report had been issued, and had encountered some criticism. But anyone who reads the Report would see that Dugard's extensive review of the authorities led him to conclude that there was no established rule in this area. The *dies ad quem* requirement which commended itself to the *Loewen* arbitrators was perhaps the least plausible of a long series of alternative candidates.[18]

[16] *Loewen*, 26 June 2003, at para. 225.
[17] International Law Commission (Dugard), First Report on Diplomatic Protection, UN Doc. A/CN.4/506/Add. 1 (2000).
[18] *Ibid.* at p. 11, para. 16. These included: (i) the date on which a government endorses the claim of a national; (ii) the date of initial diplomatic negotiations; (iii) the date of filing the claim; (iv) the date of signature of the treaty referring to the relevant forum; (v) the date of ratification of said treaty; (vi) the date of its entry into force; (vii) the date of presentation of the claim (*accord*, Guy I. F. Leigh, 'Nationality and Diplomatic Protection', (1971) 20 *International and Comparative Law Quarterly* 453, at p. 475); (viii) the date of conclusion of the oral hearings; (ix) the date of judgment (i.e. the *Loewen* solution); and (x) the most extreme, the date of settlement.

Without any indication of being aware of it, the *Loewen* arbitrators adopted the reasoning in the case of *Minnie Stevens Eschauzier (Great Britain v. US)*, 24 June 1931, V RIAA 207, whose claim was rejected because she lost her British nationality by marriage to an American between the date of the conclusion of the oral hearing and the judgment. As the Umpire (Edwin P. Parker) noted in the far more influential *Administrative Decision No. V (US v. Germany)*, 31 October 1924, VII RIAA 119: (A) the acquisition of nationality transfers allegiance but does not

The reasons given by a tribunal when it explains why it decides to devote itself to expositions unnecessary to the task at hand never fail to engage the attentive reader's curiosity. In this case, we are left to muse about the universe of hidden meaning which might lie behind the innocent-sounding preposition 'as'. That little word is used twice in a remarkable sentence, undoubtedly drafted with particular care since it appears in the second paragraph of the award:

*As* our consideration of the merits of the case was well advanced when Respondent filed this motion to dismiss and *as* we reached the conclusion that

> transport existing state obligations and, (B) at any rate, most of the decisions depend on the *lex specialis* of the relevant treaty and therefore do not reflect a general principle; 'it may well be doubted whether the alleged rule [of continuous nationality] has received such universal recognition as to justify the broad statement that it is an established rule of international law', *Ibid.* at p. 140.
>
> In the end, Professor Dugard recommended that the ILC 'reject the doctrine of continuous nationality as a substantive rule of customary international law'. ILC, First Report on Diplomatic Protection, Addendum 1 at p.14, para. 21. *Accord*, D. P. O'Connell, *International Law* (2nd edn, London: Stevens & Sons, 1970), at pp. 1035–1036. And if one were seeking to give a purposive interpretation to the *lex specialis*, i.e. NAFTA, it would seem appropriate to give weight to the objective of stimulating the mobilisation of financial resources to be employed in cross-border investment. That indeed happened. A Canadian corporate entity, Loewen Inc., invested in the US. Notions of estoppel would seem to preclude subsequent denial of the treaty protections attached to that investment. The international wrong caused to the investment occurred at a time when the corporate entity enjoyed Canadian nationality, and so, under this view, its entitlement was vested. Why should it matter that due to the scheduling vagaries of international litigation the award came to be rendered at a time when the holder of that entitlement had a different nationality?
>
> To be complete, there was another aspect of the critical nationality issue, namely the fact that before being reorganised as a US corporation, The Loewen Group, Inc., had assigned its rights to the NAFTA claim to a newly incorporated Canadian entity called Nafcanco (which the tribunal described as 'a play on the words NAFTA and Canada'; *Loewen*, 26 June 2003, at para. 220). Under *Barcelona Traction*, this might have been enough to preserve the corporate claimant's distinct nationality. At least one would have expected an in-depth discussion of the matter. The award, however, contained only the two following dismissive sentences:
>
> 'All of the benefits of any award would clearly inure to the American corporation. Such a naked entity as Nafcanco, even with its catchy name, cannot qualify as a continuing national for the purposes of this proceeding' (*ibid.* at para. 237).
>
> This affirmation is impossible to square with other, more carefully articulated decisions in the field of investment arbitration; see, e.g., *CME Czech Republic BV* v. *Czech Republic*, partial award, 13 September 2001, 9 *ICSID Reports* [forthcoming] (Schwebel, Händl, Kühn (presiding)). Drafters of bilateral investment treaties wishing to require more than what the *Loewen* arbitrators called a 'naked entity' articulate explicit requirements to that effect, e.g. that a substantial presence or principal headquarters is located in the country of incorporation.

Claimants' NAFTA claims should be dismissed on the merits, we include in this Award our reasons for this conclusion.

There it is, and that is all; what is obvious is that the arbitrators felt moved to make a statement, but how they thought this passage legitimised a thousand words *obiter dictum* remains obscure.

In other circumstances, with other tribunals, one might treat such explanations with indifference, or indeed criticise them as jurisprudentially unwise, for reasons suggested in the following comments made before the final award in *Loewen* was handed down by one of the lawyers who represented the US Government in that case:

Arbitrators in cases under investment treaties have recently demonstrated an increasing awareness that the public law nature of these cases demands a different approach than that called for in private commercial arbitrations. Certain tribunals have demonstrated a pronounced sensitivity to the importance of the issues they have been asked to decide, for example, by limiting their discussion of the issues raised by the parties to those necessary to the decision made, rather than follow the approach, not unusual in private arbitrations, of addressing every argument made by the parties, even if the ultimate grounds for the decision make such a discussion unnecessary and hypothetical.[19]

But such reservations must give way to the truly exceptional circumstances of the *Loewen* case.

First, the notoriety of this case in the field of investment arbitration cannot be overestimated; quite simply, few – if any – other international awards have been more intently anticipated. It was a case about which lawyers around the world, no matter how personally uninvolved in the proceedings, had passionate feelings. A purely technical dismissal on jurisdictional grounds would have been an unbearable let-down; *obiter* or not, the arbitrators must have felt a compelling demand to say *something* about the merits.

Secondly, each of the three arbitrators had reached the heights of the judiciary of their countries; for two of them, the *absolute* heights. As eminent national judges, they brought a noteworthy perspective to their task, when empanelled as international arbitrators, of sitting in judgment over the conduct of the national judiciary of one of their countries. The arbitrator whose country's responsibility was in question, Abner Mikva,

---

[19] B. Legum, 'Trends and Challenges in Investor-State Arbitration', (2003) 19 *Arbitration International* 143, at p. 147.

had experience not only as a judge on the District of Columbia Court of Appeals, but also as an elected member of the US House of Representatives and a White House counsel. This was, in other words, not an international tribunal likely to trample heedlessly on the prerogatives of national judges.

Thirdly, this was not a battleground for those who still labour in the desiccated vineyards of ideology and rush to consider awards in terms of global polarities. This was not a North–South conflict, but a claim brought by an investor of a capital exporting country against another capital exporting state. The interests were those of two rich neighbouring countries with functionally fused economies and similar cultures of liberal capitalism.

So what this tribunal had to say about denial of justice is bound to be studied for generations to come. As we have seen, the claim would, according to the tribunal, have failed even on the merits because the aggrieved investor had the burden to demonstrate that it had 'no reasonably available and adequate remedy' under municipal law, and failed to discharge that burden. So when the arbitrators unhesitatingly observed that the investor had been treated appallingly by American courts, in a manner violative of international law, we are dealing with an *obiter dictum* in the second degree.

In a nutshell, the Canadian investor lost a commercial dispute before the courts of Mississippi against a local competitor, the O'Keefe family, in circumstances redolent of the worst excesses of the US legal system. The commercial dispute involved less than US$10 million, but a judgment was handed down by a jury in an amount of US$500 million, of which US$400 million were punitive damages and US$75 million were on account of 'emotional distress'. The claim was prosecuted before an elected judge by a lawyer operating on a contingency-fee basis,[20] who sought, unchecked by the judge, to appeal to the jurors' parochialism and racial prejudice.

The heart of the 'disgraceful' conduct of the trial was that the judge:

failed in his duty to take control of the trial by permitting the jury to be exposed to persistent and flagrant appeals to prejudice on the part of O'Keefe's counsel and

---

[20] The remarkable career of Willie Edward Gary as a flamboyant plaintiff's lawyer, and his involvement with the O'Keefes, is recounted at length in Jonathan Harr, 'The Burial', *The New Yorker*, 1 November 1999, 70. (Harr is the author of *A Civil Action* (New York: Vintage, 1996), the best-selling non-fiction book turned into a motion picture featuring John Travolta.)

witnesses. Respondent is responsible for any failure on the part of the trial judge in failing to take control of the trial so as to ensure that it was fairly conducted in this respect.[21]

The facts that gave rise to that conclusion will be considered in the immediately following section on 'Discrimination or prejudice'.

Some aspects of the case, however, merit attention in connection with the more general topic of fundamental procedural defects.

First, the arbitral tribunal criticised the trial judge for refusing 'to give an instruction to the jury stating clearly that discrimination on the grounds of nationality, race, and class was impermissible'. Loewen requested that his instruction include an exhortation to the effect that all persons 'are equal in the eyes of the law without regard to race, ethnicity, national origin, wealth or social status' and that the foreign parties were 'entitled to the same fair trial' as the O'Keefes. The judge refused, and instead contented himself by reading a standard one-sentence instruction, given in every case, which refers to bias in general, but is explicit about neither nationality nor race:

You should not be influenced by bias, sympathy or prejudice.[22]

This, the arbitrators concluded, was 'inadequate to counter the prejudice created by the way in which O'Keefe's case had been presented'[23]:

There was a gross failure on the part of the trial judge to afford the due process due to Loewen in protecting it from the tactics employed by O'Keefe and its counsel.[24]

In other words, when the injustice in a case is initiated by a litigant for whose behaviour the state is not responsible, the court is nevertheless held to a duty to remedy the unfairness – and failure to fulfil that duty is imputable to the state.

Secondly, the arbitral tribunal was unimpressed by the US Government's argument to the effect that since it is responsible for only the conduct of its courts, and not for that of litigants, the claim should fail because Loewen did not raise objections with the judge. In this respect the arbitrators obviously drew on their considerable collective experience. They acknowledged that there had been occasions in the trial when objections or requests to strike irrelevant and prejudicial evidence could have been made, but were not.

---

[21] *Loewen*, 26 June 2003, at para. 53.   [22] *Ibid.* at para. 82.   [23] *Ibid.* at para. 85.
[24] *Ibid.* at para. 87.

In a jury trial, however, counsel are naturally reluctant to create the impression, by continuously objecting, that they are seeking to suppress relevant evidence or that they are relying on technicalities. So it is not to be expected that Loewen's counsel would object on every occasion when objectionable comment was made or inadmissible evidence was given. The question is whether Loewen's counsel sufficiently brought their objections to the attention of the trial judge and whether the trial judge was aware of the problem and should have taken action himself.[25]

...

It may well be that the trial judge's unfavourable, dismissive, abrupt responses to their objections during the *voir dire*, reinforced by similar responses during the trial, led them to make the judgment that objections would be rejected and would result in prejudice to Loewen in the eyes of the jury.[26]

Overall, they concluded:

Having regard to the history of the trial, and the way in which it was conducted by Judge Graves, we do not consider that failures to object on the part of Loewen's counsel amounted to a waiver of the grounds on which Claimants now contend that the conduct of the trial constituted a violation of NAFTA.[27]

Thirdly, the judge rather obviously mishandled the requirement under Mississippi law that trials must be procedurally bifurcated with respect to claims of punitive damages; liability and compensatory damages are to be considered first, before any evidence and arguments are presented with respect to punitive damages. O'Keefe referred to punitive damages during the course of the trial; Loewen objected, but the judge gave no instruction to the jury in that respect. A verdict was returned for US$100 million in compensatory damages and US$160 million in punitive damages. After denying a motion by Loewen for a mistrial without discussion, the judge informed the jury that he did not accept the award of punitive damages. As the arbitral tribunal put it:

The jury may well have interpreted the rejection of this award as an indication that it was inadequate.[28]

---

[25] *Ibid.* at para. 73.    [26] *Ibid.* at para. 75.    [27] *Ibid.* at para. 87.

[28] *Ibid.* at para. 96. An alternative explanation, more to the judge's credit, appears in Harr's account in *The New Yorker*: the judge was minded to let the verdict stand without going on to a separate consideration of punitive damages, but it was Loewen's legal team which insisted on doing so during a meeting in his chambers. This inevitably meant that evidence would be adduced regarding Loewen's net worth. The judge was astonished. 'I don't think you want to go back in there', he is quoted as having said. 'You already know they've given a hundred and sixty million dollars without knowing net worth.' Harr, 'The Burial' at p. 92.

At any rate, the jury was brought back to consider the amount of punitive damages. When presenting arguments on this point, O'Keefe's lawyer now asserted that Loewen would make 'over $7.9 billion' from its contract with the National Baptist Convention, a religious group including numerous African Americans, and that this profit would be made from 'just selling vaults' because black people would not be admitted to Loewen funeral homes for burial. Neither assertion was supported by evidence.

Ultimately the jury's final verdict included US$400 million in punitive damages, making the total of US$500 million – 'by far the largest [damages] ever awarded in Mississippi'.[29] The arbitrators concluded that Loewen had 'a very strong case ... that the amounts were so inflated as to invite the inference that the jury was swayed by prejudice, passion or sympathy'.[30] The first verdict showed that the jurors were prepared to award punitive damages with neither instructions nor evidence to that effect. Their initial award included compensatory damages on account of elements (oppression and fraud) not requested in counsel's closing address, as well as US$78 million on account of breach of a contract which one of O'Keefe's own witnesses had valued at only US$980,000. There had been no expert evidence of emotional distress, but merely O'Keefe's self-described 'sleepless nights, worry and stress'. The damages awarded included 'lost future revenue' whereas Mississippi law – like the law everywhere – allows only 'lost future profits'. Damages were allowed under both a settlement agreement and the contract which that agreement had purported to extinguish, an obvious duplication of recovery.

Fourthly, the arbitral tribunal rejected the objection that Loewen's own flawed trial strategy was the cause of the verdict. The US Government submitted an expert opinion to the effect that the trial had been affected by serious errors. The arbitrators agreed that with hindsight Loewen's counsel made a number of 'unwise' decisions. Moreover, four former Loewen witnesses gave evidence critical of Loewen's business practices. One of them testified that Loewen put into practice a policy of 'constant and aggressive price increases'; and gave O'Keefe in particular misleading information in 'evident breach of contract'. Finally, Loewen's conduct during the trial itself was unappealing: unfavourable evidence was

---

[29] *Harr*, 'The Burial' at p. 92, reports that several jurors revealed that with only one more vote they would have awarded one billion dollars. The largest previous verdict in Mississippi had, according to *The New Yorker*, been in the amount of $18 million. *The Wall Street Journal*'s editorial page featured the headline: 'A Small Canadian Firm Meets the American Tort Monster', *ibid.* at p. 95.

[30] *Loewen*, 26 June 2003, at para. 105.

produced belatedly, and thus highlighted; Loewen's counsel had not complied with court orders with respect to the sequestration of a witness, with the result that his testimony was struck; Raymond Loewen suffered from 'frequent claims of memory failure'; and Loewen produced contradictory evidence about its net worth.

While accepting that these matters strengthened O'Keefe's case, the arbitral tribunal concluded that they 'do not erase the prejudicial conduct at trial ... or eliminate the influence it was calculated to have on the jury'.[31]

The arbitral tribunal noted that no legal system expects to produce 'perfect trials'. Mistakes, errors and prejudice will occur from time to time. Each system has its own methods for correcting such missteps, but not every one of them is remedied; each system has its own way of defining criteria that allow 'the results of less than perfect trials' to stand. In the US, often-applied criteria include the doctrines of 'harmless error', 'invited error', and the waiver of objection.

The US Government argued that such appellate doctrines precluded the international arbitral tribunal from basing its decision 'on specific flaws that were the most egregious'. The arbitrators disagreed, stating as follows:

We need not resolve the domestic procedural disputes which arose at the trial such as the question whether Loewen was entitled to the particular instruction which it sought as to bias. The question is whether the whole trial, and its resultant verdict, satisfied minimum standards of international law, or the 'fair and equitable treatment and full protection and security' that the Contracting States pledged in Article 1105 of NAFTA.[32]

Taking the 'excessiveness of the verdict' as 'one instance of many ... methods employed by the jury and countenanced by the judge [that] were the antithesis of due process',[33] the arbitrators defined 'unfair and inequitable treatment or denial of justice amounting to a breach of international justice' as:

[m]anifest injustice in the sense of a lack of due process leading to an outcome which offends a sense of judicial propriety[34]

and concluded that:

the whole trial and its resultant verdict were clearly improper and discreditable and cannot be squared with minimum standards of international law and fair and equitable treatment.[35]

---

[31] *Ibid.* at para. 118.  [32] *Ibid.* at para. 121.  [33] *Ibid.* at para. 122.
[34] *Ibid.* at para. 132.  [35] *Ibid.* at para. 137.

The *Loewen* award was not enthusiastically received in all quarters. To the contrary, it gave rise to a torrent of unrestrained criticism, excoriating the arbitrators for cowardice and lack of realism. Although far from the most acerbic, a well-known Swiss arbitrator wrote an article expressing the views that the arbitrators' reasons 'defy the imagination', that it is a 'riddle how a distinguished Arbitral Tribunal could base its decision on such implausible grounds', that the arbitrators 'pompously asserted' that they were rescuing NAFTA from a threat to its very viability, that in thus taking upon themselves the exclusive responsibility of the governments of the concerned countries they 'blinked and shrank' from applying 'NAFTA provisions designed to redress exactly such abuses', and that they thus made the kind of 'bad law' which 'breeds disrespect and contempt among the politicians and public at large for the whole investors' protection system, weakening it rather than strengthening it'.[36]

But is it fair to conclude that *Loewen* was decided by timorous, unctuous arbitrators anxious to assist the powerful wrongdoer? Were they like Hemingway, who, F. Scott Fitzgerald is said to have said, was always willing to lend a helping hand to the one above him? Before answering yes, the arbitrators' critics should consider:

(A)  that the shocking description of the miscarriage of justice that took place in Mississippi which has impressed itself on the minds of most observers is in fact none other than the description given by the arbitrators themselves, at length and in the strongest terms – an 'outrage', and

(B)  it would have been easy for the arbitrators, as a matter of reasoning and drafting, to whitewash the defendant government by minimising the grievance, and demonstrating that the elements of the delict of denial of justice were not satisfied, for example by giving weight to the US Government's factually accurate observation that the claimants had not availed themselves of numerous opportunities to object, or to emphasise several 'unwise decisions' made by Loewen's litigating team. There is international jurisprudence to the effect that the failure to use forensic weapons at one's disposal, such as, in the *Ambatielos* case,[37] not calling a key witness, will disqualify subsequent recourse to international justice.

---

[36] Jacques Werner, 'Making Investment Protection More Certain: A Modest Proposal', (2003) 4 *Journal of World Investment* 767, at p. 777.
[37] *Greece* v. *UK*, 6 March 1956, XII RIAA 83.

A good case can be made for the proposition that the *Loewen* award advances rather than damages the cause of the rule of international law. Faced with future claims of denial of justice, international adjudicators, assuming that they have jurisdiction and that the claim is ripe, will find valuable guidance in the collective analysis of these three highly experienced judges as they uncompromisingly evaluated the complex record of this controversial case.

## Discrimination or prejudice

As the *Loewen* tribunal observed, international law attaches 'special importance to discriminatory violations of municipal law', so that:

A decision which is in breach of municipal law and is discriminatory against the foreign litigant amounts to manifest injustice according to international law.[38]

This does not, of course, mean that a discriminatory judgment is internationally inviolable if it is not in breach of municipal law. In such a case, the breach of international law is *legislative*. If the law is not discriminatory, and a discriminatory *judgment* issues which violates the law, then there has been a judicial breach of international law which need not be referred to as denial of justice. Thus, the *Loewen* tribunal spoke of 'manifest injustice'; it would be simpler to say 'breach'.

If there is proof of actual bias, there is obviously prejudice. But there may be unfairness sufficient to violate international law even in the absence of evidence of actual bias.

In a separate chapter of its award,[39] the *Loewen* tribunal concluded that there was no direct evidence of actual bias on the part of either the jury or the judge. There was 'strong reason for thinking that the jury were affected by the persistent and extravagant O'Keefe appeals to prejudice'. The judge's conduct was consistent with bias. Still, in the absence of evidence supporting a finding of actual bias, the violation of international law could be only that the judge 'failed to discharge his paramount duty to ensure that Loewen received a fair trial'.[40] In this respect:

Neither State practice, the decisions of international tribunals nor the opinion of commentators support the view that bad faith or malicious intention is an

---

[38] *Loewen*, 26 June 2003, at para. 135.    [39] *Ibid.* chap. XIX, at para. 138.    [40] *Ibid.*

essential element of unfair and inequitable treatment or denial of justice amounting to a breach of international justice.[41]

In *Loewen*, the 'disgraceful' nature of the judge's conduct of the trial was manifested in his repeatedly allowing O'Keefe's counsel to make 'extensive irrelevant and highly prejudicial references' to: (i) Loewen's foreign nationality; (ii) race-based distinctions between the two litigants; and (iii) class-based distinctions between them.

With respect to nationality, O'Keefe's case was presented 'from beginning to end on the basis that Jerry O'Keefe was a war hero and 'fighter for his country' who epitomised local business interests, and was the victim of a ruthless foreign (Canadian) corporate predator'. Loewen was depicted as financed by the 'Shanghai Bank'; O'Keefe intimated that both Loewen and the bank might be controlled by 'the Japanese'. The truth is that Loewen was *partly* financed by the Hong Kong and Shanghai Bank, which is an *English and Hong Kong* bank. Yet O'Keefe's counsel repeatedly referred to his client's fighting for his country against the Japanese and exhorted the jury members to 'do their duty as Americans and Mississippians'.

The arbitrators were not persuaded by the US Government's attempts to persuade them that these comments were justifiable comment on Loewen's use of its 'unequal financial means to oppress [O'Keefe]'. They wrote that the 'rhetoric of O'Keefe's counsel went well beyond any legitimate exercise'.

The US Government sought to convince the arbitrators that 'the vast majority' of references to nationality, when viewed in context, were intended to identify the place where relevant events took place. The tribunal was unconvinced.

The arbitrators also found that O'Keefe had engaged in a 'racial politics strategy' which went well beyond such legitimate aims as defining relevant markets for the purposes of arguments about unfair competition; they referred to 'the efforts of O'Keefe to suggest that O'Keefe did business with black and white people alike whereas Loewen did business with white people'. The judge was African American, as were eight of the twelve jurors.

As for 'class-based prejudice': the arbitrators were understandably impressed by the way in which O'Keefe's counsel concluded his address to the jurors:

Ray [Loewen] comes down here, he's got his yacht up there, he can go to cocktail parties and all that, but do you know how he's financing that? By 80 and 90 year

---

[41] *Ibid.* at para. 132.

old people who go to get to a funeral, who go to pay their life savings, goes into this here, and it doesn't mean anything to him. Now, they've got to be stopped . . .

1 billion dollars, ladies and gentlemen of the jury. You've got to put your foot down, and you may never get this chance again. And you're not just helping the people of Mississippi but you're helping poor people, grieving families everywhere. I urge you to put your foot down. Don't let them get away with it. Thank you, and may God bless you all.[42]

The arbitrators quoted counsel's statement that:

The Loewen Group, Ray Loewen, Ray Loewen is not here to-day. The Loewen Group is from Canada. He's not here to-day. Do you think that every person should be responsible and should step up to the plate and face their own actions? Let me see a show of hands if you feel that everybody in America should have the responsibility to do that.[43]

They referred to this as 'skilful use by counsel for [O'Keefe] of the opportunity to implant inflammatory and prejudicial materials in the minds of the jury'.[44] Gary (O'Keefe's lawyer) spoke of Loewen's 'descent on the State of Mississippi'. As an 'extreme' example of appeals to national prejudice, the arbitrators pointed to the testimony of a former US Secretary of Agriculture, ostensibly solicited to testify to O'Keefe's good character, who spoke of his (the Secretary's) experience as a member of government in protecting 'the American market' from Canadian *wheat farmers* who drove American producers out of the market with low prices only to inflate the prices once they had secured the market. Gary, in his closing address to the jury, repeated this remark and explicitly compared Loewen to the Canadian wheat farmers. The arbitrators described Gary's manner of 'emphasising nationalism' as follows: "'[Y]our service on this case is higher than any honor that a citizen of this country can have, short of going to war and dying for your country;" . . . He described the American jury system as one that O'Keefe "fought for and some died for," [and said that Loewen] "didn't know that this man didn't come home just as an ace who fought for his country – he's a fighter . . . He'll stand up for America and he has." Mr Gary returned to the same theme at the end of his closing address: "[O'Keefe] fought and some died for the laws of this nation, and they're [Loewen] going to put him down for being American".'[45]

---

[42] *Ibid.* at para. 68.   [43] *Ibid.* at para. 57.   [44] *Ibid.*   [45] *Ibid.* at paras. 61–62.

Finally, it may be observed that the *Loewen* tribunal's findings illustrate the general proposition that the involvement of a jury in rendering a national court judgment provides no insulation from responsibility under international law. It is, as Freeman put it, 'a link in the chain of justice which is ultimately open to inspection in all its constituents by the processes of international law'.[46]

On the other hand, jury verdicts are doubtless less likely to come into question as a potential cause of state responsibility due to the existence of corrective measures, either by the trial judge or by appellate jurisdictions, such as orders for new trials or judgments notwithstanding the verdict.

In criminal cases, the most numerous historical precedents involved *failure* by local juries to indict, let alone convict, individuals apparently guilty of the murder, or indeed lynching, of unpopular foreigners.[47] The failure of prosecution of criminal acts gives rise to the possibility of denial of justice in the same way as does any internationally defective operation of a national judicial system (see the section on 'Inadequate measures against perpetrators of crimes against foreigners' in Chapter 6).

## Corruption

A rare instance of acknowledged corruption arose in the claim of *Coles and Croswell*, espoused by the British Government on behalf of two of its nationals convicted of theft in Haiti.[48] A Special Commissioner appointed by Britain described the matter as follows in his letter to the Haitian Minister of Foreign Affairs:

The extraordinary behaviour of the jury at the trial, and the general character of the proceedings are disclosed in the Judgment of the Court of Cassation of the 30th December, 1885.

That Judgment shows that the jury, whose deliberations should, according to law, be secret, conducted themselves in the most unseemly manner by noisy disputes and contradictions in open Court, and by disorderly proceedings in the jury room. But the most remarkable feature in the case is that, on the 21st December 1885, the Public Prosecutor was committed for trial for corrupting

---

[46] Freeman at p. 363.

[47] The *Vorowski* case is particularly memorable, involving the murder of a Russian delegate to the Lausanne Conference in 1923. His apparent murderer was acquitted by a local jury, prompting a Soviet boycott on Swiss products; Arnold J. Toynbee, *Survey of International Affairs 1924* (Oxford University Press, 1928), at pp. 258–259. (This reprisal did not, it seems, create a permanent impediment to Swiss prosperity.)

[48] *Great Britain* v. *Haiti*, 31 May 1886, 78 British and Foreign State Papers 1305.

some of the jury in order to obtain a conviction, and that no less than five jurymen were similarly dealt with for having allowed themselves to be tampered with.

It is difficult to understand how a verdict, delivered by such a jury, and under such circumstances, could have been allowed to stand for a moment.

Yet the same Court of Cassation, which had on the 21st December, 1885, directed the committal of the Public Prosecutor and five of the jurymen for corruption, actually on the 30th of the same month refused to annul the sentence of the Court of Assize, which was based on an admittedly corrupt verdict. It is impossible to reconcile these two Judgments of the Court of Cassation, and a more flagrant contradiction can hardly be conceived.[49]

## Arbitrariness

Arbitrariness is not so much something opposed to a rule of law, as something opposed to the rule of law ... It is wilful disregard of due process of law, an act which shocks, or at least surprises a sense of judicial propriety.[50]

Shortly after this oft-quoted passage was written by a chamber of the International Court of Justice, the *Amco II* tribunal presided by Judge Rosalyn Higgins (as she was to become) handed down the final award in one of the earliest and longest-running cases under the aegis of the International Centre for the Settlement of Investment Disputes.

*Amco* v. *Indonesia* was brought by a group of companies which had invested in the hotel business in Jakarta. They operated under a lease and management agreement signed between Amco Asia Corp. (USA) and PT Wisma, a corporate entity controlled by the Indonesian army. Each party undertook to make capital investments and to share profits in a hotel located on a site owned by PT Wisma. That agreement contained a clause providing that disagreements should be decided by an arbitrator named by the President of the International Chamber of Commerce in Paris.

In order to operate in Indonesia, the investors applied for a licence to establish a local subsidiary under the Foreign Capital Investment Law. After the application had been examined by the Foreign Investment Board and the Foreign Investment Evaluation Body, and agreed in principle by the President of the Republic, the licence was granted by

---

[49] *Ibid.* at p. 1328.
[50] *Case concerning Elettronica Sicula SpA (ELSI) (US* v. *Italy)* 1989 *ICJ Reports* 15 at p. 76.

the Minister of Public Works. The licence provided that disputes between the licensee and the government would be referred to ICSID arbitration.

The investors had a falling out with PT Wisma, primarily due to claims by the latter concerning its profit share. Ultimately PT Wisma took over control of the hotel with the assistance of the Indonesian armed forces. It then successfully petitioned the Indonesian courts for rescission of the lease and management agreement, alleging a number of breaches by the investors, including their alleged failure to make their capital contributions in full. A jurisdictional objection to the effect that the matter should be referred to ICC arbitration in Paris was rejected. Meanwhile, PT Wisma informed the Indonesian Capital Investment Coordinating Board (known under its acronym as 'BKPM') of certain alleged irregularities by the investors. BKPM sought and obtained presidential permission to revoke the investment licence.

ICSID arbitral proceedings were commenced by the investors in 1981. The matter did not involve amounts of macroenomic significance; the claim was never put higher than US$15 million, and the ultimate award was for a principal amount of some US$2.6 million. Nevertheless, it became one of the best-known international cases of the 1980s, giving rise to lengthy decisions by three panels comprising a number of leading international lawyers. The first arbitration was concluded by an award in 1984.[51] That award was partially annulled by an *ad hoc* committee in 1986.[52] The case was then resubmitted to a new tribunal which rendered its award on the merits in 1990.[53] By that stage, the case had already traversed fundamental issues of applicable law, jurisdiction, standards of review and – perhaps uniquely – the scope of *res judicata* when it arises from an incomplete annulment.

For present purposes, however, three substantive claims addressed to the tribunal in the resubmitted case, which might conveniently be referred to as *Amco II*, are relevant:

- the revocation of the licence violated procedural rights;
- the revocation was not substantively justified;

---

[51] 20 November 1984, 1 *ICSID Reports* 413 (Foighel, Rubin, Goldman (presiding)).
[52] 16 May 1986, 1 *ICSID Reports* 509 (Feliciano, Giardina, Seidl-Hohenveldern (presiding)).
[53] 31 May 1990, 1 *ICSID Reports* 569; rectification 10 October 1990, *ibid.* 638 (Lalonde, Magid, Higgins (presiding)).

- the rescission of the agreement by the Indonesian courts was unlawful because the local courts lacked jurisdiction and there was no evidence of breach.

There were two stated grounds for revocation of the licence: failure to invest the required amount of foreign capital and improper subcontracting of the investors' obligations. The first tribunal had held that the BKPM's procedure had been unlawful. The investors had not been given 'warnings' of purported non-observance of their obligations as required by the relevant Indonesian regulations and by 'general principles of law'.[54] Moreover, BKPM accepted PT Wisma's allegations after only a perfunctory examination, without allowing the investors to produce documents or to examine and answer either a file submitted to BKPM by PT Wisma or a BKPM report recommending revocation produced within three days of PT Wisma's first complaint – and indeed the very day after receipt of the aforementioned file. Given the violation of 'due process of law', the tribunal concluded that 'the revocation of the approval of the investment application was unlawfully and therefore wrongfully decided, whatever the reasons on which it was based, and even if, as a matter of substance, said reasons could have justified it'.[55]

This finding had not been disturbed by the *ad hoc* committee, and the *Amco II* tribunal therefore took it as a *res judicata*. Reviewing the lengthy record, the arbitrators nevertheless made some observations of their own. They found that the BKPM's examination was 'rushed, over-reliant on PT Wisma's characterizations, factually careless, and insufficiently based on detailed and independent verifications with the authorities concerned . . . the whole approach to the issue of revocation of the licence was tainted by bad faith, reflected in events and procedures'.[56] They noted that the issue of fault was not entirely 'black and white'. The investors' accounts were to some extent unreliable. 'While PT Amco's behaviour contained discreditable features, that fact could not justify BKPM's approach to the question of revocation.'[57]

---

[54] 1 *ICSID Reports* 413 at para. 198. The tribunal added: 'It could not be argued, in this respect, that discussion and defence would not have changed the administration's mind; because such argument would mean that the administration had decided in advance not to take into account any argument of the investor whatsoever, which would itself amount to a refusal of due process.' *Ibid.* at para. 202.

[55] *Ibid.* at para. 201.    [56] *Amco II* at paras. 83 and 98.    [57] *Ibid.* at para. 112.

## Retroactive application of laws

The claimant in the *Mondev* case complained about the retroactive application of an allegedly new rule adopted by the Massachusetts Supreme Judiciary Court. As seen in the section on 'No responsibility for misapplication of national law' in Chapter 4, the very premise of this grievance was undermined when the international arbitral tribunal found that the state court's decision 'fell well within the interstitial scope of law-making exercised by courts such as those of the United States'.[58] But even if this had not been the case, 'it is normally a matter for local courts to determine whether and in what circumstances to apply new decisional law retrospectively'.[59]

It is necessary to test the word 'normally' in the just-quoted phrase. Unfettered discretion to apply new or modified rules retrospectively may obviously result in the negation of legal security. In the field of human rights, judicial decisions are fiercely resisted if they have the effect of creating criminal liability where none existed before. This issue has been dealt with by the European Court of Human Rights under Article 7 of the European Convention.[60] 'If there is any analogy at all,' the award in *Mondev* reasoned, 'it is much fainter in civil cases.' The arbitrators then dismissed the complaint out of hand: 'Assuming, for the sake of argument, that standards of this kind might be applicable [to a claim of unjust or inequitable treatment], in the Tribunal's view there was no contravention of any such standards in the present case.'[61]

It is not difficult to see that the retroactive application of law by judges must be characterised as a denial of justice if the courts thereby make themselves the tools of 'targeted legislation' (see the section so named in Chapter 6). The 'law' allegedly applied retroactively in *Mondev* was of a different nature. It was judge-made law of the kind particularly prevalent in the common law, described by the *Mondev* award as 'interstitial' – presumably by comparison to the framework of positive legislation or regulation. But 'decisional law' too, whether one calls it *case law* or *jurisprudence*, may be more than interstitial. Surprising departures from

---

[58] *Mondev* at para. 137.    [59] *Ibid.*

[60] See *S.W.* v. *United Kingdom* and *C.R.* v. *United Kingdom*, 22 November 1995, (1996) 21 EHRR 363, at paras. 32–36; *Streletz, Kessler & Krenz* v. *Germany*, 22 March 2001, (2001) 33 EHRR 31, at paras. 46–108.

[61] *Mondev* at para. 138, citing *Carbonara & Ventura* v. *Italy*, 30 May 2000, [2000] ECHR 205, at paras. 64–69; *Agoudimos & Cefallonian Sky Shipping Co.* v. *Greece*, 28 June 2001, [2001] ECHR 402, at paras. 29–30.

settled patterns of reasoning or outcomes, or the sudden emergence of a full-blown rule where none had existed, must be viewed with the greatest scepticism if their effect is to disadvantage a foreigner. If it is targeted, 'decisional law' is no different from statutes or decrees, and may constitute an international wrong.

## Gross incompetence

This category is intended to cover one type of the miscarriages of justice which some persist in referring to as *substantive* denial of justice. That category should be jettisoned for reasons given in the section on 'The demise of substantive denial of justice' in Chapter 4. Grossly incompetent judgments are precisely the kind of decisions which, in the words of Fitzmaurice, no 'competent judge could reasonably have made'.[62] They therefore are the embodiment of the state's violation of its duty to establish and maintain a decent system of justice.

It must be admitted that many cases do not fit neatly into the categories chosen to organise this chapter. There is considerable overlap. Is the gravamen a matter of xenophobic prejudice, or irrationality, or gross incompetence? In truth, where a denial of justice has occurred it is likely that gross incompetence coexists with other deep flaws.[63]

One case which can be put in multiple categories is *Idler*, which indeed recurs several times in this chapter. For present purposes, the following passage in the award is worth quoting. It analysed the legal theory, purporting to extend to the government the rights of a recent minor to void contracts entered into on his behalf:

A moment's reflection will show the benefit was not universally applicable to Venezuela's contracts, and that her courts were powerless to make them so. A contract or transaction subject to the right had implied in it a condition of defeasance and restoration at the option of the privileged party. It was as though it had written in the body thereof that the minor, or king, or other favored person reserved the option to disaffirm and annul it partially or altogether, and have restored him all things lost or parted with on account

---

[62] Fitzmaurice at p. 114.

[63] A similar comment may be made about *Sawtelle* v. *Waddell & Reed, Inc.*, No. 2330 (NY App. Div. 1st Dept.), 13 February 2003, where an arbitral award of punitive damages in the amount of $25 million was vacated by a New York court as *arbitrary* and *irrational*, being 'grossly disproportionate to the harm suffered'. (The claimants in *Loewen* would doubtless have liked to have their $500 million jury verdict reviewed by *that* court.)

thereof. Could such a right in Venezuela, however fully possessed by succession, affect her contractual or other obligations with other states? Had her treaties implied in them any such condition? And was the case in any wise different as to contracts with citizens of such states made therein, where the right was not in vogue?

These were North American contracts, made at Philadelphia, where the right did not obtain. When Venezuela, so to say, came there to enter into them, she came, as would Great Britain or any other person competent to contract, with not a privilege less, not one more. Her right of *restitutio* she left behind her. The Philadelphia contracts had no condition of defeasance implied in them. When sent to Venezuela for execution, none were added. No power there, judicial or other, could engraft it on them. Therefore, as to those contracts themselves, it is perfectly clear Venezuela had not the right of *restitutio in integrum*. Unless, consequently, the law was that the right pertained to judgments when it did not to their bases, these legal proceedings can not be upheld, even if otherwise valid.

To assert such to be the state of the law is to say that Venezuela, as to the contracts, was an adult, full grown and stalwart, but as to their enforcement, a – minor! Such a condition, under the ancient Roman law, would seem to have been an impossibility.[64]

There are other precedents where international adjudicators found the evidentiary approach of the local court to have been so unfair against the foreigner as to vitiate the outcome. In the *Bronner* case against Mexico, where Umpire Thornton, after observing that he was 'always most reluctant to interfere with the sentences of judicial courts', nevertheless felt bound to hold that a confiscation of the goods of an importer, on the grounds that he had intended to defraud the customs authorities, was 'so unfair as to amount to a denial of justice'.[65] The claimant had taken 'more than usual precautions . . . to prevent the possibility of any such accusation'. He could not conceivably 'have harboured an intention to deceive with the slightest hope of success', because he had submitted the amended invoices which the court had deemed to be proof of subterfuge to the Mexican consul at Liverpool with every expectation that they would be transmitted to the Mexican authorities.

A similar case was that of the *Orient*, decided by the commission created under the US–Mexico treaty of 11 April 1839.[66] It also related to the confiscation of the property of a US national, in this case a schooner and its cargo. The only evidence against the alleged offender

---

[64] *Jacob Idler* v. *Venezuela*, Moore, *Arbitrations* 3491, at p. 3510.
[65] *US* v. *Mexico*, ibid. at p. 3134.    [66] *US* v. *Mexico*, ibid. at p. 3229.

was the testimony of the revenue collector, who presented a document he claimed to be a false manifest. Four other witnesses (including the collector's own assistant) testified that he had in fact refused to take the manifest presented to him, because it was not in Spanish, and left it on the table of the master's cabin. Upholding the claim, the commissioners wrote:

> The decision of the court confiscating the vessel and cargo was thus founded on a single fact, ascertained to exist only on the testimony of a single witness, while it was expressly denied by four others, having an equal opportunity of knowing the truth and equally entitled to credit. A decision thus given in direct opposition to so strong a preponderance of the testimony cannot be entitled to respect. It indicates strongly a predetermination on the part of the judge to confiscate the property without reference to the testimony. This opinion is strengthened by the fact that fourteen days before the decision was made the judge had agreed to pay certain expenses out of the proceeds of the confiscation ... A judge who would thus, two weeks in advance of a trial and before the testimony was examined, pledge himself to make a particular decision, would not be likely to be very scrupulous in the examination of the evidence, and certainly could claim no very great degree of respect for his decision.[67]

It is important to perceive that this aspect of the international sanction of denial of justice does not seek to second-guess national authorities' interpretation of propositions of law as such. O'Connell captured it well when he wrote: 'Bad faith and not judicial error seems to be the heart of the matter, and bad faith may be indicated by an unreasonable departure from the rules of evidence and procedure.'[68]

## Pretence of form

Unscrupulous judges may cover up a multitude of sins by an abuse of form to mask an internationally wrongful purpose. Indeed, all types of denial of justice considered in this chapter could be occulted in this fashion. It is essential that international adjudicators be able to go behind empty formality if international standards are not to be overwhelmed by the handiwork of cynical intelligence.

In the First Hearing of the prisoner Rubashov in *Darkness at Noon*, the Examining Magistrate Ivanov leaves no illusions about the objective of

---

[67] *Ibid.* at p. 3231.
[68] D. P. O'Connell, *International Law* (2nd edn, London: Stevens & Sons, 1970), at p. 948.

the exercise: 'For the public, one needs, of course, a trial and legal justification.'[69] Later on, Ivanov is physically liquidated, so Rubashov is informed, for his lenient interrogation techniques. He is replaced by the implacable Gletkin. The latter ultimately breaks Rubashov's will, by a combination of endless questioning, sleep deprivation and environmental discomfort (the emblematic hard chair, blinding lights, windowless room). Yet Gletkin answers Rubashov instantly when he asks why he has not been treated with violence:

'You mean physical torture,' said Gletkin in a matter-of-fact tone. 'As you know, that is forbidden by our criminal code.'

He goes on to explain:

The political utility of your confession at the trial will lie in its voluntary character.[70]

And indeed at the trial Rubashov is duly asked whether he wants an advocate for his defence (he declines) and whether he has any complaint to be made about the investigation (he has none). When the prisoner asks for an interruption due to an intolerable toothache (from an untreated root which the prison doctor had offered to excise, but without anaesthesia) he makes it possible for the following day's newspaper to report:

It is typical of the correct procedure of revolutionary justice that the President immediately granted this wish and, with a shrug of contempt, gave the order for the hearing to be interrupted for five minutes.[71]

In a moment of candour, Gletkin explains that differences of opinion are intolerable because they may confuse and unsettle the masses; they compromise 'the imperious necessity for the Party to be united'. Therefore, Rubashov's role at the trial was:

to gild the Right, to blacken the Wrong. The policy of opposition is wrong. Your task is therefore to make the opposition contemptible; to make the masses understand that opposition is a crime and that the leaders of the opposition are criminals.[72]

---

[69] Arthur Koestler, *Darkness at Noon* (1940; trans. Daphne Hardy, London: Folio Society, 1980), at p. 94.
[70] *Ibid.* at p. 222.   [71] *Ibid.* at p. 247.   [72] *Ibid.* at p. 237.

And so Rubashov obediently admits to preposterous accusations of plotting to assassinate the Leader of the Party, and of conspiring with foreign enemies, although his true 'crime' is his 'sentimental' but intolerably 'oppositional' disapproval of the brutal methods of the regime. In return, as he is sent off to be shot in the neck, Gletkin offers him only one comfort in the form of the promise of a posthumous explanation of historical necessity:

> after the victory, one day when it can do no more harm, the material of the secret archives will be published ... And then you ... will be given the sympathy and pity which are denied today.[73]

The point of recalling Koestler's *magnum opus* is simple: if Rubashov had had the possibility of bringing an action before an international court of human rights, the Soviet Union would obviously have responded by pointing to the punctiliousness of its procedural code and of the way it was specifically applied in his case.[74] International law must go behind the form, or else international law will serve not to eradicate injustice, but to frown upon clumsiness.

## Summary

Some denials of justice may be readily recognised: refusal of access to court to defend legal rights, refusal to decide, unconscionable delay,

---

[73] *Ibid.* at p. 238.

[74] *Darkness at Noon* never once mentions the name of the country where the trial takes place. As if seeking to dispel any doubt, the Soviet Union's representative to the first session of the UN Human Rights Commission (Valentin Tepliakov) in early 1947 reacted sharply to the declaration by the Lebanese delegate to the effect that the first principle to guide the work of the Commission should be that the human person is more important than any national group to which he may belong. Any pressure from a group to coerce consent should be held to be unacceptable. Tepliakov replied that this was completely unsuitable; Summary Records, UN Doc. E/CN.4/SR 14 at p. 4.

> "I do not understand,' he said, professing puzzlement at Malik's reference to 'pressure' exerted on individuals. 'What does he mean?' The rights of the individual, he insisted, must be seen in relation to the individual's obligations to the community, which is 'the main body which provides for his existence, and the enjoyment of the human rights which belong to him.' On one point he was absolutely unambiguous: 'We cannot divide the individual from society."

> Mary Ann Glendon, *A World Made New* (New York: Random House, 2001), at p. 40. (It should not be forgotten that even some Western powers who today champion the virtues of liberal democracy, perhaps disoriented in the twilight of their colonial era, adopted a disturbingly ambiguous posture with respect to individual human rights.)

manifest discrimination, corruption, or subservience to executive pressure.

Unfairness in the hearing of a case is a more difficult matter. Disappointed litigants tend to see unfairness everywhere. Yet the varieties of legal culture that enrich the world are to be respected; a method for the reception of evidence is not unfair because a foreigner finds it odd. The legitimacy of local practice should be acknowledged by the international adjudicator as well as by the complainant. It is often surpassingly difficult to evaluate fairness without having been present; perhaps not with respect to some formal matters, like failure of notice to attend, which may be a matter of undisputable fact, but with respect to subjective matters, like an atmosphere of harassment, which are difficult to reconstitute from a written record. International adjudicators must pass judgment in a necessarily subjective manner. States are most unlikely, in any foreseeable future, to establish general international appellate jurisdictions to pass comprehensive judgment on the decisions of national courts; they would not tolerate that a similar thing entered through the back door in the guise of sanctions for denial of justice. Hence the unavoidability of formulations that are at once open-textured and indicative of the exceptional foundation necessary to make good on such claims against states. One might say that denial of justice arises when *proceedings are so faulty as to exclude all reasonable expectation of a fair decision,* but the choice of words is infinite. What they all have in common is that they lead to a debate to be resolved by appeals to experience, not to the dictionary.

How do international adjudicators then recognise a denial of justice when confronted with a given set of facts? One basic postulate is that denial of justice is not limited to cases where the doors of justice were literally shut. A system of justice may fall short of international standards in many other ways. No definitive list of instances could be presented, for it would soon be invalidated by new fact patterns, untested forms of organisation of systems of justice, and the boundless capacities of human invention. Recurring instances are unreasonable delay, politically dictated judgments, corruption, intimidation, fundamental breaches of due process, and decisions so outrageous as to be inexplicable otherwise than as expressions of arbitrariness or gross incompetence.

A further basic postulate is that some acts or omissions by governmental authorities are sufficiently closely related to the administration of justice that they must also be deemed capable of generating international delinquency under the heading of denial of justice: failures of enforcement, the implementation of sanctions against persons or property without trial, failure of investigation or indictment, lengthy imprisonment without trail, arbitrarily lenient or harsh punishment.

# 8

# Remedies and sanctions

## General principles: *restitutio, damnum emergens, lucrum cessans*

Traditionally, the issue of reparation was central to the subject of denial of justice. It was the very objective of the exercise of diplomatic protection. Yet the International Law Commission's rapporteur on Diplomatic Protection, Professor John Dugard, made it clear in his First Report[1] that his work would include no attempt to formulate principles of reparation, but rather defer to the ILC Articles on State responsibility.[2] Articles 34–36 of the ILC Articles provide:

### 34. Forms of reparation

Full reparation for the injury caused by the internationally wrongful act shall take the form of restitution, compensation and satisfaction, either singly or in combination, in accordance with the provisions of this Chapter.

### 35. Restitution

A State responsible for an internationally wrongful act is under an obligation to make restitution, that is, to re-establish the situation which existed before the wrongful act was committed, provided and to the extent that restitution:

(a)  is not materially impossible;
(b)  does not involve a burden out of all proportion to the benefit deriving from restitution instead of compensation.

---

[1]  International Law Commission (Dugard), First Report on Diplomatic Protection, UN Doc. A/CN.4/506 at p. 12, para. 35.
[2]  Report of the International Law Commission on the work of its 48th Session, 6 March – 26 July 1996, UN Doc. A/51/10 at pp. 141–142.

## 36. Compensation

1. The State responsible for an internationally wrongful act is under an obligation to compensate for the damage caused thereby, insofar as such damage is not made good by restitution.
2. The compensation shall cover any financially assessable damage including loss of profits insofar as it is established.

These Articles are important, and will inform any current discussion of remedies under international law. Yet they are not designed to cater specifically to the particular enquiries that are germane to cases of denial of justice.

Some such cases have no difficulty applying the general rule, established with venerable authority by the Permanent Court of International Justice in the *Chorzów Factory* case,[3] that the sanction of illicit acts should, to the extent possible, extinguish their consequences and re-establish the *status quo ante*. Judge de Visscher opined with specific reference to denial of justice that the 'normal' reparation should be *restitutio in integrum*.[4] The easiest case is that of payment obligations wrongfully imposed upon the claimant; they are simply annulled.[5] The ordinary case of a claimant denied the right to collect a judgment is also straightforward; the damages, as in the *Martini* case, will be the uncollected amount, plus interest.[6] It may be that the wrongful refusal to enforce a judgment leads to additional damages – such as the claimant's bankruptcy in the *Fabiani* case[7] – but such complicating factors are not unique to cases of denial of justice. They fall to be determined within the limits of the recovery of indirect losses (discussed below).

But sometimes it is impossible to unscramble the omelette. The very event of a wrongful national judgment may have set off a series of events involving third parties. Acceleration clauses may have been triggered under loan agreements. Secured rights may have matured in the guise of deemed events of default. Transactions, or entire enterprises, may have been irredeemably compromised.

Under the *restitutio* approach of the *Martini* award, Loewen would have been entitled to the reversal of the iniquitous judgment. But in the meanwhile a settlement had ensued, and the winning plaintiff had encashed

---

[3] *Germany* v. *Poland*, (1928) PCIJ, Series A, No. 17.    [4] De Visscher at p. 436.
[5] *Martini* (*Italy* v. *Venezuela*), 3 May 1930, II RIAA 975.
[6] See *Montano* (*Peru* v. *US*), Moore, *Arbitrations* 1630, at p. 1637.
[7] *Antoine Fabiani* (*no. 1*) (*France* v. *Venezuela*), Moore, *Arbitrations* 4878, at p. 4910.

$175 million – and doubtless spent much of it. Certainly tens of millions would have been paid over to Mr Gary, the contingency lawyer. The international arbitral tribunal had authority to recognise the international responsibility of the US, but no jurisdiction to order Messrs O'Keefe and Gary to disgorge sums of money obtained under a settlement agreement. The only respondent before the arbitrators was the US. *Restitutio* would surely imply a payment of $175 million, but does it not also imply that that sum must be reduced by what would, on a balance of probabilities, have happened to Loewen if the clock had indeed been turned back? For Loewen's previous situation had been that of a besieged defendant. Should the tribunal judge what a 'likely' outcome would have been in a trial not contaminated by unfairness? Or should it notionally 'purge' the actual trial of the consequences of unfairness, e.g. by considering that the amount of *compensatory*, as opposed to punitive, damages were based on creditable evidence of a contract breach and therefore represented what Loewen would have lost in the normal course of events (i.e. a proper trial). That amount would therefore fall to be discounted.

The solutions to these questions are elusive.

In reading old awards, one must also be careful to verify whether the *compromis* under which the relevant commission or tribunal had been given its authority contained limitations on either the types of liability or the measure of reparation that could be recognised. (Such limitations were the political price of obtaining assent to international adjudication.) Pleaders often miss the point, for example, that the well-known *El Triunfo* award simply could not grant damages on account of lost profits arising from the breach of the relevant maritime concession agreement because the inter-state agreement explicitly forbade any such recovery.

Adjudicators have struggled since time immemorial with the limits of compensable damages. Yet the concepts are not complex. At the one extreme are damages which demonstrably arise as the evidently direct consequence of the wrongful act. At the other extreme, there are damages which are insufficiently established either in fact or as a matter of caus-ation. They are typically referred to as 'too remote', 'unforeseeable' or 'speculative'. In between there is an area of *indirect* damages which are controversial.[8]

---

[8] See the ILC Commentary under Article 36, in James Crawford, *The International Law Commission's Articles on State Responsibility: Introduction, Text and Commentaries* (Cambridge University Press, 2002), at pp. 218–230.

That they may be recovered is beyond cavil. The difficulty is the permanent haze that overlies the boundary between what is *too remote* and what is merely indirect. In addition, there are contractual stipulations – or indeed treaty stipulations, as in the *El Triunfo* case – which exclude the award of indirect compensation, or compensation on account of lost profits. Such stipulations create their own difficulties of interpretation,[9] and moreover the risk that awards limited by them fail to be recognised as exceptions.

In principle, this passage written by Sir Hersch Lauterpacht in 1927 has lost none of its cogency or authority:

The border line between direct and indirect damages, or between prospective and merely speculative profits, is seldom clear, and its determination is often dependent upon the subjective estimate of the arbitrator, who is, in fact, guided not so much by the technical distinctions between different kinds of damages, as by the wish, perfectly justified in law, to afford full redress to the injured. But to maintain that international law disregards altogether compensation for *lucrum cessans* is as repellant to justice and common sense, as it is out of accord with the practice of international tribunals.[10]

---

[9]  Consider these hypothetical examples:

   (A)   Six ships are expropriated. Their replacement value is 100.
   (B)   A transportation company owning six ships is expropriated. It is established that a bona fide third-party purchaser was prepared to purchase the company, which benefited from a portfolio of advantageous contracts, for 200.
   (C)   Same as B, but instead of proof of a third-party offer, there is an economically irreproachable demonstration that the going-concern value to the expropriated owners is 200.

(A) is not difficult. But how is (B) different from (A)? See Crawford, *Articles*, at p. 226: 'The value of goodwill and other indicators of profitability may be uncertain, *unless derived from information provided by a recent sale or acceptable arms-length offer*' (emphasis added). And if (B) is accepted, why not (C)? The demonstrable market value of a disposed asset has been accepted by international tribunals, as in *de Sabla* (*US* v. *Panama*, 29 June 1933, VI RIAA 358) (proof of purchase offers for lots in Panama) and in this dictum in *SPP* v. *Egypt* (*Southern Pacific Properties (Middle East) Limited* v. *Egypt*, award, 20 May 1992, 3 *ICSID Reports* 189, at p. 237: an arm's-length transaction 'should, in principle, be the best indication of the value of an asset'. But that may imply the recovery of anticipated lost profits: i.e. the purchasers are willing to go beyond the replacement value of the six ships (which are not for sale) to pay an *enhanced* value based on their expectations that the transportation company has demonstrable prospects of profitable operations. What then is the difference between (B) and (C); or between enterprise value and lost profits?

[10]  Sir Hersch Lauterpacht, *Private Law Sources and Analogies of International Law* (London/ New York: Longman, 1927, repr. 2002), at pp. 148–149.

Another controversial area relates to non-material or 'moral' damages. Claims for mental suffering, injury to feelings, humiliation, shame, or injury to credit and reputation are predictable in the context of denial of justice, where the personal integrity of the victim may have been profoundly affected. A person's psyche may be ruined by unlawful commitment to a psychiatric institution[11]; a prosperous enterprise may be ruined by wrongful condemnation or the refusal to give effect to valid judgments in its favour.[12] As with indirect damages, the controversy tends to arise in cases of concrete application; the principle, as such, is well established. Non-material damages, in the words of Umpire Parker in the *Lusitania cases*, are 'very real, and the mere fact that they are difficult to measure or estimate by money standards makes them none the less real and affords no reason why the injured person should not be compensated'.[13]

A final general consideration of utmost importance is to recognise that a state may not escape international responsibility for denial of justice by relying on a judgment which recognises the wrong but purports to erase it by the grant of paltry compensation. The issue is quite similar to that of expropriation; international responsibility is not excluded by insufficient compensation. The sufficiency of compensation is necessarily within the purview of international adjudicators; otherwise the recognition of an international wrong would be an empty gesture, and states could escape liability on the flimsiest pretext. In the *Howland* case,[14] the claimants were thus able to prosecute their international claim notwithstanding an ostensibly favourable Mexican Supreme Court judgment restituting to them a significant quantity of beeswax which had been wrongfully seized by

---

[11]  See *Timofeyev* v. *Russia*, 23 October 2003, [2003] ECHR 546.
 In *Philis* v. *Greece*, which involved a less compelling victim, namely an engineer thwarted in his attempts to pursue contractual claims, the European Court of Human Rights nevertheless held: 'The feeling of frustration generated by the impossibility of assuming control of the defence of his own interests, as well as the prolonged anxiety as to the outcome of his disputes with his debtors, must have caused the applicant some non-pecuniary damage. Making an assessment on an equitable basis ... the Court awards him 1,000,000 drachmas under this head' (27 August 1991, (1991) 13 EHRR 741, at para. 73).

[12]  *Antoine Fabiani (no. 1)* (*France* v. *Venezuela*), Moore, *Arbitrations*, at p. 4878.

[13]  *US* v. *Germany*, 1 November 1923, VII RIAA 32, at p. 40, quoted with approval in Crawford, *Articles*, at pp. 223–224. For an example where a 'strenuously urged' claim for loss of credit, despite a finding of liability for the depravation of property with the complicity of officials, and evidence of a harrowing ordeal in chaotic regions of Venezuela, was disallowed as 'entirely too indefinite and uncertain', see *Poggioli* (*Italy* v. *Venezuela*), J. H. Ralston, *Venezuela Arbitrations of 1903* (Washington, DC: US Government Printing Office, 1904), 847, at p. 870.

[14]  *G. G. S. Howland* v. *Mexico*, Moore, *Arbitrations*, at p. 3227.

customs officials. (Without hearing anyone on behalf of the owners, they had decided that the wax was from Havana – and thus a prohibited import due to a war with Spain – rather than St Petersburg as duly recorded by US officials and certified by the Mexican counsel in New York.) The problem was that the wax had deteriorated during the period between its seizure and release (from December 1825 to April 1828). The Mexican commissioners argued that the Mexican judgment had finally disposed of 'the merits of the case' by ordering restitution but no compensation for damages and costs. The umpire disagreed, and ordered compensation comprising the original value of the ninety-three bales in question, plus 'duties, charges, and a moderate profit, together with the expenses incurred in the recovery of the wax',[15] as well as interest. The net recovery resulted from deducting the price finally obtained in Mexico upon the release of the deteriorated wax. There seems to be no reason for distinguishing between deterioration of the condition of the property and that of the market price; in either case the mitigation is objectively determined by the price obtained.

## Vicarious damage and deterrence

As we have seen, international law first responded to denial of justice by justifying a regime of reprisals. These sanctions were carried out by or under the authorisation of the victim's sovereign. By the beginning of the twentieth century, the favoured mechanism had become that of diplomatic protection. Coercion under the colour of the state, initiated and indeed carried out by private parties to satisfy private interests, became a thing of the past.

Nevertheless, in 1938 Freeman could still write that:

it is still undoubtedly accurate as a theoretical matter to speak of the State's right to resort to reprisals or war, if need be, to secure the justice that has been denied to its nationals.[16]

Today, even that theoretical justification has disappeared in the wake of the near-universal renunciation of force as a means of settling disputes. Instead, international law has developed the doctrine of a 'secondary obligation' to repair the damage resulting from the 'original' unlawful act. When that secondary obligation too is breached, the victim's state may be expected to intensify diplomatic pressure, including the use of economic

[15] *Ibid.* at p. 3228. [16] Freeman at p. 572.

bargaining chips and agitation in multilateral organisations, or indeed to seize international jurisdictions.

Given the vast expansion of direct access to an adjudication by litigants other than states, however, the most significant sanctions in contemporary practice are those imposed by national courts pursuant to international *res judicata* such as arbitral awards (or indeed national judgments applying international law). This involves considerations of a number of issues beyond the scope of this study, such as the scope of sovereign immunity from execution, waivers of immunity, and the role of insurance against the failure to respect awards or judgments.

What matters for present purposes is the conceptual shift in terms of the remedies granted in cases of denial of justice as the bulk of practice has shifted from diplomatic protection to direct private action against the responsible state. In Bouchard's day, and still in Freeman's, the precedents almost invariably involved the claims of a state demanding reparations for damages to its own honour, or to prejudice caused to its protected national, or both. In theory, the injured party was the claiming state, not its national; once the claiming state was satisfied, the matter was closed for the purposes of international law.

One consequence of this type of proceeding was that the state might articulate its own prejudice, such as that arising from general ill-will towards its citizens as a group, and might seek its own remedy, e.g.:

in the shape of an apology given with appropriate solemnity and, where proper, the punishment of the guilty persons, either disciplinary or otherwise.[17]

In the *Sartori* case[18] before the US – Peru Commission under the Treaty of 12 January 1863, the claimant was a US businessman residing in Chile. On a business trip to Peru, he was detained by military forces. He was confined for a duration of four months, and then released without any judicial proceedings. In the meanwhile, his business was ruined. He therefore sought compensation in the considerable amount of $118,755. The US Commissioners favoured his cause; their Peruvian colleagues did not, observing that Sartori at his arrest had been carrying a package, in itself innocent but entrusted to him by an insurrectionist military commander for delivery to a common friend. The matter went to the Umpire (General Herran), who concluded that the arrest and detention had been justified, but that 'the Government of Peru is responsible for the delay of 48 hours in taking the formal declaration of Sartori, and for not having brought him to judgment'.

---

[17] *Ibid.* at p. 575.    [18] *US* v. *Peru*, Moore, *Arbitrations*, at p. 3120.

Having concluded that there was an international wrong, the Umpire turned to the issue of damages. He found that the claimant's theory of causation was unacceptable, as encapsulated in this sentence:

Peru is not responsible for the fact that Mr. Sartori should have absented himself from Valparaiso, leaving his affairs in the hands of an agent in whose good faith he could place no reliance.[19]

He nevertheless concluded that the irregularity in Sartori's treatment should lead to financial compensation, reasoning as follows:

There is no circumstance leading to the belief that this omission was intentional on the part of the Peruvian Government. Far from this, proofs exist that they were not influenced by bad will or the spirit of persecution, and that it was their desire to give no cause of complaint to the United States; but on the principle that reparation ought to be made in cases where responsibility is incurred, however small it may be, for noncompliance with the treaty, *in order that each government may place entire confidence in the good faith of the other*, it seems to me that an equitable and reasonable indemnity ought to be granted to Mr. Sartori.[20]

The phrase in italics would of course have no place in a case where the individual private claimant has direct access against the respondent government.

A second consequence was that the injured party had no right to develop and articulate its own legal theory of remedies. The protecting state might conceive a general approach to claims of damages on account of a large group of citizens injured by the same respondent state. As was often the case before a number of the commissions and tribunals established between 1850 and 1950, that general approach would then be applied as individual claims were presented before separate bodies of adjudicators.

These features of bygone practice should be kept in mind as one considers the precedents of the time. Equally, one should not exaggerate the difficulty of referring to them. As the Permanent Court of International Justice stated in the *Chorzów Factory* case:

It is a principle of international law that the reparation of a wrong may consist in an indemnity corresponding to the damage which the *nationals* of the injured State have suffered as a result of the act which is contrary to international law. This is even the most usual form of reparation.[21]

---

[19] *Ibid.* at p. 3124.    [20] *Ibid.* at p. 3123 (emphasis added).
[21] (1928) PCIJ, Series A, No. 17, at pp. 27–28.

And as every practising international lawyer knows, the fact that the *Chorzów Factory* case involved two states litigating pursuant to the mechanism of diplomatic protection has not prevented that case from becoming a seminal precedent for the calculation of damages in a myriad of international arbitrations initiated by private parties.

## Illustrative precedents

The general rule applies here too; the reparation of an international wrong may take the form of *restitutio in integrum* or in compensatory damages calculated so as to efface the pecuniary consequences of the delict. Here as elsewhere, theory bows to the historical preference for *restitutio*, but international jurisprudence with respect to the law of claims has for many generations found few situations where it is practicable.[22]

On the other hand, there are circumstances when *restitutio* is both appropriate and practical. For example, obligations placed on a foreigner by a civil judgment vitiated by a denial of justice may simply be annulled by the relevant international jurisdiction, as in the *Martini* case.[23] Or a criminal conviction handed down in such circumstances may likewise be held without effect, with or without the possibility of a retrial depending on the circumstances.

The *Fabiani* award is a leading and venerable precedent. The French claimant had obtained an award from a private arbitral tribunal in 1880 declaring him entitled to certain sums owed by a past Venezuelan partner and the exclusive owner of certain property located in Venezuela. Fabiani's attempts to execute this award in Venezuela were comprehensively frustrated by an unjustifiable series of delays and suspensions. First, his case was halted to allow a putative appeal for which there existed no proper mechanism. Next, the pretext of a specious conflict of jurisdiction was invoked to paralyse the process. Finally, the competent court simply failed to put Fabiani's petition to enforce his award on its schedule for hearings.[24] As a result, Fabiani could not recover considerable assets to which he was legally entitled, and, exhausted by interminable and costly litigation, fell into bankruptcy. The unpaid debts which caused his

---

[22] For an exception and a learned exposition of the matter, see the award of 19 January 1977 by Professor René-Jean Dupuy, sitting as sole arbitrator in *Texaco Overseas Petroleum Company / California Asiatic Oil Co.* v. *Libya*, (1978) 17 ILM 1, at pp. 31–36.

[23] *Italy* v. *Venezuela*, 3 May 1930, II RIAA 975.

[24] Cf. *Revpower Ltd* v. *Shanghai Far-East Aero-Technology Import and Export Corporation*, discussed in the section entitled 'Refusal to judge' in Chapter 7.

bankruptcy represented sums far less than those which he would have recovered if his award had been enforced.

A substantial award was rendered in the amount of some 4.3 million francs. The largest element of the award, 1.8 million francs, was on account of losses caused by the bankruptcy and the resulting closing of his business; these were the:

immediate consequence of the denials of justice, since Fabiani was thrown into bankruptcy at Maracaibo for the non-payment of sums greatly inferior to those which execution of the [foreign] judgment would have obtained for him.[25]

The second largest element, 1.5 million francs, was 'indirect' damages, which the arbitrator considered to be due since Fabiani, given his proven capability in the local business milieu, would have expanded his profitable business but for the fact that 'by the fault of the Venezuelan judicial authorities, he lost his property and prestige altogether'. (The award also included damages in the amount owed under the original private arbitral award, as well as for Fabiani's costs.)

When awarding damages for denials of justice, international adjudicators are looking at a delict of a different nature from a breach of a commercial contract. In some cases it can be *specially* demonstrated that the breach of the contract deprived the claimant of funds which he was in a position to put to particularly advantageous use. Such awards are rare. International tribunals are seldom persuaded to give indirect damages for the loss of high-yield ventures, but rather consider that a prudent rate of return on safe money markets are the appropriate standard by which to assess the damages.

A denial of justice, however, by its nature may deprive the victim of more than a sum of money. Precisely because judicial institutions are involved, an unjust judgment may have vast deleterious consequences. In *Fabiani*, as seen, repeated denials of justice led to bankruptcy and a loss of prestige which curtailed what had until then been the claimant's successful career in Venezuela. The arbitrator awarded substantial damages on account of 'lost profits' and 'other gains by exploiting additional sources of revenue', which he declared were the 'immediate consequences' of the bankruptcy and to be distinguished from the similarly substantial indirect damages awarded because the amounts granted under the original awards had been unproductive for so many years. International lawyers today are likely to refer to both types of damage as *indirect*, and to have no difficulty in accepting the *reality* of damages flowing from the unlawful

---

[25] *Antoine Fabiani (no. 1) (France v. Venezuela)*, Moore, *Arbitrations* 4878, at p. 4913.

inaccessibility of capital; but tend to apply a rate of interest. Since the movement of the second billiard ball is the consequence of the cue striking the cue ball, the physical act of the player is the *cause* – but is nevertheless *indirect*. It is a mistake for judges or arbitrators to think that they have to 'improve' the status of the loss by declaring it to be *direct*.

The case of *Cotesworth and Powell*[26] concerned a judge in Barranquilla who colluded with an assignee in bankruptcy to rob the claimants of property held by a failed partnership, rendered decisions without a hearing, and then disappeared with all documents – making it impossible for the claimants to prove their ownership. To add injury to injury, the Colombian authorities proclaimed a decree of amnesty which prevented any action against the judge.

Aiming to grant reparations that would restore 'the state of affairs as it would have been if justice had been followed from the beginning', the award stated that:

if the Government, by means of its amnesty, relieved of responsibility the authors of the deeds forming the basis and foundation of this claim, it can be affirmed, in strict justice, that in doing so it assumed that responsibility.

Accordingly, the award was for payment of 'the value of the property unjustly attached and not returned'.

To this amount interest of 5 per cent was awarded, the commissioner stating that:

it would be absurd to assume that the legitimate property of an individual can be taken from him and kept and used for years and then returned finally without the slightest remuneration.

For all its factual complications, *Idler*[27] was a straightforward case when it came to damages. The claimant had recovered a judgment on a contractual claim against the public treasury for non-payment of deliveries under a contract. Four years later, the judgment was annulled by a court found to have been incompetent, acting without a legal basis and submissive to governmental pressure. Finding that Venezuela had been culpable of a denial of justice, the arbitral tribunal awarded the amount of the original judgment plus contractual interest (6 per cent) from the date thereof.

---

[26] *Great Britain* v. *Colombia*, Moore, *Arbitrations* at p. 2050.
[27] *Jacob Idler* v. *Venezuela*, Moore, *Arbitrations*, at p. 3491. The case is discussed at length in Chapter 6, especially in the section on 'Governmental interference'.

(The period during which interest ran, it should be noted, was among the longest in the annals of international arbitration: about seventy years.)

In *Smith* v. *Marianao*,[28] local authorities had instituted illegal expropriation proceedings and the claimant's property was partially demolished. He then obtained a judgment declaring that the process was illegal, but his subsequent petition to be restored to possession was denied. Finding a denial of justice, the arbitrators evaluated the property (giving weight to factors such as its unobstructed waterfront view), considered the duration of the claimant's deprivation of use, and his legal costs.

In *De Sabla*, the loss of property was evaluated on the basis of offers made for the land.[29]

In the French *Conseil d'Etat* case referred to in Chapter 7[30] the State was held liable – by national application of the European Convention of Human Rights – for damages caused by unreasonable delays in judging a claim under a public works contract. The court affirmed that the claimant was entitled to reparations (beyond whatever he may have recovered by virtue of the decision on the merits of his initial claim) covering all 'material and moral' damages, in particular for 'the loss of an advantage or a chance', for the belated recognition of a right, and indeed for vexation (*désagrément*) 'beyond the usual worries engendered by any law suit' in light of the plaintiff's particular situation. (The plaintiff was 72 years old when he brought his petition, the matter was deemed not to be 'particularly difficult', and judgment was not rendered for seven and a half years.)

## *Amco II* and proximate cause

As described in the section of Chapter 7 entitled 'Arbitrariness', the *Amco II* tribunal held that Indonesia committed a denial of justice when one of its administrative agencies, the Capital Investment Coordinating Board (or 'BKPM'), revoked the claimants' investment licence. This gave rise to a debate of fundamental importance when it came to assessing damages. Indonesia raised the issue how damages could follow even if the record would support a finding *by the international tribunal* that the investors' conduct justified revocation.

[28] (1930) 24 AJIL 384.
[29] *De Sabla* (*US* v. *Panama*), 29 June 1933, VI RIAA 358, at pp. 367–368.
[30] Conseil d'Etat, *Garde des sceaux, Ministre de la justice/M. Magiera*, 28 June 2002.

The claimants insisted that the 'procedurally unlawful revocation' itself should give rise to compensation 'even if BKPM's decision were substantively valid'. Indonesia argued that this could be so only if it were proved that the procedural failure had led to an unlawful *substantive* decision. No such proof could be given, so Indonesia argued, because the revocation was in any event well founded. Moreover, the investor was given later opportunities to seek revision of the revocation.[31] Therefore the claim must be rejected because ultimately the investors had not been denied what Indonesia referred to as 'substantial justice', by which Indonesia meant that the international tribunal could – and should – still determine that the investors' conduct justified cancellation of the licence.

The tribunal reviewed a number of Indonesian precedents invoked by the parties. Eight of them are individually described in the award. The arbitrators found that they did not 'clearly stipulate whether a procedurally unlawful act *per se* generates compensation; or whether a decision tainted by bad faith is necessarily unlawful', although there was 'some slight authority' that the answer 'might be answered in the affirmative'.[32] The inconclusiveness of Indonesian law led the arbitrators, pursuant to Article 42 of the ICSID Convention, to appreciate the matter under international law – a circumstance which naturally enhances the interest of this precedent for the purposes of our study.

The tribunal then turned to a number of cases which have already featured prominently in this book. The proposition for which *Martini* was cited – that an arbitral tribunal may annul obligations imposed on a foreigner by a national decision which violates international law, or award monetary reparation – did not, in the *Amco II* tribunal's view, address the issue at hand. As for *Fabiani*, it demonstrated that damages may flow if an unjust procedure causes loss, but the question was whether damages would be available absent such loss. Similarly, the arbitrators rejected the applicability of *de Sabla*, where the damages awarded could not be said to represent compensation for procedural violations since they flowed from the loss of property resulting from the defective procedures.

---

[31] This Indonesian defence is given very little attention in the award. It is difficult to avoid the impression that the arbitrators overlooked the point encapsulated by Judge Jiménez de Aréchaga when he wrote that: 'an essential condition of a State being held responsible for a judicial decision in breach of municipal law is that the decision must be a decision of a court of last resort, all remedies having been exhausted'. 'International Law in the Past Third of a Century', (1978) 159 *Recueil des cours*, vol. I, 278, at p. 282. This aspect of denial of justice is of course at the heart of Chapter 5.

[32] *Amco II* at para. 121.

And while *Idler* declared Venezuelan judgments to be a nullity due to a denial of justice (in particular lack of proper notice), the award in that case did not consider whether those judgments might have been substantively correct. In the same way, *Chattin* made no supposition about substantive guilt or otherwise; damages were awarded, in the words of the commission which decided that case, because of the 'most astonishing lack of seriousness on the part of the Court'. *Smith* v. *Marianao* involved a wrongful expropriation, with the consequence that damages were to be awarded in the event the property was not restored.

For its part, Indonesia argued that some judgments of the European Court of Human Rights suggest that 'procedural violations do not generate damages where there remains the possibility that the substantive decision might be the same'.[33] The arbitrators were not convinced, noting that there is 'a discrete jurisprudence relating to Article 50 of the European Convention that has no applicability to the issue in this case'.[34]

Having concluded its review of the international legal authorities invoked by the disputants, the *Amco II* tribunal concluded that 'the question in international law is not whether procedural irregularities generate damages *per se*. Rather, the international law test is whether there has been a denial of justice ... as Commissioner Nielson reminded in the *McCurdy* case, even if no single act constitutes a denial of justice, such denial of justice can result from "a combination of improper acts".' The arbitrators referred to the *ELSI* case, which had just been decided by the ICJ, and its distinction 'between unlawfulness in municipal law' and 'arbitrariness under international law'. This distinction, the arbitrators wrote, is 'equally germane to the distinction between procedural unlawfulness and a denial of justice'.[35]

---

[33] *Ibid.* at para. 125.
[34] *Ibid.* at para. 128. Article 50 requires 'just compensation' to be given by the European Court if the reparation permitted by local law is incomplete. It must be said that the *Amco II* Tribunal's treatment of the *Sramek* v. *Austria*, 22 October 1984, [1984] ECHR 12, seems unduly dismissive. To conclude that it does not support Indonesia's claim, the arbitrators noted that the applicant in *Sramek* had not sought the Austrian courts to compensate her for the procedural wrong (irregular composition of the tribunal), but for consequential pecuniary loss; at para. 127. But the issue was not what Sramek had sought from the Austrian courts. It was rather what one should make of the European Court's observation that 'the evidence in the file does not warrant the conclusion that had it been differently composed [the tribunal] would have arrived at a decision in Mrs Sramek's favour'.
[35] *Amco II* at para. 136.

This analysis led the arbitrators to consider whether the circumstances of their case amounted to a denial of justice regardless of the existence of substantive grounds justifying the revocation of the licence. They concluded that although 'certain' grounds of that nature 'might have existed', the 'circumstances surrounding BKPM's decision make it unlawful', and gave rise to Indonesia's liability.

The *Amco II* tribunal's review of the precedents cogently demonstrated that the authorities relied on by the parties did not in fact answer the question as framed: does international law consider that damages should be awarded solely on account of a denial of justice even if it can be demonstrated that the substantive outcome would have been justified even without the violation of due process? But having done so, the critical reader might well reflect, the *Amco II* tribunal does not appear to have answered the question either. What the arbitrators rather did is to affirm that there was a distinction between 'procedural unlawfulness' and 'denial of justice', and that in the case before them a finding of the latter under international law (in addition to the former, under local law) was justified. Having so concluded, the tribunal explicitly stated that it was not required 'to address the issue of whether Amco fulfilled its investment obligation',[36] and that it need not make legal findings of law as to whether an administrative decision may be 'substantively justifiable' by reference to grounds not cited in the decision – and this precisely 'because of its determination that BKPM's substantive decision was irrevocably tainted by bad faith'.[37] The unstated premise appears to be that if there has been an international delict, reparations are due. But that of course is not what international law affirms; *Chorzów Factory* is trite law to the effect that in the wake of a breach the damages caused must be repaired. And so the question remains: what are the damages if the outcome would have been the same even if the national authorities had acted properly?

The award says that the acts imputed to Indonesia were unlawful even though 'certain substantive grounds might have existed for the revocation of the licence'.[38] But the issue at this juncture is not the unlawfulness of the conduct, but whether it caused proximate damage. Nor is the reader assisted by the tantalising statement that there are 'indications' that the circumstances of the revocation 'tainted the proceedings irrevocably'. The acknowledgement of 'indications' sound like something short of a *finding*. More importantly, the notion of *irrevocability* is quite unhelpful. If it is taken to mean that the harm caused to the investor was irretrievable,

---

[36] *Ibid.* at para. 141.  [37] *Ibid.* at para. 143.  [38] *Ibid.* at para. 139.

there is a contradiction with the observation that the revocation might have been well founded. If it is taken to mean that the defect could not be corrected by an appellate mechanism, one would search in vain in the award for an examination of that proposition.[39] Or if it is taken to mean only that the conclusion is incontrovertible, the use of the word seems inapt.

In the section of its award dealing with issues of quantum, the *Amco II* tribunal began with the postulate that 'BKPM's decision ... caused PT Amco to lose its licence to engage in business ventures in Indonesia' and proceeded without pause to assess the value of what the investors thus had lost. Surely this was going too fast. The words just quoted indicate that the consequence of the delict was something very concrete: the loss of the right to do business. But what had caused the arbitrators to conclude that the *Martini, Fabiani, de Sabla* and *Smith* v. *Marianao* awards did not 'address the problems before this Tribunal' was *precisely* that they sought to repair the consequences of the international delict rather than to consider whether the delict *per se* gave rise to a duty to compensate. And if the investor's own conduct might have justified revocation of the licence if that issue had been examined properly – i.e. with proper notice and a right to be heard – how can one think that the BKPM's decision 'irrevocably' *caused* the investors to lose their rights to do business?

The Tribunal's answer to this question was as follows:

> To argue, as did Indonesia, that although there had been procedural irregularities, a 'fair BKPM' would still have revoked the licence, because of Amco's own shortcomings, is to misaddress causality. The Tribunal cannot pronounce upon what a 'fair BKPM' would have done. This is both speculative, and not the issue before it. Rather, it is required to characterise the acts that BKPM did engage in and to see if those acts, if unlawful, caused damage to Amco. It is not required to see if, had it acted fairly, harm might then have rather been attributed to Amco's own fault.[40]

Since BKPM's denial of justice effectively deprived the investors of their contract rights (the rescission of the lease and management agreement was chiefly based on the impossibility to carry it out without the licence) 'non-speculative profits under that contract are recoverable',[41] the

---

[39] To the contrary, para. 152 mentions parenthetically that the Indonesian Supreme Court 'was not acted' to invalidate the revocation of the investment licence when it rejected the appeal against the decision that the lease and management agreement pertaining to the hotel had been validly rescinded.

[40] *Ibid.* at para. 174.    [41] *Ibid.* at para. 178.

objective being 'to put Amco in the position it would have been in had the contract been performed'. This was evaluated according to a discounted cashflow method which both parties acknowledged as appropriate in principle – although naturally with a debate about assumptions and relevant data which is familiar in international arbitration, and is of no particular interest for our subject.

By contrast to *Amco II*, in *Lauder* v. *Czech Republic* the arbitral tribunal explicitly held that the respondent state 'took a discriminatory and arbitrary measure' against the investor when the official Media Council, after having accepted that he make a direct investment in a Czech entity (CET21) which held a valuable television licence, changed its mind as a result of political opposition 'to the granting of the licence to an entity with significant foreign capital'.[42] Lauder therefore had to invest in a new company which would have 'exclusive use' of the licence. The measure was arbitrary, said the tribunal, 'because it was not founded on reason or fact, nor on the law which expressly accepted 'applications from companies with foreign equity participation', but on mere fear reflecting national preference'.[43] The tribunal then went on to address the issue of relevance here, namely whether the breach led to damage. It held:

It is most probable that if in 1993 Mr. Lauder's investment in the Czech television could have been made directly in CET 21, the Licence holder, the possible breach of any exclusive agreements in 1999 could not have occurred in the way it did. Even if the breach therefore constitutes one of several '*sine qua non*' acts, this alone is not sufficient. In order to come to a finding of a compensable damage it is also necessary that there existed no intervening cause for the damage ...

The arbitrary and discriminatory breach by the Respondent of its Treaty obligations constituted a violation of the Treaty. The alleged harm was, however, caused in 1999 by the acts of CET 21, controlled by Mr. Železný. The 1993 breach of the Treaty was too remote to qualify as a relevant cause for the harm caused. A finding of damages due to the Claimant by the Respondent would therefore not be appropriate.[44]

---

[42] Award, 13 September 2001, 9 *ICSID Reports* [forthcoming] (Cutler, Klein, Briner (presiding)) at para. 231.

[43] *Ibid.* at para. 232.

[44] *Ibid.* at paras. 234–235. (The tribunal in *CME Czech Republic BV* v. *Czech Republic* partial award, 13 September 2001, 9 *ICSID Reports* [forthcoming] (Schwebel, Hándl, Kühn (presiding) reached a sharply different conclusion as to the facts of the case.)

If one goes back to a *locus classicus* of international law, the *Chorzów Factory* case,[45] one finds that the court identified three fundamental questions presented in this logical sequence:

(1)  The existence of the obligation to make reparation.
(2)  The existence of the damage which must serve as a basis for the calculation of the amount of the indemnity.
(3)  The extent of this damage.[46]

The PCIJ rephrased its second question somewhat more simply as, 'whether damage has resulted from the wrongful act'. If that is the question, did the *Amco II* tribunal elide it? The authorities to the effect that this question must be confronted are too numerous to mention. As examples, consider the German – US Mixed Claims Commission's statement in 1923 that proximate cause is 'a rule of general application both in private and public law';[47] the *ELSI* case, so clearly in the minds of the *Amco II* arbitrators, where the US claim was rejected because of its failure to establish that the offending acts of the Italian Government were the proximate cause of the relevant losses – rather than 'ELSI's headlong course to insolvency';[48] and the posture of the plenary Iran – US Claims Tribunal when it found a 'failure' by the US but reserved for a later stage the determination, 'whether Iran has established that it has suffered a loss as a proximate result' thereof.[49]

But the PCIJ also said, in an oft-quoted phrase, that 'it is a principle of international law, and even a general conception of law, that any breach of an engagement involves an obligation to make reparation'. It did not qualify this statement by adding *provided damages are proved*. We are thus impelled to look closer at step (2) above: 'the existence of the damage which must serve as a basis for the calculation'. Might it not be said that the damage 'which must serve as a basis' is determined by the pleadings, and that the identification of the damages to be proved may therefore be the consequence of the submissions of the claiming party? Some intimations of such a notion transpire from this passage of the judgment:

---

[45]  *Germany v. Poland* (1928) PCIJ, Series A, No. 17. This was the famous Judgment 13 of the Court, which had in fact been preceded by four other judgments (Nos. 6, 7, 8 and 9) in the same case.
[46]  *Ibid.* at p. 29.
[47]  *Administrative Decision No. II (US v. Germany)*, 1 November 1923, VII RIAA 23, at p. 29.
[48]  *Case concerning Elettronica Sicula SpA (ELSI) (US v. Italy)* 1989 *ICJ Reports* 15, at para. 101.
[49]  *Iran v. US*, Case No. A11, 597-A11-FT, award, 7 April 2000, at para. 291.

The Applicant having calculated the amount of the reparation claimed on the basis of the damage suffered by the two Companies as a result of the Polish Government's attitude, it is necessary for the Court to ascertain whether these Companies have in fact suffered damage as a consequence of that attitude.[50]

This was of course a claim by espousal. Germany had chosen to present a claim aimed at recovering the pecuniary loss of its nationals. That being the plea, it had to be proved. (And so it was.) But as we have seen, international law has also embraced the concept of deterrence, as in the *Sartori* case where an indemnity was granted to the claimant 'on the principle that reparation ought to be made in cases where responsibility is incurred, however small it may be ... in order that each government may place entire confidence in the good faith of the other'.[51] Was this the unarticulated premise of *Amco II*, that the claimant acted as a private prosecutor whose recovery served the broader interests of international law,[52] and as such dispensed from proving proximate cause? Or should the award be read as standing for the proposition that the state gets one clear chance at providing justice to the foreigner, failing which the international tribunal should not speculate about the outcome if national processes had been proper?

If a foreigner's claim before a national court was thwarted by a denial of justice, the prejudice often falls to be analysed as the loss *of a chance* – the possibility, not the certainty, of prevailing at trial and on appeal, and of securing effective enforcement against a potential judgment debtor whose credit-worthiness may be open to doubt. The questions left open by *Amco II* suggest that this dimension of the inquiry was overlooked.

At any rate, the observation must be made that a *Leitmotif* of our study courses into this chapter too; there is no magic of drafting, no improvement of legislative technique, that can allow the international legal process to dispense with the need for the judicial qualities of discernment in the light of experience, applied to the circumstances of each case.

---

[50] *Chorzów Factory case (Germany v. Poland)*, (1928) PCIJ, Series A, No. 17, at p. 30.
[51] *US v. Peru*, Moore, *Arbitrations* 3120, at p. 3123.
[52] De Visscher wrote at 414–415 that awards in favour of individuals 'in reality correspond to a social necessity ... the objective being to create an incentive for the defaulting government to ameliorate its judicial organisation, while giving the claiming government some assurance that such facts will not arise again in the future'.

## The time value of money

Given the lengthy delays that tend to bedevil so many legal systems, it is clear that the issue of whether interest runs on the amounts found to represent the compensable loss takes on a special importance in the context of denial of justice. We have already considered the extreme *Idler* case, where the dispute festered for seventy years.[53]

Far more recently, the European Court of Human Rights – not known for generous awards to claimants – recognised that 'the adequacy of the compensation would be diminished'[54] unless consideration were given to the fact that ten years had elapsed since the claimant had obtained an arbitral award against the Government of Greece only to be frustrated by a new law which purported to annul the award (see the section on 'Targeted legislation' in Chapter 6). It therefore granted interest, even though the arbitral award – which involved a substantial amount of money – had not stipulated that interest would run until payment. This realism must be approved.

## Summary

The goal of reparations in international law is to restore the victim of a breach to the position it would have enjoyed if the infraction had not occurred. That general principle applies to cases of denial of justice.

Although the formulation of the principle is uncontroversial, its concrete application raises considerable difficulties. It is not always easy to determine what the hypothetical consequences would have been if denial of justice had not occurred.

If the complainant has been deprived of a right or caused to make payment, the situation is relatively straightforward. Since this international wrong requires the failure of the national system as a whole, the finding of denial of justice necessarily means that there was no further local recourse. The rights must then be restored (if restitution is available and sufficient) or monetary reparation awarded.

The difficulties arise when the complainant was thwarted from *pursuing or defending a claim*. After all, if his case had been given a fair hearing, it may have been a poor one in any event. Similarly, the denial of justice may

---

[53] *Jacob Idler* v. *Venezuela*, Moore, *Arbitrations* at p. 3491.
[54] *Stran Greek Refineries and Stratis Andreadis* v. *Greece*, 9 December 1994, (1995) 19 EHRR 293, at para. 82.

have occurred at the national appellate level, as the complainant sought to overturn an unfavourable first judgment. The appeal may have had little chance of success even in the absence of the denial of justice. What does it then mean to put the complainant in the 'same situation'? The inquiry may be further complicated by the fact that the victim, as in *Loewen*, decided in the circumstances to compromise, and thereafter asks the international tribunal to give compensation for the shortfall on the footing that the unfavourable settlement was unavoidable due to the denial of justice.

It seems difficult to justify the conclusion that the prejudice to a claimant who was prevented from having his grievance heard should be deemed equal to whatever relief he had initially seen fit to ask. In establishing an amount so that it corresponds to what the international tribunal feels was the true loss, it may be necessary to evaluate probabilities of the outcome if the local system had proceeded in accordance with its laws but without violating international law.

The notion that no international wrong must go unpunished is arguably inconsistent with *Chorzów* if its consequence is that it leads to recovery even in the absence of demonstrable prejudice. Such recovery could only be viewed as a penalty in the interest of the international rule of law.

# 9

# The menace of 'obscure arbiters'?

We have concluded our efforts to situate denial of justice in modern international law. The book could be closed already. The reflections to be offered in this final chapter are, strictly speaking, *hors sujet*. There will be no further analysis, no illuminating synthesis. What remains are thoughts inspired by sidelong glances.

At the heart of this *post scriptum* is the simple point that the adjudication of claims of denial of justice tends to be a matter of considerable sensitivity. Our subject therefore gives rise to a formidable test of commitment to the rule of international law. True, the same can be said for the way national constituencies receive *any* international decision unfavourable to national interests. In that sense, a finding by international adjudicators that a state is guilty of denial of justice may encounter the same type of resistance as that which often confronts foreign arbitral awards arising from ordinary private commercial transactions. Yet there is something exceptionally emotive about challenges to national justice. They seem to strike at the heart of national pride. And so it seems difficult to leave the subject without considering the policy implications of international adjudications relating to this delict.

## Anti-international challenges

As the case of *Loewen* v. *United States* drew to a close, a regional US newspaper quoted critics of free trade agreements as raising the 'subtle issue' whether a 'secret tribunal' of 'obscure arbiters' should be in a position to 'trample the voice of the people'.[1] The epithet – *obscure arbiters* – is

---

[1] Stewart Yerton, 'Critics Say Agreement Tramples the Rights of Local Citizens', *The New Orleans Times Picayune*, 30 June 2003.

pejorative but meaningless. Nor need anyone fear that international arbitrators will exceed the bounds of their jurisdiction. If they do, their decisions are quashed – by annulment if the case is heard under the aegis of ICSID, otherwise by national courts.[2]

The serious question is whether they represent some form of danger even when they do respect the terms of their mandate. Have they been given licence to subvert the popular will, or to work against the public good? The evocation of anonymous cabals, however exaggerated, justifies an exploration of the scope of the *duty* and *authority* of international arbitrators.

When international tribunals pass judgment on national institutions, indignant reactions are predictable. They escape the confines of diplomatic discourse and erupt into the realm of public debate, producing much rhetoric but less informed judgment.

For there to be a denial of justice under international law, an international tribunal must find that the legal system of a country has performed badly, so badly that it falls short of international minimum standards. People everywhere vigorously criticise their own courts, but resent it when foreigners do; hence the outbursts against imagined 'obscure' villains. One doubts that the author of the philippics quoted above would have been appeased if Sir Anthony Mason, the former president of the highest court of Australia who chaired the *Loewen* tribunal, had been replaced by a celebrity lawyer. The logical inference from this type of criticism is rather that international legal claims against a state should be resolved by politicians accountable to the electorate of that state. In other words, the objection is not only a negation of the judicial process, but a rejection of the principle that a state may be held accountable under international law.

That acute sensibilities come to the fore when national justice is challenged by foreign prosecutors before international tribunals is neither surprising nor new. In the economic sphere – where the predominant issues concern the protection of property rights – the nationalistic reactions once tended to be those of Third World countries. Capital-exporting nations like the United States, on the other hand, staunchly promoted the international rule of law, and in particular the authority of international tribunals to pass judgment on the actions of national authorities, including courts.

---

[2] As in *Metalclad* (Supreme Court of British Columbia, judgment of 2 May 2001, 5 *ICSID Reports* 236) and *Attorney-General of Canada* v. *S.D. Myers, Inc.*, Federal Court of Canada, judgment of 13 January 2004, 8 *ICSID Reports* 194.

At the turn of the century, a *volte-face* in the US became perceptible in the attitudes of a number of officials, pressure groups and media, as the conduct of US organs of government came repeatedly before the bar of international law, almost entirely as a result of the application of the North American Free Trade Agreement (NAFTA).

In a much-remarked article,[3] Guillermo Aguilar Alvarez and William Park likened the new US attitude to that of a protagonist in Jules Romains' *Les hommes de bonne volonté*, who was happy to break the law but incensed that others did so as well: *c'est un homme qui aime l'honnêteté d'autrui* (a man who likes honesty in others). Aguilar and Park noted the extraordinary public outbursts of US Congressmen who in the course of a single session:

- fulminated against the possibility that the Justice Department might have to sue the State of Mississippi to enforce a hypothetical award in favour of Loewen: 'This is nuts! ... We must stand together to protect the sovereignty of American laws. We should not allow [that] American taxpayer dollars pay American lawyers to help a foreign corporation fight American state laws in court'.[4]

- expressed anxiety that the pace of globalisation might result in 'sacrificing state and local laws at the altar of ill-defined international investor rights'.[5]

- yielded to the temptation of facile polemics: 'The question ... is very clear: Should the rights of an investor come before the rights to enact a chemical ban to prevent cancer?'[6] and: 'Are my colleagues to allow families' health and that of our children, our friends and neighbors to be threatened because of foreign bureaucrats!'[7]

All of these sentiments were expressed in support of legislation in 1999[8] that would have prohibited the Department of Justice from using its budget to challenge state laws that violate NAFTA – of which, as Aguilar and Park pointed out, the Mississippi bond requirement (under

---

[3] 'The New Face of Investment Arbitration: Capital Exporters as Host States under NAFTA Chapter 11', ICCA Congress Series No. 11, 302; republished with amendments as 'The New Face of Investment Arbitration: NAFTA Chapter 11', (2003) 28 *Yale Journal of International Law* 365.
[4] Shows (Mississippi), 145 *Congressional Record* H7368 (5 August 1999).
[5] Tierney (Massachusetts), *ibid.* [6] Bonior (Michigan), *ibid.*
[7] Ros-Lehtinen (Florida), *ibid.* at p. H7370.
[8] The Kucinich–Ros-Lehtinen amendment, discussed and defeated by vote on 5 August 1999, *ibid.*

which the Loewen Corporation was given ten days to provide security in the amount of US$625 million) might be an example. The proposal failed, but by a scant margin: 196 in favour, 226 opposed.

Attacks from other sources were yet more excessive. Public Citizen, an organisation founded by Ralph Nader, the consumer advocate and environmentalist, took out full-page advertisements captioned 'Secret Courts for Corporations' and 'Taxpayer Dollars for Foreign Polluters'. They castigated NAFTA for enabling 'foreign corporations to sue the federal government in secret tribunals, demanding our tax dollars as payment for complying with US health, safety and pollution laws'. The World Wildlife Fund and the Institute for Sustainable Development sponsored and disseminated a report by a Canadian lawyer concluding that NAFTA Chapter 11 arbitrations are 'one-sided', lack 'transparency', and are 'shockingly unsuited to the task of balancing private rights against public goods'.[9] A journalist of national reputation, Bill Moyers, appearing on the ostensibly dispassionate Public Broadcasting Service, introduced one of his programmes by evoking 'a threat to democracy from an obscure provision of the North American Free Trade Agreement ... how is it that foreign corporations can trump health and safety laws in our own country?' That 'obscure provision', it turned out, was nothing other than NAFTA's Chapter 11, the investment section, which Moyers described as though it were a sinister incubator of 'secret tribunals'. It turned out that the immediate trigger for this segment of the programme was the *Methanex* case.[10] Guests invited to speak included a lawyer for the 'Earthjustice Legal Defense Fund', which had lobbied for the ban of the petrol additive MTBE; according to Methanex, a Canadian company, this ban constituted a discriminatory measure under NAFTA. In this gathering, NAFTA was lambasted as a 'sophisticated extortion racket' and 'an end run around the Constitution' in which 'secret NAFTA tribunals can force taxpayers to pay billions of dollars in lawsuits'. Democracy, it was said, 'goes out the window'.[11]

---

[9] Howard Mann, *Private Rights, Public Problems: A Guide to NAFTA's Controversial Chapter on Investor Rights* (New Providence, NI: International Institute for Sustainable Development and World Wildlife Fund, BPR Publishers, 2001), at p. 46.

[10] *Methanex Corp.* v. *United States of America*, partial award, 7 August 2002, 7 *ICSID Reports* 239 (Rowley, Christopher, Veeder (presiding)); hearings on the merits 7–17 June 2004 (with Professor W. Michael Reisman replacing Mr Christopher following the latter's resignation).

[11] *Now with Bill Moyers*, 2 January 2002, transcript available at <http://www.pbs.org/now/transcript/transcript_tdfull.html>.

## Responses to the anti-international critiques

There are of course serious controversies about the macroeconomic dislocations created by globalising policies in general and NAFTA in particular, relating for example to the scope and timing of tariff reductions, the need to retrain workers and farmers displaced by international competition, and the tradeoffs between declines in employment rates in some sectors against increases elsewhere. Such political issues are the substance of governmental policy; the *raison d'être* of a reliable legal infrastructure is purely instrumental. To be sure, using a good tool to implement misguided policies leads to poor results, but that is no reason to blame the tool. The point becomes obvious when one considers that the absence of mechanisms for implementation will inevitably frustrate the soundest and most democratic of policies.

There is more than one paradox in the kinds of denunciations described above. The multilateralist impulse from the left of the political spectrum, so vibrant when it comes to the Kyoto Protocol on transnational environmental protection, to the curtailment of the death penalty, or to the promotion of any number of laudable mechanisms for the protection of human rights, seems to evaporate when it comes to protection of property rights.[12] But when the outbursts come from the right, one cannot help but think that those who were aghast at the prospect of an international tribunal 'trampling on sovereignty' by condemning the Mississippi court's miscarriage of justice in *Loewen* would find nothing amiss if precisely such a sanction had been pronounced against precisely such a miscarriage of justice in a Third World country. That, one would imagine them saying, is precisely what international arbitration was designed to do.

The neonationalist reaction nevertheless deserves serious attention, not so much because it has merit, but because it puts into relief choices that

---

[12] History, it may be said, teaches that when leaders can do with private property as they please, they tend to engineer systems of incentive and disincentive that make all other human rights illusory. It is perhaps fitting that a much-discussed book-length treatment of this subject was authored by a noted historian of Russia, Richard Pipes, *Property and Freedom* (London: The Harvill Press, 1999).

The relationship between property rights and the fight against poverty was a key to *The Mystery of Capital* (New York: Basic Books, 2000), a book-length essay by the Peruvian economist Hernando de Soto, a member of the International Labor Organization's World Commission on the Social Dimension of Globalization and the promoter of the much-heralded effort in the 1990s to alleviate the bureaucratic obstacles to the recognition of rights created within Peru's vast informal economy.

are fundamental to the international legal order. As with the inherently difficult concept of *democratic rule*, the tradeoffs must be understood and weighed and debated continuously. Perhaps the US Congress, or the legislature of the State of Mississippi, knows what is best for the public, and for the environment, and should not have to comply with international law; but if national authorities act on such impulses they should comprehend that they are undermining the international rule of law. For it is the very essence of international law that it limits national sovereignty. It is a social contract, and requires careful consideration of long-term interests. We all like to do as we please, whenever we please. But we are not prepared to allow others that privilege. When we surrender to the discipline of general norms, therefore, we do so only because otherwise there is little prospect that others will voluntarily yield their own sovereignty. The stakes are high. If the politicians of one country insist that international tribunals should have no power to rule on the legality of economic discrimination against foreigners because the protection of local business interests is essential, and coincides with the welfare of the local community, their posture may be practically undistinguishable from that of leaders in other countries who might insist that international tribunals should have no power to rule on the legality of the curtailment of civil rights because such restrictions reflect the local conception of the will of God, or a local cultural attachment to traditional authoritarian rule.

The neonationalist currents seem most persuasive to those who are attracted by sensational allegations of conspiracies against the public interest, and are disinclined to make an effort to grasp the more complex themes of international rules and economic cooperation. The shrill voices will always be with us. They are an inevitable part of democratic debate. It would be our loss if they fell silent; they provide valuable occasions to articulate rational rebuttals of the extreme positions which underlie appeals to public prejudice.

Yet political maturity requires that propaganda be recognised as such. The open-minded search for policies that contribute to long-term benefits for the community as a whole – national, regional, international – is the nutrient of a healthy democratic diet. Not so propaganda, whose authors pursue an ultimate revealed truth, and care little about the means of advancing their cause. They have no time for inconvenient facts. Servants of their revelation, they are dismissive of what Arthur Koestler called *penultimate* truths. As the discredited Rubashov, the principal character of *Darkness at Noon*, rues in his prison cell, true believers consider that 'the question of subjective good faith is of no interest ... History has taught us that often lies serve her better than the truth.'

Ultimate revelations are of infinite variety. They may be as simple as the postulate that anything that endangers a dictatorial regime is to be combated at any cost. So, for example, inquiries by the Inter-American Commission of Human Rights as to the enslavement of local courts by the executive branch might be dismissed as an insulting infringement of national sovereignty, and the investigations by international criminal courts of the cover-up of genocide castigated as the handiwork of imperialist conspirators.

One need only recall the reaction of the Fujimori Government when Ivcher Bronstein brought proceedings against Peru before the Inter-American Court of Human Rights.[13] A naturalised Peruvian citizen, Bronstein was the majority shareholder and director of a television station which had become a thorn in the side of the regime, exposing human rights violations and corrupt practices by Vladimir Montesinos, the infamous power broker behind the throne. The government abruptly 'withdrew' Bronstein's citizenship, with the result that he was no longer qualified to own and operate a local broadcasting company; he was in effect silenced and dispossessed. Roughly at the same time, three Peruvian Constitutional Court justices initiated proceedings before the Inter-American Court of Human Rights, contending that they had been impeached because they refused to uphold the constitutionality of a law intended to allow Fujimori to run for an additional presidential term.[14] In July 1999, Peru purported to withdraw its recognition of the jurisdiction of the Inter-American Court of Human Rights. (The Court held it to be ineffective; post-Fujimori, Peru has reaffirmed its subjection to the jurisdiction of the Court.[15])

In the course of this episode, Fujimori had continued to make eloquent speeches about the crucial role of an independent judiciary to the building of a democratic and prosperous nation. As for various exceptions to due process, he said:

---

[13] *Ivcher Bronstein* v. *Peru* (Merits), 6 February 2001, Inter-American Court of Human Rights, Series C, No. 74.

[14] *Constitutional Court case* (*Aguirre Roca, Rey Terry, and Revoredo Marsano* v. *Peru* (Merits)), 31 January 2001, Inter-American Court of Human Rights, Series C, No. 71.

[15] Jo M. Pasqualucci, *The Practice and Procedure of the Inter-American Court of Human Rights* (Cambridge University Press, 2003), at pp. 115–116.

*No se trata de quebrar el Estado de Derecho, sino de adecuarlo a circunstancias de emergencia.*
(We are not toppling the State of Law, but rather adjusting it to circumstances of emergency.)

That was his way of saying: we will run *our* courts *our* way. As for the Inter-American Court of Human Rights, he left it to the Chairman of the parliamentary Judicial Commission to say that Peru would not bow to a Court – and now the inevitable phrase – 'whose conduct has obviously become politicised'. Various members and spokesmen of the Fujimori Government referred to the Judges of the Inter-American Court as *viejos decrépitos, izquierdistas infiltrados,* and *abogados y voceros del terrorismo.*[16] On one occasion Fujimori himself indulged in legal analysis: orders by an international court to conduct new trials were unconstitutional, he ventured, because of the rule of *res judicata.*[17]

A similar example was furnished by the *ad hominem* diatribes directed by Nigeria against three of the leading international jurists of their generation immediately following the judgment in *Land and Maritime Boundary Between Cameroon and Nigeria.*[18] They were accused of 'legitimising and promoting the interests of former colonial powers at our expense', solely by virtue of their having the nationalities of European former colonial

---

[16] In response, a Peruvian human rights activist referred to the rather conventional curricula vitae of the distinguished Judges to demonstrate the surrealism of describing them as 'aging and decrepit leftist infiltrators, lawyers and spokesmen of terrorism'. Javier Diez Cansero, 'Fujimori y el Sistema Interamericano de Derechos Humanos: Crónica geisha de una sesión histórica', 13 July 1999, available online at the website of the Peruvian Asociación Por Derechos Humanos, <http://www.aprodeh.org.pe/public/ciddhh.c_july23.htm>.

[17] Consciously or not, he thus echoed a dusty 'advisory opinion' rendered by the Peruvian Supreme Court in 1927 in the case of *Cantero-Herrera* v. *Canevaro Co.*, in which Cuban claims of denial of justice before Peruvian courts were met with the Supreme Court's nationalistic assertion that *res judicata* has been 'raised to the category of international law' in that 'no self-respecting country will countenance that any other country should impeach the force and legality of an executed judgment'. The episode is described by Freeman at p. 128 *et seq.*, who dismissed this primitive attempt to 'transplant into the international community a generally accepted principle of municipal law as a means of barring claims founded in distinct international wrongs', at p. 129.

Fujimori's posture had even earlier antecedents. As noted in correspondence from the US Secretary of State to his Minister in Peru on 1 November 1886, Peru expressed its willingness to accept international adjudication of claims by US citizens provided that any treaty to that effect would exclude 'all claims upon which judgment may have been pronounced by Peruvian tribunals'. The US position was straightforward: 'Such judgments are not recognised by international law as internationally binding, and cannot be so regarded by this government.' J.B. Moore, *A Digest of International Law* (8 vols., Washington, DC: US Government Printing Office, 1906), vol. VI, at p. 267.

[18] *Cameroon* v. *Nigeria,* Equatorial Guinea intervening, 2002 *ICJ Reports* 3.

powers.[19] Whatever the 'logic' of the proposition that a decision favourable to Cameroon was the product of neocolonialism, it must also be recognised as insulting to a fellow African state. The Nigerian statement went on to declare that the government would act in compliance with 'its constitutional commitment to protect its citizenry', a clear challenge to the authority of the court's judgment.

Not all true believers have a political agenda. Some are defenders of local culture, or religious traditions, against the onslaughts of the modern world. In *The Last Temptation of Christ* case before the Inter-American Court of Human Rights, involving censorship of a motion picture, Chilean church groups seeking to intervene as *amici curiae* in favour of the ban explained that they acted 'in the name of Jesus Christ, the Catholic Church and themselves'.[20] It would be a mistake to underestimate the fervour of such beliefs. How can those who hold them be expected to hesitate, if they see the choice as being between the abstract and distant benefits of the international rule of law and the imperative need to stop the devil from corrupting the hearts and minds of the children of the faithful?

To move to the economic field, the revelations fuelling anti-internationalist rhetoric may be *a priori* convictions that anything is evil if it is perceived as either favourable or disadvantageous to business, or if it does not give an attractive forum for single-issue pressure groups. Dialogue is pointless; no evidence is admissible if it does not conform to the ultimate truth. Illustrations abound whenever international bodies purport to regulate trade, whether at a regional or global level. Thus, to take but one example among legion, pending a decision by the WTO Appellate Body regarding the licitness of US steel tariffs, the Chairman of the American Iron and Steel Institute told the US Congressional Steel Caucuses that:

The WTO's abuse of power and infringement of U.S. sovereignty will undermine the international rules-based trading system if Congress does not push back.[21]

---

[19] Official statement issued by the Nigeria Information Service Centre, 7 November 2002, available online at <http://www.nigeriaembassyusa.org/110802_1.shtml>. Fortunately for regional peace, Nigeria ultimately reconsidered and seemed to accept the inevitable consequences of the judgment.

[20] *Olmedo Bustos et al.* v. *Chile* (Merits), 5 February 2001, Inter-American Court of Human Rights, Series C, No. 73, at para. 21.

[21] Remarks of Daniel R. DiMicco, ASIS Press Release, 8 April 2003, available online at <http://www.steel.org/news/pr/2003/pr030408.html>. In fact, the Appellate Body's decision went against the US Government, but was complied with, prompting

Fortunately, cooler heads tend to prevail; untruths and exaggerations are examined and exposed.

One such distortion – and a particularly harmful one – is to view international law as a conspiracy of foreign capitalists thwarting the protection of public health, the environment and other unimpeachable objectives. International tribunals obviously do not set out to curtail national legislative prerogatives of seeking ways to prevent cancer, or to give free rein to industrial polluters; they impose norms of non-discrimination, or respect for other obligations of international law. And the application of such norms does not mean that the international tribunal substitutes its judgment for that of national authorities. To the contrary, it gives effect to their own international agreements. Consider this passage from *Azinian v. Mexico*:

> The possibility of holding a State internationally liable for judicial decisions does not, however, entitle a claimant to seek international review of the national court decisions as though the international jurisdiction seised has plenary appellate jurisdiction. This is not true generally, and it is not true of NAFTA. *What must be shown is that the court decision itself constitutes a violation of the treaty.* Even if the Claimants were to convince this Arbitral Tribunal that the Mexican courts were wrong with respect to the invalidity of the Concession Contract, this would not per se be conclusive as to a violation of NAFTA. More is required; the Claimants must show either a denial of justice, or a pretence of form to achieve an internationally unlawful end.[22]

This paragraph has been cited in other investment arbitration awards, and always with approval. It has never been acknowledged by a US Congressman, nor, it would seem, by a journalist. There *is* no foreign bogeyman who wants to subvert democratic legislation. The issue is rather this: when a government enters into an agreement under international law, is it subject to the processes of international law or can it decide unilaterally how to comply with its undertakings?

But there are other readily exposed untruths, such as the allegation that Chapter 11 was an insidious hidden feature of NAFTA, slipped in without proper legislative awareness. Some things are so preposterous that they do not even deserve to be ignored – so let it be said that NAFTA was the

---

a New York Times editorialist to opine that 'this case was the rough equivalent of *Marbury v. Madison*', David Sanger, 'Backing Down on Steel Tariffs, US Strengthens Trade Group', *New York Times* (5 December 2003), 25, quoted in James Bacchus, *Freedom and Trade* (London: Cameron May 2004), at p. 296.

[22] *Robert Azinian et al.* v. *Mexico*, award, 1 November 1999, 5 *ICSID Reports* 269, at para. 99 (emphasis in the original).

product of lengthy negotiations involving large teams of negotiators representing each of the three governments; that it was not a routine bit of legislation, but a highly visible treaty; and that the US Congress, for one, is not a gathering of dupes lacking access to information and critical analysis.

Almost as nonsensical is the proposition that international tribunals comprise 'unknown' unelected decision-makers. Arbitral tribunals are *selected* in accordance with the parties' agreement. Disputants in invest-ment arbitrations think very long and hard about their choice of arbitra-tors. They might not select celebrities, but persons they believe have the requisite insight and impartiality to give proper effect to the international instrument being invoked. Of course nothing stops the respondent state from nominating well-known figures having held prominent positions of public responsibility, and this has indeed occurred. Thus, for example, the early NAFTA Tribunals included a former US Secretary of State, a former Attorney General, and a former Congressman and federal judge.

The oft-repeated complaint that arbitral tribunals are 'secret' was overcome, as we shall see, by successive measures that not only made the process more transparent, but allowed representative interest groups to make submissions to the international adjudicators. These measures were met by grudging acquiescence. Like the man who will not take *yes* for an answer, it seemed the critics were not satisfied that their concern was addressed, but unhappy to be deprived of a grievance.

As for the sensationalist claim that 'secret NAFTA tribunals can force taxpayers to pay billions of dollars in lawsuits' one can only wonder about its foundation in fact.[23] A noteworthy instance was the *Pope & Talbot* case,

---

[23] Senator Kerry argued in the US Congress that it was necessary to curb treaty-based investor protection by referring to a study which showed that 'unless we change the chapter 11 model, claims against the United States will average $32 billion annually'. 148 *Congressional Record* S4594 (21 May 2002). Senator Gramm of Texas retorted that '[i]n the 57 years that we have had investment treaties, never, ever has the United States of America lost a case. But every day those same treaties protect American investments in Central and South America, in Africa, in Asia, in the developing world, in the very countries we say we want to see develop capitalist and democratic systems' (*ibid.* at S4596). Gary H. Sampliner, a Senior Counsel in the Office of the General Counsel for International Affairs of the US Department of Treasury put it as follows: 'Like Sherlock Holmes' proverbial dog that didn't bark, the low number of NAFTA claims filed to date, and the lower number of the successful ones, may be the most eloquent testimony yet to the lack of a serious threat from the investor-state arbitration provisions of US investment agreements' ('Arbitration of Expropriation Cases Under US Investment Treaties – A Threat to Democracy or the Dog That Didn't Bark?' (2003) 18 *ICSID Review* 1, at p. 2).

which was sufficiently controversial to cause the NAFTA Free Trade Commission, headed by the Canadian Minister for International Trade, the Mexican Secretary of the Economy, and the US Trade Representative, whose interpretation of the treaty is explicitly binding on tribunals deciding investment disputes, to issue an Interpretive Note[24] purporting to direct arbitrators to adopt a particular, restrictive under-standing of international minimum standards.[25] Yet the final award against Canada in that case amounted to barely US$460,000 – less than what it cost the investor to prosecute its claim, and a thousand times less than the original claim of US$508 million.[26]

The cooler heads that prevail are those of the representatives of the relevant States. In their Joint Statement on the occasion of the tenth anniversary of NAFTA, the three governments declared as follows:

> The evidence is clear – the NAFTA has been a great success for all three Parties. It is an outstanding demonstration of the rewards that flow to outward-looking, confident countries that implement policies of trade liberalization as a way to increase wealth, improve competitiveness and expand benefits to consumers, workers and businesses. We remain committed to ensuring that the NAFTA continues to help us to strengthen the North American economy through a rules-based framework for doing business in an increasingly integrated market. Since January 1, 1994, when the NAFTA entered into force, three-way trade amongst

It is of course unacceptable to take the position that 'international law is fair only if we always win'. There will inevitably be cases where the US Government will face substantial exposure in serious cases that legitimately involve high stakes; *Methanex v. United States of America* (7 *ICSID Reports* 208) may be an example. There were however no protests from US legislators when a US investor won an award of US$354 million against the Czech Republic, even though its government's resources are incomparably more modest than those of the US and even though the Czech authorities felt that they had acted in pursuit of legitimate regulatory supervision of the television broadcasting industry; *CME Czech Republic BV v. Czech Republic*, award on damages, 14 March 2003, 9 *ICSID Reports* [forthcoming].

[24] NAFTA, Free Trade Commission, Chapter 11 Interpretation, 31 July 2001, 6 *ICSID Reports* 367.

[25] What happens if arbitrators find that the Free Trade Commission has engaged in *amendments* to NAFTA rather than *interpretations* thereof remains controversial. (In the former hypothesis, investors would doubtless raise estoppel arguments.) See the much-remarked conclusion expressed in paragraph 47 on the final award in *Pope & Talbot Inc. v. Canada*, award on damages, 31 May 2002, 7 *ICSID Reports* 148 (Greenberg, Belman, Dervaird (presiding)): '[W]ere the Tribunal required to make a determination whether the Commission's action is an interpretation or an amendment, it would choose the latter.'

[26] On the other hand, Canada's *conduct* was adjusted in the course of the proceedings in light of rulings by the arbitral tribunal; that development might be considered as a form of relief of some benefit to the claimant.

our countries has reached over US$621 billion, more than double the pre-NAFTA level. Foreign Direct Investment by other NAFTA partners in our three countries more than doubled to reach US$299.2 billion in 2000.[27]

This statement should be considered against the background that these three democratic countries had known significant governmental changes since NAFTA was negotiated. It is a permissible inference that the national interests in maintaining NAFTA were sufficient to justify the dismissal of dogmatic calls for its abolition.

The occasional costs of having offered international protection of investors' rights appear minuscule compared to the macroeconomic effects of the treaty overall.[28] If NAFTA has been successful in stimulating trade and investment, it must be so because this complex treaty *as a whole* has created effective incentives. And if the three governments had really been involved in treason against national sovereignty, presumably their electorates would have dismissed them.

As for the US complaints quoted above about the WTO's treatment of steel tariffs, it so happens that the president of the WTO Appellate Body at the very time was a former US Congressman, James Bacchus. Before he finished his mandate, he wrote this:

To anyone at all acquainted with the everyday reality of the WTO, the very thought of the WTO as some kind of would-be 'world government' is laughable. The WTO is not a government, and no one in any way involved with the WTO has even the remotest desire to make it one. The WTO is an international organization *consisting of governments*. It is a forum where governments agree by consensus on rules to lower barriers to trade, and a way for governments to ensure compliance with those rules when disputes arise about what they mean.[29]

Mr Bacchus put it more concretely as follows:

Contrary to some popular misconceptions, the WTO treaty is *not* a free trade agreement. It does not *mandate* free trade. The WTO treaty is an international

---

[27] NAFTA Free Trade Commission Joint Statement, 'Celebrating NAFTA at Ten', 7 October 2003, available online at <http://www.dfait-maeci.gc.ca/nafta-alena/statement-en.asp>.

[28] And those costs should not be exaggerated in the first place. To quote the conclusion of Sampliner's study, 'Arbitration of Expropriation Cases', at p. 43: 'while the future direction of international regulatory takings jurisprudence in investor – state arbitration is not free from doubt, the promise of enhancements to the global rule of law appears far to outweigh the threats to legitimate sovereign prerogatives posed by expropriation claims under this new form of dispute settlement'.

[29] Bacchus, *Trade*, at p. 145.

agreement for freeing trade and for preventing trade discrimination. It establishes a framework of rules that enables WTO Members to free trade by making voluntary trade concessions on a multilateral basis, and it discourages WTO Members from engaging in certain kinds of trade discrimination against trading partners that are also Members of the WTO-based multilateral trading system.[30]

What is significant is that so many states have made considerable efforts to obtain membership in the WTO. They do not seek to withdraw from membership. The important opinions are those of the representatives of the relevant states.

## The urgency of prudence

All human institutions are imperfect. There are, inevitably, grounds for complaint. A series of questions arise. First, is the matter important enough to mobilise attention and generate proposals for action? Secondly, is the proper solution repair or replacement? Thirdly, are the proposals being raised realistic? And fourthly, is there a risk of trading one set of imperfections for another set of possibly greater ones?

The objectives of those who have suggested reforms are unquestionably worthwhile: to produce better decisions; to avoid inconsistency; and to enhance the perceived legitimacy of the process. The mechanisms of international adjudication are naturally susceptible to improvement in each of these respects; the matter merits reflection.

The objectives of better and more consistent decision-making may be considered together, since the idea is not consistency at any cost, but respectable consistency. The most frequently suggested idea is that of imposing an appellate body to ensure quality and predictability. For example, Mr Jacques Werner, a Geneva lawyer and publisher, in proposing the creation of an 'appellate court', because the 'system has to become more predictable',[31] referred to the experience of 'the old GATT system' of adjudicating disputes by panels. 'Those displeased with the panels' decisions ridiculed them as having been taken by 'unelected faceless bureaucrats!' The problem, he suggested, was that they were unappealable.

---

[30] *Ibid.* at p. 39.

[31] Jacques Werner, 'Making Investment Arbitration More Certain: A Modest Proposal', (2003) 4 *Journal of World Investment* 767, at p. 783. For a more in-depth articulation of a similar proposal, see Charles H. Brower II, 'Structure, Legitimacy and NAFTA's Investment Chapter', (2003) 36 *Vanderbilt Journal of Transnational Law* 37.

He wrote that the new WTO Appellate Body has conferred 'added respectability ... and acceptability to the whole process'.

Politics makes strange bedfellows; perhaps a pro-investment lawyer like Werner finds momentary allies of the anti-globalising persuasion when he speaks of the need to reform investment arbitration. Such ostensible sympathisers would, however, be unlikely to support any proposal which credits the WTO, their *bête noire*, with 'respectability' and 'acceptability'. Business interests at the opposite end of the ideological spectrum might take a similarly critical view, as evidenced by the reaction from the US steel industry quoted above, referring to 'the WTO's abuse of power and infringement of US sovereignty'. It cannot be assumed that WTO proceedings are perceived as having greater international legitimacy than other fora applying international law.

Beyond political reactions, one should also observe that the comparison between the WTO system and the practice of investment arbitration raises more questions than it answers, with respect to the identity of decision-makers as well as the type of issues submitted to them. Surely there can be no valid comparison between 'faceless bureaucrats' *imposed* upon parties and the arbitrators *selected* by the disputants in international arbitrations involving states.

Equally, one must be conscious of the fact that WTO disputes focus on the legitimacy of general measures, whereas investment disputes often arise out of particular executive actions relating to specific transactions. To the extent that an international arbitral tribunal evaluates specific facts, there can be no complaint about inconsistent results, because those facts will not be the same as those evaluated by another tribunal.

But of course international arbitral tribunals also rule on contentions of law. What about inconsistencies in that regard? A lawyer who acted for the US Government in a number of NAFTA arbitrations, Barton Legum, has stated that:

States traditionally have provided for standing tribunals to address cases of public importance, particularly where a significant volume of claims is at issue. If the result of the next few years is a collection of disparate decisions with widely varying and case-specific approaches to the issues presented, states may be tempted to consider replacing the system of *ad hoc* tribunals with a standing one that is perhaps capable of producing more consistent and coherent results.[32]

---

[32] 'Trends and Challenges in Investor-State Arbitration', (2003) 19 *Arbitration International* 143, at 147.

But precisely what kind of permanent tribunal is envisaged? Once one begins to imagine its concrete form and method, a number of considerations give pause.

First, inconsistencies of principle are relatively rare. The two awards in the notorious cases between the Lauder Group and the Czech Republic certainly reflected different evaluations of fact between two tribunals.[33] Yet there was no fundamental disagreement as to the legal principles to be applied, only a sharp divergence as to how they applied to the facts as pleaded and proved. The claimant alleged an indirect expropriation. The two tribunals came to different views as to whether there had been regulatory interference of such a magnitude as to constitute an unlawful deprivation. There is consensus in the vast literature on indirect takings that such claims cannot be decided by applying formulae, but require an informed view of all the circumstances. It is not astonishing to find that two cases of such a nature are pleaded and decided differently when presented before two different tribunals. The Czech problem resulted rather from the happenstance that a single investment had materialised in a legal framework which did not ensure comprehensive jurisdiction in a single forum, and that the respondent state – to its ultimate embarrassment – rejected a proposal to have the two cases consolidated and heard by the tribunal constituted under the Czech–US treaty. The controversy was thus artificially divided. Such an aberration falls to be solved, or not, on its own terms, and does not justify the imposition of an appellate jurisdiction on other cases which do not present such anomalies.

Secondly, to the extent that issues of principle remain controversial – and such issues do exist – the fact that some time is needed to achieve a settled jurisprudence is not surprising in a field where so many fundamental questions involving the interpretation of investment treaties have been litigated only in the last five years. It seems naïve to speak of inconsistency or unpredictability. After all, new fields of litigation often require many years of development within national legal systems. There is no reason to think the corpus of international investment awards will take longer to crystallise; if anything, in light of the intense transnational attention generated by these awards, it may be more rapid.[34]

---

[33] *Ronald S. Lauder* v. *Czech Republic*, award rendered under Czech–US treaty, 3 September 2001, 9 *ICSID Reports* [forthcoming]; *CME Czech Republic BV* v. *Czech Republic*, award rendered under Czech–Netherlands treaty, 13 September 2001, 9 *ICSID Reports* [forthcoming].

[34] From his review of cases arising in the late 1990s, including those against his government, Sampliner, 'Arbitration of Expropriation Cases', at pp. 42–43, expects

Thirdly, even appellate or other permanent bodies are unpredictable. Their view of the definition of relevant norms tends to evolve as they consider them in the prism of different facts, and of course their views may change simply as a function of changes over time in their membership. One may wonder how much those who complain of inconsistency know about *national* law. Kenneth Waltz chided those 'who would have us settle disputes internationally as they are domestically without first understanding how disputes are settled domestically'.[35] The law, wrote Holmes, 'will become entirely consistent only when it ceases to grow'.[36]

Fourthly, the perceptions of legitimacy of yet more adjudicatory bodies involved in the application of international law is problematic. Why should persons selected through the political processes of an international organisation be more legitimate than those chosen in accordance with the agreement of the particular disputants in the particular case?[37] To take the case of the WTO Appellate Body, whatever one may make of the criticisms, they are being raised – left and right. Moreover, as Legum points out, even if it were the case that:

most participants have a generally positive view of the WTO Appellate Body, their experience has not necessarily been shared by participants before some other standing international tribunals. A standing tribunal that takes an exceedingly expansive view of its mandate and the substantive law may be more of a liability than a benefit from the perspective of the States that create it.[38]

One such practical reality has to do with the *participants* in the hypothetical corrective mechanism. The stark reality is that some governments are likely to see no need for prevailing claimants to participate in such a process, with the result that the challenge to the award would be debated only between the governments signatory to the relevant treaty. Neither

increased 'convergence between international jurisprudence and the jurisprudence of the principal legal systems of the world'.

[35] Kenneth Waltz, *Man, the State and War* (New York: Columbia University Press, 1959), at p. 116.

[36] Oliver Wendell Holmes Jr, *The Common Law* (ed. M. Howe, Mineole, NY: Dover, 1963), at p. 32.

[37] A former legal advisor of the US Department of State, reflecting back on his career, took a disabused view of the ICJ itself; Davis R. Robinson, 'The Role of Politics in the Election and the Work of the Judges of the International Court of Justice', *Proceedings of the 97th Annual Meeting of the American Society of International Law* (2003), at p. 277.

[38] Barton Legum, 'The Introduction of an Appellate Mechanism: The US Trade Act of 2002', in E. Gaillard and Y. Banifatemi (eds.), *Annulment of ICSID Awards: A New Investment Protection Regime in Treaty Arbitration* (Huntingdon, NY: Juris, 2004) 289, at p. 299.

government may in fact want the award to stand; the claimant investor would have no one to defend it. The most legally impeccable award could be sacrificed to expediency. This would be the negation of the very object of treaty-based investor protection.

Another practical reality has to do with the *composition* of the reviewing bodies. If they are to comprise only persons named by the states signatory to the relevant treaty, a fundamental disequilibrium would be created. Moreover, if the proponents of appellate review imagine that the correcting jurisdiction would somehow be composed of particularly eminent jurists towering over the first-instance arbitrators, the reality of international politics makes it unlikely that such an outcome would eventuate. Who will stop governments from appointing politically representative individuals who know little about international arbitration but a lot about the desiderata of their appointers? Does the world need more politics, or more law?

The goal is not to secure unfettered discretion for arbitrators. To the contrary, their compliance with jurisdictional requirements must be absolute, and must be reviewable, or the whole edifice will crumble. Even with respect to substantive issues, the development of an international legal order does not require that the parties suffer the consequences of grossly aberrant decisions. To recall the phrase coined by a Chief Justice of the New Zealand Court of Appeal, the determination of rights should not be left to: 'subjective views about which party "ought to win" ... or the formless void of individual moral opinion'.[39] The domain of international law is particularly inappropriate for intuitive justice, because the cultural baggage of the decision-makers is so unlikely to be homogenous.

This is certainly a serious problem, given the high degree of finality of arbitral awards. But that leads to a fifth observation, namely that the instruments pursuant to which international law in this field is applied *themselves* contain corrective mechanisms as a part of their rules of dispute resolution. Article 1126 of NAFTA, for example, provides for consolidation if more than one arbitration challenges the legitimacy of the same

---

[39] Lord Justice Cooke, in *Aquaculture Corp.* v. *New Zealand Green Mussel Co. Ltd*, [1990] 3 *NZLR* 299. *Cf.* James Bacchus, The Strange Death of Sir Francis Bacon: The Do's and Don'ts of Appellate Advocacy in the WTO, lecture reproduced in Bacchus, *Trade*, at p. 383: '*Don't* bother arguing that the Appellate Body should embrace some "teleological" approach to interpretation that would enable the members to impose their purely personal views on the meaning of the "covered agreements". They don't. They won't.'

governmental measure. They may thus be merged into a single super-arbitration where the result will be binding on one and all. Inconsistency is inconceivable. And in the ordinary run of cases to which that mechanism does not apply, review procedures are available under the relevant arbitration rules. That is precisely how the Canadian courts, for example, came to deal with the *Metalclad* v. *Mexico*,[40] *Feldman* v. *Mexico*[41] and *S. D. Myers* v. *Canada*[42] awards.

Criticism to the effect that international arbitration is overly burdensome – too time-consuming, too expensive – is a different matter. Justice is unlikely ever to come instantly at no cost to the deserving party, but that observation does not justify complacency. Still, to evaluate cost-effectiveness can be a daunting task. Comparisons between the WTO Appellate Body and individual arbitral tribunals are hazardous. Investment arbitrations and multilateral systems for resolving trade disputes are quite different things. In arbitration, there is usually an extensive and controversial narrative to be examined by reference to a particular transaction, leading to time-consuming fact-finding through oral as well as documentary evidence. A ruling on a trade dispute may, on the other hand, be prepared in the abstract; when fact-finding is necessary, it is of a completely different, macroeconomic nature. Most of all, the premises of a one-off arbitration between a private party and a state are fundamentally different from those of a standing multilateral body comprising only states, who may be either claimants or defendants, whose relationships are by definition permanent, and whose propensity for settling individual controversies are affected by a complex variety of considerations. An investor who feels there is nothing left to lose, on the other hand, may be impelled by pure burn-my-bridges intractability.[43]

---

[40] Supreme Court of British Columbia, judgment of 2 May 2001, 5 *ICSID Reports* 236.
[41] *Mexico* v. *Feldman Karpa*, Superior Court of Justice, Ontario, judgment of 3 December 2003, 8 *ICSID Reports* 500.
[42] Federal Court of Canada, judgment of 13 January 2004, 8 *ICSID Reports* 194.
[43] None of those observations should detract from the fundamental proposition that both state-to-state trade controversies and investor–state disputes are elements of the vast task of building the international rule of law. In 2000, Julio Lacarte-Muró, the Uruguayan jurist who served as the first Chairman of the WTO Appellate Body from 1995 to 1997, co-wrote (with Petina Gappah) an article entitled 'Developing Countries and the WTO Legal and Dispute Settlement System: A View From the Bench', which concluded as follows: 'It has often been said that the WTO dispute settlement system provides an opportunity for economically weak smaller countries to challenge trade measures taken by more economically powerful Members. This point deserves some emphasis. The Appellate Body is an integral part of a rules based,

Nor is it easy to make good on claims that arbitrations are overly lengthy. As practitioners know, proceedings are often interrupted by negotiation, and over-eager arbitrators may be put in their place by the parties' joint indication that the exigencies of the case require more elaborate and time-consuming case management. When both an investor and the respondent state make such representations, it is not easy for an arbitrator to disregard their wishes.

These observations are confirmed by consideration of the operations of the unique *ad hoc* committees constituted to deal with requests for annulments of awards under the ICSID Convention. Unlike most ICSID tribunals, these committees are constituted only of members appointed by ICSID, and are therefore assuredly comprised of non-partisan, experienced international adjudicators. Their task is not to conduct a *de novo* review of the dispute, but to determine whether the award is vitiated by any of the five strictly limited defects defined in Article 52 of the Convention. Yet requests for annulment invariably lead to substantial briefing and hearings. The proceedings usually last more than a year. These are intrinsically complex matters.

Those who think in terms of short-term interests, or are interested in pursuing single objectives without heed to their effect on others, tend to be quick to identify the causes of their disappointment and to propose instant cures. They seem to have little patience for examining the kinds of factors just described. That their proposed cures have been tried in the past and found wanting, or that they run counter to fundamental values that have emerged over many generations, seems ignored. National initiatives intended to curtail the reach of international law must therefore be viewed with scepticism.

For example, in March 2002 the Chairman of the US Senate Finance Committee wrote to the US Trade Representatives proposing: (i) that foreign investors should be denied any substantive rights not given to Americans; (ii) to establish an appellate review of NAFTA awards; and (iii) to support government screening of arbitration requests.[44] Senator John Kerry of Massachusetts argued that the home country of the investor should be able to prohibit attempts to initiate

---

"judicialized" dispute settlement mechanism which ensures transparency and predictability. This system works to the advantage of all Members, but it especially gives security to the weaker Members who often, in the past, lacked the political or economic clout to enforce their rights and to protect their interests. In the WTO, *right* perseveres over *might*.' ((2000) *Journal of International Economic Law* 395, at pp. 400–401; emphasis in the original.)

[44] Aguilar Alvarez and Park, 'New Face', at pp. 385–386.

international arbitration if its officials determine that it 'lacks legal merit'.[45]

If ensuring that foreigners receive no greater substantive rights than nationals means that the legislators will see to it that nationals have *as much protection* as that given by international law, who can object? But if it means that international law is to be *cut down* to national treatment, it means that the Yankees have belatedly become converts to the Calvo Doctrine. International law would suffer.

At any rate, the US Trade Act of 2002,[46] as finally adopted, while asserting in its preamble that the US 'provides a high level of protection for investment', defines the 'negotiating objectives' of the government's trade negotiators as ensuring that foreigners receive no 'greater substantive rights with respect to investment protections' than domestic investors by providing, *inter alia*, for 'mechanisms to eliminate frivolous claims', for an appellate body 'or similar mechanism' to 'provide coherence to the interpretation of investment provisions in trade agreements', and for public arbitral proceedings and the admissibility of *amicus curiae* submissions from non-governmental organisations and interest groups.[47] The objectives are intended to serve as criteria to be examined by Congress before it decides whether to approve any new agreement negotiated by the executive branch.

These ideas raise a host of problems. For example, the pursuit of an appropriate appellate body will not only face the questions raised above, but also the plain fact that most investment arbitrations arise from a very large number of bilateral treaties containing separate dispute resolution provisions; to establish a single body with jurisdiction over all of them would be difficult.[48] Would the expense and delays associated with a swarm of new adjudicatory bodies, involving inevitably high fixed costs but uncertain levels of activity, truly be of value to the international community? Strictly speaking, the question is irrelevant to the present study, which focuses on the authority of international

---

[45] 148 *Congressional Record* S4504 (16 May 2002).

[46] Public Law No. 107–210, 116 *Stat.* 933 (6 August 2002).

[47] See *ibid.*, Division B, Title XXI, of the Act. This development gave Mr Legum the impetus to return to the subject of permanent tribunals and appellate review, and to consider its potential concrete implications; in Legum, 'Appellate Mechanism', at p. 5. In particular, he opined that it is 'not immediately apparent' how an appellate body could comfortably coexist with the New York Convention.

[48] Cf. Hugo Perezcano, 'Investment Protection Agreements – Should a Multilateral Approach be Reconsidered', (2003) 4 *Journal of World Investment* 929.

adjudicators as opposed to national authorities, irrespective of how the former operate, but it is impossible not to be concerned about the spectre of unintended potential consequences which may hamper the fulfilment of the rule of law.

The desire to achieve consistency and to avoid misconduct in international adjudication is legitimate, but it did not suddenly emerge for the first time when the US Congress turned to the matter in 2002. Generations of scholars and practitioners have wrestled with these questions. It should not be too much to ask that would-be reformers ask themselves seriously whether they are rushing off to replace an imperfect but functioning model with a visibly flawed one.

If an international tribunal's application of international law is overruled by a national court, the most important objective of the arbitral process, namely neutrality, may be compromised. It is fortunate that the dominant worldwide trend is not to allow national courts to review arbitral awards for alleged errors of fact or law. National courts therefore tend to control the work of international arbitrators only insofar as they have exceeded their mandate or violated a fundamental rule of due process.

Thus, consideration of appellate review in the international domain focuses on the usefulness of creating *additional international bodies* which might review awards.

There is no impediment to such bodies, and they have existed for a long time in the sphere of purely private arbitrations. They have, for example, been conceived as useful in the framework of trade associations, where the first level decision would be made on a rough-and-ready basis; if either side wished to take the matter further, it could advance to a more elaborate appellate level, where perhaps more experienced persons would ensure more sophisticated decisions. Under such systems, there is no reason not to have an unlimited power to revise the first decision.[49] Nevertheless, such procedures have typically been limited to dispute resolution mechanisms established by commodities industries and have involved routine disputes among parties engaged in a high volume of similar transactions. It is safe to say that for

---

[49] The German Supreme Court once upheld an award against a German party by an appellate tribunal under the European Wholesale Potato Trade Rules, sitting in Brussels; the claim had previously been rejected by a first-level tribunal sitting in Hamburg. Decision of 9 March 1978, *Wertpapier-Mitteilungen* 573 (1978).

most lawyers involved in international arbitration, two-tiered arbitration is a curiosity.

More relevant to current international practice is the role of *ad hoc* committees under the ICSID system and that of the International Court of Arbitration in arbitrations under the International Chamber of Commerce Rules. The essential feature in each case is that the deciding organ has the same degree of neutrality *vis-à-vis* the parties as does the initial tribunal; it is not a national authority. The ICC Court 'scrutinises' each award before it is delivered to the parties. The Court has the authority to *modify* matters of form, but only to make *comment* on points of substance for the arbitrators' consideration. There is evidence that this function enhances the bona fides of ICC awards in the eyes of national courts called on to recognise or enforce them.[50]

ICSID *ad hoc* committees have broader authority; they may *annul* awards. Still, their power is limited to determining whether the tribunal had indeed been given the mandate it exercised, and whether it accomplished all of its mission – but no more – while respecting due process. Whether the right balance was struck in the initial experiences with ICSID *ad hoc* committees, in cases involving Cameroon[51] and Indonesia,[52] is debatable,[53] but since then a proper understanding of the annulment mechanism appears to have been achieved.[54]

In investment arbitrations, some fundamental issues recur frequently. One is that of the jurisdictional posture of an investor having grievances under both contract and treaty. It is important that consistency is achieved in terms of understanding how international tribunals should resolve the complex and crucial issues that arise in such circumstances. There is much to be said for ensuring that a proper corrective function is carried out by a panel of experienced specialists not named by the parties.[55]

---

[50] W. Laurence Craig, William W. Park and Jan Paulsson, *International Chamber of Commerce Arbitration* (3rd edn, Dobbs Ferry, NY: Oceana, 2000), at pp. 380–383.

[51] *Klöckner Industrie-Anlagen GmbH et al.* v. *Cameroon and SOCAME*, annulment decision, 3 May 1985, 2 *ICSID Reports* 95 (El-Kosheri, Seidl-Hohenveldern, Lalive (presiding)).

[52] *Amco Asia Corp. et al.* v. *Indonesia*, annulment decision, 16 May 1986, 1 *ICSID Reports* 509.

[53] Alan Redfern, 'ICSID: Losing Its Appeal?' (1987) 3 *Arbitration International* 98.

[54] Jan Paulsson, 'ICSID's Achievements and Prospects', (1991) 6 *ICSID Review* 380; Christoph Schreuer, 'Three Generations of ICSID Annulment Proceedings', in E. Gaillard and Y. Banifatemi (eds.), *Annulment of ICSID Awards: A New Investment Protection Regime in Treaty Arbitration* (Huntington, NY: Juris, 2004).

[55] *Vivendi* is a salient example of the establishment by an *ad hoc* committee of the proper approach to a central issue – contract claims v. treaty claims – which arises with

In contrast to the inchoate proposals described above, important and well-considered reforms have been implemented with respect to the transparency of the arbitral process. The NAFTA Free Trade Commission has twice addressed the concerns of third parties in this regard. In 2001, it declared with binding effect that NAFTA does not impose a 'general duty of confidentiality on the disputing parties to a Chapter Eleven arbitration'.[56] This decision led the way to the practically open-book basis on which NAFTA investment arbitrations have been conducted thereafter. Written submissions and evidence produced by the parties, procedural orders and substantive decisions rendered by the arbitrators, and indeed transcripts of the proceedings become public, it seems, in an electronic instant.[57] And in 2003 the Commission announced:

- an affirmation of the authority of investor – state tribunals to accept written submissions (*amicus curiae* briefs) by non-disputing parties, coupled with recommended procedures for tribunals on the handling of such submissions; and
- endorsement of a standard form for the Notices of Intent to initiate arbitration that disputing investors are required to submit under Article 1119 of the NAFTA.[58]

The Commission urged tribunals to 'determine the appropriate logistical arrangements for open hearings in consultation with disputing parties ... use of closed-circuit television systems, Internet webcasting, or other forms of access'. It laid down guidelines to determine on what basis third parties should be deemed to have a legitimate reason to make representations to arbitral tribunals, and to ensure that those representations do not make the process unmanageable.

---

inevitable regularity; *Compañía de Aguas del Aconquija and Vivendi Universal* v. *Argentina*, annulment decision, 3 July 2002, 6 *ICSID Reports* 340; 42 ILM 1135 (2002).

[56] NAFTA, Free Trade Commission, Chapter 11 Interpretation, 31 July 2001, 6 *ICSID Reports* 567.

[57] The *Methanex* case may have been the first instance of an investor – state arbitration in which facilities were provided for members of the public to view and hear the proceedings through closed-circuit video (in June 2004). The auditorium was crowded on the first day, but soon thereafter emptied as tedium took its toll. The striving for transparency does not arise from the public's craving for the arcana of decision-making, but from its aversion to the thought that it is occult.

[58] NAFTA Free Trade Commission Statement on Transparency, 7 October 2003, (2005) 44 ILM 796.

## Respect for the 'obscure arbiter' as a test of commitment to the international rule of law

What does it mean to favour international adjudication? Whether one *should* favour it is a different question, and one which will not detain us at all, in the spirit of Sir Elihu Lauterpacht's words as he ended the 1990 lectures in memory of his father:

> It has simply been assumed – as being beyond discussion and as being in the best interests of our international society – that negotiated, but principled, settlement, or if no negotiated settlement can be reached, then the judgment or recommendation of a third party, is far, far better than the use of force. That is why, when gloom pervades, as occasionally it must, there is still virtue in attempting, by critical analysis and creative proposal, to promote improvement in the machinery of international justice.[59]

When examining claims of denial of justice, international tribunals must ultimately apply concepts which are inherently elastic. No one has been able to define the international delict of denial of justice without using abstractions such as 'egregious' or 'unacceptable' or 'manifestly iniquitous'. Such is the nature of the thing. International adjudicators are not robots. Even if they were, there is no formula according to which they could be programmed to evaluate the facts of all cases in a uniform manner.

It should be obvious that when international adjudicators rule upon a claim of denial of justice, judge they should and judge they must, bringing to bear their cultural and intellectual baggage, applying their predispositions and experience. *Subjective* does not mean *arbitrary*. It is not the reflection of a purely personal taste or attitude. It refers to the fact that the quality of the judgment to be made depends on the individual understanding, knowledge and detachment of the decider. That is why a diligent child whom one might well trust to watch a machine and 'judge' when a cursor reaches a red line would nevertheless not be allowed to judge whether drivers involved in an automobile accident exercised due care. There is no mechanistic way of applying, as already noted, concepts which, whenever a difficult case takes us away from the comfortable certainties of their core meaning, permit inconsistent yet defensible

---

[59] E. Lauterpacht, *Aspects of the Administration of International Justice* (Cambridge: Grotius 1991), at p. xiii.

conclusions. Consider, for example, the italicised words in this passage from the well-known decision from 1927 in the *Chattin* case (*US* v. *Mexico*):

Irregularity of court proceedings is proven with reference to absence of *proper* investigations, *insufficiency* of confrontations, withholding from the accused the opportunity to know all of the charges brought against him, *undue* delay of the proceedings, making the hearings in open court a *mere formality*, and a *continued* absence of *seriousness* on the part of the Court.[60]

Or the italicised words in the formulation of a European scholar who sought, in 1949, to distil the following definition of the procedural rights protected by international law:

the right to a *fair, non-discriminatory* and *unbiased* hearing, the right to a *just* decision rendered in *full* compliance with the laws of the State within a *reasonable* time.[61]

One might as well rewrite this as a formula, using $J$ for the value 'adequate justice' and the other symbols replacing each of the italicised words in the order they appear:

No $J$ if none of [$A$, $B$, or $C$] or neither of [($X$ and $Y$) with $Z$], where $A$, $B$, $C$, $X$, $Y$, and $Z$ can assume any values within a wide range.[62]

Nor could it be objected that such expressions reflected early developments in international law, and that contemporary jurisprudence has developed objective and predictable standards. One need only consider that the *Mondev* v. *US* award, handed down in 2002, set down a test to the effect that a judicial decision runs afoul of the international standard if it was 'clearly improper and discreditable';[63] or that the *Loewen* tribunal's articulation of the delict in 2003 finally boiled down to this: 'a lack of due process leading to an outcome which offends a sense of judicial propriety'.[64]

One may, and should, insist on integrity and independence, but it is futile to imagine a vast cohort of international arbitrators who would decide every case identically. Such is the function of judging, and the

---

[60] *Chattin* (*US* v. *Mexico*), 23 July 1927, IV RIAA 282, at para. 30.
[61] Andreas Roth, *The Minimum Standard of International Law Applied to Aliens* ( Leiden: A.W. Sijthoff, 1949), at p. 185 (emphasis added).
[62] The conceit is inspired by the one reproduced in H.L.A. Hart, *The Concept of Law* (2nd edn, Oxford University Press, 1994), at p. 13.
[63] *Mondev* at para. 127. 'This is admittedly a somewhat open-ended standard, but it may be that in practice no more precise formula can be offered to cover the range of possibilities.'
[64] *Loewen*, 26 June 2003, at para. 132; the *Loewen* award also explicitly approved the *Mondev* formulation, in para. 133.

# Denial of Justice in International Law

person who does not accept that proposition simply does not accept international adjudication.[65]

If states are to be held accountable for breaches of international law, they cannot be the ultimate judges of the breach alleged. To say that the international examination of national judgments would be an impermissible infringement of sovereignty is to advocate the negation of international law, which by its nature is conceived as a limitation on the behaviour of states. If the problem is a mistrust of international adjudicators, it merits examination as such. The principle should not suffer because its applier is mistrusted. The question then becomes: do the relevant adjudicators merit mistrust?

The quality of decision-making is naturally paramount. The selection of judges and arbitrators must be punctiliously consistent with the relevant international agreements. The impartiality and quality of their judgments and awards must command respect. Otherwise, their claims to legitimacy will founder either on the Scylla of suspicion that they are but the agents of occult forces who wish to undo the policy determinations of democratic governments, or on the Charybdis of contempt on the part of those who would see them as too timorous to impose the full force of international law on powerful states.

The history of the adjudication of complaints of denial of justice before international bodies does not show that legal theory was skewed to suit powerful states. This proposition may be demonstrated in four ways. First, the annals of international arbitration are replete with instances of claims by one western country against another, founded on denial of justice, with no suggestion that the claimant's conception of the delict was less rigorous than the one invoked against weaker states.

In an essay entitled 'International Responsibility of States for Acts of the Judiciary',[66] Judge Jiménez de Arèchaga reproduced the salient

---

[65] This observation would be equally apposite with respect to any number of substantive issues. For example, one of the most vexing contemporary issues in the international law of foreign investment relates to the distinction to be drawn between compensatable state action that is 'tantamount to expropriation', on the one hand, and police-power regulation or tax that does not give rise to an obligation to compensate, on the other. In a passage characteristic of the approach of international tribunals in this area, the award in *Feldman* v. *Mexico*, after reciting a number of specific findings of facts, concluded in para. 111: 'While none of these factors alone is necessarily conclusive, in the Tribunal's view taken together they tip the expropriation/regulation balance away from a finding of expropriation.' (Award, 16 December 2002, 7 *ICSID Reports* 339.)

[66] In W.G. Friedmann, L. Henkin and O.J. Lissitzyn (eds.), *Transnational Law in a Changing Society – Essays in Honor of Philip C. Jessup* (New York: Columbia University Press, 1972), at p. 171.

254

pleadings of the *Barcelona Traction* case[67] in which he had participated as a member of Spain's legal team. *Barcelona Traction* was of course disposed of by the success of Spain's preliminary objection, but that objection had been joined to the merits, with the result that the substantive case was fully pleaded in memorials and oral hearings. Belgium submitted that all the acts of the Spanish authorities which underlay its grievance were part of a series of denials of justice. Jiménez de Aréchaga's essay illustrates how these two states, neither of whom could be said to hold a neocolonialist ascendancy over the other – albeit of course it was in Spain's interest to disprove the existence of any denial of justice – and although their versions of the facts were irreductibly opposed, in the course of the refinements of their arguments, thrusting and parrying, asserting and conceding in this momentous case, eventually reached substantially common ground as to the definition of the basis for determining the liability of states for acts of their judiciaries.

Secondly, as seen, many claims failed although they were brought against relatively weak Latin American states. Of the cases discussed in this book, *North American Dredging* and *Neer* were salient instances. But the examples are legion.[68]

Thirdly, in cases involving claims between equally powerful countries there is no sign that judges, arbitrators, or commissioners applied different standards from those followed when the respondent state was weak.[69]

---

[67] *Case concerning the Barcelona Traction, Light and Power Company (Belgium v. Spain)* (New Application: 1962), Second Phase, 1970 *ICJ Reports* 4.

[68] In the addendum on the Calvo Clause to The International Law Commission (Dugard), Third Report on Diplomatic Protection, UN Doc. A/CN.4/523/Add. 1, Professor Dugard referred to cases in which mixed claims commissions 'displayed a remarkable leniency to Mexico in finding that there had been no denial of justice on the facts', at para. 30.

[69] See, e.g., *Spanish Zone of Morocco (UK v. Spain)*, 29 May 1923, II RIAA 617; *Robert E. Brown (US v. Great Britain)*, 23 November 1923, VI RIAA 120, holding that 'all three branches of the Government conspired to ruin [the claimant's] enterprise', at p. 129.

There are of course bad cases. It is hard to deny that the *Pelletier case (US v. Haiti)*, Moore, *Arbitrations* at p. 1757, arose in scandalous circumstances. A resourceful US claimant was able to mobilise political support for imposing an arbitration agreement upon a Haitian government powerless to resist. An award was rendered against Haiti by an arbitrator of US nationality. But it is equally important to note that although the arbitrator was a former Justice of the US Supreme Court, the US Government quickly decided to treat the award as a nullity – explicitly described as such by the Secretary of State – and accepted Haiti's 'remonstrance' against the award. A concise description of the record of this case is found in W.M. Reisman, *Nullity and Revision: The Review and Enforcement of International Judgments and Awards* (New Haven, CT: Yale University Press, 1971), at pp. 401–404 and 435–437.

Fourthly, for all the abstract pronouncements of Latin Americans about the appropriateness of a narrow definition of denial of justice, their pleadings in actual cases, when espousing the claim of their own nationals, are undistinguishable from those propounded by the traditionally claiming states.[70]

## The early American example

It is worthwhile reflecting on the early American experiences with international law and contrast it with some current attitudes in the United States, where recent political debate seems to lack both a historical perspective and an understanding of the reasons for bowing to international adjudication.

The great US Secretary of State, Elihu Root, in his opening address before the third annual meeting of the American Society of International Law in 1909, observed that 'proud independent sovereign commonwealths like Virginia and Pennsylvania and New York and Massachusetts', which 'revered their judges', had nevertheless accepted a Constitution which recognised that courts are likely 'to be affected by local sentiment, prejudice, and pressure'. Thus:

We have provided in the third article of the Constitution of the United States that in controversies between states or between citizens of different states the

---

[70] See the examples cited by Freeman, at 132, note 3, and in particular the following liberal definition of denial of justice articulated by counsel for Cuba in the *Cantero-Herrera* claim against Peru: 'by denying access to the courts, by an undue procrastination in the court proceedings in open violation of the adjective laws of the country, by the non-existence of courts, by want of a sufficient number of officials to dispatch the business of the courts, by not offering proper guaranties due to their use as means of oppression against aliens, or by removing the judges after they have taken cognizance of the cases, or by the excuses of the judges to dictate sentences, or by their handing down of unjust sentences in violation of the substantive laws of the country, or by refusing to comply with the provisions of a law in accordance with the interpretation given by the courts, or by refusing to execute a final sentence, or by amnesty laws protecting crimes to the prejudice of the interests of aliens, or lastly by any other means which deny redress to the injured alien who has suffered in his interests.' For a more recent example of the weaker state subscribing to a broad conception of denial of justice, see the *Ambatielos Claim (Greece v. UK)*, 6 March 1956, XII RIAA 83, at p. 102. Greece went so far as to contend, unsuccessfully, that in withholding allegedly material documents the British Government denied Ambatielos 'access to the [English] Courts' because such access should perforce be understood to include 'the obligation to make it possible for [the foreign national] to avail himself of all the documents necessary for the defence of his rights'. (*Ibid.* at pp. 110–111; the case has more than a dose of irony, considering that it arose a century after the *Don Pacifico* affair, with the tables turned.)

determination of what is just shall not be confined to the courts of justice of either state, but may be brought in the Federal tribunals, selected and empowered by the representatives of both states and of all the states – true arbitral tribunals in the method of their creation and the office they perform.[71]

Root's point was that at the international level as well, 'in order to avoid the danger of denials of justice, and to prevent the belief that justice had not been done', states should accept, by international agreement, that the decisions of their courts be reviewed by international tribunals. He pointed to no less than twelve cases where matters already decided by the US Supreme Court had subsequently been submitted to international tribunals, six of them reaching opposite results[72] and all of them complied with by the US Government.

There may be many instances where government officials dutifully accept that national sovereignty is restricted not only by international law, and moreover by international adjudicators who may apply international law in a manner adverse to the government's position. But it would be foolish to ignore that there are also many instances when government officials challenge the authority of international adjudicators. International judgments or awards may be politically sensitive and highly unpopular in countries affected by the decision. Of all international adjudicators, arbitrators may seem to be the most fragile. After all, in their capacity as arbitrators they are neither elected officials nor even international civil servants.

But was the American acceptance of the international adjudication really a matter of highmindedness? Or did the US Government understand that it had no choice in the matter, lest it harm an international legal order from which the US too stood to benefit – and had done so in the past?

To understand why the US accepted that its Supreme Court's decisions be disregarded by international adjudicators, it is appropriate to go back to the previous century, and more particularly the so-called Jay Treaty of 19 November 1794 between the UK and the US.[73] The Treaty provided

---

[71] E. Root, 'The Relations between International Tribunals of Arbitration and the Jurisdiction of National Courts', (1909) 3 AJIL 529, at p. 534.

[72] *Ibid.* at p. 535: *the Hiawatha* (2 Black), *the Circassian* (2 Wallace), *the Springbock* (5 Wallace), *the Sir William Peel* (5 Wallace), *the Volant* (5 Wallace) and *the Science* (5 Wallace)'; all cited with further references in Jackson H. Ralston, *The Law and Procedure of International Tribunals* (Stanford University Press, 1926), at p. 114.

[73] 8 *Stat.* 116. The Treaty was named after John Jay, who negotiated and signed the Treaty and subsequently became the first Chief of Justice of the US Supreme Court. In 'Federalism, NAFTA Chapter Eleven and the Jay Treaty of 1794', (2001) 18 *ICSID*

for three five-member commissions: one to resolve a controversy concerning the border between the US and Canada, and two to adjudicate the claims of British and American creditors, respectively. A number of British claims arose from confiscations carried out against persons who had supported the Crown during the Revolutionary War. The commission dealing with American grievances was faced with a number of claims concerning the capture of US merchant vessels and their cargo. The forfeiture of the claimants' property as prizes under international law had been determined by the English courts, and the agent of the UK argued thus:

a solemn decision of the high court of appeals, which is the supreme court of the law of nations in this kingdom, ought to be respected and confirmed by other authorities proceeding on the same law.[74]

The US Commissioners secured a rejection of this position (by a majority vote). Thus, in the important case of *The Betsey*, decided on 13 April 1797, one of them (Christopher Gore) wrote as follows, in an oft-quoted passage:

But that the decision of any court, however respectable its members, is conclusive on foreign governments, as to the law of nations, and that the principles on which it is founded may not be rightfully contested, as contrary to that law, is not, in my belief, warranted by just ideas of the equal independence of nations or by their practice.[75]

William Pinckney expressed himself to the same effect, but in greater detail:

the jurisdiction of the court of the capturing nation is complete upon the *point of property* ... its sentence forecloses all controversy *between claimant and captor and*

*News* 6, Barton Legum noted the five following characteristics of investor – state arbitration under NAFTA: 'First, it allows foreign investors to sue the United States government for damages under international, and not domestic, law;
Second, it allows those investors to claim that state governments within the United States have taken their property or otherwise violated international law;
Third, it requires the federal government of the United States, and not the state governments, to assume liability for those state-government acts;
Fourth, it requires the federal government's liability to be decided not by judges appointed by the President with the advice and consent of the Senate, but by a panel of international arbitrators; and
Fifth, it contemplates a panel of arbitrators that may be composed of United States nationals, nationals of the State of the foreign investor and a presiding arbitrator who is presumptively selected by agreement.' He then observed that each of these five characteristics was also extant under the 1794 Jay Treaty between the US and Great Britain.
[74] *The Betsey (US v. Great Britain)*, Moore, *Arbitrations*, at p. 3161.   [75] *Ibid.* at p. 3162.

*those claiming under them*, and . . . if it do not appear unjust on the face of it, it suffices *to terminate forever all ordinary judicial inquiry* upon the matter of it. These are unquestionable effects of a final admiralty sentence, and in these respects it is unimpeachable. But [Britain's] objection reaches infinitely further. It swells an incidental jurisdiction over *things* into a direct, complete, and unqualified control over nations and their citizens. The author I have just quoted [Rutherford, *Institutes of Natural Law*] proves incontestably . . . that this doctrine is absurd and inadmissible; that neither the United States nor the claimants its citizens are bound to take for just the sentence of the lords, if in fact it is not so; and that the affirmance of an illegal condemnation, so far from legitimating the wrong done by the original seizure and precluding the neutral from seeking reparation for it against the British nation, is peculiarly that very act which consummates the wrong and indisputably perfects the neutral's right of demanding that reparation through the medium of his own government.[76]

In his *International Law Digest* published 89 years later, Francis Wharton wrote as follows:

It was maintained before the British and American Mixed Commission sitting in London under the treaty of 1794 that a decision of a British prize court estopped the party against whom it was made from proceedings, when a foreigner, through his own government. This was contested by Mr. Pinkney, and his position was affirmed by the arbitration acting under the advice of Lord Chancellor Loughborough, and is now accepted law.[77]

So by the time of the six cases invoked by Mr Root as examples of US compliance with international law, it would have been difficult for the US government to insist that its own courts – even the Supreme Court – would have the last word with respect to claims by British subjects that their goods had been wrongfully captured in connection with blockades during the American Civil War. These were all prize cases – dealing with the validity under international law of the seizure at sea of vessels and cargo – that arose before the British–American Claims Commission

---

[76] *Ibid.* at pp. 3184–3185.

[77] F. Wharton (ed.), *A Digest of the International Law of the United States*, (3 vols., 2nd edn, Washington, DC: US Government Printing Office, 1887), vol. II, at p. 695. In the *Garrison* case decided by the US–Mexican Commission created under a Treaty of 4 July 1868, the Umpire (Francis Lieber) reached further back in time: 'It is objected that the case has been adjudicated by the proper Mexican court and can not be reopened before this Commission; that therefore it ought to be dismissed. It is true that it is a matter of the greatest political and international delicacy for one country to disacknowledge the judicial decisions of a court of another country, which nevertheless the law of nations universally allows in extreme cases. *It has done so from the times of Hugo Grotius.*' (Moore, *Arbitrations*, at p. 3129; emphasis added.)

operating under the Washington Treaty of 1871. The fundamental principle was established in the following way:

The question was early raised, on the part of the United States, as to the jurisdiction of these prize cases by the commission, both in respect to cases where the decision of the ultimate appellate tribunal of the United States had been had, and to those in which no appeal had been prosecuted on the part of the claimants to such ultimate tribunal. As to the former class of cases, the undersigned [Hale] may properly state that he personally entertained no doubt of the jurisdiction of the commission, as an international tribunal, to review the decisions of the prize courts of the United States, where the parties alleging themselves aggrieved had prosecuted their claims by appeal to the court of last resort. As this jurisdiction, however, had been sometimes questioned, he deemed it desirable that a formal adjudication by the commission should be had upon this question. The commission unanimously sustained their jurisdiction in this class of cases, and as will be seen, all the members of the commission at some time joined in awards against the United States in such cases.[78]

These echoes of history may suggest that respect for international adjudication is not a dangerous adventure sponsored by the naïve, or a betrayal of sovereignty fomented by the concupiscent, but the rediscovery of an old virtue of national restraint arising from the recognition of an international community of interests.

True, this virtue may often prove powerless against unilateralist expediency and calculation. True, there may be disheartening periods in international life when the flame flickers feebly. But it would be wrong to doom the international rule of law on the grounds that it requires unrealistic self-sacrifice. To obtain the benefits and protections of a community, one must accept some restraints. This is not a matter of good faith or idealism, but of insight. If a community fails, and proves itself unable to deliver, its calls for discipline are likely to go unheeded.

[78] *Hale's Report*, quoted in Ralston, *International Arbitration from Athens to Locarno* (Stanford University Press, 1929), at p. 112. When the US and France by the Treaty of 15 January 1880 established a claims commission, neither wanted to open up matters already decided by the national authorities of either state. To achieve this result required an unusual restriction on an international adjudicatory body. Accordingly the treaty contained an exceptional provision excluding claims which had been 'diplomatically, judicially or otherwise by competent authorities heretofore disposed of by either government'. A number of the claims which had given impetus to the treaty were thus necessarily withdrawn once this wording was accepted. The lone attempt to disregard this extraordinary limitation was dismissed by the Commission's decision not to assert jurisdiction; *G.A. Le More & Co. v. US*, No. 211, Moore, *Arbitrations* 3232, at p. 3233.

Large parts of our world may seem impervious to international law. That does not prevent anyone from understanding what international law is, or from seeing that it is generally respected in large parts of the globe, to the advantage, it would seem, of those who live there. So what if the emergent law-based international community is fragmented, unsteady, vulnerable? How is that different from the development of national communities?

## Conclusions

The proposition that states may be held accountable under international law by arbitral tribunals created by treaty is neither new nor radical. There were hundreds of such cases in the nineteenth century. The defendant states were of all types: rich and powerful, European or ex-colonial. International tribunals held the United States responsible for actions which its Supreme Court had declared not to be breaches of international law. Those awards were nevertheless respected by the United States.[79] When one of the most illustrious of all awards was handed down against Great Britain in the *Alabama Claims* case (1872), the British arbitrator (Sir Alexander Cockburn) issued a harsh dissent, calling the award of some US$15 million in gold 'unjust', but his government – far more powerful at the time than the US – nevertheless paid the amount awarded.[80]

---

[79] See Note 72 of this chapter above.

[80] The *Alabama Claims* concerned damages caused by the *Alabama* and other Confederate cruisers and privateers to Northern merchant ships during the US Civil War. They had been equipped and provisioned in English ports. The British arbitrator refused to sign the award and insisted hopelessly that a state is not responsible for the acts of its citizens; the other four arbitrators considered that Great Britain had failed to comply with its duties to maintain neutrality with due diligence. The three neutral arbitrators were eminent individuals appointed by the Emperor of Brazil, the King of Italy and the President of Switzerland. The literature on the *Alabama Claims* is perhaps the most abundant of all in the field of international arbitration. One worthwhile account appeared in pages 64–91 of the French professor A. Mérignac's lively monograph, *Traité théorique et pratique de l'arbitrage international* (Paris: Larose, 1895).

Twenty-five years after the *Alabama Claims* award, a question was put in Parliament to the Under Foreign Secretary, George Curzon (as he then was) whether it was true that a substantial amount of the amount collected by the US had not in fact been paid over to private parties having claimed losses. Curzon answered that this appeared to be the case, but: 'It would be contrary to the undertakings of Great Britain in the treaty of Washington, made in 1871, to request the return of any sum left over after the claims against the award had been satisfied.

Mr. Bowles – Is there any prospect of the United States Government offering to repay any surplus?

This tradition of respect for international law as applied by international tribunals should be kept in mind by contemporary critics of investment arbitration who sometimes imagine that such tribunals can be paralysed by declarations of municipal courts that the treaties creating international jurisdiction are contrary to national constitutions. It has thus been argued that the US Constitution 'does not empower the federal government to subject either the federal courts or the state courts to review by an international tribunal'.[81] In response, one might say preliminarily that international law does not so much *review* national court decisions, in the sense of correcting them, as regarding them as lacking decisive effect. More importantly, the debate about the enforceability of international decisions within the US is different from the proposition that international adjudicators may disregard national decisions.[82]

To suggest that the alleged requirements of a nation's own constitution may neutralise the international undertakings of its government flies in the face of international law itself. It may happen that such undertakings are an excess of power under national arrangements. They may give rise to sanctions under municipal law. But they do not (provided of course that the appearance of authority is sufficient for the purposes of international law[83]) disentitle reliance on those undertakings on the international plane.

Mr. Curzon – I am afraid that I cannot speak for the United States Government. [Laughter.]' (*Parl. Deb.*, vol. 46, ser. 4, col. 1253, 25 February 1897.)

[81] Mark Weisburd, 'International Courts and American Courts', (2000) 21 *Michigan Journal of International Law* 877, at p. 938. As a result, he contends, the US Supreme Court was right in not deferring to the International Court of Justice in the *Beard* case involving the Paraguayan national executed in Virginia; and the US is precluded from accepting the jurisdiction of the Inter-American Court of Human Rights.

[82] Professor Weisburd's attempt to minimise the implications of the awards rendered under the Treaty of Washington, arguing *ibid.* at p. 898 that they did not 'disturb [the] effects' of the Supreme Court judgments as to title to captured properties, was anticipated and answered by Commissioner Pinckney in 1797, and does not in the least detract from the latter's successful submissions against the position advanced by Great Britain; see Note 78 of this chapter.

[83] Ever since the analysis by the Permanent Court of International Justice of the famous Ihlen declaration, involving the renunciation of territorial claims by a Foreign Minister, in the *Eastern Greenland case* (*Denmark* v. *Norway*) (1933) PCIJ Series A/B, No. 53, any notion that the binding force of NAFTA or of bilateral investment treaties could be challenged on the international level by the US by reference to national constitutional strictures appears quite implausible.

The key passage from the PCIJ decision, at p. 71, is well known: 'The Court considers it beyond all dispute that a reply of this nature given by the Minister for Foreign Affairs on behalf of his Government in response to a request by the diplomatic representative of a foreign Power, in regard to a question falling within his province, is

To develop constitutional arguments to invalidate international agreements is to follow in the footsteps of Iran, which unsuccessfully sought to escape international arbitration by invoking Article 139 of the Constitutional Law of the Islamic Republic (forbidding state entities to agree with foreign parties in 'significant' cases without special parliamentary approval). Whatever their force as a matter of national law, such arguments evaporate on the international plane.[84]

As Judge Keba Mbaye (former Vice-President of the International Court of Justice and former First President of the Supreme Court of Senegal) put it: 'A state must not be allowed to cite the provisions of its law in order to escape from an arbitration that it has already accepted.'[85] Lord Mustill has suggested that: 'Perhaps it should be classed as a principle of international *ordre public*.'[86] This concept was firmly endorsed in a landmark arbitration brought by a German private party against Belgium.[87] It has even been incorporated into the *municipal* law of Switzerland, where a state party to an arbitration agreement 'cannot rely on its own law to contest the arbitrability of a dispute or its own capacity to be a party to an arbitration'.[88]

Criticism of international tribunals on the grounds that they impede democratic policies – whether protection of the environment or the labour market – is misdirected. International tribunals do not establish policy. They give affect to international agreements. To deny the authority of international tribunals is to deprive states of the power to make meaningful promises.[89]

binding upon the country to which the Minister belongs.' The following sentence from Judge Anzilotti's Dissenting Opinion, at pp. 91–92, is less often cited, but deserves the fullest attention because it takes the matter one step further (and is in full agreement with the majority as to the binding effect of the declaration): 'As regards the question whether Norwegian constitutional law authorised the Minister for Foreign Affairs to make the declaration, that is a point which, in my opinion, does not concern the Danish Government: it was Mr Ihlen's duty to refrain from giving his reply until he had obtained any assent that might be requisite under the Norwegian laws.'

[84] See Craig, Park and Paulsson, *ICC Arbitration*, at pp. 44–46; Jan Paulsson, 'May a State Invoke its Internal Law to Repudiate Consent to International Commercial Arbitration?' (1986) 2 *Arbitration International* 90.

[85] K. Mbaye, *ICC International Arbitration: 60 Years On: A Look at the Future* (Paris: ICC Publications No. 412, 1984), at p. 296.

[86] M. Mustill, 'The New Lex Mercatoria: The First Twenty-Five Years', (1988) 4 *Arbitration International* 86, at p. 112, footnote 91.

[87] *Benteler v. Belgium* (1984) *Journal des Tribunaux* 230.

[88] Art. 177(2) *Loi Fédérale sur le droit international privé*.

[89] Readers of French do well to study the lengthy and fundamental article published by Pierre Mayer under the title 'La neutralisation du pouvoir normative de l'Etat en matière de contrats d'Etat', (1986) 113 *Journal du droit international* 5 where he asks: 'Is it

Criticism of international tribunals on the grounds that they should operate more efficiently, transparently, coherently, and fairly are entirely legitimate. But no human institutions are perfect. International arbitral tribunals have existed for many generations; complaints by those disappointed in their awards have existed for precisely as long. One must be careful to recognise criticism which is only a cover for the disinclination to obey international norms, and careful too in not rushing to implement ostensible reforms which will have the effect only of paralysing their effective application.

It thus seems that many of those who challenge the legitimacy of international adjudication are taking aim at the wrong target. They criticise the principle of the supremacy of international law when their real complaint has to do with the political choices made by their own government in making the bargains reflected in international treaties. The mistake is a dangerous one. For what will happen if they destroy the authority of international law? What then does it matter if they are right about the policy? What will they do once they have prevailed – once they have achieved agreement as to rules for the protection of the environment, the elimination of child labour, the proper treatment of persons accused of crime, an adjustment of the terms of trade in favour of impoverished producers denied access to markets? What a hollow victory indeed, to stand there empty-handed, soon to long for the shattered tool.

not paradoxical that the exaltation of sovereignty over natural resources implies preventing the sovereign State from entrusting their temporary exploitation by a foreign corporation possessed of the necessary capital and technology, on the grounds that the State cannot validly accord the guarantees required by the corporation?' *Id.* at p. 44 (the present author's translation). He adds *ibid.*: 'to allow States to undo their commitments means in practice to forbid them from making undertakings in the future' [permettre aux Etats de se délier, c'est en pratique leur interdire de se lier dans le futur].

When France wanted to ensure that the Walt Disney Corporation would build Eurodisneyland outside Paris and not in Spain, the Parliament passed a special law to authorise the government to accept ICSID jurisdiction in agreements 'with foreign corporations for the implementation of operations having a national interest' (Art. 9, Law No. 86972 of 19 August 1986, *Journal officiel*, 22 August 1986, 10190). The US corporation was adamant about a neutral jurisdiction in the event of a dispute with the government. That law was thought to overcome legal objections of the Conseil d' Etat and the political objections of those who were hostile to the project on cultural grounds. *See* Matthieu de Boisséson, 'Interrogations et doutes sur une évolution législative: L'article 9 de la loi de 19 août 1986', (1987) *Revue de l'arbitrage* 3. (The fact that the law was in all likelihood not required under a proper reading of the *Code civil* is irrelevant for present purposes; see Thomas Clay, 'Une erreur de codification dans le Code civil: les dispositions sur l'arbitrage', in *Le Code civil: 1804–2004* (Paris: Dalloz, 2004), 693, at 706.)

## Summary

The mechanism of holding states accountable by international tribunals is not a new invention. It was much used in the nineteenth century. Disputes between Great Britain and the United States are particularly illustrative.

In the field of international investments, arbitral tribunals are instruments of the rule of law. Their purpose is not to favour the rich, but to enable states to make reliable promises. To undermine that reliability is to deprive the state of a valuable tool.

Arbitral tribunals are not to be blamed for the contents of treaties.

International tribunals tend to irritate respondent states – whether they are rich or poor – in individual cases; yet their decisions should be respected in order to achieve the long-term benefits of the rule of law. Respect for settled and legitimate expectations is a precondition for healthy international relations.

# Bibliography

Abs, Herman and Shawcross Hartley W., Draft Convention on Investments Abroad, (1960) 9 *Journal of Public Law* 115.

Abdurrasyid, Priyatna H., 'They Said I was going to be Kidnapped', (2003) 18(6) *Mealey's International Arbitration Report* 29.

Adede, A. O., 'A Fresh Look at the Meaning of the Doctrine of Denial of Justice under International Law', 1976 *Canadian Yearbook of International Law* 86.

Aguilar, Alvarez Guillermo and Park, William, 'The New Face of Investment Arbitration: Capital Exporters as Host States under NAFTA Chapter 11', ICCA Congress Series No. 11, 302; republished with amendments as 'The New Face of Investment Arbitration: NAFTA Chapter 11', (2003) 28 *Yale Journal of International Law* 365.

Amerasinghe, C. F., *State Responsibility for Injuries to Aliens* (Oxford: Clarendon, 1967).

Auer, Andres, Malinverni, Giagio and Hottelier, Michel, *Droit Constitutionnel Suisse* (2 vols., Bern: Staempfli Editions, 2000).

Bacchus, James, *Freedom and Trade* (London: Cameron May, 2004).

Bagge, A., 'Intervention on the Ground of Damage Caused to Nationals, with Particular Reference to Exhaustion of Local Remedies and the Rights of Shareholders', (1958) 34 *BYIL* 162.

Baty, T., *The Canons of International Law* (London: John Murray, 1930).

Bevilaqua, Clovis, *Direito publico internacional – A synthese dos principios e a contribuiçao do Brazil* (Rio de Janeiro: Livraria Francisco Alves, 1910).

Borchard, Edwin, 'Decisions of Claims Commissions, United States and Mexico', (1926) 10 *AJIL* 536.

    *The Diplomatic Protection of Citizens Abroad* (New York: The Banks Law Publishing Co., 1916).

Brower, Charles H. II, 'Structure, Legitimacy and NAFTA's Investment Chapter', (2003) 36 *Vanderbilt Journal of Transnational Law* 37.

Brownlie, Ian, *Principles of Public International Law* (6th edn, Oxford University Press, 2003).

Cadiet, Loïc, *Droit judiciaire privé* (3rd edn, Paris: Litec, 2000).

Cançado Trindade, A. A., 'Denial of Justice and its Relationship to Exhaustion of Local Remedies in International Law', (1978) 53 *Philippine Law Journal* 404.

   *The Application of the Rule of Exhaustion of Local Remedies in International Law: Its Rationale in the International Protection of Individual Rights* (Cambridge University Press, 1983).

Cheng, Bin *General Principles of Law as Applied by International Tribunals* (Cambridge: Grotius, 1953, reprinted in 1987).

Clay, Thomas, 'Une erreur de codification dans le Code civil: les dispositions sur l'arbitrage', *in Le Code civil: 1804–2004* (Paris: Dalloz, 2004) 693.

Craig, Laurence, W., Park, William, W. and Paulsson, Jan, *International Chamber of Commerce Arbitration* (3rd edn, Dobbs Ferry: Oceana, NY, 2000).

Crawford, James, *The International Law Commission's Articles on State Responsibility: Introduction, Text and Commentaries* (Cambridge University Press, 2002).

Dalrymple, C. K., 'Politics and Foreign Direct Investment: The Multilateral Investment Guarantee Agency and the Calvo Clause', (1996) 29 *Cornell International Law Journal* 161.

Darby, Evans, W., *International Tribunals: A Collection of Various Schemes Which Have Been Propounded, and of Instances since 1815* (London: Peace Society, 1899).

Davis J. B., *Treaties and Conventions concluded between the United States of America and other Powers since July 4, 1776* (Washington, DC: US Government Printing Office, 1889).

de Boisséson, Matthieu, 'Interrogations et doutes sur une évolution législative: L'article 9 de la loi de 19 août 1986', (1987) *Revue de l'arbitrage* 3.

de Lapradelle, A., and Politis, N., *Recueil des arbitrages internationaux*, (2 vols., Paris: Pedone, 1905 (vol. I); 1923 (vol. II)).

de Soto, Hernando, *The Mystery of Capital* (New York: Basic Books, 2000).

de Visscher, Charles, 'Le déni de justice en droit international' (1935) 54 *Recueil des cours* 370.

Drago, Louis, 'State loans and their relation to international policy', (1907) 1 *AJIL* 692.

Dugard, John, 'Chief Justice versus President: Does the Ghost of Brown v. Leyds NO Still Haunt Our Judges?' *De Rebus* (September 1981).

Dupuis, C., 'Liberté des voies de communication et les Relations internationales' (1924) *Recueil des Cours*, vol. I at p. 129.

Eagleton, Clyde, 'Denial of Justice in International Law', (1928) 22 *AJIL* 538.

   *The Responsibility of States in International Law* (New York University Press, 1928).

Emberland, Marius, 'The Usefulness of Applying Human Rights Arguments in International Commercial Arbitration', (2003) 20 *Journal of International Arbitration* 355.

# Bibliography

Fawcett, James, 'The Exhaustion of Local Remedies: Substance or Procedure?' (1954) 31 *BYIL* 452.

*Feuille Fédérale (Journal Officiel) de la Confédération Suisse*, 1997.

Fitzmaurice, Sir Gerald, 'Hersch Lauterpacht – The Scholar as Judge', (1961) 37 *BYIL* 53.

'The Meaning of the Term "Denial of Justice"' (1932) 13 *BYIL* 93.

Freeman, A. V., *The International Responsibility of States for Denial of Justice* (London/ New York: Longman, 1938).

Gallo, Klaus, *De la invasión al reconocimiento – Gran Bretaña y el Río de la Plata 1806–1826* (Buenos Aires: A–Z Editores, 1994).

García-Amador, Francisco V., 'State Responsibility: Some New Problems', (1958) 94 *Recueil des Cours*, vol. II, at p. 369.

Sohn, Louis B. and Baxter, R. R., *Recent Codification of the Law of State Responsibility for Injuries to Aliens* (Dobbs Ferry, NY: Oceana, 1974).

Glendon, Mary Ann, *A World Made New* (New York: Random House, 2001).

Grotius, Hugo, *De Jure Belli ac Pacis libri tres* (Oxford: Clarendon, 1925).

Guerrero, Gustavo, *Annex to Questionnaire No. 4*, Committee of Experts for the Progressive Codification of International Law, Report of the Sub-committee, League of Nations Document C.196.M.70.1927.V (the 'Guerrero Report').

Harr, Jonathan, *A Civil Action* (New York: Vintage, 1996).

'The Burial', *The New Yorker*, 1 November 1999, at p. 93.

Hart, H. L. A., *The Concept of Law* (2nd edn, Oxford University Press, 1994).

Hersley, A. S., 'The Calvo and Drago Doctrines', (1907) 1 *AJIL* 26.

Holmes, Oliver Wendell, Jr, *The Common Law* (ed., M. Howe, Mineole Dover, 1963).

Hunt, B. L., *American and Panamanian General Claims Arbitration under the Conventions between the United States and Panama of July 28, 1926, and December 17, 1932* (Washington, DC: US Department of State Arbitration Series, No. 6, 1934).

Hyde, C. C., *International Law Chiefly as Interpreted and Applied by the United States* (2 vols., Boston, MA: Little, Brown, and Co., 1922).

International Conferences of American States, First Supplement, 1933–1940 (Washington DC: Carnegie Endowment for International Peace, 1940).

International Law Commission (ILC), Draft Articles on State Responsibility, Comments and Observations Received from Governments, UN Doc.A/ CN.4/488 (1998).

(Crawford), Second Report on State Responsibility, UN Doc. A/CN.4/498 (1999).

(Dugard), First Report on Diplomatic Protection, UN Doc. A/CN.4/506 (2000).

(Dugard), Second Report on Diplomatic Protection, UN Doc. A/CN.4/514 (2001).

(Dugard), Third Report on Diplomatic Protection, UN Doc. A/CN.4/523 (2002).

(Dugard), The Addendum to the Third Report on Diplomatic Protection, UN Doc. A/CN.4/523/Add.1 (2002).

(Amador García), Sixth Report on State Responsibility, Addendum, UN Doc. A/CN.4/134/Add. 1 (1961).

*ILC Yearbook* 1977.

Report of the International Law Commission on the work of its 48th Session, 6 March – 26 July 1996, UN Doc. A/51/10.

Irizarry y Puente, J., 'The Concept of 'Denial of Justice' in Latin America', (1944) 43 *Michigan Law Review* 383.

Jaksic, Aleksandar, *Arbitration and Human Rights* (Frankfurt am Main: Peter Lang Publishing, 2002).

Jennings, Sir Robert, 'State Contracts in International Law', (1961) 37 *BYIL* 156.

Jennings, Sir Robert and Watts, Sir Arthur, (eds.), *Oppenheim's International Law* (9th edn, 2 vols., Harlow: Longman, 1992).

Jiménez de Aréchaga, E., 'International Law in the Past Third of a Century', (1978) 159 *Recueil des Cours*, vol. I, at p. 278.

'International Responsibility' in M. Sørensen (ed.), *Manual of Public International Law* (London: Macmillan, 1968).

'International Responsibility of States for Acts of the Judiciary', in Friedmann, W. G., Henkin, L. and Lissitzyn, O. J. (eds.), *Transnational Law in a Changing Society – Essays in Honor of Philip C. Jessup* (New York: Columbia University Press, 1972).

Kagan, Robert, *Of Paradise and Power: America and Europe in the New World Order* (New York: Alfred A. Knopf, 2003).

Koestler, Arthur, *Darkness at Noon* (1940; trans. Daphne Hardy, London: Folio Society, 1980).

Lacarte-Muró, Julio, and Gappah, Petina, 'Developing Countries and the WTO Legal and Dispute Settlement System: A View From the Bench', (2000) *Journal of International Economic Law* 395.

Lauterpacht, E., *Aspects of the Administration of International Justice* (Cambridge: Grotius, 1991).

Lauterpacht, Sir Hersch, *International Law and Human Rights* (London: Stevens & Sons, 1950).

*Private Law Sources and Analogies of International Law* (London/New York: Longman, 1927, repr. 2002).

*The Function of Law in the International Community* (Oxford: Clarendon, 1933).

Legum, B., 'Federalism, NAFTA Chapter Eleven and the Jay Treaty of 1794', (2001) 18 *ICSID News* 6.

'The Introduction of an Appellate Mechanism: The US Trade Act of 2002', in Gaillard, E., and Banifatemi, Y., (eds.) *Annulment of ICSID Awards: A New Investment Protection Regime in Treaty Arbitration* (Huntingdon, NY: Juris, 2004), 289.

'Trends and Challenges in Investor-State Arbitration', (2003) 19 *Arbitration International* 143.

Leigh, Guy, I. F., 'Nationality and Diplomatic Protection', (1971) 20 *International and Comparative Law Quarterly* 453.

Lemaître, Eduardo, *A Brief History of Cartagena* (Bogotá: Editorial Colina, 1994).

Lipstein, K., 'The Place of the Calvo Clause in International Law', (1945) 22 *BYIL* 130.

Lissitzyn, Oliver J., 'The Meaning of the Term Denial of Justice in International Law', (1936) 30 *AJIL* 632.

Mann, Howard, *Private Rights, Public Problems: A Guide to NAFTA's Controversial Chapter on Investor Rights* (New Providence, NJ: International Institute for Sustainable Development and World Wildlife Fund, BPR Publishers, 2001).

Mayer, Pierre, *Droit international privé* (6th edn, Paris: Montchrestien, 1998).

'La neutralisation du pouvoir normative de l'Etat en matière de contrats d'Etat', (1986) 113 *Journal du droit international* 5.

Mbaye, K., *ICC International Arbitration: 60 Years On: A Look at the Future* (No.412, Paris: ICC Publications 1984).

Mérignac, A., *Traité théorique et pratique de l'arbitrage international* (Paris: Larose, 1895).

Moore, J. B., *A Digest of International Law* (8 vols., Washington, DC: US Government Printing Office, 1906).

*History and Digest of International Arbitrations to which the United States Has Been a Party* (6 vols., Washington, DC: US Government Printing Office, 1898).

Mummery David, R., 'The Content of the Duty to Exhaust Local Remedies', (1965) 59 *AJIL* 398.

Murgerwa, Nkmabo, 'Subjects of International Law', in Max Sørensen (ed.), *Manual of Public International Law* (London: Macmillan, 1968).

Mustill, M., 'The New Lex Mercatoria: The First Twenty-Five Years', (1988) 4 *Arbitration International* 86.

Nielsen Fred, K., *American and British Claims Arbitration under the Special Agreement of August 18, 1910* (Washington, DC: US Government Printing Office, 1926).

O'Connell, D. P., *International Law* (2nd edn, London: Stevens & Sons, 1970).

Okoye, Felix Chuks, *International Law and the New African States* (London: Sweet & Maxwell, 1972).

Orrego, Francisco Vicuña, 'Individuals and Non-State Entities before International Courts and Tribunals', in J. A. Frowein and R. Wolfrum (eds.), *Max Planck Yearbook of United Nations Law* (The Hague: Kluwer, 2001), vol. V, at p. 53.

Park, Joseph, H., *British Prime Ministers of the Nineteenth Century: Policies and Speeches* (New York University Press, 1916).

Pasqualucci, Jo M., *The Practice and Procedure of the Inter-American Court of Human Rights* (Cambridge University Press, 2003).

Paulsson, J., 'Arbitration Without Privity', (1995) 10 *ICSID Review* 232.
  'ICSID's Achievements and Prospects', (1991) 6 *ICSID Review* 380.
  'May a State Invoke its Internal Law to Repudiate Consent to International Commercial Arbitration?' (1986) 2 *Arbitration International* 90.
Paulsson, J., and Crawford, Alastair, '1994 Revision of CIETAC Rules Promises Increased Neutrality in Arbitration in China', (1994) 9(6) *Mealey's International Arbitration Report* 17.
Perezcano, Hugo, 'Investment Protection Agreements – Should a Multilateral Approach be Reconsidered', (2003) 4 *Journal of World Investment* 929.
Petrochilos, Georgios, *Procedural Law in International Arbitration* (Oxford University Press, 2004).
Pipes, Richard, *Property and Freedom* (London: The Harvill Press, 1999).
Podesta Costa, L. A., and Ruda, José Maria (eds.), *Derecho internacional público* (2 vols., Buenos Aires: TEA, 1984).
Ralston, J. H., *International Arbitration from Athens to Locarno* (Stanford University Press, 1929).
  *The Law and Procedure of International Tribunals* (Stanford University Press, 1926).
  *Venezuelan Arbitrations of 1903* (Washington, DC: US Government Printing Office, 1904).
*Recueil officiel des Arrêts du Tribunal Fédéral* (Switzerland), 119 Ia 4.
Reed, Lucy, Paulsson, Jan and Blackaby, Nigel, *Guide to ICSID Arbitration* (The Hague: Kluwer, 2004).
Redfern, Alan, 'ICSID: Losing Its Appeal?' (1987) 3 *Arbitration International* 98.
Reisman, W., Michael, *Nullity and Revision: The Review and Enforcement of International Judgments and Awards* (New Haven, CT: Yale University Press, 1971).
Robinson, Davis, R., 'The Role of Politics in the Election and the Work of the Judges of the International Court of Justice', *Proceedings of the 97th Annual Meeting of the American Society of International Law* (2003).
Rogers, William, D., 'Of Missionaries, Fanatics and Lawyers: Some Thoughts on Investment Disputes in the Americas', (1978) 72 *AJIL* 1.
Root, Elihu, 'The Basis of Protection to Citizens Residing Abroad' (1910) 4 *AJIL* 517.
  'The Relations between International Tribunals of Arbitration and the Jurisdiction of National Courts', (1909) 3 *AJIL* 529.
Roth, Andreas, *The Minimum Standard of International Law Applied to Aliens* (Leiden: A. W. Sijthoff, 1949).
Roy, S. N., Guha, 'Is the Law of Responsibility of States for Injuries to Aliens a Part of Universal International Law?'(1961) 55 *AJIL* 866.
Sampliner, Gary, 'Arbitration of Expropriation Cases Under US Investment Treaties – A Threat to Democracy or the Dog That Didn't Bark?' (2003) 18 *ICSID Review* 1.
Schwarzenberger, G., 'The Abs-Shawcross Draft Convention on Investments Abroad', (1961) 14 *Current Legal Problems* 213.

271

Schreuer, Christoph, 'Three Generations of ICSID Annulment Proceedings', in Gaillard, E., and Banifatemi, Y. (eds.), *Annulment of ICSID Awards: A New Investment Protection Regime in Treaty Arbitration* (Huntington, NY: Juris, 2004).

Schwebel, Stephen M., 'Injunction of Arbitral Proceedings and Truncation of the Tribunal', (2003) 18(4) *Mealey's International Arbitration Report* 33.

*International Arbitration: Three Salient Problems* (Cambridge: Grotius, 1987).

*Justice in International Law: Selected Readings* 171 (Cambridge: Grotius, 1994).

Schwebel, Stephen M., and Wetter, J. Gillis, 'Arbitration and the Exhaustion of Local Remedies', (1966) 60 *AJIL* 484.

Scott, G. W., 'Hague Convention Restricting the Use of Force to Recover Contract Claims', (1908) 2 *AJIL* 78.

Shea, Donald, R., *The Calvo Clause: A Problem of Inter-American and International Law and Diplomacy* (Minneapolis: University of Minnesota Press, 1955).

Shihata, Ibrahim, 'Towards a Greater Depoliticization of Investment Disputes: The Roles of ICSID and MIGA', (1986) 1 *ICSID Review* 1.

Toynbee, Arnold, J., *Survey of International Affairs 1924* (Oxford University Press, 1928).

Ubertazzi, L. C., Galli, P. and Sanna, F., *Codice del diritto d'autore* (Milan: Giuffrè, 2003).

Udombana, Nsongurua, 'So Far, So Fair: The Local Remedies Rule in the Jurisprudence of the African Commission on Human and Peoples' Rights, (2003) 97 *AJIL* 1.

Union of International Associations, *2001/2002 Yearbook of International Organizations* (Munich: KG Saur, 2001).

Vattel, Emer (or Emmerich) de, *The Law of Nations or the Principles of Natural Law (Le droit des gens, ou principes de la loi naturelle)*, Classics of International Law (1916; trans. Charles G. Fenwick, 3 vols., Buffalo, NY: William S. Hein & Co., 1995).

Veeder, V. V., 'The Natural Limits to the Truncated Tribunal: The German Case of the Soviet Eggs and the Dutch Abduction of the Indonesian Arbitrator', in R. Briner, L. Y. Fortier, K. P. Berger and J. Bredow (eds.), *Law of International Business and Dispute Settlement in the 21st Century – Liber Amicorum Karl-Heinz Böckstiegel* (Cologne: Bredow, 2001).

Leandro, Vieira Silva, 'Latin America and the Concept of "Denial of Justice"' (thesis for an LL M in public international law, Leiden University, 2000, unpublished).

Waltz, Kenneth, *Man, the State and War* (New York: Columbia University Press, 1959).

Weisburd Mark, 'International Courts and American Courts', (2000) 21 *Michigan Journal of International Law 877*.

Werner, Jacques, 'Making Investment Arbitration More Certain: A Modest Proposal', (2003) 4 *Journal of World Investment* 767.

Wharton, F. (ed.), *A Digest of the International Law of the United States* (3 vols., 2nd edn, Washington, DC: US Government Printing Office, 1887).

Yerton, Stewart, 'Critics Say Agreement Tramples the Rights of Local Citizens', *The New Orleans Times Picayune*, 30 June 2003 (business section).

# *Index*

# Index

# Index

Lightning Source UK Ltd.
Milton Keynes UK

175075UK00002B/20/P